STUDY GUIDE
&
SELECTED SOLUTIONS

Susan E. McMurry

D0117776

Fundamentals of General, Organic, and Biological

Chemistry

Seventh Edition

McMurry

Ballantine

Hoeger

Peterson

Boston   Columbus   Indianapolis   New York   San Francisco   Upper Saddle River
Amsterdam   Cape Town   Dubai   London   Madrid   Milan   Munich   Paris   Montréal   Toronto
Delhi   Mexico City   São Paulo   Sydney   Hong Kong   Seoul   Singapore   Taipei   Tokyo

Editor in Chief: Adam Jaworski

Executive Editor: Jeanne Zalesky

Senior Marketing Manager: Jonathan Cottrell

Assistant Editor: Lisa R. Pierce

Managing Editor, Chemistry and Geosciences: Gina M. Cheselka

Production Project Manager, Science: Wendy Perez

Operations Specialist: Jeffrey Sargent

Cover Designer: Seventeenth Street Studios

Cover Photograph: *Close-up of eye*: Don Hammond/Design Pics, Inc. / Alamy; *Fireworks*: Patrakov Fedor / Shutterstock

1 2 3 4 5 6 7 8 9 10—**EB**— 15 14 13 12

www.pearsonhighered.com   ISBN 10: 0-321-77610-0; ISBN 13: 978-0-321-77610-5

Contents

Preface

How is food digested? What is DNA fingerprinting? How do anesthetics work?

For all of these questions, chemistry provides an answer. Chemistry, the study of matter, is essential for understanding the physical world, from acid rain to gene therapy to the ozone layer. Chemical laboratory tests are a routine part of medical care. The functioning of our bodies is a result of thousands of biochemical reactions. To study life, you must first study chemistry.

Both the textbook and this *Study Guide and Selected Solutions Manual* are designed to be as helpful as possible to you in your chemistry course. The textbook contains numerous solved problems that show you techniques for solving specific types of chemistry problems. In addition, the text includes applications of the material in each chapter to contemporary science problems. This *Study Guide* consists of several types of study aids: detailed solutions to all textbook problems, outlines of the chapters, and self-tests.

The following suggestions may help you:

1. *Attend all classes.* Although it's possible to learn chemistry just by reading the textbook and study guide, a lecturer makes difficult topics much easier to understand and ties together seemingly unrelated topics.

2. *Read the textbook.* The best way to study is to skim the chapter to be covered before class, and then to read it more thoroughly after the lecturer has discussed the material. Use the textbook to help you understand subjects you find especially difficult. It is also helpful to use the chapter outlines in the *Study Guide* after reading the textbook.

3. *Work the problems.* Start by reading carefully the Solved Problems in the textbook. Next, try to work the Practice Problems, using the steps outlined in the Solved Problems. Finally, attempt the Additional Problems at the end of the chapter. Although this *Study Guide and Selected Solutions Manual* has detailed solutions to all text problems, it's better to use the solutions in this book as a last resort. You will learn more if you first struggle a bit with a problem before checking its answer than if you look up the answer right away.

4. Use the supplementary material in the *Study Guide* to help you review each chapter. The chapter outlines organize and restate both the major themes of each chapter and the detailed contents. Go over the list of key terms in the textbook to make sure that you know the meaning of each important term. Test yourself with the self-tests, which include multiple choice, sentence completions, matching, and true/false questions.

Acknowledgments

I would like to thank the following people for their assistance with this book: John McMurry (of course), David Ballantine, Carl Hoeger, Virginia Peterson, Lisa Pierce, and Richard Jarman. I am grateful to my entire family for their patience and support.

Chapter 1   Matter and Measurements

Chapter Outline

I. Matter and its properties (Sections 1.1–1.2).
   A. Matter is anything that is physically real (Section 1.1).
   B. Properties are the characteristics of matter.
      1. Physical properties are those properties that can be measured without altering the identity of a substance. Examples include mass, melting point, boiling point, and color.
      2. Chemical properties must be determined by changing the identity of the substance. Examples include rusting, combustion, and chemical reactivity.
      3. A physical change does not alter the identity of a substance.
      4. A chemical change is a process in which one or more substances undergoes a change in identity.
   C. States of matter (Section 1.2).
      1. The states of matter are solid, liquid, and gas.
         a. Solids have definite volume and definite shape.
         b. Liquids have definite volume and indefinite shape.
         c. Gases have indefinite volume and indefinite shape.
      2. Changes of state are melting, boiling, condensing, and freezing.
II. Classification of matter (Sections 1.3–1.6).
   A. Mixtures (Section 1.3).
      1. Mixtures vary in composition and properties.
      2. Mixtures can be separated by physical methods.
   B. Pure substances.
      1. Pure substances include chemical compounds and chemical elements.
      2. Pure substances don't vary in composition and properties.
      3. Chemical compounds can be broken down to elements by chemical change.
      4. Chemical elements can't be broken down.
   C. Chemical elements (Sections 1.4–1.5).
      1. There are 118 elements; 91 of them occur naturally (Section 1.4).
      2. Elements are represented by one- or two-letter symbols.
      3. The symbols for elements can be combined to produce chemical formulas.
      4. Elements are presented in a table—the periodic table (Section 1.5).
      5. Elements can be classified as metals, nonmetals, or metalloids.
         a. Metals are solids that are lustrous, brittle, malleable, and good conductors of heat and electricity.
         b. Nonmetals may be solid, liquid, or gas and are poor conductors.
         c. Metalloids have characteristics intermediate between metals and nonmetals.
   D. Chemical reactions (Section 1.6).
         a. A chemical reaction represents a chemical change between pure substances.
         b. In a chemical reaction, the reactants are written on the left, the products are written on the right, and an arrow connects them.
III. Measurements (Sections 1.7–1.8).
   A. Physical quantities (Section 1.7).
      1. All physical quantities consist of a number plus a unit.
         a. SI units, the standard units for scientists, are the kilogram, the meter, and the kelvin.
         b. Metric units are the gram, the meter, the liter, and the degree Celsius.

      c. Other units, such as those for speed and concentration, can be derived from SI and metric units.

   2. Prefixes are used with units to indicate multiples of 10.

 B. Measuring mass, length, and volume (Section 1.8).

   1. Measuring mass.

      a. Mass is the amount of matter in a substance.

      b. Mass differs from weight (a measure of the gravitational pull exerted on an object).

      c. The SI unit of mass is the kilogram, but in chemistry the gram and milligram are more often used.

   2. Measuring length.

      a. The meter is the standard unit for length.

   3. Measuring volume.

      a. Volume is the amount of space that a substance occupies.

      b. Units for volume are the liter (L) and the cubic meter (m^3)—the SI unit.

IV. Numbers in measurement (Sections 1.9–1.11).

 A. Significant figures (Section 1.9).

   1. All measurements have a degree of uncertainty.

   2. For any measurement, the number of digits known with certainty, plus one digit considered uncertain, is known as the number of significant figures.

   3. Rules for significant figures:

      a. Zeroes in the middle of a number are always significant.

      b. Zeroes at the beginning of a number are never significant.

      c. Zeroes at the end of a number but after a decimal point are significant.

      d. Zeroes at the end of a number but before an implied decimal point may or may not be significant.

   4. Some numbers are exact and have an unlimited number of significant figures.

 B. Scientific notation (Section 1.10).

   1. In scientific notation, a number is written as the product of a number between 1 and 10 times 10 raised to a power.

      a. For numbers greater than 10, the power of 10 is positive.

      b. For numbers less than 1, the power of 10 is negative.

   2. Scientific notation is helpful in indicating the number of significant figures in a number.

 C. Rounding off numbers (Section 1.11).

   1. Numbers must be rounded off if they contain more digits than are significant.

   2. Rounding in calculations.

      a. In multiplication or division, the result can't have more significant figures than any of the original numbers.

      b. In addition or subtraction, the result can't have more digits to the right of the decimal point than any of the original numbers.

   3. Rules of rounding:

      a. If the digit to be removed is 4 or less, drop it and remove all following digits.

      b. If the digit to be removed is 5 or greater, add 1 to the digit to the left of the digit you drop.

      c. Round off after all steps in a calculation have been carried out.

 D. Problem solving (Section 1.12).

   1. Converting a quantity from one unit to another.

      a. In the *factor-label* method:

      (quantity in old units) x (conversion factor) = (quantity in new units).

         i. The conversion factor is a fraction that converts one unit to another.

         ii. All conversion factors are equal to 1.

      b. In the factor-label method, units are treated as numbers.

      c. In the factor-label method, all unwanted units cancel.

2. Problem solving techniques.
    a. Identify the information known.
    b. Identify the information needed in the answer.
    c. Use conversion factors to convert the given information to the answer.
    d. Make a "ballpark" estimate of the answer and compare it to the calculated answer.
V. Temperature, heat, and energy (Section 1.13).
    A. Measuring temperature.
        1. Units of temperature are the degree Fahrenheit, the degree Celsius, and the kelvin.
        2. Temperature in °C = Temperature in K – 273.15°.
        3. $°F = \left(\dfrac{9\,°F}{5\,°C} \times °C\right) + 32\,°F.$
        4. $°C = \dfrac{5\,°C}{9\,°F} \times (°F - 32\,°F).$
    B. Energy and heat.
        1. All chemical reactions are accompanied by a change in energy.
            a. Potential energy is stored energy.
            b. Kinetic energy is the energy of motion.
        2. Heat is the energy transferred from a hotter object to a cooler object when the two are in contact.
        3. Units of energy are the joule (SI) and the calorie.
        4. Specific heat $= \dfrac{\text{calories}}{\text{grams} \times °C}$
VI. Density and specific gravity (Section 1.14).
    A. Density.
        1. Density = Mass (g) / Volume (mL or cm^3).
        2. Density is temperature dependent.
    B. Specific gravity.
        1. Specific gravity $= \dfrac{\text{density of substance (g/mL)}}{\text{density of water (1 g/mL)}}.$
        2. Specific gravity has no units.

Solutions to Chapter 1 Problems

1.1   *Change in physical properties*:   (a) grinding of a metal   (d) a puddle evaporating
       Change in chemical properties: (b) fruit ripening   (c) wood burning

1.2   At 10°C, acetic acid is a solid.

1.3   *Mixtures*: (a) concrete (heterogeneous);   (d) wood (heterogeneous)
       Pure substances: (b) helium (element);   (c) a lead weight (element)

1.4   *Physical changes*: (a) dissolving sugar in water
       Chemical change: (b) production of carbon dioxide by heating limestone; (c) frying an egg; (d) conversion of salicylic acid to acetylsalicylic acid

1.5   The process is a chemical change because the product is different in composition from the reactant.

1.6   (a) 2 (Na); (b) 1 (W); (c) 6 (Sr); (d) 5 (Ti); (e) 4 (F);   (f) 3 (Sn).

1.7   (a) Ammonia (NH_3) contains one nitrogen atom and three hydrogen atoms.
       (b) Sodium bicarbonate ($NaHCO_3$) contains one sodium atom, one hydrogen atom, one carbon atom, and three oxygen atoms.
       (c) Octane (C_8H_{18}) contains eight carbon atoms and eighteen hydrogen atoms.
       (d) Vitamin C ($C_6H_8O_6$) contains six carbon atoms, eight hydrogen atoms, and six oxygen atoms.

1.8

Element	Name	Number in Periodic Table
(a) B	boron	5
(b) Si	silicon	14
(c) Ge	germanium	32
(d) As	arsenic	33
(e) Sb	antimony	51
(f) Te	tellurium	52

The metalloids appear on a diagonal boundary between metals and nonmetals.

1.9   Mercury is a metal. Physical properties that lead to its toxicity include the solubility of mercury-containing compounds and the persistence of mercury vapor. Chemical properties include the tendency of mercury and mercury vapor to form soluble toxic compounds.

1.10   (a) 1 cm = 1 centimeter = 0.01 m   (b) 1 dg = 1 decigram = 0.1 g
        (c) 1 km = 1 kilometer = 1000 m   (d) 1 μs = microsecond = 0.000 001 s
        (e) 1 ng = 1 nanogram = 0.000 000 001 g

1.11   *Number   Significant Figures   Reason*

Number	Significant Figures	Reason
(a) 3.45 m	3	
(b) 0.1400 kg	4	Rule 3
(c) 10.003 L	5	Rule 1
(d) 35 cents	Exact	

1.12 32.3 °C. The answer has three significant figures.

1.13 In scientific notation, a number is written as the product of a number between 1 and 10 times 10 raised to a power. In (a), 58 g = 5.8 x 10^1 g.

Value	Scientific Notation
(a) 0.058 g	5.8 x 10^{-2} g
(b) 46,792 m	4.6792 x 10^4 m
(c) 0.006 072 cm	6.072 x 10^{-3} cm
(d) 345.3 kg	3.453 x 10^2 kg

1.14
Value in Scientific Notation	Value in Standard Notation
(a) 4.885 x 10^4 mg	48,850 mg
(b) 8.3 x 10^{-6} m	0.000 0083 m
(c) 4.00 x 10^{-2} m	0.0400 m

1.15 (a) 6.3000 x 10^5 (b) 1.30 x 10^3 (c) 7.942 x 10^{11}

1.16 (a) 2.30 g   (b) 188.38 mL   (c) 0.009 L   (d) 1.000 kg

1.17 Remember:
(1) The sum or difference of two numbers can't have more digits to the right of the decimal point than either of the two numbers.
(2) The product or quotient of two numbers can't have more significant figures than either of the two numbers.

Calculation	Rounded to:
(a) 4.87 mL + 46.0 mL = 50.87 mL	50.9 mL
(b) 3.4 x 0.023 g = 0.0782 g	0.078 g
(c) 19.333 m − 7.4 m = 11.933 m	11.9 m
(d) 55 mg − 4.671 mg + 0.894 mg = 51.223 mg	51 mg
(e) 62,911 ÷ 611 = 102.96399	103

1.18

(a) 16.0 oz x $\dfrac{28.35 \text{ g}}{1 \text{ oz}}$ = 454 g   (b) 2500 mL x $\dfrac{1 \text{ L}}{1000 \text{ mL}}$ = 2.5 L

(c) 99.0 L x $\dfrac{1 \text{ qt}}{0.9464 \text{ L}}$ = 105 qt

1.19

0.840 quart x $\dfrac{1 \text{ L}}{1.057 \text{ quart}}$ x $\dfrac{1000 \text{ mL}}{1 \text{ L}}$ = 795 mL

1.20 This is a *long* unit conversion! Remember that all units must cancel at the end, except for the units needed in the final answer (meters and seconds). Nautical miles must be converted to meters, and hours must be converted to seconds. Also remember the definition of a knot—1 nautical mile per hour.

$\dfrac{14.3 \text{ naut. mi}}{1 \text{ hr}}$ x $\dfrac{6076.1155 \text{ ft}}{1 \text{ naut. mi}}$ x $\dfrac{0.3048 \text{ m}}{1 \text{ ft}}$ x $\dfrac{1 \text{ hr}}{60 \text{ min}}$ x $\dfrac{1 \text{ min}}{60 \text{ s}}$ = 7.36 m/s

1.21

$$2 \times 0.324 \text{ g} \times \frac{1000 \text{ mg}}{1 \text{ g}} \times \frac{1}{135 \text{ lb}} \times \frac{2.205 \text{ lb}}{1 \text{ kg}} = 10.6 \frac{\text{mg}}{\text{kg}}$$

$$2 \times 0.324 \text{ g} \times \frac{1000 \text{ mg}}{1 \text{ g}} \times \frac{1}{40 \text{ lb}} \times \frac{2.205 \text{ lb}}{1 \text{ kg}} = 36 \frac{\text{mg}}{\text{kg}}$$

1.22 From Section 1.13, we find the formula:

$$(\text{°F} - 32 \text{ °F}) \times \frac{5 \text{ °C}}{9 \text{ °F}} = \text{°C}$$

Substituting 136°F into the preceding formula:

$$(136 \text{ °F} - 32 \text{ °F}) \times \frac{5 \text{ °C}}{9 \text{ °F}} = 57.8 \text{ °C}$$

To find the temperature in kelvins, add the temperature in degrees Celsius to 273.15 since the size of a degree is the same in both kelvins and degrees Celsius.

$$(273.15 + 57.8) \text{ K} = 331.0 \text{ K}$$

1.23 39 °C = 102 °F

1.24

$$\text{Heat (cal)} = \text{mass (g)} \times \text{temperature change (°C)} \times \text{specific heat} \left(\frac{\text{cal}}{\text{g} \cdot \text{°C}} \right)$$

$$= 350 \text{ g} \times (25 \text{ °C} - 3 \text{ °C}) \times \frac{1.0 \text{ cal}}{\text{g} \cdot \text{°C}}$$

$$= 7700 \text{ cal} = 7.7 \times 10^3 \text{ cal}$$

Ballpark check: The temperature change is approximately 20 °C. The mass of Coca-Cola times the temperature change equals 7000, a number close to the exact solution.

1.25

$$\text{Specific heat} = \frac{\text{calories}}{\text{grams} \times \text{°C}}$$

$$\text{Specific heat} = \frac{161 \text{ cal}}{75 \text{ g} \times 10.0 \text{ °C}} = \frac{0.21 \text{ cal}}{\text{g} \cdot \text{°C}}, \quad \frac{674 \text{ J}}{75 \text{ g} \times 10.0 \text{ °C}} = \frac{0.90 \text{ J}}{\text{g} \cdot \text{°C}}$$

1.26

$$\text{Density} = \frac{\text{Mass}}{\text{Volume}} = \frac{17.4 \text{ g}}{27.3 \text{ cm}^3} = \frac{0.637 \text{ g}}{\text{cm}^3}$$

The sample will float since it is less dense than water.

1.27

$$12.37 \text{ g} \times \frac{1 \text{ mL}}{1.474 \text{ g}} = 8.392 \text{ mL}$$

Ballpark check: Since the density of chloroform is approximately 1.5, the volume needed is about two-thirds of the mass needed.

1.28 Battery acid is more dense than water.

Understanding Key Concepts

1.30 Green: boron (B) – metalloid
Blue: bromine (Br) – nonmetal
Red: vanadium (V) – metal

1.32 The specific gravity is found by reading the liquid level on the scale of the hydrometer.
(a) The specific gravity of this solution is 0.978.
(b) The answer has three significant figures.
(c) The solution is less dense than water.

1.34 The length of the pencil is either 8.0 cm or 3 1/8 in.

1.36 If two identical hydrometers are placed in ethanol and in chloroform, the hydrometer in chloroform will float higher. Since a hydrometer bulb sinks until it displaces a volume of liquid equal to its mass, it displaces a smaller volume of chloroform, the denser liquid, and the bulb floats higher.

Chemistry and the Properties of Matter

1.38 *Physical changes:* (a) boiling water; (d) breaking of glass
Chemical changes: (b) decomposing water by passing a current through it; (c) exploding of potassium when placed in water

States and Classification of Matter

1.40 A *gas* is a substance that has no definite shape or volume.
A *liquid* has no definite shape but has a definite volume.
A *solid* has a definite volume and a definite shape.

1.42 Sulfur dioxide is a gas at 298 K (25 °C).

1.44 *Mixtures:* (a) pea soup; (b) seawater; (d) urine; (f) multivitamin tablet
Pure substances: (c) propane (C_3H_8); (e) lead

1.46 *Reactant*   *Products*

Hydrogen peroxide ⟶ Water + Oxygen
chemical compound   *chemical compound*   *element*

Elements and Their Symbols

1.48 *Metals* are elements that are solids at room temperature (except for Hg), are lustrous and malleable, and are good conductors of heat and electricity.

Nonmetals are elements that are gases or brittle solids (except for Br) and are poor conductors.

Metalloids are elements that have properties intermediate between those of metals and nonmetals.

1.50 (a) Gadolinium (Gd); (b) Germanium (Ge); (c) Technetium (Tc); (d) Arsenic (As); (e) Cadmium (Cd)

1.52 (a) The symbol for bromine is Br (the second letter in a symbol is never capitalized).
(b) The symbol for manganese is Mn (Mg is the symbol for magnesium).
(c) The symbol for carbon is C (Ca is the symbol for calcium).
(d) The symbol for potassium is K; (Po is the symbol for polonium).

1.54 Carbon, hydrogen, nitrogen, and oxygen are present in glycine. The formula $C_2H_5NO_2$ represents 10 atoms.

1.56 Ibuprofen: $C_{13}H_{18}O_2$

Physical Quantities: Definitions and Units

1.58 A *physical quantity* is a physical property that can be measured; it consists of a number plus a unit.

1.60 (a) cubic centimeter (b) decimeter (c) millimeter (d) nanoliter
(e) milligram (f) cubic meter

1.62

$$1 \text{ mg} \times \frac{10^{-3} \text{ g}}{1 \text{ mg}} \times \frac{10^{12} \text{ pg}}{1 \text{ g}} = 10^9 \text{ pg}$$

$$35 \text{ ng} \times \frac{10^{-9} \text{ g}}{1 \text{ ng}} \times \frac{10^{12} \text{ pg}}{1 \text{ g}} = 3.5 \times 10^4 \text{ pg}$$

Scientific Notation and Significant Figures

1.64 (a) 9.457×10^3 (b) 7×10^{-5} (c) 2.000×10^{10}
(d) 1.2345×10^{-2} (e) 6.5238×10^2

1.66 (a) six (b) three (c) three (d) four
(e) 1–5 (f) 2–3

1.68 (a) 7926 mi; 7900 mi; 7926.38 mi (b) $7.926\,381 \times 10^3$ mi

1.70 (a) 12.1 g (b) 96.19 cm (c) 263 mL (d) 20.9 mg

Unit Conversions and Problem Solving

1.72 (a) 0.3614 cg (b) 0.0120 ML (c) 0.0144 mm (d) 60.3 ng (e) 1.745 dL
(f) 1.5×10^5 cm

1.74 (a) 97.8 kg (b) 0.133 mL (c) 0.46 ng (d) 2.99 Mm

1.76

(a) $\dfrac{100 \text{ km}}{1 \text{ hr}} \times \dfrac{0.6214 \text{ mi}}{1 \text{ km}} = \dfrac{62.1 \text{ mi}}{1 \text{ hr}}$

(b) $\dfrac{62.1 \text{ mi}}{1 \text{ hr}} \times \dfrac{5280 \text{ ft}}{1 \text{ mi}} \times \dfrac{1 \text{ hr}}{60 \text{ min}} \times \dfrac{1 \text{ min}}{60 \text{ s}} = \dfrac{91.1 \text{ ft}}{1 \text{ s}}$

1.78

(a) $6 \times 10^{-6}\,m \times \dfrac{10^2\,cm}{1\,m} = 6 \times 10^{-4}\,cm$

(b) $1\,cm \times \dfrac{1\,cell}{6 \times 10^{-4}\,cm} = 2 \times 10^3\,cells$

$1\,in. \times \dfrac{1\,cell}{6 \times 10^{-6}\,m} \times \dfrac{1\,m}{39.37\,in} = 4 \times 10^3\,cells$

1.80

$\dfrac{200\,mg}{1\,dL} \times \dfrac{10\,dL}{1\,L} \times 5\,L = 10^4\,mg; \quad 10^4\,mg \times \dfrac{1\,g}{10^3\,mg} = 10\,g\ cholesterol$

1.82

$\dfrac{1.2 \times 10^4\,cells}{1\,mm^3} \times \dfrac{10^6\,mm^3}{1\,L} \times 5\,L = 6 \times 10^{10}\,cells$

Energy, Heat, and Temperature

1.84

Heat (cal) = mass (g) $\times$ temperature change (°C) $\times$ specific heat $\left(\dfrac{cal}{g \cdot °C}\right)$

$= 30.0\,g \times (30.0\,°C - 10.0\,°C) \times \dfrac{0.895\,cal}{g \cdot °C} = 537\,cal = 0.537\,kcal$

$537\,cal \times \dfrac{4.18\,J}{1\,cal} = 2240\,J = 2.24\,kJ$

1.86

Specific heat $= \dfrac{cal}{g \cdot °C} = \dfrac{23\,cal}{5.0\,g \times 50\,°C} = 0.092\,\dfrac{cal}{g \cdot °C} = 0.38\,\dfrac{J}{g \cdot °C}$

1.88

For mercury: Temperature change (°C) $= \dfrac{250\,cal}{150\,g \times 0.033\,\dfrac{cal}{g \cdot °C}} = 51\,°C$

Final temp $= 25\,°C + 51\,°C = 76\,°C$

For iron: Temperature change (°C) $= \dfrac{250\,cal}{150\,g \times 0.106\,\dfrac{cal}{g \cdot °C}} = 15.7\,°C$

Final temp $= 25.0\,°C + 15.7\,°C = 40.7\,°C$

Density and Specific Gravity

1.90

$250\,mg \times \dfrac{1\,g}{10^3\,mg} \times \dfrac{1\,cm^3}{1.40\,g} = 0.179\,cm^3$

1.92 To find the density of lead, divide the mass of lead by the volume of the bar in cm^3.
0.500 cm x 1.55 cm x 25.00 cm = 19.38 cm^3.

$$\frac{220.9 \text{ g}}{19.38 \text{ cm}^3} = 11.4 \frac{\text{g}}{\text{cm}^3}$$

1.94 The density of ethanol at 25 °C is equal to its specific gravity at 25 °C times the density of water at 25 °C.

$$0.787 \text{ x } \frac{0.997 \text{ g}}{1 \text{ mL}} = 0.785 \frac{\text{g}}{\text{mL}}; 125 \text{ g x } \frac{1 \text{ mL}}{0.785 \text{ g}} = 159 \text{ mL}$$

Chemistry in Action

1.96 ASA contains nine carbons, eight hydrogens, and four oxygens, totaling 21 atoms. It is a solid at room temperature.

1.98

$$(28 \text{ °F} - 32 \text{ °F}) \text{ x } \frac{5 \text{ °C}}{9 \text{ °F}} = -2.2 \text{ °C } = 271 \text{ K}$$

1.100 (a) BMI = 29   (b) BMI = 23.7   (c) BMI = 24.4

Individual (a), with a body mass index that borders on obese, is most likely to have increased health risks.

General Questions and Problems

1.102 Element 117 lies beneath astatine in the periodic table. It is expected to be a nonmetallic, nonconducting solid and to have chemical behavior similar to the elements above it.

1.104

$$3.125 \text{ in. } \text{ x } \frac{2.54 \text{ cm}}{1 \text{ in.}} = 7.94 \text{ cm}$$

The difference in the calculated length (7.94 cm) and the measured length (8.0 cm) is due to the lack of precision of the ruler and to rounding.

1.106

(a) $350 \text{ kcal } \text{ x } \frac{1 \text{ x } 10^3 \text{ cal}}{1 \text{ kcal}} = 3.50 \text{ x } 10^5 \text{ cal}; 3.50 \text{ x } 10^5 \text{ cal } \text{ x } \frac{4.18 \text{ J}}{\text{cal}} = 1.46 \text{ x } 10^6 \text{ J}$

(b) Temperature change (°C) = $\dfrac{\text{heat (cal)}}{\text{mass (g) x specific heat}\left(\dfrac{\text{cal}}{\text{g} \cdot \text{°C}}\right)}$

mass = 35.5 kg = $3.55 \text{ x } 10^4$ g; heat = $3.50 \text{ x } 10^5$ cal

Temperature change (°C) = $\dfrac{3.50 \text{ x } 10^5 \text{ cal}}{3.55 \text{ x } 10^4 \text{ g } \text{ x } 1.00 \left(\dfrac{\text{cal}}{\text{g} \cdot \text{°C}}\right)} = 9.86 \text{ °C}$

1.108 3.9×10^{-2} g/dL iron, 8.3×10^{-3} g/dL calcium, 2.24×10^{-1} g/dL cholesterol

1.110

$$75\,\frac{mL}{beat} \times 72\,\frac{beats}{min} \times 60\,\frac{min}{hr} \times 24\,\frac{hr}{day} = 7.8 \times 10^6\,\frac{mL}{day}$$

1.112

$$0.14\text{ mL} \times \frac{0.963\text{ g}}{1\text{ mL}} = 0.13\text{ g}$$

1.114

$$\frac{85\text{ mg}}{100\text{ mL}} \times \frac{1\text{ g}}{10^3\text{mg}} \times \frac{10^3\text{ mL}}{1\text{ L}} \times \frac{0.9464\text{ L}}{1\text{ qt}} \times \frac{1\text{ qt}}{2\text{ pt}} \times 11\text{ pt} = 4.4\text{ g}$$

$$4.4\text{ g} \times \frac{1\text{ lb}}{454\text{ g}} = 0.0097\text{ lb}$$

1.116

$$\left(\frac{100\text{ mL}}{1\text{ kg}} \times 10\text{ kg}\right) + \left(\frac{50\text{ mL}}{1\text{ kg}} \times 10\text{ kg}\right) + \left(\frac{20\text{ mL}}{1\text{ kg}} \times 35\text{ kg}\right) = 2200\text{ mL}$$

1.118

Heat (cal) = mass (g) x temperature change (°C) x specific heat $\left(\frac{cal}{g \cdot °C}\right)$

For water: specific heat = 1.00 cal /(g·°C);

$$\text{mass} = 3.00\text{ L} \times \frac{10^3\text{ mL}}{1\text{ L}} \times \frac{1.00\text{ g}}{1\text{ mL}} = 3.00 \times 10^3\text{ g};$$

temperature change = 90.0 °C – 18.0 °C = 72.0 °C

Calories needed = 3.00×10^3 g x 72.0°C x $\frac{1.00\text{ cal}}{g \cdot °C}$ = 2.16×10^5 cal = 216 kcal

$$216\text{ kcal} \times \frac{1.0\text{ tbsp}}{100\text{ kcal}} = 2.2\text{ tbsp butter}$$

1.120

$$\frac{1620\text{ g}}{205\text{ mL}} = 7.90\,\frac{g}{mL}$$

The value calculated for density very nearly agrees with the density of iron (7.86 g/mL).

1.122 Use the dimensions of the cork and of the lead to find their respective volumes. Multiply the volume of each substance by its density to arrive at the mass of each.
Volume of cork: 1.30 cm x 5.50 cm x 3.00 cm = 21.5 cm^3
Volume of lead: $(1.15\text{ cm})^3 = 1.52$ cm^3

Mass of cork: Mass of lead:
21.5 cm^3 x $\frac{0.235\text{ g}}{1\text{ cm}^3}$ = 5.05 g cork   1.52 cm^3 x $\frac{11.35\text{ g}}{1\text{ cm}^3}$ = 17.3 g lead
Add the two masses, and divide by the sum of the two volumes to find the density of the combination.

$$\text{Density} = \frac{5.05\text{ g} + 17.3\text{ g}}{21.5\text{ cm}^3 + 1.52\text{ cm}^3} = \frac{22.40\text{ g}}{23.0\text{ cm}^3} = 0.974\text{ g/cm}^3$$

The combination will float because its density is less than the density of water.

Self-Test for Chapter 1

1.   Write the full name of these units:
      (a) μm   (b) dL   (c) Mg   (d) L   (e) ng

2.   Write the abbreviation for each of the following units:
      (a) kiloliter   (b) picogram   (c) centimeter   (d) hectoliter

3.   *Quantity*   *Significant Figures?*

      (a) 1.0037 g
      (b) 0.0080 L
      (c) 0.008 L
      (d) 2 aspirin
      (e) 273,000 mi

4.   Express the following in scientific notation:
      (a) 0.000 070 3 g   (b) 137,100 m   (c) 0.011 L   (d) 18,371,008 mm
      How many significant figures do each of these quantities have?
      7.03×10^{-5} g 13.71×10^{4} m 1.1×10^{-2}

5.   Round the following to three significant figures:
      (a) 807.3 L   (b) 4,773,112 people   (c) 0.00127 g   (d) 10370 μm
      Express each of these quantities in scientific notation.

6.   Convert the following quantities:
      (a) 256 g = _____ lb   (b) 417 mm = _____ m
      (c) 2.0 gallons = _____ L   (d) 2.17 m = _____ inches
      (e) 35 °C = _____ °F   (f) 298 K = _____ °C
      (g) 175 mL = _____ fl oz   (h) 175 mg = _____ oz

7.   If the specific heat of gold is 0.031 cal/g °C, how many calories does it take to heat 10 g of
      gold from 0 °C to 100 °C? $10 \times .031 \times 100 = \boxed{31 \text{ cal}}$

8.   If the density of ethanol is 0.7893 g/mL, how many grams does 275 mL of ethanol weigh?

Multiple Choice

1.   Which of the following is not an SI unit?
      (a) kg   (b) L   (c) m   (d) K

2.   How many significant figures does the number 4500 have?
      (a) 2   (b) 3   (c) 4   (d) any of the above

3.   Which of the following quantities is larger than a gram?
      (a) 1 nanogram   (b) 1 dekagram   (c) 1 centigram   (d) 1 microgram

4.   Which of the following conversion factors do you need for converting 3.2 lb/qt to kg/L?
      (a) $\dfrac{1 \text{ kg}}{2.2 \text{ lb}} \times \dfrac{1 \text{ qt}}{0.95 \text{ L}}$ (b) $\dfrac{2.2 \text{ lb}}{1 \text{ kg}} \times \dfrac{1 \text{ qt}}{0.95 \text{ L}}$ (c) $\dfrac{2.2 \text{ lb}}{1 \text{ kg}} \times \dfrac{0.95 \text{ L}}{1 \text{ qt}}$ (d) $\dfrac{1 \text{ kg}}{2.2 \text{ lb}} \times \dfrac{0.95 \text{ L}}{1 \text{ qt}}$

5.   When written in scientific notation, the exponent in the number 0.000 007 316 is:
      (a) 10^{-6} (b) 6   (c) –6   (d) 10^{6}

6. The change of state that occurs when a gas is cooled to a liquid is called:
   (a) boiling   (b) melting   (c) evaporation   (d) condensation

7. How many zeros are significant in the number 0.007 006?
   (a) 1   (b) 2   (c) 3   (d) 4

8. All of the following have uniform composition except: (a) element   (b) solution   (c) pure substance   (d) chemical compound

9. To measure the amount of heat needed to raise the temperature of a given substance, you need to know all of the following except:
   (a) the mass of the substance   (b) the specific heat of the substance   (c) the density of the substance   (d) the initial and final temperature

10. For which of the following is specific gravity a useful measure?
    (a) to describe the amount of solids in urine   (b) to indicate the amount of heat necessary to raise the temperature of one gram of a substance by 1°C   (c) to determine if an object will float on water

Sentence Completion

1. The fundamental SI units are _____, _____, _____, and _____.

2. Physical quantities are described by a _____ and a _____.

3. The amount of heat necessary to raise the temperature of one gram of a substance by one degree is the substance's _____ _____.

4. _____ is the symbol for the element bismuth.

5. The number 0.003 06 has _____ significant figures.

6. To convert from grams to pounds, use the conversion factor _____.

7. A _____ substance can be beaten or rolled into different shapes.

8. The method used for converting units is called the _____ _____ method.

9. _____ _____ is the density of a substance divided by the density of water at the same temperature.

10. The size of a degree is the same in both _____ and _____ units.

True or False

1.   The units of specific gravity are g/mL.

2.   The number 0.07350 has four significant figures.

3.   The sum of 57.35 and 1.3 has four significant figures.

4.   The conversion factor 1.057 quarts/liter is used to convert quarts into liters.

5.   Rust formation is a chemical change.

6.   The temperature in °C is always a larger number than the temperature in K.

7.   Raising the temperature of 10 g of water by 10 °C takes less heat than raising the temperature of 10 g of gold by 10 °C.

8.   Mass measures the amount of matter in an object.

9.   Ice is more dense than water.

10.   A nanogram is larger than a picogram.

Match each entry on the left with its partner on the right.

1.   50037   (a) Converts pounds to kilograms

2.   1 centimeter   (b) 0.1 grams

3. $\dfrac{2.205 \text{ lb}}{1 \text{ kg}}$ (c) Larger than one inch

4.   263 K   (d) −17.8 °C

5.   1 dekagram   (e) Five significant figures

6.   0.048   (f) SI unit of volume measure

7.   1 m^3 (g) Converts kilograms to pounds

8.   1 liter   (h) 10 grams

9.   1 decimeter   (i) −10 °C

10. $\dfrac{1 \text{ kg}}{2.205 \text{ lb}}$ (j) Smaller than one inch

11.   0°F   (k) Metric unit of volume measure

12.   1 decigram   (l) Two significant figures

Chapter 2   Atoms and the Periodic Table

Chapter Outline

I. Atomic Theory (Sections 2.1–2.3).
    A. Fundamental assumptions about atoms (Section 2.1).
        1. All matter is composed of atoms.
        2. The atoms of each element are different from the atoms of all other elements.
        3. Chemical compounds consist of elements combined in definite proportions.
        4. Chemical reactions only change the way that atoms are combined in compounds; the atoms themselves are unchanged.
    B. Nature of the atom (Sections 2.1).
        1. Atoms are very small ($\sim 10^{-11}$ m in diameter).
        2. Atoms consist of subatomic particles.
        a. A proton is positively charged and has a mass of 1.6726×10^{-24} g.
        b. A neutron has no charge and has a mass of 1.6749×10^{-24} g.
        c. An electron is negatively charged and has a mass of 9.1093×10^{-28} g.
        3. The masses of atoms are expressed in relative terms.
        a. Under this system, a carbon atom with six protons and six neutrons is given a mass of exactly 12 atomic mass units (amu).
        b. Consequently, a proton and a neutron each have a mass of approximately 1 amu.
        4. Atoms are held together by the interplay of attractive and repulsive forces of positively charged protons and negatively charged electrons.
        5. Protons and neutrons are located in the nucleus of an atom, and electrons move about the nucleus.
        6. The size of the nucleus is small compared to the size of the atom.
    C. Composition of atoms (Section 2.2).
        1. Atoms of different elements differ from each other according to how many protons they contain.
        2. Z stands for the number of protons an atom has and is known as the atomic number.
        3. The number of electrons in an atom is the same as the number of protons.
        4. The mass number A stands for the number of protons plus the number of neutrons.
    D. Isotopes and atomic weight (Section 2.3).
        1. Isotopes are atoms of the same element that differ only in the number of neutrons.
        2. Isotopes are represented by showing the mass number as a superscript on the left side of the symbol for the chemical element; the atomic number is shown as a subscript on the left side.
        3. Most elements occur in nature as a mixture of isotopes.
        4. The atomic weight of an element can be calculated if the percent of contributing isotopes is known.
II. The Periodic Table (Sections 2.4–2.5).
    A. The periodic table is a classification of elements according to their properties (Section 2.4).
        1. Elements are arranged by increasing atomic number in seven rows called periods.
        2. Elements are also arranged in 18 vertical columns called groups.
        a. Main group elements occur on the left and right of the periodic table.
        b. Transition metal groups occur in the middle of the periodic table.
        c. Inner transition metal groups are shown separately at the bottom.
        3. The elements in each group have similar chemical properties.

B. Chemical characteristics of groups of elements (Section 2.5).
  1. Group 1A—Alkali metals (Li, Na, K, Rb, Cs, Fr).
  a. Shiny, soft, low-melting.
  b. React violently with water.
  2. Group 2A—Alkaline earth metals (Be, Mg, Ca, Sr, Ba, Ra).
  a. Lustrous, shiny metals.
  b. Less reactive than metals in group 1A.
  3. Group 7A—Halogens (F, Cl, Br, I, At).
  a. Corrosive, nonmetals (except At).
  b. Found in nature only in combination with other elements.
  4. Group 8A—Noble gases (He, Ne, Ar, Kr, Xe, Rn). Extremely unreactive.
C. Neighboring groups have similar behaviors.
  1. Metals.
  a. Found on the left side of the periodic table.
  b. Silvery, ductile, good conductors.
  2. Nonmetals.
  a. Found on the right side of the periodic table.
  b. Eleven of the 17 nonmetals are gases.
  c. Solid nonmetals are brittle and are poor conductors of electricity.
  3. Metalloids.
  a. Occur on the boundary between metals and nonmetals.
  b. Have intermediate chemical behavior.
III. Electrons (Sections 2.6–2.9).
  A. The properties of the elements are due to the distribution of electrons in their atoms (Section 2.6).
  B. Location of electrons.
  1. Electrons are located in specific regions about the nucleus.
  2. The energies of electrons are quantized.
  3. The locations of electrons are described by shells, subshells and orbitals.
  a. Shells.
    i. Shells describe the energy level of an electron.
    ii. Shells are related to an electron's distance from the nucleus.
  b. Subshells.
    i. Subshells describe the energy levels of electrons within each shell.
    ii. The four types of subshell are *s*, *p*, *d*, and *f*.
  c. Orbitals.
    i. Orbitals are the regions of subshells in which electrons of a specific energy can be found.
    ii. An *s* subshell contains one orbital, a *p* subshell contains three orbitals, a *d* subshell contains five orbitals, and an *f* subshell contains seven orbitals.
    iii. Each orbital can hold two electrons, and they must be of opposite spin.
    iv. An *s* orbital is spherical, and a *p* orbital is dumbbell-shaped.
  4. Since the exact position of electrons can't be specified, orbitals are often referred to as electron clouds.
  C. Electron configurations (Section 2.7).
  1. The specific arrangement of electrons in an atom's shells and subshells is known as its electron configuration.
  2. This arrangement can be predicted by using three rules.
  a. Electrons occupy the lowest orbitals available within each subshell.
    i. Within each shell, the subshell energy levels increase in the order *s*, *p*, *d*, *f*.
  b. Each orbital can hold only two electrons, and they must be of opposite spin.
  c. If two or more orbitals have the same energy, each orbital is half filled before any orbital is completely filled.

3. The number of electrons in each subshell is given by a superscript.
D. Electron configuration and the periodic table (Sections 2.8–2.9).
   1. Properties of elements are determined by their location in the periodic table (Section 2.8).
   2. The periodic table is divided into four regions.
      a. Elements in groups 1A and 2A are *s*-block elements because they result from filling *s* orbitals.
      b. Groups 3A–8A are *p*-block elements.
      c. Transition metals are *d*-block elements.
      d. Inner transition metals are *f*-block elements.
   3. The periodic table can be used as a reminder of the order of orbital filling.
   4. Elements within a group of the periodic table have similar electronic configurations of their valence electronic shells and thus similar chemical behavior.
   5. The valence electrons in a compound can be represented by electron dots (Section 2.9).

Solutions to Chapter 2 Problems

2.1

$$150 \times 10^{12} \text{ atoms} \times \frac{56 \text{ amu}}{1 \text{ atom}} \times \frac{1.660\ 539 \times 10^{-24} \text{ g}}{1 \text{ amu}} = 1.39 \times 10^{-8} \text{ g}$$

2.2

(a) $1.0 \text{ g} \times \dfrac{1 \text{ amu}}{1.660\ 539 \times 10^{-24} \text{ g}} \times \dfrac{1 \text{ atom}}{1.0 \text{ amu}} = 6.0 \times 10^{23} \text{ atoms}$

(b) $12.0 \text{ g} \times \dfrac{1 \text{ amu}}{1.660\ 539 \times 10^{-24} \text{ g}} \times \dfrac{1 \text{ atom}}{12.0 \text{ amu}} = 6.02 \times 10^{23} \text{ atoms}$

(c) $23.0 \text{ g} \times \dfrac{1 \text{ amu}}{1.660\ 539 \times 10^{-24} \text{ g}} \times \dfrac{1 \text{ atom}}{23.0 \text{ amu}} = 6.02 \times 10^{23} \text{ atoms}$

2.3 In each of the preceding examples, the mass in grams equals the mass in amu, and the number of atoms in all three samples is identical.

2.4 In comparing the volume of the nucleus to the volume of the atom, the terms 4/3 π cancel.
$(radius_{nucleus})^3 \div (radius_{atom})^3 = (1.5 \times 10^{-15} \text{ m}^3)^3 \div (1.44 \times 10^{-10})^3 \times 100\%$

$$= (3.375 \times 10^{-45} \text{ m}^3) \div (2.986 \times 10^{-30}) \times 100\%$$

$$= 1.1 \times 10^{-13}\%$$

Thus, $1.1 \times 10^{-13}\%$ of the volume of a gold atom is occupied by the nucleus.

2.5 (a) Re   (b) Sr   (c) Te

2.6 Recall that the *atomic number* (Z) shows how many protons an atom contains. Cobalt, with an atomic number of 27, thus contains 27 protons.
Cobalt also contains 27 electrons, since the number of protons equals the number of electrons.
The *mass number* (A) shows the number of protons plus the number of neutrons. To find the number of neutrons in an atom, subtract the atomic number from the mass number.
For cobalt: Mass number – atomic number = 60 – 27 = 33.
The cobalt atom has 33 neutrons.

2.7   Contribution from ^{39}K: 93.12% of 38.96 amu = 36.28 amu
Contribution from ^{41}K: 6.88% of 40.96 amu =   2.82 amu

                                    Atomic weight = 39.10 amu

The calculated value agrees exactly with the reported value.

2.8   Both bromine isotopes have 35 protons. The isotope with mass number 79 has 44 neutrons, and the isotope with mass number 81 has 46 neutrons.
The atomic number is written at the lower left of the element symbol, and the mass number is written at the upper left.

$^{79}_{35}$Br   and $^{81}_{35}$Br

2.9

$^{35}_{17}$Cl $^{37}_{17}$Cl

2.10   Aluminum is in group 3A (or 13) and period 3.

2.11   The group 1B element in period 5 is silver (Ag).
The group 2A element in period 4 is calcium (Ca).

2.12   *Group 5A Element*   *Period*

    Nitrogen (N)   2
    Phosphorus (P)   3
    Arsenic (As)   4
    Antimony (Sb)   5
    Bismuth (Bi)   6

2.13   Metals: titanium (Ti), scandium (Sc)
Nonmetals: selenium (Se), argon (Ar), astatine (At)
Metalloids: tellurium (Te)

2.14   (a) Krypton: (ii) nonmetal; (iv) main group element; (v) noble gas
(b) Strontium: (i) metal; (iv) main group element
(c) Nitrogen: (ii) nonmetal; (iv) main group element
(d) Cobalt: (i) metal; (iii) transition element

2.15   Thirteen He-4 nuclei, plus four neutrons, would be needed.

2.16   (a) Sodium; Group 1A; Period 3; metal   (b) Oxygen; Group 6A; Period 2; nonmetal

2.17   Twelve electrons are present in this atom, which is magnesium.

2.18   Sulfur is a main-group element (Group 6A) that is a nonmetal. The last electron is found in a $3p$ orbital.

2.19   To find the electron configuration of an atom, first find its atomic number. For C (carbon), the atomic number is 6; thus, carbon has 6 protons and 6 electrons. Then assign electrons to the proper orbitals. For carbon, the electron configuration is $1s^2\, 2s^2\, 2p^2$.

Element	Atomic Number	Electron Configuration
(a) C (carbon)	6	$1s^2\, 2s^2\, 2p^2$
(b) P (phosphorus)	15	$1s^2\, 2s^2\, 2p^6\, 3s^2\, 3p^3$
(c) Cl (chlorine)	17	$1s^2\, 2s^2\, 2p^6\, 3s^2\, 3p^5$
(d) K (potassium)	19	$1s^2\, 2s^2\, 2p^6\, 3s^2\, 3p^6\, 4s^1$

2.20   Element 33 (As): $1s^2\, 2s^2\, 2p^6\, 3s^2\, 3p^6\, 4s^2\, 3d^{10}\, 4p^3$. The $4p$ subshell is incompletely filled. Notice that only one electron occupies each orbital of the $4p$ subshell.

     ↑ ↑ ↑ $4p^3$

2.21   The atom has 31 electrons (and 31 protons) and can be identified as gallium.

2.22   (a) F: $1s^2\, 2s^2\, 2p^5$; [He] $\mathbf{2s^2\, 2p^5}$ (b) Al: $1s^2\, 2s^2\, 2p^6\, 3s^2\, 3p^1$; [Ne] $\mathbf{3s^2\, 3p^1}$

     (c) As: $1s^2\, 2s^2\, 2p^6\, 3s^2\, 3p^6\, 4s^2\, 3d^{10}\, 4p^3$; [Ar] $\mathbf{4s^2\, 3d^{10}\, 4p^3}$
(Valence electrons are bold.)

2.23   In group 2A, all elements have the outer-shell configuration ns^2.

2.24   Chlorine, in group 7A (17), has seventeen electrons. Its electron configuration is $1s^2\, 2s^2\, 2p^6\, 3s^2\, 3p^5$. Two electrons are in shell 1, eight electrons are in shell 2, and seven electrons are in shell 3. The outer shell configuration is $3s^2\, 3p^5$.

2.25   The elements form group 6A (16) and have the general valence-shell configuration $ns^2 np^4$.

2.26

     ·Ẋ·

2.27

     :R̈n: ·Ṗb·   :Ẍe: ·Ra·

2.28   The wavelength of red light lies between 700–780 nm, and the wavelength of blue light lies between 400–480 nm. Blue light is associated with higher energy.

Understanding Key Concepts

2.30   The element marked in red is a gas (fluorine—group 7A).
The element marked in blue has atomic number 79 (gold).
All elements in group 2A have chemical behavior similar to the element marked in green (calcium). These include beryllium, magnesium, strontium, barium, and radium.

2.32   Selenium (Z = 34) is the element whose orbital-filling diagram is shown. Notice that it is possible to identify the element by counting its electrons, which equal the number of protons and give the value of Z.

Atomic Theory and the Composition of Atoms

2.34   (1) All matter is composed of atoms.
(2) The atoms of a given element differ from the atoms of all other elements.
(3) Chemical compounds consist of atoms combined in specific proportions.
(4) Chemical reactions change only the way that atoms are combined in compounds; the atoms themselves are unchanged.

2.36

(a) Bi: $208.9804 \text{ amu} \times \dfrac{1.660\ 539 \times 10^{-24} \text{ g}}{1 \text{ amu}} = 3.470201 \times 10^{-22} \text{ g}$

(b) Xe: $131.29 \text{ amu} \times \dfrac{1.660\ 539 \times 10^{-24} \text{ g}}{1 \text{ amu}} = 2.1801 \times 10^{-22} \text{ g}$

(c) He: $4.0026 \text{ amu} \times \dfrac{1.660\ 539 \times 10^{-24} \text{ g}}{1 \text{ amu}} = 6.6465 \times 10^{-24} \text{ g}$

2.38

$6.022 \times 10^{23} \text{ atoms} \times \dfrac{1.660\ 539 \times 10^{-24} \text{ g}}{1 \text{ amu}} \times \dfrac{14.01 \text{ amu}}{1 \text{ atom}} = 14.01 \text{ g}$

2.40

$15.99 \text{ g} \times \dfrac{1 \text{ amu}}{1.660\ 539 \times 10^{-24} \text{ g}} \times \dfrac{1 \text{ atom}}{15.99 \text{ amu}} = 6.022 \times 10^{23} \text{ atoms}$

2.42

Particle	Mass in amu	Charge
Proton	1.007 276	+1
Neutron	1.008 665	0
Electron	$5.485\ 799 \times 10^{-4}$	−1

2.44

Isotope	Argon-36	Argon-38	Argon-40
Number of neutrons	18	20	22

2.46 Symbols (a) and (c) represent isotopes because they have the same atomic number but different mass numbers.

2.48

(a) $^{14}_{6}C$ (b) $^{39}_{19}K$ (c) $^{20}_{10}Ne$

2.50

$^{12}_{6}C$ – six neutrons $^{13}_{6}C$ – seven neutrons $^{14}_{6}C$ – eight neutrons

2.52 Contribution from ^{63}Cu: 69.17% of 62.93 amu = 43.53 amu
Contribution from ^{65}Cu: 30.83% of 64.93 amu = 20.02 amu

The Periodic Table

2.54 The third period in the periodic table contains 8 elements because 8 electrons are needed to fill the s subshell (2 electrons) and p subshell (6 electrons) of the third shell.

2.56 Americium (Am; atomic number 95) is a metal.

2.58 (a) They are metals.
(b) They are transition metals.
(c) The $3d$ subshell is being filled.

2.60 (a) Rubidium: (i) metal; (v) main group element; (vii) alkali metal
(b) Tungsten: (i) metal; (iv) transition element
(c) Germanium: (iii) metalloid; (v) main group element
(d) Krypton: (ii) nonmetal; (v) main group element; (vi) noble gas

2.62 Selenium is chemically similar to sulfur.

2.64 The alkali metal family is composed of lithium, sodium, potassium, rubidium, cesium, and francium.

Electron Configuration

2.66 A maximum of two electrons can go into an orbital.

2.68 First shell—2 electrons
Second shell—8 electrons
Third shell—18 electrons

2.70 The third shell contains three subshells: $3s$, $3p$, $3d$. The fourth shell contains four subshells: $4s$, $4p$, $4d$, $4f$. The fifth shell contains five subshells: $5s$, $5p$, $5d$, $5f$, and an additional subshell.

2.72 Ten electrons are present; the element is neon.

2.74 (a) Sulfur   (b) Bromine   (c) Silicon

$\uparrow\downarrow$ $\uparrow$ $\uparrow$ $\uparrow\downarrow$ $\uparrow\downarrow$ $\uparrow$ $\uparrow$ $\uparrow$ _

$3p^4$ $4p^5$ $3p^2$

2.76

Element	Sulfur	Bromine	Silicon	Rubidium	Niobium	Rhodium
Number of unpaired electrons	2	1	2	1	3	3

2.78 The element with atomic number 12 (Mg) has two electrons in its valence shell.

$\cdot$Mg$\cdot$

2.80 Beryllium: $2s$ Arsenic: $4p$

2.82

Element:	(a) Kr	(b) C	(c) Ca	(d) K	(e) B	(f) Cl
Number of valence-shell electrons:	8	4	2	1	3	7

:Kr: $\cdot$C$\cdot$ $\cdot$Ca$\cdot$ $\cdot$K $\cdot$B$\cdot$:Cl$\cdot$

Chemistry in Action

2.84 A normal light microscope can't reach the degree of precision of a scanning tunneling microscope.

2.86 Hydrogen and helium are the first two elements made in stars.

2.88

	Higher Energy	*Lower Energy*
(a)	ultraviolet	infrared
(b)	gamma waves	microwaves
(c)	X rays	visible light

General Questions and Problems

2.90 Helium, neon, argon, krypton, xenon, and radon make up the noble gas family.

2.92 Tellurium has a greater atomic weight because its nuclei contain, on the average, more neutrons than an iodine nucleus.

2.94 Pb: $1s^2\,2s^2\,2p^6\,3s^2\,3p^6\,4s^2\,3d^{10}\,4p^6\,5s^2\,4d^{10}\,5p^6\,6s^2\,4f^{14}\,5d^{10}\,6p^2$
Shell 1: 2 electrons   Shell 2: 8 electrons   Shell 3: 18 electrons
Shell 4: 32 electrons   Shell 5: 18 electrons   Shell 6: 4 electrons

2.96   Contribution from ^{79}Br: 50.69% of 78.92 amu = 40.00 amu
Contribution from ^{81}Br: 49.31% of 80.91 amu = 39.90 amu
_____
Average atomic weight = 79.90 amu

2.98   The unidentified element is strontium, which occurs directly below calcium in group 2A and thus has similar chemical behavior. Strontium is a metal, has 38 protons, and is in the fifth period.

· Sr ·

2.100 Tin, a metal, has an electron configuration by shell of 2 8 18 18 4.

2.102 (a) Electrons must fill the $4s$ subshell before entering the $3d$ subshell. The correct configuration:

$$1s^2 \, 2s^2 \, 2p^6 \, 3s^2 \, 3p^6 \, 4s^2 \, 3d^8$$

(b) Electrons must fill the $2s$ subshell before entering the $2p$ subshell. The correct configuration:

$$1s^2 \, 2s^2 \, 2p^3$$

(c) Silicon has 14 electrons. The p orbitals must be half-filled before any one orbital is completely filled. The correct configuration:

$$1s^2 \, 2s^2 \, 2p^6 \, 3s^2 \; \underset{3p}{\uparrow \; \uparrow} \; \text{\_}$$

(d) The $3s$ electrons must have opposite spins. The correct configuration:

$$1s^2 \, 2s^2 \, 2p^6 \; \underset{3s}{\uparrow\downarrow}$$

2.104 An electron will fill or half-fill a d subshell instead of filling an s subshell of a higher shell.

2.106 The last orbital filled in element 117 is $7p$.

Self-Test for Chapter 2

Multiple Choice

1. Which of the following is a metalloid?
   (a) carbon   (b) aluminum   (c) silicon   (d) phosphorus

2. Which of the following has a partially filled d subshell?
   (a) calcium   (b) vanadium   (c) zinc   (d) arsenic

3. Which of the following is not a part of atomic theory?
   (a) All metal is composed of atoms.   (b) The atoms of each element are different from the atoms of other elements.   (c) In chemical compounds, atoms are combined in specific proportions.   (d) Chemical reactions only change the way that atoms are combined.

4. How many isotopes of hydrogen are there?
   (a) one   (b) two   (c) three   (d) can't be determined

5. What holds protons and neutrons together in the nucleus?
   (a) attraction   (b) repulsion   (c) electrons   (d) internuclear forces

6. Which of the following has a mass number of 33?
   (a) $^{74}_{33}\text{As}$ (b) $^{35}_{17}\text{Cl}$ (c) $^{32}_{16}\text{S}$ (d) $^{33}_{16}\text{S}$

7. In which order are subshells usually filled?
   (a) s, p, d, f (b) d, f, p, s (c) s, p, f, d (d) s, d, p, f

8. The element with atomic number 38 is:
   (a) an alkali metal   (b) an alkaline earth metal   (c) a transition metal   (d) a metalloid

9. The element that has atomic weight $= 91$ and has 40 electrons is:
   (a) protactinium   (b) niobium   (c) antimony   (d) zirconium

10. The element that has electron configuration $1s^2\, 2s^2\, 2p^6\, 3s^2\, 3p^6\, 4s^2\, 3d^7$ is:
    (a) copper   (b) rhodium   (c) arsenic   (d) cobalt

11. An element that has electrons in its f subshell is:
    (a) europium   (b) technetium   (c) antimony   (d) xenon

12. $^{195}_{78}\text{X}$ is the symbol for:
    (a) gold   (b) platinum   (c) iridium   (d) iron

Sentence Completion

1. A _____ orbital is dumbbell-shaped.

2. An atomic mass unit is also known as a _____.

3. The nucleus of an atom is made up of _____ and _____.

4.   The _____ _____ indicates the number of protons in an atom.

5.   The electrons in an atom are grouped by energy into _____.

6.   Elements belonging to the same _____ have similar chemical properties.

7.   The atomic number of aluminum is _____.

8.   Protons, neutrons, and electrons are known as _____ _____.

9.   Atoms having the same number of protons but different numbers of neutrons are called _____.

10.   The third shell contains _____ electrons.

11.   The word _____ means that electrons can have certain energy values and no others.

True or False

1.   Bismuth is a metal.

2.   The mass of an electron is approximately 1 amu.

3.   A 4*s* electron is higher in energy than a 3*d* electron.

4.   Isotopes have the same number of protons but different numbers of neutrons.

5.   An atom's atomic number indicates the number of protons and neutrons the atom has.

6.   Elements in group 2A are more reactive than elements in group 1A.

7.   Elements in the same period have similar chemical properties.

8.   More elements are metals than are nonmetals.

9.   All compounds consist of atoms combined in specific proportions.

10.   A subshell contains only two electrons.

11.   An element can have the same number of protons, neutrons, and electrons.

12.   Atomic weight always increases with atomic number.

Match each entry on the left with its partner on the right.

1. $1s^2\ 2s^2$ (a) Mendeleev

2. Group   (b) Number of protons in an element

3. Atomic mass unit   (c) Reactive metals

4. Formulated the periodic   (d) Average mass of a large number of an
    table   element's atoms

5. Neutron   (e) Column in the periodic table

6. $^{28}_{14}\text{Si}$ (f) Row in the periodic table

7. Group 1A   (g) Element with atomic mass of 14 amu

8. Atomic number   (h) Electron configuration of beryllium

9. $^{29}_{14}\text{Si}$ (i) Element having 15 neutrons

10. Atomic weight   (j) Subatomic particle with zero charge

11. $^{14}_{7}\text{N}$ (k) Dalton

12. Period   (l) Element with atomic number 14

Chapter 3   Ionic Compounds

Chapter Outline

I. Ions (Sections 3.1–3.2).
   A. Ions are formed when a neutral atom either gains an electron (to form an anion) or loses an electron (to form a cation).
      1. Ionization energy measures the ease with which an atom gives up an electron.
         a. Energy must be supplied in order to remove an electron.
         b. Elements on the far left of the periodic table have smaller ionization energies and lose electrons more easily.
         c. Elements on the far right of the periodic table have larger ionization energies and lose electrons with difficulty.
      2. Electron affinity measures the ease with which an atom gains an electron.
         a. Energy is released when an atom gains an electron.
         b. Elements on the far right of the periodic table have larger electron affinities and gain electrons easily.
         c. Elements on the far left of the periodic table have smaller electron affinities and gain electrons less easily.
   B. Main group elements in the middle of the periodic table neither lose or gain electrons easily.
II. Formation of ionic compounds (Sections 3.3–3.5).
   A. Compounds formed between an element on the far left side of the periodic table and an element on the far right of the periodic table are electronically neutral (Section 3.3).
      1. These compounds consist of a large number of cations and anions packed together in a regular arrangement in a crystal.
      2. The bonds between ions in the crystal are known as ionic bonds.
      3. The crystal is known as an ionic solid.
   B. Properties of ionic compounds (Section 3.4).
      1. Ionic compounds are crystalline.
      2. Solutions of ionic compounds conduct electricity.
      3. Ionic compounds are high-melting.
      4. Many, but not all, ionic compounds are water-soluble.
   C. The octet rule (Section 3.5).
      1. Main group elements undergo reactions that leave them with eight valence electrons – an octet.
III. Ions of some common elements (Sections 3.6–3.8).
   A. Cations (Section 3.6).

      1. Group 1A $M\cdot \longrightarrow M^+ + e^-$

      2. Group 2A $\cdot M\cdot \longrightarrow M^{2+} + 2e^-$
      3. Group 3A Al^{3+} is the only common cation.
      4. Transition metals form cations, but the charge on these cations is not as predictable as it is for main group elements.

B. Anions.

    1. Group 6A $:\overset{\cdot\cdot}{\underset{\cdot\cdot}{X}}: \; + \; 2\,e^- \longrightarrow \; :\overset{\cdot\cdot}{\underset{\cdot\cdot}{X}}:^{2-}$

    2. Group 7A $:\overset{\cdot}{\underset{\cdot\cdot}{X}}: \; + \; e^- \longrightarrow \; :\overset{\cdot\cdot}{\underset{\cdot\cdot}{X}}:^{-}$

C. Group 4A, group 5A, and group 8A elements don't usually form cations or anions.
D. Naming ions (Section 3.7).
    1. Main group cations are named by identifying the metal and then adding the word "ion."
    2. Transition metal cations are named by identifying the metal, specifying the charge, and adding the word "ion."
    3. Anions are named by replacing the end of the name of the element with -*ide* and adding the word "ion."
    4. Polyatomic ions (Section 3.8).
        a. Polyatomic ions are composed of more than one atom.
        b. Subscripts in polyatomic ions indicate how many of each ion are present in the formula unit (no subscripts are necessary if only one ion is present).
        c. The names of polyatomic ions should be memorized.
IV. Ionic compounds (Sections 3.9–3.11).
  A. Formulas of ionic compounds (Section 3.9).
    1. Formulas are written so that the number of positive charges equals the number of negative charges.
        a. Cations are listed first, anions second.
        b. It is not necessary to write the charges of the ions.
        c. Use parentheses around a polyatomic ion if it has a subscript.
    2. A formula unit shows the simplest neutral unit of an ionic compound.
  B. Naming ionic compounds (Section 3.10).
    1. Ionic compounds are named by citing the cation and then the anion, with a space between the two words.
    2. If the cation can exhibit more than one charge, the charge must be specified.
  C. Acids and bases (Section 3.11).
    1. Acids are compounds that provide H^+ ions in solution.
    2. Bases are compounds that provide OH^- ions in solution.
    3. Some acids and bases can each provide more than one H^+ or OH^- ion in solution.

Solutions to Chapter 3 Problems

3.1   The Mg^{2+} ion is a cation.

3.2   The S^{2-} ion is an anion.

3.3   The ion shown, O^{-2}, is an anion because it has two more negative charges than positive charges.

3.4   Figure 3.1 shows approximate ionization energies for helium, neon, argon and krypton. In line with this trend, it is predicted that the ionization energy of xenon should be somewhat less than that of krypton but greater than the ionization energy of most other elements.

3.5 (a) According to Figure 3.1, B ($Z = 5$) loses an electron more easily than Be ($Z = 4$).
(b) Ca ($Z = 20$) loses an electron more easily than Co ($Z = 27$).
(c) Sc ($Z = 21$) loses an electron more easily than Se($Z = 34$).

3.6 (a) According to Figure 3.1, H gains an electron more easily than He. Because the electron affinity for He is zero, it does not accept an electron.
(b) S gains an electron more easily than Si.
(c) Cr gains an electron more easily than Mn.

3.7 *Ionic liquids:*   *Other ionic substances:*
Liquid or low-melting at room temperature   High-melting solids
High viscosity   Low viscosity
Low to moderate electrical conductivity   Highly conducting if molten or in solution

3.8 Potassium (atomic number 19): $1s^2\ 2s^2\ 2p^6\ 3s^2\ 3p^6\ 4s^1$
Argon (atomic number 18): $1s^2\ 2s^2\ 2p^6\ 3s^2\ 3p^6$
Potassium can attain the noble-gas configuration of argon by losing an electron from its $4s$ subshell, forming the K^+ cation.

3.9 Aluminum (atomic number 13): $1s^2\ 2s^2\ 2p^6\ 3s^2\ 3p^1$
Neon (atomic number 10): $1s^2\ 2s^2\ 2p^6$
Aluminum can attain the noble-gas configuration of neon by losing three electrons, two from its $3s$ subshell and one from its $3p$ subshell, resulting in the formation of the Al^{3+} ion.

3.10

$$X\!: \ + \ :\!\ddot{Y}\!: \ \longrightarrow \ X^{2+} \ + \ :\!\ddot{\ddot{Y}}\!:^{2-}$$

Y gains electrons, and X loses electrons.

3.11 Molybdenum, a transition metal, is more likely to form a cation than an anion.

3.12

(a) $:\!\dot{\ddot{Se}}\!\cdot \ + \ 2\,e^- \ \longrightarrow \ :\!\ddot{\ddot{Se}}\!:^{2-};\quad Se \ + \ 2\,e^- \ \longrightarrow \ Se^{2-}$

(b) $\cdot Ba\cdot \ \longrightarrow \ Ba^{2+} \ + \ 2\,e^-;\quad Ba \ \longrightarrow \ Ba^{2+} \ + \ 2\,e^-$

(c) $:\!\ddot{Br}\!\cdot \ + \ e^- \ \longrightarrow \ :\!\ddot{\ddot{Br}}\!:^{-};\quad Br \ + \ e^- \ \longrightarrow \ Br^-$

3.13

$$\frac{1\ L}{35\ g}\ \times\ \frac{454\ g}{1\ lb}\ \times\ \frac{1\ gal}{3.79\ L}\ =\ \frac{3.4\ gal}{1\ lb}$$

3.14 (a) Cu^{2+} copper(II) ion (cupric ion)   (b) F^- fluoride ion
(c) Mg^{2+} magnesium ion   (d) S^{2-} sulfide ion

3.15 (a) Ag^+ (b) Fe^{2+} (c) Cu^+ (d) Te^{2-}

3.16 Na^+ sodium ion; K^+ potassium ion;
        Ca^{2+} calcium ion; Cl^- chloride ion

3.17 (a) NO_3^- nitrate ion   (b) CN^- cyanide ion
        (c) OH^- hydroxide ion   (d) HPO_4^{2-} hydrogen phosphate ion

3.18 *Group 1A*: Na^+, K^+ *Group 2A*: Mg^{2+}, Ca^{2+}
        Transition metal: Fe^{2+} *Halogen*: Cl^-

3.19 (a) The two ions are Ag^+ and I^-. Since they have the same charge, only one of each ion is
        needed. The formula is AgI.
        (b) Ions: Ag^+, O^{2-}. Two Ag^+ ions will balance the O^{2-} ion. The formula is Ag_2O.
        (c) The ions are Ag^+ and PO_4^{3-}. Three Ag^+ ions are needed to balance the charge of the
        PO_4^{3-} anion. The formula is Ag_3PO_4.

3.20 (a) Na_2SO_4 (b) $FeSO_4$ (c) $Cr_2(SO_4)_3$

3.21 $(NH_4)_2CO_3$

3.22 $Al_2(SO_4)_3$ $Al(CH_3CO_2)_3$

3.23 Use the periodic table to identify the elements present and use the rules described in
        Section 3.10 to write the formulas. The formulas are K_2S (blue), $BaBr_2$ (red), and Al_2O_3
        (green).

3.24 Since there are three calcium ions for every two nitride ions, the formula is Ca_3N_2.
        Calcium ion has a +2 charge, and nitride ion has a –3 charge.

3.25 Ag_2S—silver(I) sulfide. The charge on silver is +1.

3.26 (a) SnO_2 tin(IV) oxide   (b) $Ca(CN)_2$ calcium cyanide
        (c) Na_2CO_3 sodium carbonate   (d) Cu_2SO_4 copper(I) sulfate
        (e) $Ba(OH)_2$ barium hydroxide   (f) $Fe(NO_3)_2$ iron(II) nitrate

3.27 (a) Li_3PO_4 (b) $CuCO_3$ (c) $Al_2(SO_3)_3$ (d) CuF   (e) $Fe_2(SO_4)_3$ (f) NH_4Cl

3.28 Cr_2O_3 chromium(III) oxide

3.29 Acids provide H^+ ions when dissolved in water.
        Bases provide OH^- ions when dissolved in water.

        Acids: HF $\xrightarrow{\text{dissolve in water}}$ H^+ + F^-

                HCN $\xrightarrow{\text{dissolve in water}}$ H^+ + CN^-

        Bases: $Ca(OH)_2$ $\xrightarrow{\text{dissolve in water}}$ Ca^{2+} + $2\ OH^-$

                LiOH $\xrightarrow{\text{dissolve in water}}$ Li^+ + OH^-

3.30 Solution (a) represents HCl; the drawing shows that there are equal numbers of cations and
        anions in solution. Solution (b) represents H_2SO_4; two cations are present for each anion.

Understanding Key Concepts

3.32

⫿⫿⫿ elements that commonly form +2 ions
☰ elements that commonly form −2 ions
■ an element that forms a +3 ion

3.34 Drawing (a) represents a sodium atom, and drawing (b) represents an Na⁺ ion. The Na atom is larger because its 3s electron lies in an orbital that is farther from the nucleus.

3.36 $FeCl_2$: iron (II) chloride or ferrous chloride $FeCl_3$: iron (III) chloride or ferric chloride
FeO: iron (II) oxide or ferrous oxide Fe_2O_3: iron (III) oxide or ferric oxide
$PbCl_2$: lead (II) chloride $PbCl_4$: lead (IV) chloride
PbO: lead (II) oxide PbO_2: lead (IV) oxide

Ions and Ionic Bonding

3.38 (a) $Ca \rightarrow Ca^{2+} + 2e^-$ (b) $Au \rightarrow Au^+ + e^-$
(c) $F + e^- \rightarrow F^-$ (d) $Cr \rightarrow Cr^{3+} + 3e^-$

3.40 (a) False. A cation is formed by *loss* of one or more electrons from an atom. (b), (c) False. Group 4A elements rarely form ions. (d) True.

Ions and the Octet Rule

3.42 The *octet rule* states that main group atoms undergo reactions in order to achieve a noble gas electron configuration with eight outer-shell electrons.

3.44 Se^{2-} An ion with 34 protons and 36 electrons has a −2 charge.

3.46 (a) $X^{2+} = Sr^{2+}$; $X = Sr$ The strontium ion has the same electron configuration as the noble gas krypton.
(b) $X^- = Br^-$; $X = Br$ The bromide ion also has the same electron configuration as the noble gas krypton.

3.48 (a) Rb^+ $1s^2 2s^2 2p^6 3s^2 3p^6 4s^2 3d^{10} 4p^6$
(b) Br^- $1s^2 2s^2 2p^6 3s^2 3p^6 4s^2 3d^{10} 4p^6$
(c) S^{2-} $1s^2 2s^2 2p^6 3s^2 3p^6$
(d) Ba^{2+} $1s^2 2s^2 2p^6 3s^2 3p^6 4s^2 3d^{10} 4p^6 5s^2 4d^{10} 5p^6$
(e) Al^{3+} $1s^2 2s^2 2p^6$

Periodic Properties and Ion Formation

3.50 (a) O   (b) Li   (c) Zn   (d) N

3.52 None of the ions are stable because all lack eight outer-shell electrons.

3.54 Cr^{2+}: $1s^2\, 2s^2\, 2p^6\, 3s^2\, 3p^6\, 3d^4$
Cr^{3+}: $1s^2\, 2s^2\, 2p^6\, 3s^2\, 3p^6\, 3d^3$

3.56   The ionization energy of Li^+ is much greater than that of Li. Li readily loses an electron to form an ion with eight outer-shell electrons, but Li^+ would need to lose one electron from a stable octet in order to form the Li^{2+} cation.

Symbols, Formulas, and Names for Ions

3.58   (a) S^{2-} sulfide ion   (b) Sn^{2+} tin(II) ion   (c) Sr^{2+} strontium ion
(d) Mg^{2+} magnesium ion   (e) Au^+ gold(I) ion

3.60   (a) Se^{2-} (b) O^{2-} (c) Ag^+

3.62   (a) OH^- (b) HSO_4^- (c) $CH_3CO_2^-$ (d) MnO_4^- (e) OCl^- (f) NO_3^-
(g) CO_3^{2-} (h) $Cr_2O_7^{2-}$

Names and Formulas for Ionic Compounds

3.64   (a) $Al_2(SO_4)_3$ (b) Ag_2SO_4 (c) $ZnSO_4$ (d) $BaSO_4$

3.66   (a) $NaHCO_3$ (b) KNO_3 (c) $CaCO_3$ (d) NH_4NO_3

3.68

	S^{2-}	Cl^-	PO_4^{3-}	CO_3^{2-}
Copper(II)	CuS	$CuCl_2$	$Cu_3(PO_4)_2$	$CuCO_3$
Ca^{2+}	CaS	$CaCl_2$	$Ca_3(PO_4)_2$	$CaCO_3$
NH_4^+	$(NH_4)_2S$	NH_4Cl	$(NH_4)_3PO_4$	$(NH_4)_2CO_3$
Ferric ion	Fe_2S_3	$FeCl_3$	$FePO_4$	$Fe_2(CO_3)_3$

3.70   copper(II) sulfide   copper(II) chloride   copper(II) phosphate   copper(II) carbonate
calcium sulfide   calcium chloride   calcium phosphate   calcium carbonate
ammonium sulfide   ammonium chloride   ammonium phosphate ammonium carbonate
ferric sulfide   ferric chloride   ferric phosphate   ferric carbonate

3.72   (a) $MgCO_3$ magnesium carbonate   (b) $Ca(CH_3CO_2)_2$ calcium acetate
(c) $AgCN$ silver(I) cyanide   (d) $Na_2Cr_2O_7$ sodium dichromate

3.74 $Ca_3(PO_4)_2$ (d) is the correct formula because the six positive charges from the three Ca^{2+} ions are balanced by the six negative charges of the two PO_4^{3-} ions.

Acids and Bases

3.76   An acid provides H^+ ions when dissolved in water. A base provides OH^- ions when dissolved in water.

3.78

(a) $H_2CO_3 \xrightarrow{\text{dissolve in water}} 2\,H^+ + CO_3^{2-}$

(b) $HCN \xrightarrow{\text{dissolve in water}} H^+ + CN^-$

(c) $Mg(OH)_2$ $\xrightarrow{\text{dissolve in water}}$ Mg^{2+} + 2 OH^-

(d)   KOH $\xrightarrow{\text{dissolve in water}}$ K^+ + OH^-

Chemistry in Action

3.80   The bulky cations can't pack in an orderly way and thus don't crystallize at room temperature.

3.82   The RDI for sodium is 2300 mg, which is equivalent to 4 g of table salt.

3.84   Sodium protects against fluid loss and is necessary for muscle contraction and transmission of nerve impulses.

3.86

Ion	*Name*	*Charge*	*Total Charge*
Ca^{2+}	calcium ion	2+	10 x (2+) = 20+
$PO_4{}^{3-}$	phosphate ion	3–	6 x (3–) = 18–
OH^-	hydroxide ion	1–	2 x (1–) = 2–

The formula correctly represents a neutral compound because the number of positive charges equals the number of negative charges.

General Questions and Problems

3.88   The hydride ion has the same electron configuration ($1s^2$) as the noble gas helium.

3.90   (a) CrO_3 (b) VCl_5 (c) MnO_2 (d) MoS_2

3.92   (a) A gluconate ion has one negative charge.
(b) Three gluconate ions are in one formula unit of iron(III) gluconate, and the formula is $Fe(gluconate)_3$.

3.94   (a) $Co(CN)_2$ (b) UO_3 (c) $SnSO_4$ (d) MnO_2 (e) K_3PO_4 (f) Ca_3P_2
(g) $LiHSO_4$ (h) $Al(OH)_3$

3.96   (a) X is likely to be a metal, because metals are more likely to form cations.
(b) Y is likely to be a nonmetal.
(c) The formula for the product is X_2Y_3.
(d) X is likely to be in Group 3A or Group 3B (or to be a transition metal) and Y is likely to be in Group 6A.

Self-Test for Chapter 3

Multiple Choice

1. How many atoms does a formula unit of Li_2CO_3 contain?
   (a) 3   (b) 4   (c) 5   (d) 6

2. How many ions are produced when a formula unit of Li_2CO_3 is dissolved in water?
   (a) 3   (b) 4   (c) 5   (d) 6

3. Which of the following is not a property of ionic compounds?
   (a) crystalline   (b) conductor of electricity   (c) high melting   (d) 1:1 ratio of cations to anions

4. Which of the following is the correct name for $Fe(NO_3)_3$?
   (a) ferrous nitrate   (b) iron nitrate   (c) iron(III) nitrate   (d) iron(II) nitrate

5. Bromine has a:
   (a) large ionization energy and large electron affinity   (b) large ionization energy and small electron affinity   (c) small ionization energy and large electron affinity   (d) small ionization energy and small electron affinity

6. H_2CrO_4 is an acid that:
   (a) can provide one H^+ ion when dissolved   (b) can provide two H^+ ions when dissolved
   (c) can provide one OH^- when dissolved   (d) H_2CrO_4 is not an acid.

7. An element that loses three electrons to attain the electron configuration of argon is:
   (a) titanium   (b) scandium   (c) calcium   (d) potassium

8. The formula for gold(III) chloride is:
   (a) Au_3Cl (b) $AuCl$ (c) $AuCl_2$ (d) $AuCl_3$

9. Which of the following anions is not biologically important?
   (a) Cl^- (b) Br^- (c) HCO_3^- (d) HPO_4^-

10. The redness of rubies is due to which ion?
    (a) iron   (b) titanium   (c) aluminum   (d) chromium

Sentence Completion

1. _____ _____ measures the ease with which an atom gives up an electron.

2. The name of K_3PO_4 is _____ _____.

3. Radium (atomic number 88) loses _____ electrons to achieve a noble gas configuration.

4. NO_3^- is an example of a _____ ion.

5. The formulas of ionic compounds are _____ formulas.

6. Atoms of main group elements tend to combine in chemical compounds so that they attain _____ outer-shell electrons.

7. A _____ provides OH^- ions in water.

8. _____ is the principal mineral component of bone.

9. Ionic compounds are usually _____ solids.

10. The first three elements in group ____A form neither cations nor anions.

True or False

1. Zinc can form ions with different charges.

2. Na^+ and F^- have the same electron configuration.

3. Ionization energy measures the amount of energy released when an ion is formed from a neutral atom.

4. $Co(CO_3)_2$ is a possible compound.

5. A solution of H_3PO_4 contains only H^+ and $H_2PO_4^-$ ions.

6. Ionic crystals conduct electricity.

7. Cuprous ion is the same as copper(II) ion.

8. Many ionic compounds are not water-soluble.

9. Group 5A consists of metals and nonmetals.

10. Elements in group 7A have the largest ionization energies.

11. The octet rule is limited to main group elements.

12. Both men and women suffer the same percent bone loss over their lifetimes.

Match each entry on the left with its partner on the right.

1. $FeBr_2$ (a) Sulfite anion

2. S^{2-} (b) Electron-dot symbol

3. NH_4^+ (c) Alkali metal

4. SO_3^{2-} (d) Has the same electron configuration as Na^+

5. Ca   (e) Iron(II) bromide

6. $FeBr_3$ (f) Transition metal

7. Ar   (g) Sulfate anion

8. ·Be·   (h) Alkaline earth metal

9. Co   (i) Has the same electron configuration as Cl^-

10. SO_4^{2-} (j) Iron(III) bromide

11. Ne   (k) Polyatomic cation

12. K   (l) Sulfide anion

Chapter 4   Molecular Compounds

Chapter Outline

I. Covalent bonds (Sections 4.1–4.4).
   A Formation of covalent bonds (Section 4.1).
      1. Covalent bonds occur when two atoms share electrons.
      2. Electron sharing results from the overlap of orbitals of two atoms.
      3. The optimum distance between nuclei of two atoms is the bond length.
      4. Seven elements exist as diatomic molecules: H_2, N_2, O_2, F_2, Cl_2, Br_2, I_2.
   B. Covalent bonds and the periodic table (Section 4.2).
      1. Molecular compounds result when atoms form covalent bonds to another atom or to more than one atom.
      2 The octet rule states that each atom in a molecular compound shares the number of electrons necessary to achieve a noble-gas configuration.
      3 Most main group elements form from one to four covalent bonds and obey the octet rule.
         a. Boron forms only three bonds because it has only three valence electrons.
         b. Sulfur and phosphorus may form five or six bonds if they use *d* orbitals.
   C. Multiple covalent bonds (Section 4.3).
      1. Some atoms can share more than one electron pair to form multiple bonds.
         a. A double bond is formed when two pairs are shared.
         b. A triple bond is formed when three pairs are shared.
      2. Even when multiple bonds occur, the atoms still obey the octet rule.
   D. Coordinate bonds occur when one atom donates both of the shared electrons (Section 4.4).
II. Molecular compounds (Sections 4.5–4.8).
   A. Characteristics of molecular compounds (Section 4.5).
      1. Molecular compounds are electrically neutral and have no charged particles.
      2. Molecular compounds have low melting and boiling points.
      3. Molecular compounds may be solids, liquids, or gases.
      4. Molecular compounds are usually insoluble in water and do not conduct electricity.
   B. Molecular formulas (Section 4.6).
      1. Molecular formulas show the numbers and kinds of atoms in one molecule of a compound.
      2. Structural formulas show how atoms are connected.
      3. Lewis structures are structural formulas that show electron lone pairs (Section 4.7).
         a. One approach to drawing Lewis structures involves knowing common bonding patterns.
         b. The other approach is a general method.
            i.   Find the number of valence electrons for all atoms.
            ii. Draw a line between each pair of connected atoms to represent an electron pair.
            iii. Place lone pairs around all peripheral atoms to give them octets.
            iv. Place remaining electrons around the central atom.
            v.   If the central atom doesn't have an octet, use an electron pair from a neighboring atom to form a multiple bond to the central atom.
      4. Some larger organic molecules are written as condensed structures.
   C. Molecular shapes can be predicted by using the VSEPR model (Section 4.8).
      1. Draw a Lewis structure of the molecule, and identify the atom whose geometry you want to know.
      2. Count the number of charge clouds around the atom.

3. Predict shape by assuming that the charge clouds orient in space so that they are as far apart as possible.
    a. If there are two charge clouds, the geometry is linear.
    b. If there are three charge clouds, the geometry is trigonal planar or bent.
    c. If there are four charge clouds, the geometry is tetrahedral, trigonal pyramidal, or bent.
III. Polar covalent bonds (Sections 4.9–4.11).
    A. Polar covalent bonds occur when the electrons in a covalent bond are attracted more to one atom than another (Section 4.9).
        1. The ability of an atom to attract electrons is called electronegativity.
        2. Atoms with electronegativity differences between 0.5 and 1.9 form polar covalent bonds.
        3. Atoms with electronegativity differences > 1.9 form ionic bonds.
    B. Molecules containing polar covalent bonds can be polar (Section 4.10).
        1. Molecular polarity depends on both the presence of polar covalent bonds and on molecular shape.
        2. Polarity has a dramatic effect on molecular properties.
    C. Naming binary molecular compounds (Section 4.11).
        1. The less electronegative element is always written first.
        2. Name the first element in the compound, using a prefix if necessary.
        3. Name the second element, using an -ide ending and using a prefix if necessary.

Solutions to Chapter 4 Problems

4.1

shared electron pair

:I:I:

Each iodine atom achieves the noble gas configuration of xenon.

4.2   (a) PH_3 hydrogen—one covalent bond;   phosphorus—three covalent bonds
            (b) H_2Se hydrogen—one covalent bond;   selenium—two covalent bonds
            (c) HCl   hydrogen—one covalent bond;   chlorine—one covalent bond
            (d) SiF_4 fluorine—one covalent bond;   silicon—four covalent bonds

4.3   Lead is a member of group 4A and should form four covalent bonds, as do carbon and silicon. $PbCl_4$ is thus a more likely formula for a covalent compound, and $PbCl_2$ is the formula for an ionic compound.

4.4   (a) CH_2Cl_2. Carbon forms four covalent bonds. Two bonds form between carbon and hydrogen, and the other two form between carbon and chlorine.
            (b) BH_3. Boron forms three covalent bonds.
            (c) NI_3. Nitrogen forms three covalent bonds.
            (d) $SiCl_4$. Silicon, like carbon, forms four covalent bonds.

4.5   In acetic acid, all hydrogen atoms have two outer-shell electrons and all carbon and oxygen atoms have eight outer-shell electrons.

Acetic acid

4.6

4.7 $AlCl_3$ is a covalent molecular compound, and Al_2O_3 is ionic.

4.8   C and N must be bonded to each other. After drawing the C—N bond and all bonds to hydrogens, two electrons remain; they are a lone pair on nitrogen. All atoms now have a noble gas configuration.

CH_5N: 14 valence electrons

$$H-\overset{\overset{\displaystyle H}{|}}{\underset{\underset{\displaystyle H}{|}}{C}}-\overset{\overset{\displaystyle \cdot\cdot}{}}{\underset{\underset{\displaystyle H}{|}}{N}}-H$$

4.9

(a)

$$H-\overset{\overset{\displaystyle H}{|}}{\underset{\underset{\displaystyle H}{|}}{C}}-\overset{\cdot\cdot}{\underset{\cdot\cdot}{O}}-H$$

(b)

$$:N\equiv C-\overset{\overset{\displaystyle H}{|}}{\underset{\underset{\displaystyle H}{|}}{C}}-H$$

(c)

$$\overset{\displaystyle :\overset{\cdot\cdot}{Cl}:}{\underset{\displaystyle :\overset{\cdot\cdot}{Cl}:}{\overset{|}{\underset{|}{N}}}}-\overset{\cdot\cdot}{\underset{\cdot\cdot}{Cl}}:$$

4.10   (a) For phosgene, $COCl_2$:

Step 1:   Total valence electrons
$4 e^-$ (from C) $+ 6 e^-$ (from O) $+ 2 \times 7 e^-$ (from Cl) $= 24 e^-$

Step 2:   Six electrons are involved in the covalent bonds.

$$\begin{array}{c} O \\ | \\ Cl-C-Cl \end{array}$$

Step 3:   The other 18 electrons are placed in nine lone pairs.

$$\begin{array}{c} :\ddot{O}: \\ | \\ :\ddot{C}l-C-\ddot{C}l: \end{array}$$

Step 4:   All electrons are used up in the preceding structure, but carbon doesn't have an electron octet, so one electron pair must be moved from oxygen to form a carbon–oxygen double bond.

Step 5:   The 24 electrons have been used up, and all atoms have a complete octet.

$$\begin{array}{c} :O: \\ \| \\ :\ddot{C}l-C-\ddot{C}l: \end{array}$$

(b) For OCl^-:

Step 1:   Total valence electrons
$6 e^-$ (from O) $+ 7 e^-$ (from Cl) $+ 1 e^-$ (negative charge) $= 14 e^-$

Step 2:   Two electrons used.   O—Cl

Step 3:   Twelve additional electrons used. $:\ddot{O}-\ddot{C}l:^-$

Step 4:   The above structure uses 14 valence electrons, and all atoms have complete octets.

(c) For H_2O_2:

Step 1: $2 e^-$ (from 2 H) $+ 2 \times 6 e^-$ (from O) $= 14$ electrons

Step 2:   Six electrons are involved in covalent bonds.   H—O—O—H

Step 3:   The other eight electrons are placed in four lone pairs. $H-\ddot{O}-\ddot{O}-H$

Step 4:   The 14 electrons have been used up, and all atoms have complete octets.

(d) For SCl_2: 20 electrons

$$:\ddot{C}l-\ddot{S}-\ddot{C}l:$$

4.11

HNO₃: 24 electrons

$$:\overset{\displaystyle :\!\overset{\ddots}{O}\!:}{\underset{\displaystyle }{\overset{\parallel}{\underset{}{:\ddot{O}-N-\ddot{O}-H}}}}$$

4.12   (a) The molecular formula for methyl methacrylate is $C_6H_{10}O_2$.
(b) Methyl methacrylate has two double bonds and four electron lone pairs.

   Methyl methacrylate

4.13

:C≡O: :N̈=Ö:

CO is reactive because it can form coordinate covalent bonds with compounds that can accept an electron pair. NO is reactive because it has an unpaired electron.

4.14

$$\left[\; :\!\ddot{F}\!:\!\!-\!\!\underset{\underset{\displaystyle :\ddot{F}:}{\displaystyle |}}{\overset{\overset{\displaystyle :\ddot{F}:}{\displaystyle |}}{B}}\!\!-\!\!:\!\ddot{F}\!: \;\right]^{-}$$ tetrahedral

4.15   Carbon, the central atom, is surrounded by four bonds. Referring to Table 4.2, we see that chloroform has tetrahedral geometry.

   Chloroform

Each carbon of dichloroethylene is surrounded by three charge clouds. Dichloroethylene is planar, with 120° bond angles.

$$\underset{Cl}{\overset{Cl}{\diagdown}}C=C\underset{H}{\overset{H}{\diagup}}$$ Dichloroethylene

4.16 The geometry at (a) is tetrahedral, and the geometry at (b) is trigonal planar.

4.17 Both molecules are bent and have bond angles of approximately 90°.

4.18

Methionine

a. bent
b. tetrahedral
c. tetrahedral
d. trigonal planar
e. pyramidal

4.19 Use Figure 4.6 to predict electronegativity:

Least electronegative — — — — — —> *Most electronegative*

H (2.1), P (2.1) < S (2.5) < N (3.0) < O (3.5)

4.20 | *Electronegativity* | | *Difference* | *Type of Bond* |
|---|---|---|---|
| (a) I (2.5), | Cl (3.0) | 0.5 | polar covalent |
| (b) Li (1.0), | O (3.5) | 2.5 | ionic |
| (c) Br (2.8), | Br (2.8) | 0 | covalent |
| (d) P (2.1), | Br (2.8) | 0.7 | polar covalent |

(a) $\delta+$ $\delta-$ (b)   (d) $\delta+$ $\delta-$
    I—Cl   Li$^+$ O$^-$ P—Br

The Br–Br bond (c) is nonpolar.

4.21

$$H \xrightarrow{} $$

      H
       \\
        C=Ö
       /
      H $\delta+$ $\delta-$

Formaldehyde is polar because of the polarity of the carbon–oxygen bond and because of the two electron lone pairs.

4.22 The —CH₃ portions of diethyl ether are tetrahedral. The C–O–C portion is bent and has a bond angle of 112°. The molecule has the indicated polarity because of the polar C–O bonds and because of the two lone pairs of electrons.

4.23

 The difference in electronegativity between Li (1.0) and C (2.5) indicates that the bond between them is polar covalent, with carbon the more electronegative atom. The electrostatic potential map shows that carbon is electron-rich (red) and lithium is electron-poor (blue).

4.24 (a) S_2Cl_2 Disulfur dichloride   (b) ICl   Iodine monochloride
       (c) ICl_3 Iodine trichloride

4.25 (a) SeF_4 Selenium tetrafluoride   (b) P_2O_5 Diphosphorus pentoxide
       (c) BrF_3 Bromine trifluoride

4.26

$$\underset{\displaystyle CH_3\overset{\displaystyle \overset{CH_3}{|}}{C}=CHCH_2CH_2\overset{\displaystyle \overset{CH_3}{|}}{C}=CHCH_2OH}{}$$

Geraniol $C_{10}H_{18}O$

Understanding Key Concepts

4.28 All models except (c) represent a molecule with a tetrahedral central atom. In models (b) and (d), some atoms are hidden.

4.30

Vitamin C

4.32

Acetamide

The electrostatic potential maps show that oxygen is the most electron-rich atom (red) in acetamide. The hydrogens are most electron-poor (blue).

Covalent Bonds

4.34 In a covalent bond, each atom donates an electron to the bond. Both electrons in a coordinate covalent bond come from the same atom.

4.36 Form covalent bonds: (a) aluminum and bromine; (b) carbon and fluorine
Form ionic bonds: (c) cesium and iodine; (d) zinc and fluorine; (e) lithium and chlorine

4.38 Tellurium, a group 6A element, forms two covalent bonds, as do oxygen, sulfur, and other members of group 6A.

4.40 If the central atom is expected to form fewer bonds than appear in the formula, the compound probably contains a coordinate covalent bond.
Coordinate covalent bonds: (b) $Cu(NH_3)_4^{2+}$ (c) NH_4^+

4.42 Since tin is a member of group 4A, it forms four covalent bonds. $SnCl_4$ is the most likely formula for a molecular compound of tin and chlorine.

4.44 The indicated bond is coordinate covalent because both electrons in the bond come from nitrogen.

$:N\equiv N\!-\!\underset{..}{\overset{..}{O}}:$ coordinate covalent

Structural Formulas

4.46 (a) A *molecular formula* shows the numbers and kinds of atoms in a molecule; a *structural formula* shows how the atoms in a molecule are bonded to one another.
(b) A *structural formula* shows the bonds between atoms; a *condensed structure* shows central atoms and the atoms connected to them written as groups but does not show bonds.
(c) A *lone pair* of valence electrons is a pair that is not shared; a *shared pair* of electrons is shared between two atoms as a covalent bond.

4.48 (a) N_2 10 valence electrons N_2 contains a triple bond.
(b) NOCl   18 valence electrons   N and O are joined by a double bond.
(c) CH_3CH_2CHO 24 valence electrons   C and O form a double bond.
(d) OF_2 20 valence electrons

4.50 A compound with the formula C_2H_8 can't exist because any structure drawn would violate the rules of valence.

4.52

(a)

(b)

(c)

4.54 (a) $CH_3CH_2CH_3$ (b) $H_2C=CHCH_3$ (c) CH_3CH_2Cl

4.56 CH_3COOH

Drawing Lewis Structures

4.58

(a)

(b)

(c)

H—Ö—N̈=Ö Ö=Ö—Ö: H H
                              | |
                          H—C—C=Ö
                              |
                              H

4.60

  Dimethyl ether

4.62

  Tetrachloroethylene contains a double bond.

4.64

H—N̈—Ö—H Hydroxylamine
     |
     H

4.66

(a)
$$\left[\begin{array}{c} :O: \\ \parallel \\ H-C-\ddot{O}: \end{array}\right]^{-}$$

(b)
$$\left[\begin{array}{c} :\ddot{O}: \\ \vert \\ :\ddot{O}-S-\ddot{O}: \end{array}\right]^{2-}$$

(c)
$$\left[:\ddot{S}-C{\equiv}N:\right]^{-}$$

(d)
$$\left[\begin{array}{c} :\ddot{O}: \\ \vert \\ :\ddot{O}-P-\ddot{O}: \\ \vert \\ :\ddot{O}: \end{array}\right]^{3-}$$

(e)
$$\left[:\ddot{O}-\ddot{C}l=\ddot{O}\right]^{-}$$

Molecular Geometry

4.68 As in the previous problem, use Table 4.2.

Molecule	Number of bonds	Number of Lone Pairs	Shape	Bond Angle
(a) AB_4	4	0	tetrahedral	109°
(b) AB_3E	3	1	pyramidal	109°
(c) AB_2E_2	2	2	bent	109°

4.70

Molecule	Number of Bonding Pairs Around Central Atom	Number of Lone Pairs	Shape	Bond Angle
(a) SiF_4	4	0	tetrahedral	109°
(b) CF_2Cl_2	4	0	tetrahedral	109°
(c) SO_3	3*	0	trigonal planar	120°
(d) BBr_3	3	0	trigonal planar	120°
(e) NF_3	3	1	pyramidal	109°

* For determining shape, the double bond counts as one bond pair, and the number of bonds is three.

4.72

Vinyl acetate

All carbons are trigonal planar, except for the starred carbon, which is tetrahedral.

Polarity of Bonds and Molecules

4.74 Using the periodic table, count up from element 114. Element 119 should occur under francium and accordingly should be one of the least electronegative elements, with an electronegativity of 0.8.

4.76 *More electronegative ———> Less electronegative*
         Cl > C > Cu > Ca > Cs

4.78 Bonds in (b), (c), and (d) are nonpolar.

(a) $\overset{\delta-\ \ \delta+}{O-Cl}$ (e) $\overset{\delta+\ \ \delta-}{C-O}$

4.80 Use Figure 4.6 to determine bond polarities.

Least polar bonds ———> Most polar bonds

$$PH_3 < HCl < H_2O < CF_4$$

4.82

(a)

H—Cl

polar

(b)

H--P—H
   H

polar

(c)

H--O

   H

polar

(d) nonpolar

4.84 Both molecules are polar because of the lone pair electrons. Water is more polar because the bonds between oxygen and hydrogen are polar covalent, but the bonds between sulfur and hydrogen are nonpolar.

Names and Formulas of Molecular Compounds

4.86 (a) SeO_2 selenium dioxide   (b) XeO_4 xenon tetroxide
     (c) N_2S_5 dinitrogen pentasulfide   (d) P_3Se_4 triphosphorus tetraselenide

4.88 (a) $SiCl_4$ silicon tetrachloride   (b) NaH sodium hydride
     (c) SbF_5 antimony pentafluoride   (d) OsO_4 osmium tetroxide

Chemistry in Action

4.90 A vasodilator is a chemical that relaxes arterial walls, causing a drop in blood pressure.

4.92 Carbohydrates, proteins, and DNA are all examples of polymers that occur in nature.

4.94 $(CH_3)_2C=CHCH_2CH_2CH(CH_3)CH_2CH_2OH$

General Questions and Problems

4.96

(a)

(b) The C=O carbon atoms have trigonal planar geometry, and the other carbons have tetrahedral geometry.   (c) The C=O bonds are polar.

4.98   Consult Figure 4.3 for help.

(a) Carbon forms four bonds. The correct formula is CCl_4.
(b) Nitrogen forms three bonds. The correct formula is N_2H_4.
(c) Sulfur forms two bonds. The correct formula is H_2S.
(d) C_2OS *could* actually be correct (S=C=C=O), but compounds with such adjacent double bonds are rare. More likely is the formula COS, a structural relative of carbon dioxide (S=C=O).

4.100

(a)

(b) Phosphonium ion is tetrahedral.

(c) Phosphorus donates its lone pair of electrons to H^+ to form a coordinate covalent bond.
(d) Number of electrons: 15 (from P) + 3 (from 3 H) = 18
   Number of protons: 15 (from P) + 4 (from 4 H) = 19
PH_4^+ is positive because the number of protons exceeds the number of electrons by one.

4.102

Compound	Name
(a) $CaCl_2$	calcium chloride
(b) $TeCl_2$	tellurium dichloride
(c) BF_3	boron trifluoride
(d) $MgSO_4$	magnesium sulfate
(e) K_2O	potassium oxide
(f) FeF_3	iron(III) fluoride
(g) PF_3	phosphorus trifluoride

4.104

Chloral hydrate

4.106

      Oxalic acid

4.108

(a)   (b)

Self-Test for Chapter 4

Multiple Choice

1. Which of these diatomic molecules contains a double bond?
    (a) H_2 (b) I_2 (c) O_2 (d) N_2

2. Which of these molecules is pyramidal?
    (a) CBr_4 (b) $AlCl_3$ (c) SF_6 (d) PH_3

3. Choose the element that forms three covalent bonds and has one lone pair of electrons.
    (a) C   (b) N   (c) O   (d) F

4. How many charge clouds does the molecule H_2S have?
    (a) 2   (b) 3   (c) 4   (d) can't tell

5. Which of the following double bonds is not likely to be found in organic molecules?
    (a) O=O   (b) C=C   (c) C=O   (d) C=N

6. All of the following are true about the polyatomic ion BF_4^- except:
    (a) All atoms don't have electron octets.   (b) It has polar covalent bonds.   (c) It contains a coordinate covalent bond.   (d) It has a tetrahedral shape.

7. One of these molecules doesn't contain a polar covalent bond. Which is it?
    (a) $BeBr_2$ (b) PCl_3 (c) CO_2 (d) CS_2

8. Which of the following compounds is polar?
    (a) $BeBr_2$ (b) PCl_3 (c) CO_2 (d) CS_2

9. A name for S_2F_2 is:
    (a) sulfur fluoride   (b) sulfur difluoride   (c) disulfur fluoride   (d) disulfur difluoride

10. Which of the following is not true for molecular compounds?
    (a) They are water-soluble.   (b) They can be solids, liquids, or gases.   (c) They are composed of nonmetals.   (d) They have low melting points.

Sentence Completion

1. An _____ element strongly attracts electrons.

2. A molecular compound that occurs in living organisms is called a _____ .

3. In Lewis structures, a line represents a _____ bond.

4. _____ and _____ are the most common triple bonds in chemical compounds.

5. The formula X_2 represents a _____ molecule.

6. A molecule whose central atom forms three bonds and has no lone pairs has a _____ _____ shape.

7. _____ orbitals in sulfur and phosphorus can be used for covalent bonds.

8. N_2 contains a _____ bond.

9. _____ molecular compounds are formed from only two elements.

10. Many molecular compounds are soluble in _____ liquids.

11. Large organic molecules are often written as _____ structures.

True or False

1. Br_2 is a molecular compound.

2. Six electrons are used to form a triple bond.

3. Coordinate covalent bonds occur only in cations or anions, not in neutral compounds.

4. The first step in drawing a Lewis structure is to find the total number of electrons in the combined atoms.

5. $AlCl_3$ is a pyramidal molecule.

6. The shape of ionic compounds can be predicted by the VSEPR model.

7. Electronegativity decreases in going down the periodic table.

8. CI_4 contains polar covalent bonds.

9. Both planar and bent molecules have bond angles of 120°.

10. Group 7A elements can form more than one covalent bond.

11. Bent compounds may have either one or two lone pairs.

Match each entry on the left with its partner on the right.

1. BCl_3 (a) Contains a pure covalent bond

2.   Planar molecule   (b) $BeCl_2$

3.   Bent molecule   (c) Central atom has more than an electron octet

4. Cl_2 (d) NH_3

5. BCl_4^- (e) Contains a triple bond

6.   NaI   (f) H_2O

7.   C≡O   (g) Contains a double bond

8. SF_6 (h) Central atom doesn't have an electron octet

9.   Linear molecule   (i) Contains an ionic bond

10. O=C=O   (j) $AlCl_3$

11. Pyramidal molecule   (k) Contains a coordinate covalent bond

12. CH_3Cl (l) Contains a polar covalent bond

Chapter 5   Classification and Balancing
of Chemical Reactions

Chapter Outline

I. Chemical equations (Sections 5.1–5.2).
  A. Writing chemical equations (Section 5.1).
    1. A chemical equation describes a chemical reaction.
      a. The reactants are written on the left.
      b. The products are written on the right.
      c. An arrow goes between them to indicate the chemical change.
    2. The number and kinds of atoms must be the same on both sides of the equation.
      a. This is known as the law of conservation of mass.
    3. Numbers that are placed in front of formulas are called coefficients.
    4. States of matter (s), (g), (l) are often placed after chemical formulas.
  B. Balancing chemical equations (Section 5.2).
    1. Write an unbalanced equation using the correct formulas for all substances.
    2. Add appropriate coefficients to balance the atoms of each type, one at a time.
    3. Check to make sure that the numbers and kinds of atoms are balanced.
    4. Make sure all coefficients are reduced to their lowest whole-number values.
II. Chemical reactions (Sections 5.3–5.8).
  A. Classes of chemical reactions (Section 5.3).
    1. Precipitation reactions occur when an insoluble solid is formed.
    2. Acid–base reactions occur when an acid and a base react to yield water and a salt.
    3. Redox reactions occur when electrons are transferred between reaction partners.
  B. Precipitation reactions (Section 5.4).
    1. To predict whether a precipitation reaction occurs, you must know the solubilities of the products.
    2. Table 5.1 gives general solubility rules to predict if a precipitation reaction will occur.
  C. Acid–base reactions (Section 5.5).
    1. Acid–base reactions are known as neutralization reactions because when the reaction is complete the solution is neither acidic nor basic.
    2. An example: $HA(aq) + MOH(aq) \longrightarrow H_2O(l) + MA(aq)$
    3. When a carbonate or bicarbonate is one of the reactants, CO_2 is also produced.
  D. Redox reactions (Sections 5.6–5.7).
    1. Definition of redox reactions (Section 5.6).
      a. A redox reaction occurs when electrons are transferred from one atom to another.
      b. The substance that loses electrons is oxidized and is known as the reducing agent.
      c. The substance that gains electrons is reduced and is known as the oxidizing agent.
      d. Oxidation and reduction always occur together.
        i. In the reaction of a metal with a nonmetal, the metal loses electrons, and the nonmetal gains electrons.
        ii. In the reaction of two nonmetals, the "more metallic" element loses electrons, and the "less metallic" element gains electrons.
      e. Redox reactions occur during corrosion, combustion, respiration, and photography.

2. Recognizing redox reactions (Section 5.7).
   a. With some substances, it isn't obvious if a redox reaction has occurred.
   b. In a neutral compound, oxidation numbers are assigned to each element to indicate electron ownership.
   c. To assign oxidation numbers:
      i. An atom in its elemental state has an oxidation number of zero.
      ii. A monatomic ion has an oxidation number equal to its charge.
      iii. In a molecular compound, an atom usually has the same oxidation number that it would have if it were a monatomic ion.
      iv. The sum of the oxidation numbers in a neutral compound is zero.
      v. The oxidation number of oxygen is usually –2; the oxidation number of hydrogen is usually +1.
E. Net ionic equations (Section 5.8).
   1. A molecular equation shows reactants and products as molecules and doesn't indicate if they are ions.
   2. An ionic equation is written if ions are involved and shows all ionic reactants and products.
   3. A net ionic equation includes only the ions that undergo change and deletes spectator ions.

Solutions to Chapter 5 Problems

5.1   (a) Solid cobalt(II) chloride plus gaseous hydrogen fluoride yield solid cobalt(II) fluoride plus gaseous hydrogen chloride.

      (b) Aqueous lead(II) nitrate plus aqueous potassium iodide yield solid lead(II) iodide plus aqueous potassium nitrate.

5.2   An equation is balanced if the number and types of atoms on the left side equals the number and types of atoms on the right side.

   (a) On the left: 2 H + Cl + K + O
       On the right: 2 H + Cl + K + O The equation is balanced.
   (b) On the left: 1 C + 4 H + 2 Cl
       On the right: 1 C + 3 H + 3 Cl The equation is not balanced.
   (c) Balanced
   (d) Not balanced in H, O.

5.3   *Step 1*: Write the unbalanced equation.

$$O_2 \longrightarrow O_3$$

   Step 2: Balance the atoms of each type, one by one.

$$3\,O_2 \longrightarrow 2\,O_3$$ The equation is balanced.

5.4   (a) $Ca(OH)_2 + 2\,HCl \longrightarrow CaCl_2 + 2\,H_2O$

      (b) $4\,Al + 3\,O_2 \longrightarrow 2\,Al_2O_3$

      (c) $2\,CH_3CH_3 + 7\,O_2 \longrightarrow 4\,CO_2 + 6\,H_2O$

      (d) $2\,AgNO_3 + MgCl_2 \longrightarrow 2\,AgCl + Mg(NO_3)_2$

5.5   *Step 1:* $A + B_2 \longrightarrow A_2B_2$

   Step 2: $2A + B_2 \longrightarrow A_2B_2$ The equation is balanced.

5.6   (a) $AgNO_3(aq) + KCl(aq) \longrightarrow AgCl(s) + KNO_3(aq)$
   Precipitation: Solid AgCl is formed.

   (b) $2Al(s) + 3Br_2(l) \longrightarrow 2AlBr_3(s)$
   Redox reaction: Al^{+3} is formed from Al, and Br^- is formed from Br_2.

   (c) $Ca(OH)_2(aq) + 2HNO_3(aq) \longrightarrow 2H_2O(l) + Ca(NO_3)_2(aq)$
   Acid–base neutralization.

5.7 $6CO_2(g) + 6H_2O(l) \longrightarrow C_6H_{12}O_6(s) + 6O_2(g)$

5.8   Use Table 5.1 for solubility guidelines.

Insoluble
(a) $CdCO_3$ (most carbonates are insoluble)
(c) $PbSO_4$ (exception to the rule that sulfates are soluble)
(e) Hg_2Cl_2 (exception to the rule that chlorides are soluble)

Soluble
(b) Na_2S
(d) $(NH_4)_3PO_4$

5.9   As in Worked Example 5.6, identify the products, and use Table 5.1 to predict their solubility. If the products are insoluble, a precipitation reaction will occur.

   (a) $NiCl_2(aq) + (NH_4)_2S(aq) \longrightarrow 2NH_4Cl(aq) + NiS(s)$
   A precipitation reaction will occur.

   (b) $2AgNO_3(aq) + CaBr_2(aq) \longrightarrow Ca(NO_3)_2(aq) + 2AgBr(s)$
   A precipitation reaction will occur.

5.10 $CaCl_2(aq) + Na_2C_2O_4(aq) \longrightarrow 2NaCl(aq) + CaC_2O_4(s)$

5.11   (a) $2CsOH(aq) + H_2SO_4(aq) \longrightarrow Cs_2SO_4(aq) + 2H_2O(l)$

   (b) $Ca(OH)_2(aq) + 2CH_3CO_2H(aq) \longrightarrow Ca(CH_3CO_2)_2(aq) + 2H_2O(l)$

   (c) $NaHCO_3(aq) + HBr(aq) \longrightarrow NaBr(aq) + CO_2(g) + H_2O(l)$

5.12

	Oxidized Reactant/ Reducing Agent	*Reduced Reactant/ Oxidizing Agent*
(a)	Fe	Cu^{2+}
(b)	Mg	Cl_2
(c)	Al	Cr_2O_3

The oxidizing agent is the reduced reactant, and the reducing agent is the oxidized reactant.

5.13 $\underset{\textit{Reducing agent}}{2K(s)} + \underset{\textit{Oxidizing agent}}{Br_2(l)} \longrightarrow 2KBr(s)$

5.14   Lithium is oxidized, and iodine is reduced.

5.15

Compound	Oxidation Number of Metal	Name
(a) VCl_3	+3	vanadium(III) chloride
(b) $SnCl_4$	+4	tin(IV) chloride
(c) CrO_3	+6	chromium(VI) oxide
(d) $Cu(NO_3)_2$	+2	copper(II) nitrate
(e) $NiSO_4$	+2	nickel(II) sulfate

5.16 Oxidation numbers are written above the atoms.

(a) $\overset{+1-2}{Na_2S}(aq) + \overset{+2-1}{NiCl_2}(aq) \longrightarrow 2\,\overset{+1-1}{NaCl}(aq) + \overset{+2-2}{NiS}(s)$
This reaction is not a redox reaction because no atoms change oxidation numbers.

(b) $2\,\overset{0}{Na}(s) + 2\,\overset{+1-2}{H_2O}(l) \longrightarrow 2\,\overset{+1-2+1}{NaOH}(aq) + \overset{0}{H_2}(g)$
Sodium is oxidized and hydrogen is reduced in this reaction.

(c) $\overset{0}{C}(s) + \overset{0}{O_2}(g) \longrightarrow \overset{+4-2}{CO_2}(g)$
Carbon is oxidized and oxygen is reduced in this redox reaction.

(d) $\overset{+2-2}{CuO}(s) + 2\,\overset{+1-1}{HCl}(aq) \longrightarrow \overset{+2-1}{CuCl_2}(aq) + \overset{+1-2}{H_2O}(l)$
This is not a redox reaction because no atoms change oxidation number.

(e) $2\,\overset{+7-2}{MnO_4^-}(aq) + 5\,\overset{+4-2}{SO_2}(g) + 2\,\overset{+1-2}{H_2O}(l) \longrightarrow 2\,\overset{+2}{Mn^{2+}}(aq) + 5\,\overset{+6-2}{SO_4^{2-}}(aq) + 4\,\overset{+1}{H^+}(aq)$
In this redox reaction, the oxidation number of Mn changes from +7 to +2 and the oxidation number of S changes from +4 to +6.

5.17

Reducing agent		Oxidizing agent
(b)	Na	H_2O
(c)	C	O_2
(e)	SO_2	MnO_4^-

5.18 (a) Write the equation, including all ions.

$Zn(s) + Pb^{2+} + 2\,NO_3^- \longrightarrow Zn^{2+} + 2\,NO_3^- + Pb(s)$
The nitrate ions on each side cancel.

$Zn(s) + Pb^{2+}(aq) \longrightarrow Zn^{2+}(aq) + Pb(s)$

(b) $OH^-(aq) + H^+(aq) \longrightarrow H_2O(l)$
K^+ and SO_4^{2-} cancel, and coefficients are reduced.

(c) $2\,Fe^{3+}(aq) + Sn^{2+}(aq) \longrightarrow 2\,Fe^{2+}(aq) + Sn^{4+}(aq)$
The chloride ions cancel.

5.19 Reactions (a) and (c) are redox reactions, and (b) is a neutralization reaction.

Understanding Key Concepts

5.20   Product mixture (d) is the only mixture that contains the same number of atoms as (a).

5.22   (d) $\longrightarrow$ (c)
reactants   products

5.24   The observed product is a precipitate that contains two cations per anion. From the list of cations, Ag^+ is the only one that forms precipitates and has a 2:1 cation/anion ratio with the anions listed. The anion can be either CO_3^{2-} or CrO_4^{2-}, since both form precipitates with Ag^+. Thus, the possible products are Ag_2CO_3 and Ag_2CrO_4.

Balancing Chemical Equations

5.26   A balanced equation is an equation in which the number of atoms of each kind is the same on both sides of the reaction arrow.

5.28   (a) $SO_2(g) + H_2O(g) \longrightarrow H_2SO_3(aq)$

(b) $2\,K(s) + Br_2(l) \longrightarrow 2\,KBr(s)$

(c) $C_3H_8(g) + 5\,O_2(g) \longrightarrow 3\,CO_2(g) + 4\,H_2O(g)$

5.30   (a) $2\,C_2H_6(g) + 7\,O_2(g) \longrightarrow 4\,CO_2(g) + 6\,H_2O(l)$

(b) balanced

(c) $2\,Mg(s) + O_2(g) \longrightarrow 2\,MgO(s)$

(d) $2\,K(s) + 2\,H_2O(l) \longrightarrow 2\,KOH(aq) + H_2(g)$

5.32   (a) $Hg(NO_3)_2(aq) + 2\,LiI(aq) \longrightarrow 2\,LiNO_3(aq) + HgI_2(s)$

(b) $I_2(s) + 5\,Cl_2(g) \longrightarrow 2\,ICl_5(s)$

(c) $4\,Al(s) + 3\,O_2(g) \longrightarrow 2\,Al_2O_3(s)$

(d) $CuSO_4(aq) + 2\,AgNO_3(aq) \longrightarrow Ag_2SO_4(s) + Cu(NO_3)_2(aq)$

(e) $2\,Mn(NO_3)_3(aq) + 3\,Na_2S(aq) \longrightarrow Mn_2S_3(s) + 6\,NaNO_3(aq)$

5.34   (a) $2\,C_4H_{10}(g) + 13\,O_2(g) \longrightarrow 8\,CO_2(g) + 10\,H_2O(l)$

(b) $C_2H_6O(g) + 3\,O_2(g) \longrightarrow 2\,CO_2(g) + 3\,H_2O(l)$

(c) $2\,C_8H_{18}(g) + 25\,O_2(g) \longrightarrow 16\,CO_2(g) + 18\,H_2O(l)$

5.36 $4\,HF + SiO_2 \longrightarrow SiF_4 + 2\,H_2O$

Types of Chemical Reactions

5.38 (a) $Mg(s) + 2\,HCl(aq) \longrightarrow MgCl_2(aq) + H_2(g)$ redox reaction

(b) $KOH(aq) + HNO_3(aq) \longrightarrow KNO_3(aq) + H_2O(l)$ neutralization reaction

(c) $Pb(NO_3)_2(aq) + 2\,HBr(aq) \longrightarrow PbBr_2(s) + 2\,HNO_3(aq)$ precipitation reaction

(d) $Ca(OH)_2(aq) + 2\,H_2SO_4(aq) \longrightarrow 2\,H_2O(l) + CaSO_4(aq)$ neutralization reaction

5.40

(a) $Ba^{2+}(aq) + 2\,NO_3^-(aq) + 2\,K^+(aq) + SO_4^{2-}(aq) \rightarrow BaSO_4(s) + 2\,K^+(aq) + 2\,NO_3^-(aq)$
$$Ba^{2+}(aq) + SO_4^{2-}(aq) \rightarrow BaSO_4(s)$$
(b) $Zn(s) + 2\,H^+(aq) + SO_4^{2-}(aq) \rightarrow Zn^{2+}(aq) + H_2(g) + SO_4^{2-}(aq)$
$$Zn(s) + 2\,H^+(aq) \rightarrow Zn^{2+}(aq) + H_2(g)$$

5.42 redox: (b), (c); precipitation: (a), (d), (e)

5.44 Use Section 5.4 as a guide.
Only $Ba(NO_3)_2$ is soluble in water.

5.46 If the products consist of soluble ions, no reaction will occur. No reaction occurs in (b) and (c).

(a) $2\,NaBr(aq) + Hg_2(NO_3)_2(aq) \longrightarrow Hg_2Br_2(s) + 2\,NaNO_3(aq)$

(d) $(NH_4)_2CO_3(aq) + CaCl_2(aq) \longrightarrow CaCO_3(s) + 2\,NH_4Cl(aq)$

(e) $2\,KOH(aq) + MnBr_2(aq) \longrightarrow Mn(OH)_2(s) + 2\,KBr(aq)$

(f) $3\,Na_2S(aq) + 2\,Al(NO_3)_3(aq) \longrightarrow Al_2S_3(s) + 6\,NaNO_3(aq)$

5.48 (a) $2\,Au^{3+}(aq) + 3\,Sn(s) \longrightarrow 3\,Sn^{2+}(aq) + 2\,Au(s)$

(b) $2\,I^-(aq) + Br_2(l) \longrightarrow 2\,Br^-(aq) + I_2(s)$

(c) $2\,Ag^+(aq) + Fe(s) \longrightarrow Fe^{2+}(aq) + 2\,Ag(s)$

5.50 (a) The net ionic equation is the same as 5.49 (a) because no ions are spectator ions.

(b) $S^{2-}(aq) + Zn^{2+}(aq) \longrightarrow ZnS(s)$

Redox Reactions and Oxidation Numbers

5.52 The most easily reduced elements are found in groups 6A and 7A. The most easily oxidized elements are in groups 1A and 2A.

5.54 Oxidation number increases: (b) reducing agent, (c) substance undergoing oxidation
Oxidation number decreases: (a) oxidizing agent, (d) substance undergoing reduction

5.56 (a) Co: +3 (b) Fe: +2 (c) U: +6 (d) Cu: +2 (e) Ti: +4 (f) Sn: +2

5.58

	(a)	(b)	(c)	(d)
Oxidized	S	Na	Zn	Cl
Reduced	O	Cl	Cu	F

5.60 (a) $N_2O_4(l) + 2 N_2H_4(l) \longrightarrow 3 N_2(g) + 4 H_2O(g)$
(b) $CaH_2(s) + 2 H_2O(l) \longrightarrow Ca(OH)_2(aq) + 2 H_2(l)$
(c) $2 Al(s) + 6 H_2O(l) \longrightarrow 2 Al(OH)_3(s) + 3 H_2(g)$

5.62

	Reducing agent	Oxidizing agent
(a)	N_2H_4	N_2O_4
(b)	CaH_2	H_2O
(c)	Al	H_2O

Chemistry in Action

5.64 (a) $2 C_5H_4N_4 + 3 O_2 \longrightarrow 2 C_5H_4N_4O_3$
(b) This is a redox reaction in which purine is oxidized and O_2 is reduced.

5.66 Elemental zinc is the reducing agent and Mn^{+4} is the oxidizing agent.

General Questions and Problems

5.68 (a) $Li_2O(s) + H_2O(g) \longrightarrow 2 LiOH(s)$
(b) This is not a redox reaction because the oxidation numbers of reactant and product atoms remain the same.

5.70 (a) $Al(OH)_3(aq) + 3 HNO_3(aq) \longrightarrow Al(NO_3)_3(aq) + 3 H_2O(l)$ neutralization
(b) $3 AgNO_3(aq) + FeCl_3(aq) \longrightarrow 3 AgCl(s) + Fe(NO_3)_3(aq)$ precipitation
(c) $(NH_4)_2Cr_2O_7(s) \longrightarrow Cr_2O_3(s) + 4 H_2O(g) + N_2(g)$ redox
(d) $Mn_2(CO_3)_3(s) \longrightarrow Mn_2O_3(s) + 3 CO_2(g)$ none

5.72 (a) $2 SO_2(g) + O_2(g) \longrightarrow 2 SO_3(g)$
(b) $SO_3(g) + H_2O(g) \longrightarrow H_2SO_4(l)$
(c) The oxidation number of sulfur is +4 in SO_2 and is +6 in both SO_3 and H_2SO_4.

5.74 (a) The oxidation number of chromium in dichromate is +6.
(b) The oxidation number of carbon in C_2H_5OH is –2; the oxidation number of carbon in CO_2 is +4.
(c) The oxidizing agent is dichromate, and the reducing agent is C_2H_5OH.

5.76 $Fe^{3+}(aq) + 3 NaOH(aq) \longrightarrow Fe(OH)_3(s) + 3 Na^+(aq)$

$Fe^{3+}(aq) + 3\ ^-OH(aq) \longrightarrow Fe(OH)_3(s)$

5.78 $2 Bi^{3+}(aq) + 3S^-(aq) \longrightarrow Bi_2S_3(s)$

5.80 $CO_2(g) + 2 NH_3(g) \longrightarrow NH_2CONH_2(s) + H_2O(l)$

5.82 (a) Reactants: Mn = +4, I = –1; Products: Mn = +2, I = 0
(b) MnO_2 is the oxidizing agent, and I^- is the reducing agent.

Self-Test for Chapter 5

Multiple Choice

1.   Which of the following salts is soluble in water?
        (a) $FeSO_4$ (b) $BaSO_4$ (c) $SrSO_4$ (d) $PbSO_4$

2.   Which of the following compounds has sulfur in a +1 oxidation state?
        (a) S_2F_2 (b) H_2SO_4 (c) SO_2 (d) Na_2S

3.   Which of the following is a treatment for gout?
        (a) oxalate (b) purine (c) allopurinol (d) urate

4.   Which of the following is not a component of a dry cell battery?
        (a) MnO_2 (b) I_2 (c) NH_4Cl (d) Zn

5.   When the equation $SiCl_4 + H_2O \longrightarrow SiO_2 + HCl$ is balanced, the coefficients are:
        (a) 1,1,1,1 (b) 1,1,1,2 (c) 1,2,1,2 (d) 1,2,1,4

6.   Which of the following is not a redox process?
        (a) respiration (b) corrosion (c) neutralization (d) combustion

7.   If you wanted to remove Ba^{2+} from solution, which reagent would you add?
        (a) CH_3CO_2H (b) NaOH (c) H_2SO_4 (d) HCl

8.   In the reaction $2\ Ca + O_2 \longrightarrow 2\ CaO$, calcium is:
        (a) reduced/oxidizing agent (b) oxidized/reducing agent (c) reduced/reducing agent
        (d) oxidized/oxidizing agent

9.   When HCl is added to a solution, bubbles of gas appear. Which compound is probably
        present in the solution?
        (a) $SrCO_3$ (b) $Ca(OH)_2$ (c) AgBr (d) K_2SO_4

10.   Which lead-containing compound is probably soluble in water?
        (a) PbS (b) $PbSO_4$ (c) $PbCl_2$ (d) $Pb(NO_3)_2$

Sentence Completion

1. The numbers placed in front of formulas to balance equations are called _____.

2. A _____ is a solid that forms during a reaction.

3. Ions that appear on both sides of the reaction arrow are _____ ions.

4. The substances in a reaction can be solids, liquids, or gases, or they can be in _____ solution.

5. When acid is added to a solution, bubbles of gas are evolved if either _____ or _____ ions are present.

6. _____ is the science of extracting and purifying metals.

7. In a chemical equation, _____ are shown on the left of the reaction arrow.

8. The oxidation state of gold in $AuCl_3$ is _____.

9. In the reaction $2\,Mg + O_2 \longrightarrow 2\,MgO$, Mg is the _____ agent.

10. A reaction between an acid and a base is a _____ reaction.

True or False

1. Lithium and iodine are the redox components of a dry cell battery

2. If the chloride of a cation is water-insoluble, the bromide and iodide of that cation are also insoluble.

3. Limestone ($CaCO_3$) can be dissolved by treatment with HNO_3.

4. In a redox equation, the oxidizing agent is oxidized and the reducing agent is reduced.

5. If all coefficients in a chemical equation are even numbers, the equation is not properly balanced.

6. In a redox reaction, a reducing agent becomes more negative

7. In the reaction between K and Cl_2, K is the oxidizing agent.

8. Increased urate concentration in urine leads to gout.

9. Most sodium salts are soluble in water.

10. The same compound can be both oxidized and reduced in a reaction.

Match each entry on the left with its partner on the right.

1. Zn

2. $C_3H_8O + O_2 \longrightarrow C_3H_6O + H_2O$

3. Respiration

4. $H^+ + OH^- \longrightarrow H_2O$

5. $CoCO_3$

6. $S + O_2 \longrightarrow SO_2$

7. $HCl + NaOH \longrightarrow NaCl + H_2O$

8. Corrosion

9. $KMnO_4$

10. MnO_2

11. $AgNO_3 + NaCl \longrightarrow AgCl + NaNO_3$

12. $CoCl_2$

(a) Net ionic equation

(b) Deterioration of a metal by oxidation

(c) Redox reaction

(d) Precipitation reaction

(e) Salt soluble in water

(f) Unbalanced equation

(g) Manganese has an oxidation number of +7

(h) Oxidized in a battery

(i) Salt insoluble in water

(j) Neutralization reaction

(k) Biological redox reaction

(l) Reduced in a battery

Chapter 6   Chemical Reactions: Mole and Mass Relationships

Chapter Outline

I. The mole (Section 6.1).
   A. Molecular weight is the sum of the atomic weights of atoms in a molecule.
   B. Formula weight is the sum of the atomic weights of atoms in a formula unit.
   C. One mole of any pure substance has a mass equal to its molecular or formula weight in grams.
      1. Avogadro's number (6.022×10^{23}), known as the mole, represents the number of formula units that has a mass in grams equal to its weight in amu.
II. Mole–mass relationships (Section 6.2–6.4).
   A. Gram–mole conversions (Section 6.2).
      1. Molar mass is the mass in grams of one mole of any substance.
      2. Molar mass is a conversion factor that allows calculation of moles from grams and of grams from moles.
   B. Mole relationships and chemical equations (Section 6.3).
      1. The coefficients in an equation tell how many moles of reactant or product are involved in the reaction.
      2. The coefficients can be put in a mole ratio, which can be used as a conversion factor.
   C. Mass relationships and chemical equations (Section 6.4).
      1. Mole–mole conversions are made by using mole ratios.
      2. Mole–mass conversions are made by using molar mass as a conversion factor.
      3. Mass–mass conversions can be made by a mass–mole conversion of one substance, mole ratios, and a mole–mass conversion of the other substance.
   D. A summary of calculations using mole–mass relationships:
      1. Write the balanced equation.
      2. Choose mole–mass relationships and mole ratios to calculate the desired quantity.
      3. Set up the factor-label method to calculate the answer.
      4. Check the answer with a ballpark solution.
III. Limiting reagent and percent yield (Section 6.5).
   A. In a reaction, the reactant that is consumed first is the limiting reagent.
   B. Percent yield = actual yield/theoretical yield x 100%.
   C. Theoretical yield is found by using a mass–mass calculation.

Solutions to Chapter 6 Problems

6.1   (a) For ibuprofen, $C_{13}H_{18}O_2$:

$$
\begin{aligned}
\text{At. wt of 13 C} &= 13 \times 12.0\ \text{amu} = 156.0\ \text{amu} \\
\text{At. wt of 18 H} &= 18 \times 1.0\ \text{amu} = 18.0\ \text{amu} \\
\underline{\text{At. wt of } 2\,\text{O}} &= \underline{2 \times 16.0\ \text{amu} = 32.0\ \text{amu}} \\
\text{MW of } C_{13}H_{18}O_2 &= 206.0\ \text{amu}
\end{aligned}
$$

(b) For phenobarbital, $C_{12}H_{12}N_2O_3$:

At. wt of 12 C = 12 x 12.0 amu = 144.0 amu
At. wt of 12 H = 12 x 1.0 amu = 12.0 amu
At. wt of 2 N = 2 x 14.0 amu = 28.0 amu
At. wt of 3 O = 3 x 16.0 amu = 48.0 amu

MW of $C_{12}H_{12}N_2O_3$ = 232.0 amu

6.2   At. wt of 6 C = 6 x 12.0 amu = 72.0 amu
At. wt of 8 H = 8 x 1.0 amu = 8.0 amu
At. wt of 6 O = 6 x 16.0 amu = 96.0 amu

MW of $C_6H_8O_6$ = 176.0 amu

Since the molecular weight of ascorbic acid is 176.0 amu, 6.022×10^{23} molecules have a mass of 176 g.

$$500 \text{ mg ascorbic acid } \times \frac{1 \text{ g}}{10^3 \text{ mg}} \times \frac{6.022 \times 10^{23} \text{ molecules}}{176 \text{ g}} = 1.71 \times 10^{21} \text{ molecules}$$

A 500 mg tablet contains 1.71×10^{21} molecules of ascorbic acid.

6.3   At. wt of 9 C = 9 x 12.0 amu = 108.0 amu
At. wt of 8 H = 8 x 1.0 amu = 8.0 amu
At. wt of 4 O = 4 x 16.0 amu = 64.0 amu

MW of $C_9H_8O_4$ = 180.0 amu

$$5.0 \times 10^{20} \text{ molecules } \times \frac{180.0 \text{ g}}{1 \text{ mol}} \times \frac{1 \text{ mol}}{6.022 \times 10^{23} \text{ molecules}} = 0.15 \text{ g}$$

5.0×10^{20} molecules of aspirin weigh 0.15 g.

6.4

Cytosine $C_4H_5N_3O$

At. wt of 4 C = 4 x 12.0 amu = 48.0 amu
At. wt of 5 H = 5 x 1.0 amu = 5.0 amu
At. wt of 3 N = 3 x 14.0 amu = 42.0 amu
At. wt of 1 O = 1 x 16.0 amu = 16.0 amu

MW of $C_4H_5N_3O$ = 111.0 amu

6.5   Molar mass of C_2H_6O = 46.0 g/mol

10.0 g x $\dfrac{1 \text{ mol}}{46.0 \text{ g}}$ = 0.217 mol in a 10.0 g sample

Ballpark check: The sample size, 10.0 g, is about 1/5 mol, or about 0.2 mol.

0.10 mol x $\dfrac{46.0 \text{ g}}{1 \text{ mol}}$ = 4.6 g in a 0.10 mol sample

6.6   Molar mass of acetaminophen = 151 g

0.0225 mol x $\dfrac{151 \text{ g}}{1 \text{ mol}}$ = 3.40 g

5.00 g acetaminophen weighs more than 0.0225 mol.

6.7   The number of molecules in Step 2 would be greater because the value of l^2 is smaller for a sphere than for a cube. If the density were less, the mass in Step 3, and the number of moles in Step 4, would be less. The net result in Step 5 would be an increase in the value of Avogadro's number.

6.8   (a) $Ni(s) + 2\,HCl(aq) \longrightarrow NiCl_2(aq) + H_2(g)$

9.81 mol HCl x $\dfrac{1 \text{ mol Ni}}{2 \text{ mol HCl}}$ = 4.91 mol Ni

(b) 6.00 mol Ni x $\dfrac{1 \text{ mol NiCl}_2}{1 \text{ mol Ni}}$ = 6.00 mol $NiCl_2$ from 6.00 mol Ni

12.00 mol HCl x $\dfrac{1 \text{ mol NiCl}_2}{2 \text{ mol HCl}}$ = 6.00 mol $NiCl_2$ from 12.00 mol HCl

6.00 mol $NiCl_2$ can be formed from 6.00 mol Ni and 12.00 mol HCl.

6.9 $6\,CO_2 + 6\,H_2O \longrightarrow C_6H_{12}O_6 + 6\,O_2$

15.0 mol glucose x $\dfrac{6 \text{ mol CO}_2}{1 \text{ mol glucose}}$ = 90.0 mol CO_2

6.10 (a) This is a mole-to-mole problem.

$$9.90 \text{ mol SiO}_2 \times \frac{4 \text{ mol HF}}{1 \text{ mol SiO}_2} = 39.6 \text{ mol HF}$$

(b) This is a mass-to-mass problem.

$$23.0 \text{ g SiO}_2 \times \frac{1 \text{ mol SiO}_2}{60.1 \text{ g SiO}_2} \times \frac{2 \text{ mol H}_2\text{O}}{1 \text{ mol SiO}_2} \times \frac{18.0 \text{ g H}_2\text{O}}{1 \text{ mol H}_2\text{O}} = 13.8 \text{ g H}_2\text{O}$$

Ballpark check: About 1/3 mol SiO_2 is used to produce 2/3 mol H_2O. Since the molar mass of H_2O is 18 g, we expect about 12 g H_2O, which is reasonably close to the calculated answer.

6.11 For WO_3:

$$5.00 \text{ g W} \times \frac{1 \text{ mol W}}{183.8 \text{ g W}} \times \frac{1 \text{ mol WO}_3}{1 \text{ mol W}} \times \frac{231.8 \text{ g WO}_3}{1 \text{ mol WO}_3} = 6.31 \text{ g WO}_3$$

For H_2:

$$5.00 \text{ g W} \times \frac{1 \text{ mol W}}{183.8 \text{ g W}} \times \frac{3 \text{ mol H}_2}{1 \text{ mol W}} \times \frac{2.02 \text{ g H}_2}{1 \text{ mol H}_2} = 0.165 \text{ g H}_2$$

6.31 g WO_3 and 0.165 g H_2 are needed to produce 5.00 g W.

Ballpark check: About 3/4 of the mass of WO_3 is composed of W. Thus, 5.00 g W comes from about 4/3 x 5.00 g W = 6.33 g WO_3, a result almost identical to the calculated result.

6.12 First, find the limiting reagent.

$$19.4 \text{ g C}_2\text{H}_4 \times \frac{1 \text{ mol C}_2\text{H}_4}{28.0 \text{ g C}_2\text{H}_4} = 0.693 \text{ mol C}_2\text{H}_4; \quad 50 \text{ g HCl} \times \frac{1 \text{ mol HCl}}{36.5 \text{ g HCl}} = 1.4 \text{ mol HCl}$$

Ethylene is the limiting reagent.

$$19.4 \text{ g ethylene} \times \frac{1 \text{ mol ethylene}}{28.0 \text{ g ethylene}} \times \frac{1 \text{ mol ethyl chloride}}{1 \text{ mol ethylene}} \times \frac{64.5 \text{ g ethyl chloride}}{1 \text{ mol ethyl chloride}}$$

$$= 44.7 \text{ g ethyl chloride}$$

$$\frac{25.5 \text{ g ethyl chloride actually formed}}{44.7 \text{ g theoretical yield of ethyl chloride}} \times 100\% = 57.0\%$$

Ballpark check: The amount of ethylene reactant corresponds to about 2/3 mol. The theoretical yield of product is about 2/3 mol ethyl chloride (somewhat more than 40 g). Since the actual yield is 25.5 g, the percent yield should be around 60%.

6.13   Note: to save space, ethylene oxide will be represented as EO, and ethylene glycol as EG.

$$35.0 \text{ g EO } \times \frac{1 \text{ mol EO}}{44.0 \text{ g EO}} \times \frac{1 \text{ mol EG}}{1 \text{ mol EO}} \times \frac{62.0 \text{ g EG}}{1 \text{ mol EG}} = 49.3 \text{ g ethylene glycol}$$

This quantity represents the maximum possible amount of ethylene glycol that can be produced. If the reaction occurs in 96.0% yield, then 49.3 g EG x 0.960 = 47.3 g EG is actually formed.

Ballpark check: A bit more than 3/4 mol EO is used to produce the same number of mol of EG, corresponding to about 47 g EG, close to the calculated result. The percent yield is also in close agreement.

6.14

$$8.0 \text{ mg } \times \frac{1 \text{ g}}{10^3 \text{ mg}} \times \frac{1 \text{ mol}}{55.8 \text{ g}} = 1.4 \times 10^{-4} \text{ mol for adult males}$$

$$18 \text{ mg } \times \frac{1 \text{ g}}{10^3 \text{ mg}} \times \frac{1 \text{ mol}}{55.8 \text{ g}} = 3.2 \times 10^{-4} \text{ mol for premenopausal women}$$

6.15   According to the equation $A_2 + 2 B_2 \longrightarrow 2 AB_2$, two B_2 are needed for each A_2. In the illustration, there are seven A_2 and 17 B_2. Since the seven A_2 can consume only 14 B_2, A_2 is the limiting reagent.

Understanding Key Concepts

6.16   Methionine: $C_5H_{11}NO_2S$
At. wt of 5 C =   5 x 12.0 amu =   60.0 amu
At. wt of 11 H = 11 x 1.0 amu =   11.0 amu
At. wt of   N =   =   14.0 amu
At. wt of 2 O =   2 x 16.0 amu =   32.0 amu
At. wt of   S =   =   32.1 amu

MW of $C_5H_{11}NO_2S$ = 149.1 amu

6.18   There are 10 molecules of A and 7 molecules of B_2. According to the equation, 10 molecules of AB can theoretically be formed, with two molecules of B_2 left over.

6.20   *Note:* To save space, ethylene oxide will be represented as EO, and ethylene glycol as EG.

$$9.0 \text{ g H}_2\text{O} \times \frac{1 \text{ mol H}_2\text{O}}{18.0 \text{ g H}_2\text{O}} \times \frac{1 \text{ mol EO}}{1 \text{ mol H}_2\text{O}} \times \frac{44.0 \text{ g EO}}{1 \text{ mol EO}} = 22 \text{ g ethylene oxide}$$

$$9.0 \text{ g H}_2\text{O} \times \frac{1 \text{ mol H}_2\text{O}}{18.0 \text{ g H}_2\text{O}} \times \frac{1 \text{ mol EG}}{1 \text{ mol H}_2\text{O}} \times \frac{62.0 \text{ g EG}}{1 \text{ mol EG}} = 31 \text{ g ethylene glycol}$$

Molar Masses and Moles

6.22 Molecular weight is the sum of the atomic weights of the individual atoms in a molecule. Formula weight is the sum of the atomic weights of the individual atoms in a formula unit of any compound, whether molecular or ionic. Molar mass is the mass in grams of 6.022×10^{23} molecules or formula units of any substance.

6.24 Each formula unit of K_2SO_4 contains three ions—two K^+ ions and one SO_4^{2-} ion. Thus, one mole of K_2SO_4 contains three moles of ions, and

$$1.75 \text{ mol } K_2SO_4 \times \frac{3 \text{ mol ions}}{1 \text{ mol } K_2SO_4} = 5.25 \text{ mol ions}$$

6.26

$$2.68 \times 10^{22} \text{ atoms } \times \frac{1 \text{ mol}}{6.022 \times 10^{23} \text{ atoms}} \times \frac{238.0 \text{ g}}{1 \text{ mol}} = 10.6 \text{ g uranium}$$

6.28 *Compound (moles C):* (a) $CaCO_3$ (1mol) (b) $CO(NH_2)_2$ (1 mol) (c) $C_2H_6O_2$ (2 mol)

6.30 Molar mass of caffeine $= 194$ g

$$125 \text{ mg caffeine } \times \frac{1 \text{ g}}{10^3 \text{ mg}} \times \frac{1 \text{ mol caffeine}}{194 \text{ g caffeine}} = 6.44 \times 10^{-4} \text{ mol caffeine}$$

6.32 Molar mass of $C_{16}H_{13}ClN_2O$:

$$(16 \times 12.0 \text{ g}) + (13 \times 1.0 \text{ g}) + (35.5 \text{ g}) + (2 \times 14.0 \text{ g}) + 16.0 \text{ g} = 284.5 \text{ g/ mol Valium}$$

6.34

Compound	Molar Mass	Number of Moles in 4.50 g
(a) $Al_2(SO_4)_3$	342.3 g	0.0131 mol
(b) $NaHCO_3$	84.0 g	0.0536 mol
(c) $C_4H_{10}O$	74.0 g	0.0608 mol
(d) $C_{16}H_{18}N_2O_5S$	350.1 g	0.0129 mol

Note: Slightly different values for molar mass result when exact atomic weights are used.

6.36 Molar mass of aspirin $= 180$ g

$$0.0015 \text{ mol aspirin } \times \frac{180 \text{ g aspirin}}{1 \text{ mol aspirin}} = 0.27 \text{ g aspirin}$$

$$0.0015 \text{ mol } \times \frac{6.022 \times 10^{23} \text{ molecules}}{1 \text{ mol}} = 9.0 \times 10^{20} \text{ molecules aspirin}$$

6.38

$$8.5 \times 10^{20} \text{ formula units } \times \frac{1 \text{ mol}}{6.022 \times 10^{23} \text{ formula units}} = 1.4 \times 10^{-3} \text{ mol}$$

$$0.0014 \text{ mol } CaC_2O_4 \times \frac{128 \text{ g } CaC_2O_4}{1 \text{ mol } CaC_2O_4} = 0.18 \text{ g } CaC_2O_4$$

Mole and Mass Relationships from Chemical Equations

6.40 (a) $C_4H_8O_2(l) + 2\,H_2(g) \longrightarrow 2\,C_2H_6O(l)$

(b) 3.0 mol of ethyl alcohol are produced from 1.5 mol of ethyl acetate.

(c) $1.5\text{ mol }C_4H_8O_2 \times \dfrac{2\text{ mol }C_2H_6O}{1\text{ mol }C_4H_8O_2} \times \dfrac{46.0\text{ g }C_2H_6O}{1\text{ mol }C_2H_6O} = 138\text{ g }C_2H_6O$

(d) $12.0\text{ g }C_4H_8O_2 \times \dfrac{1\text{ mol }C_4H_8O_2}{88.0\text{ g }C_4H_8O_2} \times \dfrac{2\text{ mol }C_2H_6O}{1\text{ mol }C_4H_8O_2} \times \dfrac{46.0\text{ g }C_2H_6O}{1\text{ mol }C_2H_6O}$

$= 12.5\text{ g }C_2H_6O$

(e) $12.0\text{ g }C_4H_8O_2 \times \dfrac{1\text{ mol }C_4H_8O_2}{88.0\text{ g }C_4H_8O_2} \times \dfrac{2\text{ mol }H_2}{1\text{ mol }C_4H_8O_2} \times \dfrac{2.02\text{ g }H_2}{1\text{ mol }H_2} = 0.551\text{ g }H_2$

6.42 (a) $N_2(g) + 3\,H_2(g) \longrightarrow 2\,NH_3(g)$

(b) $16.0\text{ g }NH_3 \times \dfrac{1\text{ mol }NH_3}{17.0\text{ g }NH_3} \times \dfrac{1\text{ mol }N_2}{2\text{ mol }NH_3} = 0.471\text{ mol }N_2$

(c) $75.0\text{ g }N_2 \times \dfrac{1\text{ mol }N_2}{28.0\text{ g }N_2} \times \dfrac{3\text{ mol }H_2}{1\text{ mol }N_2} \times \dfrac{2.02\text{ g }H_2}{1\text{ mol }H_2} = 16.2\text{ g }H_2$

6.44 (a) $Fe_2O_3(s) + 3\,CO(g) \longrightarrow 2\,Fe(s) + 3\,CO_2(g)$

(b) $3.02\text{ g }Fe_2O_3 \times \dfrac{1\text{ mol }Fe_2O_3}{159.7\text{ g }Fe_2O_3} \times \dfrac{3\text{ mol }CO}{1\text{ mol }Fe_2O_3} \times \dfrac{28.0\text{ g }CO}{1\text{ mol }CO} = 1.59\text{ g }CO$

(c) $1.68\text{ mol }Fe_2O_3 \times \dfrac{3\text{ mol }CO}{1\text{ mol }Fe_2O_3} \times \dfrac{28.0\text{ g }CO}{1\text{ mol }CO} = 141\text{ g }CO$

6.46 $TiO_2(s) \longrightarrow Ti(s) + O_2(g)$

$95\text{ kg Ti} \times \dfrac{1\text{ mol Ti}}{47.9\text{ g Ti}} \times \dfrac{1\text{ mol }TiO_2}{1\text{ mol Ti}} \times \dfrac{79.9\text{ g }TiO_2}{1\text{ mol }TiO_2} = 158\text{ kg }TiO_2$

6.48

$4 \times 10^8\text{ kg }SO_2 \times \dfrac{10^3\text{ g}}{1\text{ kg}} \times \dfrac{1\text{ mol}}{64\text{ g}} = 6 \times 10^9\text{ mol}$

$6 \times 10^9\text{ mol }H_2SO_4 \times \dfrac{98\text{ g}}{1\text{ mol}} \times \dfrac{1\text{ kg}}{1 \times 10^3\text{ g}} = 6 \times 10^8\text{ kg }H_2SO_4$

6.50 Two moles of SO_2 are produced from each mole of pyrite.

$$1.0 \text{ kg FeS}_2 \text{ x } \frac{10^3 \text{ g}}{1 \text{ kg}} \text{ x } \frac{1 \text{ mol FeS}_2}{119.7 \text{ g}} \text{ x } \frac{2 \text{ mol SO}_2}{1 \text{ mol FeS}_2} = 17 \text{ mol SO}_2$$

Percent Yield

6.52

(a) $25.0 \text{ g CO } \text{ x } \frac{1 \text{ mol CO}}{28.0 \text{ g CO}} = 0.893 \text{ mol CO}; \ 6.00 \text{ g H}_2 \text{ x } \frac{1 \text{ mol H}_2}{2.02 \text{ g H}_2} = 2.97 \text{ mol H}_2$

Carbon monoxide is the limiting reagent.

(b) $10.0 \text{ g CO } \text{ x } \frac{1 \text{ mol CO}}{28.0 \text{ g CO}} \text{ x } \frac{1 \text{ mol CH}_3\text{OH}}{1 \text{ mol CO}} \text{ x } \frac{32.0 \text{ g CH}_3\text{OH}}{1 \text{ mol CH}_3\text{OH}} = 11.4 \text{ g CH}_3\text{OH}$

(c) $\frac{9.55 \text{ g}}{11.4 \text{ g}} \text{ x } 100\% = 83.8\% \text{ yield}$

6.54 (a) $CH_4(g) + 2 Cl_2(g) \longrightarrow CH_2Cl_2(l) + 2 HCl(g)$

(b) $50.0 \text{ g CH}_4 \text{ x } \frac{1 \text{ mol CH}_4}{16.0 \text{ g CH}_4} \text{ x } \frac{2 \text{ mol Cl}_2}{1 \text{ mol CH}_4} \text{ x } \frac{71.0 \text{ g Cl}_2}{1 \text{ mol Cl}_2} = 444 \text{ g Cl}_2$

(c) If the reaction occurred in 100% yield:

$$50.0 \text{ g CH}_4 \text{ x } \frac{1 \text{ mol CH}_4}{16.0 \text{ g CH}_4} \text{ x } \frac{1 \text{ mol CH}_2\text{Cl}_2}{1 \text{ mol CH}_4} \text{ x } \frac{85.0 \text{ g CH}_2\text{Cl}_2}{1 \text{ mol CH}_2\text{Cl}_2} = 266 \text{ g CH}_2\text{Cl}_2$$

Since the reaction occurs in 76% yield:

266 g x 0.76 = 202 g CH_2Cl_2 are actually formed.

6.56

(a) $75 \text{ g C}_6\text{H}_6 \text{ x } \frac{1 \text{ mol C}_6\text{H}_6}{78 \text{ g C}_6\text{H}_6} = 0.96 \text{ mol C}_6\text{H}_6$

$27.5 \text{ g HNO}_3 \text{ x } \frac{1 \text{ mol HNO}_3}{63.0 \text{ g HNO}_3} = 0.437 \text{ mol HNO}_3$

Nitric acid is the limiting reagent.

(b) $0.437 \text{ mol HNO}_3 \text{ x } \frac{1 \text{ mol C}_6\text{H}_5\text{NO}_2}{1 \text{ mol HNO}_3} \text{ x } \frac{123 \text{ g}}{1 \text{ mol C}_6\text{H}_5\text{NO}_2} = 53.8 \text{ g C}_6\text{H}_5\text{NO}_2$

Chemistry in Action

6.58 The most serious error in calculating Avogadro's number by spreading oil on water is the estimate of the size of the area the oil covered. Some approximations that Franklin made, but that can be determined with reasonable precision, are the volume of oil, the mass of the oil, its density and its molar mass. Other assumptions, involving the thickness of the oil layer and the arrangement of oil molecules on the surface of the water, are also sources of error.

6.60 The formula for ferrous sulfate is $FeSO_4$. Its molar mass is 151.9 g/mol.

$$250 \text{ mg FeSO}_4 \times \frac{55.8 \text{ g Fe}}{151.9 \text{ g FeSO}_4} = 91.8 \text{ mg Fe}$$

General Questions and Problems

6.62 Molar mass of batrachotoxin ($C_{31}H_{42}N_2O_6$) = 538 g/mol

$$0.05 \text{ µg} \times \frac{1 \text{ g}}{10^6 \text{ µg}} \times \frac{1 \text{ mol}}{538 \text{ g}} \times \frac{6.022 \times 10^{23} \text{ molecules}}{1 \text{ mol}} = 6 \times 10^{13} \text{ molecules}$$

6.64 (a) $C_{12}H_{22}O_{11}(s) \longrightarrow 12 \text{ C}(s) + 11 \text{ H}_2O(l)$

(b) $60.0 \text{ g sucrose} \times \dfrac{1 \text{ mol sucrose}}{342 \text{ g sucrose}} \times \dfrac{12 \text{ mol C}}{1 \text{ mol sucrose}} \times \dfrac{12.0 \text{ g C}}{1 \text{ mol C}} = 25.3 \text{ g carbon}$

(c) $6.50 \text{ g C} \times \dfrac{1 \text{ mol C}}{12.0 \text{ g C}} \times \dfrac{11 \text{ mol H}_2O}{12 \text{ mol C}} \times \dfrac{18.0 \text{ g H}_2O}{1 \text{ mol H}_2O} = 8.94 \text{ g H}_2O$

6.66

(a) $1.50 \text{ g C}_2H_6O \times \dfrac{1 \text{ mol C}_2H_6O}{46.0 \text{ g C}_2H_6O} \times \dfrac{2 \text{ mol K}_2Cr_2O_7}{3 \text{ mol C}_2H_6O} \times \dfrac{294.2 \text{ g K}_2Cr_2O_7}{1 \text{ mol K}_2Cr_2O_7}$

$= 6.40 \text{ g K}_2Cr_2O_7$

(b) $80.0 \text{ g C}_2H_6O \times \dfrac{1 \text{ mol C}_2H_6O}{46.0 \text{ g C}_2H_6O} \times \dfrac{3 \text{ mol C}_2H_4O_2}{3 \text{ mol C}_2H_6O} \times \dfrac{60.0 \text{ g C}_2H_4O_2}{1 \text{ mol C}_2H_4O_2}$

$= 104 \text{ g C}_2H_4O_2$

6.68 (a) $4 \text{ NH}_3(g) + 5 \text{ O}_2(g) \longrightarrow 4 \text{ NO}(g) + 6 \text{ H}_2O(g)$

(b) $17.0 \text{ g NH}_3 \times \dfrac{1 \text{ mol NH}_3}{17.0 \text{ g}} \times \dfrac{1 \text{ mol NO}}{1 \text{ mol NH}_3} \times \dfrac{30.0 \text{ g NO}}{1 \text{ mol NO}} = 30.0 \text{ g NO}$

6.70 (a) $BaCl_2(aq) + Na_2SO_4(aq) \longrightarrow BaSO_4(s) + 2 \text{ NaCl}(aq)$

(b) $27.4 \text{ g Na}_2SO_4 \times \dfrac{1 \text{ mol Na}_2SO_4}{142 \text{ g Na}_2SO_4} \times \dfrac{1 \text{ mol BaSO}_4}{1 \text{ mol Na}_2SO_4} \times \dfrac{233 \text{ g BaSO}_4}{1 \text{ mol BaSO}_4}$

$= 45.0 \text{ g BaSO}_4$

6.72

(a) $47 \text{ g } C_7H_6O_3 \times \dfrac{1 \text{ mol } C_7H_6O_3}{138 \text{ g } C_7H_6O_3} = 0.34 \text{ mol } C_7H_6O_3$

$25 \text{ g } C_4H_6O_3 \times \dfrac{1 \text{ mol } C_4H_6O_3}{102 \text{ g } C_4H_6O_3} = 0.25 \text{ mol } C_4H_6O_3$

Acetic anhydride is the limiting reagent.

$0.25 \text{ mol } C_4H_6O_3 \times \dfrac{1 \text{ mol } C_9H_8O_4}{1 \text{ mol } C_4H_6O_3} \times \dfrac{180 \text{ g } C_9H_8O_4}{1 \text{ mol } C_9H_8O_4} = 45 \text{ g } C_9H_8O_4$

(b) $\dfrac{35 \text{ g}}{45 \text{ g}} \times 100\% = 78\%$

6.74 (a) $P_4(s) + 10 \text{ } Cl_2(g) \longrightarrow 4 \text{ } PCl_5(s)$

(b) $15.2 \text{ g } P_4 \times \dfrac{1 \text{ mol } P_4}{124 \text{ g } P_4} \times \dfrac{4 \text{ mol } PCl_5}{1 \text{ mol } P_4} \times \dfrac{208 \text{ g } PCl_5}{1 \text{ mol } PCl_5} = 102 \text{ g } PCl_5$

6.76 (a) $6 \text{ } NH_4ClO_4(s) + 10 \text{ } Al(s) \longrightarrow 4 \text{ } Al_2O_3(s) + 2 \text{ } AlCl_3(s) + 12 \text{ } H_2O(g) + 3 \text{ } N_2(g)$

(b) $14.5 \times 10^3 \text{ g } NH_4ClO_4 \times \dfrac{1 \text{ mol } NH_4ClO_4}{117 \text{ g } NH_4ClO_4} \times \dfrac{15 \text{ mol gases}}{6 \text{ mol } NH_4ClO_4} = 310 \text{ mol gases}$

Remember that both water and nitrogen are gases in this problem.

Self-Test for Chapter 6

Multiple Choice

1. What mass of $CaCO_3$ has the same number of molecules as 21 g of NaF?
    (a) 10 g   (b) 20 g   (c) 50 g   (d) 100 g

2. Consider the following equation: $LiOH + CO_2 \longrightarrow LiHCO_3$. In which situation is LiOH the limiting reagent?
    (a) 6 g $LiOH$ + 11 g CO_2 (b) 10 g $LiOH$ + 16 g CO_2
    (c) 4 g $LiOH$ + 7 g CO_2 (d) 9 g $LiOH$ + 17 g CO_2

3. In the equation $P_2O_5 + 3 \text{ } H_2O \longrightarrow 2 \text{ } H_3PO_4$ the mole ratio of product to H_2O is:
    (a) 2:1   (b) 2:3   (c) 3:2   (d) 1:2

4. In the reaction $2 \text{ } Ca + O_2 \longrightarrow 2 \text{ } CaO$, how many grams of CaO can be produced from 20 g of Ca? (a) 20 g   (b) 28 g   (c) 40 g   (d) 56 g

5. $3 \text{ } NO_2 + H_2O \longrightarrow 2 \text{ } HNO_3 + NO$

    All the following statements about this reaction are true except:
    (a) The starting material is both oxidized and reduced.
    (b) NO_2 in the atmosphere might contribute to acid rain.
    (c) At least 6 g of H_2O are needed to react completely with 46 g of $NO_2.$
    (d) 92 g of NO_2 produces 28 g of NO.

True or False

1.   A mole of oxygen atoms has the same mass as a mole of nitrogen atoms.

2.   The coefficients in chemical reactions show the relative numbers of moles of reactants and products.

3.   Percent yield is the amount of a substance that can theoretically be produced divided by the amount actually produced.

4.   Mole ratios are used to convert between moles and grams of a compound.

5.   In the reaction $4 Al + 3 O_2 \rightarrow 2 Al_2O_3$, the mole ratio of product to Al is 2.

Match each entry on the left with its partner on the right.

1.   42.0 amu   (a) Converts moles Na to grams Na

2.   23.0 g sodium / 1 mol   (b) Molar mass of NaF

3.   42.0 g   (c) Converts grams Na to moles Na

4.   1 mol / 23.0 g sodium   (d) Avogadro's number

5. 6.02×10^{23} (e) Formula weight of NaF

Chapter Outline

I. Energy (Sections 7.1–7.4).
   A. Energy and chemical bonds (Section 7.1).
      1. There are two kinds of energy.
         a. Potential energy is stored energy.
         b. Kinetic energy is the energy of motion.
      2. Chemical bonds are a form of potential energy.
      3. Whether a reaction occurs, and how much heat is associated, depends on the potential energy of reactants and products.
   B. Heat changes during chemical reactions (Section 7.2).
      1. Bond dissociation energies measure the strength of covalent bonds.
         a. Bond breaking requires heat and is endothermic.
         b. Bond formation releases heat and is exothermic.
      2. The reverse of an endothermic process is exothermic, and the reverse of an exothermic process is endothermic.
      3. The law of conservation of energy states that energy can neither be created nor destroyed during any physical or chemical change.
      4. The difference between the energy needed for breaking bonds and the energy released in forming bonds is the heat of reaction, also known as enthalpy (ΔH).
   C. Exothermic and endothermic reactions: ΔH (Section 7.3).
      1. In exothermic reactions, the bond dissociation energies of the products are greater than the bond dissociation energies of the reactants, and ΔH is negative.
      2. In endothermic reactions, the bond dissociation energies of the products are smaller than the bond dissociation energies of the reactants, and ΔH is positive.
      3. The amount of heat released in the reverse of a reaction is equal to that absorbed in the forward reaction, but ΔH has the opposite sign.
      4. The heat of reaction can be determined by the formula:
$$\Delta H = \Sigma \text{ (bond dissociation energies)}_{reactants} - \Sigma(\text{bond dissociation energies})_{products}$$
   D. Free energy: ΔG (Section 7.4).
      1. Spontaneous processes.
         a. A spontaneous process proceeds without any external influence.
         b. A nonspontaneous process needs a constant external source of energy.
      2. Entropy (ΔS) measures the amount of disorder in a system.
         a. If disorder increases, ΔS is positive.
         b. If disorder decreases, ΔS is negative.
      3. The absorption of heat and the increase or decrease in disorder determine if a reaction is spontaneous.
         a. $\Delta G = \Delta H - T\Delta S$.
         b. If ΔG is negative, the process is spontaneous, and the reaction is exergonic.
         c. If ΔG is positive, the process isn't spontaneous, and the reaction is endergonic.
      4. ΔG for the reverse of a reaction is equal in value to ΔG for the forward reaction, but the sign is changed.
      5. Some nonspontaneous processes become spontaneous when temperature increases.
II. Reaction rates (Sections 7.5–7.6).
   A. How reactions occur (Section 7.5).
      1. In addition to the value of ΔG, other factors determine if a reaction will occur.
         a. Reactants must collide in the correct orientation.
         b. The energy of collision must be great enough to cause bond breaking.

      c. Many reactions with a favorable free energy don't occur at room temperature, and heat must be added to get them started.
    2. The energy changes during a reaction can be graphed on a reaction energy diagram.
    3. The amount of energy needed to produce favorable collisions is the activation energy E_{act}.
       a. E_{act} determines the reaction rate.
       b. The size of E_{act} is unrelated to the size of ΔH.
  B. Factors that affect reaction rate (Section 7.6).
    1. Increasing temperature increases reaction rate.
    2. Increasing the concentration of reactants increases reaction rate.
    3. Catalysts increase the reaction rate by lowering E_{act}.
III. Chemical equilibrium (Sections 7.7–7.9).
  A. Reversible reactions (Section 7.7).
    1. Some reactions proceed to virtual completion.
    2. Other reactions go to partial completion, at which point products begin to reform starting material.
       a. These reactions are reversible.
       b. The reaction from left to right is the forward reaction.
       c. The reaction from right to left is the reverse reaction.
    3. At some point the rate of the forward reaction equals the rate of the reverse reaction, and equilibrium is established.
    4. It is not necessary for the concentrations of products and reactants to be equal at equilibrium.
  B. Equilibrium (Section 7.8).
    1. Equilibrium equations.
       a. For the reaction $a\,A + b\,B \longrightarrow c\,C + d\,D$,

$$K = \frac{[C]^c[D]^d}{[A]^a[B]^b}$$

       b. K = equilibrium constant.
       c. Expression on the right = equilibrium constant expression.
       d. The concentrations of pure solids or liquids are omitted from the equilibrium expression.
    2. The value of K determines the position of equilibrium.
       a. When $K \gg 1$, reaction goes to completion.
       b. When $K > 1$, the forward reaction is favored.
       c. When K is of intermediate value, significant amounts of reactants and products are present at equilibrium.
       d. When $K < 1$, the reverse reaction is favored.
       e. When $K \ll 1$, there is essentially no reaction.
  C. Effect of changing reaction conditions (Section 7.9).
    1. Le Châtelier's principle: When a stress is applied to a system, the equilibrium shifts to remove the stress.
    2. Effect of changing concentration.
       a. Increasing the concentration of reactants favors the forward reaction.
       b. Increasing the concentration of products favors the reverse reaction.
    3. Effect of changing temperature.
       a. Decreasing temperature favors an exothermic reaction.
       b. Increasing temperature favors an endothermic reaction.
    4. Effect of changing pressure.
       a. There is no effect unless one of the reactants or products is a gas.
       b. Increasing pressure shifts the equilibrium in the direction that produces fewer gas molecules.

Solutions to Chapter 7 Problems

7.1   (a) Use the following expression to calculate ΔH:

$\Delta H = \Sigma$ (bond dissociation energies)$_{reactants}$ – Σ(bond dissociation energies)$_{products}$

Σ (bond dissociation energies)$_{reactants}$ = 12(C=O) + 12(O–H)
= 12(191 kcal/mol) + 12(112 kcal/mol)
= 3636 kcal/mol

Σ(bond dissociation energies)$_{products}$ = 5(C–C) + 7(C–H) + 7(C–O) + 5(O–H) + 6(O=O)
= [5(83) + 7(99) + 7(86) + 5(112) + 6(119)] kcal/mol
= 2984 kcal/mol

ΔH = 3636 kcal/mol – 2984 kcal/mol = +652 kcal/mol
652 kcal/mol x 4.18 kJ/kcal = 2730 kJ/mol

(b) The reaction is endothermic because ΔH is positive.

7.2   (a) The reaction is endothermic because ΔH is positive.

(b) $\dfrac{801 \text{ kcal}}{4 \text{ mol Al}}$ x 1.00 mol Al = 200 kcal (836 kJ) required

(c) 10.0 g Al x $\dfrac{1 \text{ mol Al}}{27.0 \text{ g Al}}$ x $\dfrac{801 \text{ kcal}}{4 \text{ mol Al}}$ = 74.2 kcal (310 kJ) required

7.3

127 g NO x $\dfrac{1 \text{ mol}}{30.0 \text{ g NO}}$ x $\dfrac{43 \text{ kcal}}{2 \text{ mol NO}}$ = 91 kcal (380 kJ) absorbed

7.4 $\Delta H = \Sigma$ (bond dissociation energies)$_{reactants}$ – Σ(bond dissociation energies)$_{products}$

Σ (bond dissociation energies)$_{reactants}$ = (C–C) + 5(C–H) + (C–O) + (O–H) + 3(O=O)
= [83 + 5(99) + 86 + 112 + 3(119)] kcal/mol
= 1133 kcal/mol
Σ(bond dissociation energies)$_{products}$ = 4(C=O) + 6(O–H)
= [4(191) + 6(112)] kcal/mol = 1436 kcal/mol
ΔH = 1133 kcal/mol – 1436 kcal/mol = –303 kcal/mol

$\dfrac{303 \text{ kcal}}{1 \text{ mol}}$ x $\dfrac{1 \text{ mol}}{46 \text{ g}}$ x $\dfrac{1 \text{ Cal}}{1 \text{ kcal}}$ = $\dfrac{6.59 \text{ Cal}}{1 \text{ g}}$

This value agrees fairly well with the caloric value of alcohol (7.1 Cal/g) shown in Table 7.1

7.5   (a) Entropy increases because the number of molecules increases.
(b) Entropy decreases because disorder decreases when gases condense.
(c) Entropy decreases because two moles of gaseous product are formed from three moles of gaseous reactants.

7.6   (a) $\Delta G = \Delta H - T\Delta S$: $\Delta H = +42.6$ kcal/mol $\Delta S = +38.6$ cal/(mol · K) $T = 298$ K
$\Delta G = +42.6$ kcal/mol $-$ [298 K x 38.6 cal/(mol · K) x 1 kcal/10^3 cal]
      $= +42.6$ kcal/mol $-$ 11.5 kcal/mol $= +31.1$ kcal/mol $= 130$ kJ/mol
The reaction is not spontaneous at 25 °C.

(b) The reaction is spontaneous at higher temperatures. In the expression $\Delta G = \Delta H - T\Delta S$, the term $T\Delta S$ becomes larger at high temperature and causes ΔG to become negative.

7.7 $\Delta G = \Delta H - T\Delta S$: $\Delta H = +1.44$ kcal/mol $\Delta S = +5.26$ cal/(mol · K)
(a) If $T = 263$ K,
$$T\Delta S = 263 \text{ K} \times \frac{5.26 \text{ cal}}{\text{mol K}} \times \frac{1 \text{ kcal}}{10^3 \text{ cal}} = \frac{1.38 \text{ kcal}}{\text{mol}}$$

$\Delta G = 1.44$ kcal/mol $-$ 1.38 kcal/mol $= +0.06$ kcal/mol $= +0.25$ kJ/mol
At 263 K, melting is not spontaneous because ΔG is positive.

(b) If $T = 273$ K,
$$T\Delta S = 273 \text{ K} \times \frac{5.26 \text{ cal}}{\text{mol K}} \times \frac{1 \text{ kcal}}{10^3 \text{ cal}} = \frac{1.44 \text{ kcal}}{\text{mol}}$$

$\Delta G = 1.44$ kcal/mol $-$ 1.44 kcal/mol $= +0.00$ kcal/mol
At 273 K, $\Delta G = 0$, and melting and freezing are in equilibrium.

(c) If $T = 283$ K,
$$T\Delta S = 283 \text{ K} \times \frac{5.26 \text{ cal}}{\text{mol K}} \times \frac{1 \text{ kcal}}{10^3 \text{ cal}} = \frac{1.49 \text{ kcal}}{\text{mol}}$$

$\Delta G = 1.44$ kcal/mol $-$ 1.49 kcal/mol $= -0.05$ kcal/mol $= -0.21$ kJ/mol
At 283 K, melting is spontaneous because ΔG is negative.

7.8   (a) The sign of ΔS is positive because disorder increases from reactant to products.
(b) In the expression $\Delta G = \Delta H - T\Delta S$, ΔH is a negative number. Because ΔS is positive, $(-T\Delta S)$ is negative at all temperatures. Thus, ΔG is negative at all temperatures, and the reaction is spontaneous at all temperatures.

7.9

In this reaction, E_{act} is large, the reaction is slow, and the free-energy change is large and negative.

7.10

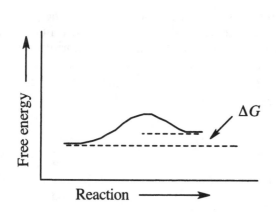

In this reaction, ΔG is small and positive. E_{act} can be small or large, but it is always larger than ΔG.

7.11

(a)

In this reaction, E_{act} is large, and ΔG is small and negative.

(b) The rate of reaction can be increased by either increasing concentration of reactants, increasing the temperature, or adding a catalyst.

7.12   Evaporation of 1.0 g sweat cools the body by 540 cal (0.540 kcal). Removing 678 kcal requires the evaporation of:

$$678 \text{ kcal } \times \frac{1.0 \text{ g}}{0.540 \text{ kcal}} = 1260 \text{ g sweat}$$

7.13

$$K = \frac{[\text{products}]}{[\text{reactants}]}$$

(a) $K = \dfrac{[NO_2]^2}{[N_2O_4]}$ (b) $K = \dfrac{[H_2O]^2}{[H_2S]^2[O_2]}$ (c) $K = \dfrac{[Br_2][F_2]^5}{[BrF_5]^2}$

Don't forget that the coefficients of the reactants and products appear as exponents in the equilibrium expression. In (b), the concentration of solid sulfur doesn't enter into the equation.

7.14   If K is greater than 1, the reaction favors products. If K is less than 1, the reaction favors reactants.
(a) Products are strongly favored.
(b) Reactants are strongly favored.
(c) Products are somewhat favored.

7.15   In the expression for the equilibrium constant, the concentration of the product HI is squared in the numerator. The concentrations of the reactants appear in the denominator. Substitute the given concentrations into the expression. The equilibrium favors products.

$$K = \frac{[\text{HI}]^2}{[\text{H}_2][\text{I}_2]} = \frac{[0.507]^2}{[0.0510][0.174]} = 29.0$$

7.16

(a) $K = \dfrac{[\text{AB}]^2}{[\text{A}_2][\text{B}_2]}$; $K = \dfrac{[\text{AB}]^2}{[\text{A}_2][\text{B}]^2}$

(b) $K = \dfrac{[1]^2}{[3][3]} = 0.11$; $K = \dfrac{[4]^2}{[2][3]^2} = \dfrac{16}{18} = 0.89$

7.17   High pressure favors the production of SO_3 because increasing the pressure shifts the equilibrium in the direction that decreases the number of molecules in the gas phase. Low temperature favors the production of SO_3 because exothermic reactions are favored by lower temperatures.

7.18   (a) Increasing the temperature shifts the equilibrium to the left, favoring reactants.
(b) Increasing the pressure shifts the equilibrium to the right, favoring product.
(c) Removing CH_4 from the reaction vessel causes more CH_4 to be formed and shifts the equilibrium toward the right, favoring product.

7.19 $Cu_2O(s) + C(s) \longrightarrow 2\,Cu(s) + CO(g)$ $\Delta G = -3.8$ kJ (−1.0 kcal)

Understanding Key Concepts

7.20 ΔH is positive because energy must be supplied in order to break the attractive forces between molecules of the crystal. ΔS is also positive because the molecules of gas are more disordered than the molecules of solid. ΔG is negative because it is stated in the problem that the reaction is spontaneous.

7.22   (a) $2\,A_2 + B_2 \longrightarrow 2\,A_2B$

(b) ΔG is negative because the reaction is spontaneous. ΔS is negative because the product mixture has fewer gas molecules and less disorder than the reactant mixture. ΔH must be negative in order for ΔG to be negative since ($-T\,\Delta S$) is positive.

7.24

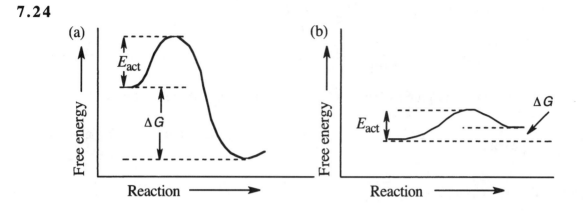

(a)

E_{act}

Free energy

ΔG

Reaction

(b)

Free energy

E_{act}

ΔG

Reaction

Enthalpy and Heat of Reaction

7.26   In an endothermic reaction, the total enthalpy of the reactants is greater than the total enthalpy of the products. In other words, the reactants have stronger bonds and are more stable, while the products have weaker bonds and are less stable. Energy must therefore be supplied for the reaction to take place.

7.28   (a) ΔH is positive. $Br_2(l) + 7.4$ kcal/mol $\longrightarrow Br_2(g)$

(b) 5.8 mol Br_2 x $\dfrac{7.4 \text{ kcal}}{1 \text{ mol } Br_2}$ = 43 kcal needed

(c) 82 g Br_2 x $\dfrac{1 \text{ mol } Br_2}{159.8 \text{ g } Br_2}$ x $\dfrac{31.0 \text{ kJ}}{1 \text{ mol } Br_2}$ = 15.9 kJ needed

7.30   (a) $2\ C_2H_2(g) + 5\ O_2(g) \longrightarrow 4\ CO_2(g) + 2\ H_2O(g)$

(b) $\Delta H = \Sigma$ (bond dissociation energies)$_{reactants} - \Sigma$(bond dissociation energies)$_{products}$

Σ (bond dissociation energies)$_{reactants}$ = $4(C–H) + 2(C\equiv C) + 5(O=O)$
$= [4(99) + 2(201) + 5(119)]$ kcal/mol
$= 1393$ kcal/mol (5820 kJ/mol)

Σ(bond dissociation energies)$_{products}$ = $8(C=O) + 4(O–H)$
$= [8(191) + 4(112)]$ kcal/mol
$= 1976$ kcal/mol (8260 kJ/mol)

$\Delta H = 1393$ kcal/mol $- 1976$ kcal/mol $= -583$ kcal/mol $= -2440$ kJ/mol

(c)

$\dfrac{2440 \text{ kJ}}{1 \text{ mol}}$ x $\dfrac{1 \text{ mol}}{2 \text{ mol } C_2H_2}$ x $\dfrac{1 \text{ mol } C_2H_2}{26 \text{ g } C_2H_2}$ = $\dfrac{46.9 \text{ kJ}}{1 \text{ g } C_2H_2}$

This value is similar to the energy values for gasoline and natural gas and indicates that acetylene is one of the best fuels.

7.32   (a) $C_6H_{12}O_6 + 6\,O_2 \longrightarrow 6\,CO_2 + 6\,H_2O$

(b) $\dfrac{-3.8\text{ kcal}}{1\text{ g glucose}} \times \dfrac{180\text{ g glucose}}{1\text{ mol glucose}} \times 1.50\text{ mol glucose} = -1.0 \times 10^3\text{ kcal} = -4.2 \times 10^3\text{ kJ}$

(c) The production of glucose from CO_2 and H_2O is an endothermic process.

$\dfrac{3.8\text{ kcal}}{1\text{ g glucose}} \times 15.0\text{ g glucose} = 57\text{ kcal (238 kJ) needed to produce 15 g glucose}$

Entropy and Free Energy

7.34   Increase in entropy: (a)
Decrease in entropy: (b), (c)

7.36   The two factors that influence the spontaneity of a reaction are: (1) the release or absorption of heat, and (2) the increase or decrease in entropy.

7.38   The free-energy change (ΔG) of a chemical reaction shows whether or not a reaction is spontaneous. If the sign of ΔG is negative, the reaction is spontaneous. Of the two factors that contribute to ΔG (ΔH and ΔS), ΔH is usually larger at low temperatures. Thus if a reaction is spontaneous (negative ΔG) it is usually exothermic (negative ΔH).

7.40   (a) Dissolution of NaCl is endothermic since ΔH is positive.
(b Entropy increases because disorder increases.
(c) Since the dissolution of NaCl is spontaneous, ΔG for the reaction must be negative. Because we already know that ΔH is positive, it must be true that $T\Delta S$ is the major contributor to ΔG.

7.42   (a) $H_2(g) + Br_2(l) \longrightarrow 2\,HBr(g)$

(b) Entropy increases because the number of gaseous product molecules is greater than the number of gaseous reactant molecules, and thus the sign of ΔS is positive.

(c) The process is spontaneous at all temperatures because ΔH is negative and ΔS is positive.

(d) $\Delta G = \Delta H - T\Delta S$; $\Delta H = -17.4\text{ kcal/mol}$; $\Delta S = 27.2\text{ cal/(mol}\cdot\text{K)}$; $T = 300\text{ K}$

$T\Delta S = 300\text{ K} \times \dfrac{27.2\text{ cal}}{\text{mol K}} \times \dfrac{1\text{ kcal}}{10^3\text{ cal}} = \dfrac{8.16\text{ kcal}}{\text{mol}} \left(\dfrac{34.1\text{ kJ}}{\text{mol}}\right)$

$\Delta G = -17.4\text{ kcal/mol} - 8.16\text{ kcal/mol} = -25.6\text{ kcal/mol (}-107\text{ kJ/mol)}$

Rates of Chemical Reactions

7.44   The *activation energy* of a reaction is the amount of energy needed for reactants to surmount the energy barrier to reaction.

7.46

7.48 A catalyst is a substance that increases reaction rate by lowering the activation energy barrier, yet remains unchanged when the reaction is completed.

7.50 (a) The negative value of ΔG indicates that diamonds spontaneously turn into graphite at 25°C.
(b) Because this behavior is not observed, the activation energy of the reaction must be extremely high and the reaction rate must be extremely slow.

Chemical Equilibria

7.52 In a reversible reaction, chemical equilibrium is a state in which the rates of the forward reaction and the reverse reaction are equal. The amounts of reactants and products need not be equal at equilibrium.

7.54 Remember that solids and pure liquids don't appear in the equilibrium expression
(a) $K = \dfrac{[CO_2]^2}{[CO]^2[O_2]}$ (b) $K = \dfrac{[MgCl_2][H_2]}{[HCl]}$

(c) $K = \dfrac{[H_3O^+][F^-]}{[HF]}$ (d) $K = \dfrac{[SO_2]}{[O_2]}$

7.56

$$K = \frac{[NO_2]^2}{[N_2O_4]} = \frac{(0.0325 \text{ mol/L})^2}{(0.147 \text{ mol/L})} = 7.19 \times 10^{-3} \text{ Reactants are favored.}$$

7.58

(a) $K = 7.19 \times 10^{-3} = \dfrac{(0.0250 \text{ mol/L})^2}{[N_2O_4]}$; $[N_2O_4] = 0.0869 \text{ mol/L}$

(b) $K = 7.19 \times 10^{-3} = \dfrac{[NO_2]^2}{(0.0750 \text{ mol/L})}$; $[NO_2] = 0.0232 \text{ mol/L}$

7.60   If the pressure is raised, relatively more reactants than products are found at equilibrium, because high pressure favors the reaction that produces fewer gas molecules.

Le Châtelier's Principle

7.62   (a) The reaction is endothermic.
(b) Reactants are favored at equilibrium.
(c) (1) Increasing pressure favors formation of ozone, since increased pressure shifts the equilibrium in the direction of the reaction that produces fewer gas molecules.
(2) Increasing the O_2 concentration increases the amount of O_3 formed.
(3) Increasing the concentration of O_3 shifts the equilibrium to the left.
(4) A catalyst has no effect on the equilibrium.
(5) Increasing the temperature shifts the equilibrium to the right because the reaction is endothermic.

7.64   According to Le Châtelier's principle, an increase in pressure shifts the equilibrium in the direction that decreases the number of molecules in the gas phase.
(a) The concentration of products decreases.
(b) The concentration of products remains the same.
(c) The concentration of products increases.

7.66 $$CO(g) + H_2O(g) \rightleftharpoons CO_2(g) + H_2(g) \quad \Delta H = -9.8 \text{ kcal/mol } (-41 \text{ kJ/mol})$$

Because it has a negative value of ΔH, the reaction is exothermic, and the equilibrium favors products. Decreasing the temperature increases the amount of H_2.

7.68 $$H_2(g) + I_2(g) \rightleftharpoons 2\,HI(g) \quad \Delta H = -2.2 \text{ kcal/mol } (-9.2 \text{ kJ/mol})$$

(a) Adding I_2 to the reaction mix increases the equilibrium concentration of HI.
(b) Removing H_2 causes the equilibrium concentration of HI to decrease.
(c) Addition of a catalyst does not change the equilibrium concentration of HI.
(d) Increasing the temperature decreases the concentration of HI.

Chemistry in Action

7.70   A gram of fat contains more energy (9 kcal/g) than a gram of carbohydrate (4 kcal/g).

7.72   Body temperature is regulated by the thyroid gland and by the hypothalamus region of the brain.

7.74   Add the two reactions, cancel all quantities common to both sides of the equation, and add the two values of ΔG to arrive at the value of ΔG for the coupled reactions.

$$ADP + HOPO_3{}^{2-} + PEP + H_2O \longrightarrow ATP + H_2O + \text{pyruvate} + HOPO_3{}^{2-}$$
$$ADP + \text{phosphoenolpyruvate} \longrightarrow ATP + \text{pyruvate} \quad \Delta G = -31.4 \text{ kJ/mol}$$

General Questions and Problems

7.76   (a) $C_2H_5OH + 3\,O_2 \longrightarrow 2\,CO_2 + 3\,H_2O + 327\ \text{kcal}$

     (b) ΔH is negative because energy is released.

     (c) $5.00\ \text{g }C_2H_5OH \ \times\ \dfrac{1\ \text{mol }C_2H_5OH}{46.0\ \text{g }C_2H_5OH}\ \times\ \dfrac{327\ \text{cal}}{1\ \text{mol}} = 35.5\ \text{kcal}$

     (d) Calories needed $=$ specific heat of H_2O x mass (g) x temperature change (°C)
        Specific heat of water $=$ 1.00 cal /(g · °C); mass of 500 mL $H_2O = 500$ g;
        Temperature change $= 80.0\ °C$

       Calories $= \dfrac{1.00\ \text{cal}}{\text{g} \cdot °\text{C}}$ x 500.0 g x 80.0 °C $= 4.00$ x 10^4 cal $= 40.0$ kcal

       40.0 kcal x $\dfrac{5.00\ \text{g }C_2H_5OH}{35.5\ \text{kcal}} = 5.63\ \text{g }C_2H_5OH$

     (e) $\dfrac{35.5\ \text{kcal}}{5.00\ \text{g }C_2H_5OH}$ x $\dfrac{0.789\ \text{g }C_2H_5OH}{1\ \text{mL }C_2H_5OH} = 5.60\ \text{kcal/mL}$

7.78   (a) $Fe_3O_4(s) + 4\,H_2(g) \longrightarrow 3\,Fe(s) + 4\,H_2O(g)$ $\Delta H = +36$ kcal/mol (151 kJ/mol)

     (b) 55 g Fe x $\dfrac{1\ \text{mol Fe}}{55.8\ \text{g Fe}}$ x $\dfrac{36\ \text{kcal}}{1\ \text{mol }Fe_3O_4}$ x $\dfrac{1\ \text{mol }Fe_3O_4}{3\ \text{mol Fe}} = 12$ kcal (50 kJ)

     (c) 75 g Fe x $\dfrac{1\ \text{mol Fe}}{55.8\ \text{g Fe}}$ x $\dfrac{4\ \text{mol }H_2}{3\ \text{mol Fe}}$ x $\dfrac{2.0\ \text{g }H_2}{1\ \text{mol }H_2} = 3.6\ \text{g }H_2$

     (d) Reactants are favored in this reaction.

7.80

     (a)

     (b) Σ (bond dissociation energies)$_{\text{reactants}}$ $= (C=O) + 2(C–N) + 4(N–H) + 2(O–H)$
                                            $= [178 + 2(73) + 4(93) + 2(112)]$ kcal/mol
                                            $= 920$ kcal/mol
        Σ(bond dissociation energies)$_{\text{products}}$ $= 2(C=O) + 4(N–H)$
                                            $= [2(191) + 6(93)]$ kcal/mol $= 940$ kcal/mol
        $\Delta H = 920$ kcal/mol $- 940$ kcal/mol $= -20$ kcal/mol (-84 kJ/mol)

7.82 (a) $4\,NH_3(g) + 5\,O_2(g) \rightleftharpoons 4\,NO(g) + 6\,H_2O(g) + heat$

(b) $K = \dfrac{[NO]^4\,[H_2O]^6}{[NH_3]^4\,[O_2]^5}$

(c) (1) Raising the pressure shifts the equilibrium to the left and favors reactants.
(2) Adding $NO(g)$ shifts the equilibrium to the left and favors reactants.
(3) Decreasing NH_3 shifts the equilibrium to the left and favors reactants.
(4) Lowering the temperature shifts the equilibrium to the right and favors products.

7.84

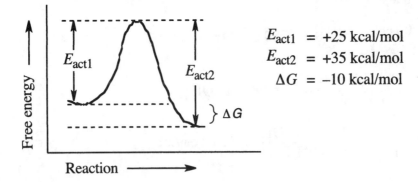

$$E_{act1} = +25\ kcal/mol$$
$$E_{act2} = +35\ kcal/mol$$
$$\Delta G = -10\ kcal/mol$$

(a) The forward process is exergonic.

(b) $\Delta G = -10$ kcal/mol (-4.2 kJ/mol)

7.86

$$1.00\ g\ \times\ \frac{1\ mol\ Na}{23.0\ g}\ \times\ \frac{-88.0\ kcal}{2\ mol\ Na}\ =\ -1.91\ kcal\ (-7.99\ kJ/mol)$$

1.91 kcal of heat is evolved. The reaction is exothermic.

Self-Test for Chapter 7

Multiple Choice

1. In which of the following processes does entropy decrease?
   (a) $C_6H_{12}O_6(s) + 6\,O_2(g) \longrightarrow 6\,CO_2(g) + 6\,H_2O(l)$

   (b) $2\,Na(s) + 2\,H_2O(l) \longrightarrow 2\,NaOH(aq) + H_2(g)$

   (c) $2\,Mg(s) + O_2(g) \longrightarrow 2\,MgO(s)$

   (d) $Zn(s) + CuSO_4(aq) \longrightarrow Cu(s) + ZnSO_4(aq)$

2. The reaction that will proceed at any temperature has:
   (a) negative ΔH, negative ΔS (b) negative ΔH, positive ΔS (c) positive ΔH, positive ΔS
   (d) positive ΔH, negative ΔS

3. Which of the conditions in Problem 2 indicates the reaction with the largest positive value of ΔG?

4. In the reaction $CH_3CO_2H + CH_3OH \rightleftharpoons CH_3CO_2CH_3 + H_2O$, the yield of $CH_3CO_2CH_3$ can be improved by:
   (a) distilling off the $CH_3CO_2CH_3$ (b) removing the water   (c) using more CH_3CO_2H and CH_3OH (d) all of the above

5. The equilibrium expression for the reaction $C_6H_6 + 3\,H_2 \longrightarrow C_6H_{12}$ is:

   (a) $\dfrac{[C_6H_{12}]}{[C_6H_6]\,[H_2]}$ (b) $\dfrac{[C_6H_{12}]}{[C_6H_6]\,[H_2]^3}$ (c) $\dfrac{[C_6H_{12}]}{[C_6H_6]\,[3\,H_2]}$ (d) $\dfrac{[C_6H_6]\,[H_2]^3}{[C_6H_{12}]}$

6. A reaction with which of the following K values is most likely to go to completion at room temperature?
   (a) $K = 10^5$ (b) $K = 10^2$ (c) $K = 10^{-1}$ (d) $K = 10^{-4}$

7. In which of the following reactions will increasing the pressure decrease the yield of product?
   (a) $2\,Mg(s) + O_2(g) \longrightarrow 2\,MgO(s)$
   (b) $H_2C{=}CH_2(g) + H_2(g) \longrightarrow CH_3CH_3(g)$
   (c) $C(s) + H_2O(g) \longrightarrow CO(g) + H_2(g)$
   (d) $3\,O_2(g) \longrightarrow 2\,O_3(g)$

8. According to Le Châtelier's principle, which of the following changes also changes the value of K?
   (a) changing temperature   (b) changing concentration   (c) changing pressure   (d) all of the above

9. All of the following statements are true about the reaction $3\,O_2(g) \longrightarrow 2\,O_3(g)$ (heat of formation = +34 kcal/mol at 25°C) except :
   (a) The reaction is endothermic.   (b) ΔS is negative.   (c) ΔG is positive.   (d) The rate of the reverse reaction increases with temperature.

10. In the reaction $Si + O_2 \longrightarrow SiO_2$ ($\Delta H = -218$ kcal/mol at 25°C), what is ΔH in kcal when 80 g of O_2 reacts with 70 g of Si?
    (a) 218 kcal   (b) –218 kcal   (c) –436 kcal   (d) –545 kcal

Sentence Completion

1. A reaction that has equal amounts of reactants and products at equilibrium has $K =$ ___.

2. The law of ___ ___ ___ states that energy can be neither created nor destroyed.

3. Addition of a ___ increases the rate of a reaction.

4. A reaction that easily proceeds in either direction is ___.

5. A reaction that absorbs heat from the surroundings is an ___ reaction.

6. An ___ ___ ___ gives the relationship between the concentrations of products and reactants at equilibrium.

7. The rate of a reaction can be increased by increasing ___ or ___ or by adding a ___.

8. The reactions that continually take place in the body are known as ___.

9. ___ ___ is unrelated to reaction spontaneity.

10. For a chemical reaction to occur, reactant molecules must ___.

True or False

1. The caloric value of food tells how much energy is absorbed when food is burned in oxygen.

2. In a chemical equilibrium, both product and reactant concentrations remain constant.

3. According to Le Châtelier's principle, changing pressure only affects equilibrium if gaseous reactants or products are involved.

4. In an exothermic reaction, the bond dissociation energies of the products are greater than the bond dissociation energies of the reactants.

5. A reaction with a large E_{act} will probably have a large heat of reaction.

6. Raising the temperature of a reaction always increases the rate of reaction.

7. A very unfavorable reaction may take place if the temperature is high enough.

8. Catalysts increase the rate of a reaction by increasing the number of collisions between reactants.

9. At chemical equilibrium, all chemical reaction stops.

10. At low temperatures, the spontaneity of a reaction is determined by ΔH.

Match each entry on the left with its partner on the right.

1. Enzyme   (a) Shows energy relationships in a reaction

2. Exergonic reaction   (b) A reaction that gives off heat

3. K (c) Reduces the size of E_{act}

4. Enthalpy   (d) Energy needed for a reaction to occur

5. Reaction energy diagram   (e) Measure of the amount of disorder in a reaction.

6. Free energy   (f) Reaction that is not spontaneous

7. Exothermic reaction   (g) Reaction that can go in either direction

8. Endergonic reaction   (h) Reaction that absorbs heat

9. E_{act} (i) Difference in energy of products and reactants

10. Entropy   (j) Reaction that is spontaneous

11. Reversible reaction   (k) Determines if a reaction is spontaneous

12. Endothermic reaction   (l) Measures the ratio of products to reactants

Chapter Outline

I. Introduction to gases, liquids, and solids (Section 8.1).
  A. Phases of matter are determined by the attractive forces between molecules.
     1. In gases, attractive forces are very weak.
     2. In liquids, attractive forces are strong.
     3. In solids, forces are so strong that atoms are held in place.
  B. During changes of phase, also known as changes of state, heat is either absorbed or released.
     1. Every change of state is characterized by a free-energy change, ΔG.
        a. ΔG consists of an enthalpy term and an entropy term.
        b. The enthalpy term is a measure of the heat absorbed or released during a phase change.
        c. The entropy change is a measure of the change in molecular disorder.
     2. At the temperature where a change of phase occurs, two states are in equilibrium.
     3. At the change from solid to liquid, two phases are at equilibrium at the melting point.
     4. At the change from liquid to gas, two phases are at equilibrium at the boiling point.
II. Intermolecular forces (Section 8.2).
  A. Intermolecular forces are the forces that act between molecules.
  B. In an ideal gas, intermolecular forces are unimportant.
  C. Three types of intermolecular forces are important in liquids and solids.
     1. Dipole–dipole forces occur when the positive end of a polar molecule is attracted to the negative end of a second molecule.
     2. London forces.
        a. Short-lived polarity in molecules causes a temporary attraction between molecules.
        b. London forces increase with increasing molecular weight and vary with molecular shape.
     3. Hydrogen bonding.
        a. Hydrogen bonds occur between a hydrogen atom bonded to an electronegative atom (O, N, F) and an unshared electron pair of a second electronegative atom.
        b. In hydrogen bonds, the hydrogen atom is partially bonded to two different electronegative atoms.
        c. Hydrogen bonds can be quite strong, and hydrogen bonding is responsible for elevated boiling points.
III. Gases (Sections 8.3–8.11).
  A. The kinetic–molecular theory explains the behavior of gases (Section 8.3).
     1. A gas consists of a great many molecules moving about with no attractive forces.
     2. The amount of space that molecules occupy is much smaller than the space between molecules.
     3. The energy of the molecules is related to Kelvin temperature.
     4. When molecules collide, their total kinetic energy is conserved.
     5. A gas that obeys all these behaviors is an ideal gas.
  B. Pressure (Sections 8.4).
     1. Pressure is defined as force per unit area.
     2. Units of pressure are mmHg, Pascal (in the SI system), atmosphere, and pounds per square inch (psi).
     3. Gas pressure can be measured by using a barometer or a manometer.

C. Gas laws (Sections 8.5–8.11).
   1. Boyle's law (for a fixed amount of gas at constant T) (Section 8.5).
      a. The pressure of a gas is inversely proportional to its volume.
      b. $P_1V_1 = P_2V_2$.
   2. Charles's law (for a fixed amount of gas at constant P) (Section 8.6).
      a. The volume of a gas is directly proportional to its temperature in K.
      b. $V_1/T_1 = V_2/T_2$.
   3. Gay-Lussac's law (for a fixed amount of gas at constant V) (Section 8.7).
      a. Pressure is directly proportional to temperature in K.
      b. $P_1/T_1 = P_2/T_2$.
   4. Combined gas law (Section 8.8).
      a. $P_1V_1/T_1 = P_2V_2/T_2$ for a fixed amount of gas.
   5. Avogadro's law (at constant T and P) (Section 8.9).
      a. The volume of a gas is directly proportional to its molar amount at constant T and P.
      b. $V_1/n_1 = V_2/n_2$.
      c. Standard temperature and pressure = 273.15 K and 1 atm.
      d. Standard molar volume of a gas = 22.4 L.
   6. Ideal gas law (Section 8.10).
      a. $PV = nRT$, where R is a gas constant.
   7. Dalton's law of partial pressure (Section 8.11).
      a. Mixtures of gases behave the same as a pure gas.
      b. The partial pressure of a gas in a mixture is the same as the gas would have if it were alone.
IV. Liquids and solids (Sections 8.12–8.15).
   A. Liquids (Section 8.12–8.13).
      1. Evaporation occurs when molecules near the surface of a liquid escape into the gaseous state.
         a. When molecules are in the gaseous state, they obey gas laws.
      2. The contribution of the partial pressure of the escaped gas to the total pressure is known as vapor pressure.
         a. Vapor pressure rises with increasing temperature.
      3. The normal boiling point of a liquid is at 760 mmHg.
         a. The boiling point rises or falls with atmospheric pressure.
      4. Viscosity and surface tension are properties of liquids.
         a. Viscosity is a liquid's resistance to flow.
         b. Surface tension is the resistance of a liquid to spread out.
      5. Water is a unique liquid (Section 8.13).
         a. Water has very high specific heat, high heat of vaporization, and strong hydrogen bonding.
         b. Solid water is less dense than liquid water.
   B. Solids (Section 8.14).
      1. A crystalline solid has atoms, molecules, or ions rigidly held in an orderly arrangement.
         a. Categories of crystalline solids include ionic solids, molecular solids, covalent network solids, and metallic solids.
      2. Particles in an amorphous solid do not have an orderly arrangement.
   C. Changes of phase (Section 8.15).
      1. The heat needed to completely melt a solid is the heat of fusion.
      2. The heat needed to completely vaporize a liquid is the heat of vaporization.

Solutions to Chapter 8 Problems

8.1   (a) The change of state from liquid to gas is disfavored by ΔH (positive sign) but is favored by ΔS (large positive value).

(b) $\Delta G = \Delta H - T\Delta S : \Delta H = +9.72$ kcal/mol; $\Delta S = +26.1$ cal/(mol $\cdot$ K); $T = 373$ K

$$T\Delta S = 373 \text{ K} \times \frac{26.1 \text{ cal}}{\text{mol K}} \times \frac{1 \text{ kcal}}{10^3 \text{ cal}} = \frac{9.74 \text{ kcal}}{\text{mol}} = \frac{40.7 \text{ kJ}}{\text{mol}}$$

$\Delta G = 9.72$ kcal/mol $- 9.74$ kcal/mol $= -0.02$ kcal/mol $= 0.08$ kJ/mol

(c) For the change from gas to liquid, $\Delta H = -9.72$ kcal/mol (-40.1 kJ/mol) and $\Delta S = -26.1$ cal/mol$\cdot$K (-109 kJ/mol$\cdot$K).

8.2   Boiling points generally increase with increasing molecular (or atomic) weight because of London dispersion forces.

(a) Kr, Ar, Ne. This series is arranged in order of decreasing boiling point.
(b) Cl_2, Br_2, I_2. This series is arranged in order of increasing boiling point.

8.3   Methyl alcohol (a) and methylamine (c) are capable of hydrogen bonding because each contains a hydrogen atom bonded to an electronegative atom. Ethylene (b) does not form hydrogen bonds.

8.4   (a) *London forces* are the only intermolecular forces between nonpolar ethane molecules, and thus ethane has a low boiling point.
(b) The major intermolecular force between ethyl alcohol molecules is *hydrogen bonding*, which causes ethyl alcohol to be high boiling. Dipole–dipole interactions and London forces are also present but are weaker than hydrogen bonding.
(c) *Dipole–dipole* interactions are the principal forces between ethyl chloride molecules and cause the boiling point of ethyl chloride to be higher than that of ethane. London forces are also present.

8.5   Use the appropriate conversion factor from Section 8.4.

$$0.289 \text{ atm} \times \frac{760 \text{ mmHg}}{1 \text{ atm}} = 220 \text{ mmHg}$$

$$0.289 \text{ atm} \times \frac{14.7 \text{ psi}}{1 \text{ atm}} = 4.25 \text{ psi}$$

$$0.289 \text{ atm} \times \frac{101,325 \text{ Pa}}{1 \text{ atm}} = 2.93 \times 10^4 \text{ Pa}$$

8.6   Shifting to biomass-based fuels would decrease dependence on fossil fuels but would have little effect on current atmospheric CO_2 levels. However, biosynthesis of biomass fuels would consume CO_2, which would later be burned and released back into the atmosphere, setting up an equilibrium in which CO_2 levels would remain constant.

8.7   The pressure of the gas inside the manometer is greater than atmospheric pressure because the mercury level is higher in the open arm of the manometer than in the closed end. Since atmospheric pressure is 750 mmHg and since the difference in mercury levels in the manometer arm is 250 mmHg, the pressure of the gas inside the manometer is 750 mm + 250 mm = 1000 mmHg.

8.8   If the variables in the problem are pressure and volume, Boyle's law must be used.

Solution: $P_1 \times V_1 = P_2 \times V_2$

$$V_2 = \frac{P_1 \times V_1}{P_2} = \frac{(90 \text{ atm})(5.0 \text{ L})}{(1.0 \text{ atm})} = 450 \text{ L}$$

Ballpark check: Since the pressure is reduced by almost 100 times, the volume must increase by almost 100 times, from 5 L to 500 L.

The ballpark solution and the detailed solution agree.

8.9   *Solution:* $P_1 \times V_1 = P_2 \times V_2$

$$V_2 = \frac{P_1 \times V_1}{P_2} = \frac{(4.0 \text{ atm})(3.2 \text{ L})}{(10.0 \text{ atm})} = 1.3 \text{ L}$$

Ballpark check: Since the pressure increases by three times, the volume must decrease by the same amount, from 4.0 L to 1.3 L.

At a pressure of 0.70 atm: $V_2 = \dfrac{P_1 \times V_1}{P_2} = \dfrac{(4.0 \text{ atm})(3.2 \text{ L})}{(0.70 \text{ atm})} = 18 \text{ L}$

8.10

$112 \text{ mmHg} \times \dfrac{14.7 \text{ psi}}{760 \text{ mmHg}} = 2.17 \text{ psi}; \quad 75 \text{ mmHg} \times \dfrac{14.7 \text{ psi}}{760 \text{ mmHg}} = 1.45 \text{ psi}$

Blood pressure would be recorded as 2.17/1.45.

8.11   Charles's law is used to calculate volume or temperature changes when pressure and quantity remain constant.

Solution:

$$\frac{V_1}{T_1} = \frac{V_2}{T_2}$$

$$T_2 = \frac{V_2 \times T_1}{V_1} = \frac{(1.0 \text{ L})(273 \text{ K})}{0.30 \text{ L}} = 910 \text{ K } (637 \,^\circ\text{C})$$

Ballpark check: Since the volume increases threefold, the temperature must also increase threefold, from 273 K to around 900 K.

If $V_2 = 0.20$ L: $T_2 = \dfrac{V_2 \times T_1}{V_1} = \dfrac{(0.20 \text{ L})(273 \text{ K})}{0.30 \text{ L}} = 182 \text{ K } (-91 \,^\circ\text{C})$

8.12 Use Gay-Lussac's law when pressure and temperature vary, and volume and quantity are unchanged. Don't forget to change temperature from °C to K.

Solution:

$$\frac{P_1}{T_1} = \frac{P_2}{T_2}$$

$$P_2 = \frac{P_1 \times T_2}{T_1} = 30 \text{ psi} \times \frac{318 \text{ K}}{288 \text{ K}} = 33 \text{ psi}$$

Ballpark check: Since the temperature increase is about 10%, the pressure increase is also expected to be approximately 10%.

8.13 In this problem, P, V, and T vary.

$$\frac{P_1 V_1}{T_1} = \frac{P_2 V_2}{T_2}; \qquad P_1 = 752 \text{ mmHg}; \ T_1 = 295 \text{ K}; \ V_1 = 275 \text{ L}$$

$$P_2 = 480 \text{ mmHg}; \ T_2 = 241 \text{ K}; \ V_2 = ?$$

$$V_2 = \frac{P_1 V_1 T_2}{P_2 T_1} = \frac{(752 \text{ mmHg})(275 \text{ L})(241 \text{ K})}{(480 \text{ mmHg})(295 \text{ K})} = 352 \text{ L}$$

8.14 The temperature increase [from 18 °C (291 K) to 50 °C (323 K)] increases the volume by about 10%. The pressure increase (from 1 atm to 2 atm) decreases the volume by half. The resulting balloon volume should be somewhat more than half the original volume, as represented by balloon (a).

8.15 Use Avogadro's Law; the quantity on the left side of the equation is the standard molar volume of a gas, 22.4 L/mol.

$$\frac{V_1}{n_1} = \frac{V_2}{n_2}$$

$$n_2 = \frac{V_2 \times n_1}{V_1} = 1.00 \times 10^5 \text{ L CH}_4 \times \frac{1.0 \text{ mol}}{22.4 \text{ L}} = 4.46 \times 10^3 \text{ mol CH}_4$$

The same container could also hold 4.46×10^3 moles of CO_2.

$$4.46 \times 10^3 \text{ mol CH}_4 \times \frac{16.0 \text{ g CH}_4}{1 \text{ mol CH}_4} = 7.14 \times 10^4 \text{ g CH}_4$$

$$4.46 \times 10^3 \text{ mol CO}_2 \times \frac{44.0 \text{ g CO}_2}{1 \text{ mol CO}_2} = 1.96 \times 10^5 \text{ g CO}_2$$

Ballpark Check: Since one mole of a gas occupies 22.4 L at STP, a 100,000 L container holds 100,000/22.4 moles, or about 4500 moles. Thus, the ballpark solution and the exact solution agree.

8.16 $PV = nRT$; $P = nRT/V$

$n = 3.2 \text{ g} \times \dfrac{1 \text{ mol}}{44.0 \text{ g}} = 0.073 \text{ mol}$; $R = 0.0821 \dfrac{\text{L} \cdot \text{atm}}{\text{mol} \cdot \text{K}}$

$T = 20°C = 293 \text{ K}$; $V = 350 \text{ mL} = 0.35 \text{ L}$

$P = \dfrac{0.073 \text{ mol} \times \dfrac{0.0821 \text{ L} \cdot \text{atm}}{\text{mol} \cdot \text{K}} \times 293 \text{ K}}{0.35 \text{ L}} = 5.0 \text{ atm}$

8.17 $PV = nRT$; $n = PV/RT$

$P = 150 \text{ atm}$; $V = 180 \text{ L He}$; $R = 0.0821 \dfrac{\text{L} \cdot \text{atm}}{\text{mol} \cdot \text{K}}$; $T = 25°C = 298 \text{ K}$

$n = \dfrac{150 \text{ atm} \times 180 \text{ L He}}{0.0821 \dfrac{\text{L} \cdot \text{atm}}{\text{mol} \cdot \text{K}} \times 298 \text{ K}} = 1.1 \times 10^3 \text{ mol He}$

$1.1 \times 10^3 \text{ mol He} \times \dfrac{4.0 \text{ g}}{1 \text{ mol He}} = 4.4 \times 10^3 \text{ g He}$

8.18 We can use the ideal gas law to compare the volumes of two gases: Since the piston is moveable, $P = 1$ atm in all cases.

(a) The increase in temperature increases the volume to 450/300 = 3/2 of the original volume, and the decrease in amount decreases the volume to 0.200/0.300 = 2/3 of the original value. Since 3/2 x 2/3 = 1, the two changes exactly cancel, and the final volume is the same as the original volume.

$T_1 = 300 \text{ K}$; $n_1 = 0.300 \text{ mol}$; $T_2 = 450 \text{ K}$; $n_2 = 0.200 \text{ mol}$; $V_1/V_2 = ?$

$\dfrac{V_1}{V_2} = \dfrac{n_1 T_1 P_2}{n_2 T_2 P_1} = \dfrac{n_1 T_1}{n_2 T_2}$; $\dfrac{V_1}{V_2} = \dfrac{(0.300 \text{ mol})(300 \text{ K})}{(0.200 \text{ mol})(450 \text{ K})} = 1$

(b) The decrease in temperature decreases the volume to 200/300 = 2/3 of the original, and the increase in amount increases the volume to 0.400/0.300 = 4/3 of the original volume. Since 2/3 x 4/3 = 8/9, the final volume is a bit less than the original volume.

$T_1 = 300 \text{ K}$; $n_1 = 0.300 \text{ mol}$; $T_2 = 200 \text{ K}$; $n_2 = 0.400 \text{ mol}$; $V_1/V_2 = ?$

$\dfrac{V_1}{V_2} = \dfrac{(0.300 \text{ mol})(300 \text{ K})}{(0.400 \text{ mol})(200 \text{ K})} = \dfrac{9}{8}$ The volume in (b) is 8/9 of the original volume.

$P = 1$ atm   (a)   (b)

$T = 300 \text{ K}$ $T = 450 \text{ K}$ $T = 200 \text{ K}$

$n = 0.300 \text{ mol}$ $n = 0.200 \text{ mol}$ $n = 0.400 \text{ mol}$

8.19   0.98 x 9.5 atm = 9.3 atm He
0.020 x 9.5 atm = 0.19 atm O_2

The partial pressure of oxygen in diving gas (0.19 atm) is approximately equal to the partial pressure of oxygen in air (0.21 atm).

8.20

$$\frac{573 \text{ mmHg}}{760 \text{ mmHg}} \text{ x } 100\% = 75.4\% \text{ N}_2; \qquad \frac{100 \text{ mmHg}}{760 \text{ mmHg}} \text{ x } 100\% = 13.2\% \text{ O}_2$$

$$\frac{40 \text{ mmHg}}{760 \text{ mmHg}} \text{ x } 100\% = 5.3\% \text{ CO}_2; \qquad \frac{47 \text{ mmHg}}{760 \text{ mmHg}} \text{ x } 100\% = 6.2\% \text{ H}_2\text{O}$$

8.21   We know from the previous problem that the partial pressure of O_2 in the lungs at atmospheric pressure is 13.2%. Thus, at 265 mmHg,

265 mmHg x 0.132 = 35.0 mmHg

8.22   The ratio of He molecules/ Xe molecules is 8/4 or 2/1. Since 2/3 of the molecules are He, P_{He} = 2/3(750 mmHg) = 500 mmHg. P_{Xe} = 250 mmHg.

8.23   To melt isopropyl alcohol:

$$1.50 \text{ mol } \text{x } \frac{60.0 \text{ g}}{1 \text{ mol}} \text{ x } \frac{21.4 \text{ cal}}{1 \text{ g}} \text{ x } \frac{1 \text{ kcal}}{10^3 \text{ cal}} = 1.93 \text{ kcal}$$

To boil isopropyl alcohol:

$$1.50 \text{ mol } \text{x } \frac{60.0 \text{ g}}{1 \text{ mol}} \text{ x } \frac{159 \text{ cal}}{1 \text{ g}} \text{ x } \frac{1 \text{ kcal}}{10^3 \text{ cal}} = 14.3 \text{ kcal}$$

8.24

$$2.50 \text{ mol H}_2\text{O x } \frac{18.0 \text{ g}}{1 \text{ mol H}_2\text{O}} \text{ x } \frac{2260 \text{ J}}{1 \text{ g}} \text{ x } \frac{1 \text{ kJ}}{10^3 \text{ J}} = 102 \text{ kJ}$$

8.25   At 25 °C and 50 atm, CO_2 is probably close to a gas/liquid phase equilibrium (solid line on graph).

Understanding Key Concepts

8.26

(a) According to Charles's law, the volume of a gas at fixed pressure is directly proportional to its temperature. Since the temperature increases by 50% (from 300 K to 450 K), volume also increases by 50%.

(b) Boyle's law states that the volume of a gas is inversely proportional to its pressure. Doubling the pressure halves the volume.

(c) For changes in both pressure and temperature, the combined gas law states that PV/T is constant. Thus, reducing both the pressure and the temperature by one-third leaves the volume unchanged.

8.28 Drawing (a) shows the sample of water as a solid, its state at 200 K. At 300 K, water is a liquid with a very low vapor pressure (as shown in Figure 8.20), represented by (c).

8.30 Both sides of the manometer have equal heights because both sides have equal pressure.

8.32 Refer to Problem 8.18 for an approach to solving this problem. Note the quantities that change and those that remain constant; these differ in each part of the problem. Be sure to convert temperature to kelvins.

(a) $\dfrac{V_2}{V_1} = \dfrac{n_2 T_2 P_1}{n_1 T_1 P_2} = \dfrac{T_2}{T_1}; \quad \dfrac{V_2}{V_1} = \dfrac{(323\ \text{K})}{(298\ \text{K})} = 1.08$

(b) $\dfrac{V_2}{V_1} = \dfrac{n_2 T_2 P_1}{n_1 T_1 P_2} = \dfrac{T_2 P_1}{T_1 P_2}; \quad \dfrac{V_2}{V_1} = \dfrac{(448\ \text{K})(0.92\ \text{atm})}{(298\ \text{K})(2.7\ \text{atm})} = 0.51$

(c) $\dfrac{V_2}{V_1} = \dfrac{n_2 T_2 P_1}{n_1 T_1 P_2} = \dfrac{n_2 P_1}{n_1 P_2}; \quad \dfrac{V_2}{V_1} = \dfrac{(0.22\ \text{mol})(0.92\ \text{atm})}{(0.075\ \text{mol})(2.7\ \text{atm})} = 1.0$

$T = 298\ \text{K}$
$n = 0.075\ \text{mol}$
$P = 0.92\ \text{atm}$

(a)
$T = 323\ \text{K}$
$n = 0.075\ \text{mol}$
$P = 0.92\ \text{atm}$

(b)
$T = 448\ \text{K}$
$n = 0.075\ \text{mol}$
$P = 2.7\ \text{atm}$

(c)
$T = 298\ \text{K}$
$n = 0.22\ \text{mol}$
$P = 2.7\ \text{atm}$

Intermolecular Forces

8.34 (a) All molecules exhibit London forces, which increase in strength with increasing molecular weight.
(b) Dipole–dipole interactions are important for molecules that are polar.
(c) Hydrogen bonding occurs between an unshared electron pair on an electronegative atom (O, N, or F) and a hydrogen atom bonded to a second electronegative atom (O, N, F).

8.36 Ethanol is higher boiling than dimethyl ether because of hydrogen bonding. Since molecules of ethanol are strongly attracted to each other, the boiling point of ethanol is higher than that of dimethyl ether, whose molecules are held together by weaker dipole–dipole interactions.

Gases and Pressure

8.38 One atmosphere is the amount of pressure needed to hold a column of mercury 760 mm high.

8.40 (1) A gas consists of many tiny particles moving about at random with no attractive forces between particles.

(2) The amount of space occupied by gas molecules is much smaller than the amount of space between molecules.

(3) The average kinetic energy of gas particles is proportional to Kelvin temperature.

(4) When molecules collide, they spring apart elastically, and their total energy is constant.

8.42

(a) $1 \text{ atm} \times \dfrac{760 \text{ mmHg}}{1 \text{ atm}} = 760 \text{ mmHg}$

(b) $25.3 \text{ psi} \times \dfrac{760 \text{ mmHg}}{14.7 \text{ psi}} = 1310 \text{ mmHg}$

(c) $7.5 \text{ atm} \times \dfrac{760 \text{ mmHg}}{1 \text{ atm}} = 5.7 \times 10^3 \text{ mmHg}$

(d) $28.0 \text{ in.Hg} \times \dfrac{25.4 \text{mm}}{1 \text{ in.}} = 711 \text{ mmHg}$

(e) $41.8 \text{ Pa} \times \dfrac{760 \text{ mmHg}}{101{,}325 \text{ Pa}} = 0.314 \text{ mmHg}$

8.44 When the level in the arm connected to the container is 176 mm (17.6 cm) lower than the level open to the atmosphere, the pressure in the gas container is greater than atmospheric pressure.

$754.3 \text{ mmHg} + 176 \text{ mmHg} = 930 \text{ mmHg} = 1.22 \text{ atm}$

Boyle's Law

8.46 Boyle's law: Volume varies inversely with pressure at constant temperature and number of moles, that is, $P_1V_1 = P_2V_2$.

8.48 $P_1V_1 = P_2V_2$; $P_1 = 65.0 \text{ mmHg}$; $P_2 = 385 \text{ mmHg}$; $V_1 = 600.0 \text{ mL} = 0.600 \text{ L}$; $V_2 = ?$

$V_2 = \dfrac{P_1V_1}{P_2} = \dfrac{65.0 \text{ mmHg} \times 0.600 \text{ L}}{385 \text{ mmHg}} = 0.101 \text{ L} = 101 \text{ mL}$

8.50 $P_1V_1 = P_2V_2$; $P_1 = 5.0 \text{ atm}$; $P_2 = 1.0 \text{ atm}$; $V_1 = 0.350 \text{ L}$; $V_2 = ?$

$V_2 = \dfrac{P_1V_1}{P_2} = \dfrac{5.00 \text{ atm} \times 0.350 \text{ L}}{1.00 \text{ atm}} = 1.75 \text{ L}$

Charles's Law

8.52 Charles's law: Volume varies directly with temperature at constant pressure and number of moles; that is, $V_1/T_1 = V_2/T_2$.

8.54

$$\frac{V_1}{T_1} = \frac{V_2}{T_2}; \qquad V_1 = 960 \text{ L}; \ V_2 = 1200 \text{ L}; \ T_1 = 291 \text{ K}; \ T_2 = ?$$

$$T_2 = \frac{V_2 T_1}{V_1} = \frac{1200 \text{ L} \times 291 \text{ K}}{960 \text{ L}} = 364 \text{ K} = 91°C$$

8.56

$$\frac{V_1}{T_1} = \frac{V_2}{T_2}; \qquad V_1 = 185 \text{ mL}; \ V_2 = ?; \ T_1 = 38 \ °C = 311 \text{ K}; \ T_2 = 97 \ °C = 370 \text{ K}$$

$$V_2 = \frac{V_1 T_2}{T_1} = \frac{185 \text{ mL} \times 370 \text{ K}}{311 \text{ K}} = 220 \text{ mL}$$

Gay-Lussac's Law

8.58 Gay-Lussac's law: Pressure varies directly with temperature at constant volume and number of moles; that is, $P_1/T_1 = P_2/T_2$.

8.60

$$\frac{P_1}{T_1} = \frac{P_2}{T_2}; \qquad P_1 = 0.95 \text{ atm}; \ P_2 = ?; \ T_1 = 25 \ °C = 298 \text{ K}; \ T_2 = 117 \ °C = 390 \text{ K}$$

$$P_2 = \frac{P_1 T_2}{T_1} = \frac{0.95 \text{ atm} \times 390 \text{ K}}{298 \text{ K}} = 1.2 \text{ atm}$$

Combined Gas Law

8.62

$$\frac{P_1 V_1}{T_1} = \frac{P_2 V_2}{T_2}; \qquad P_1 = 760 \text{ mmHg}; \ V_1 = 2.84 \text{ L}; \ T_1 = 273 \text{ K}$$
$$P_2 = 520 \text{ mmHg}; \ V_2 = 7.50 \text{ L}; \ T_2 = ?$$

$$T_2 = \frac{P_2 V_2 T_1}{P_1 V_1} = \frac{520 \text{ mmHg} \times 7.50 \text{ L} \times 273 \text{ K}}{760 \text{ mmHg} \times 2.84 \text{ L}} = 493 \text{ K} = 220 \ °C$$

8.64

$$\frac{P_1 V_1}{T_1} = \frac{P_2 V_2}{T_2}; \qquad P_1 = 748 \text{ mmHg}; \ V_1 = 75.4 \text{ mL}; \ T_1 = 23 \ °C = 296 \text{ K}$$
$$P_2 = 760 \text{ mmHg}; \ V_2 = ?; \ T_2 = 0 \ °C = 273 \text{ K}$$

$$V_2 = \frac{P_1 V_1 T_2}{T_1 P_2} = \frac{748 \text{ mmHg} \times 75.4 \text{ mL} \times 273 \text{ K}}{296 \text{ K} \times 760 \text{ mmHg}} = 68.4 \text{ mL}$$

8.66 (a) For one mole of gas, the combined gas law states that P is proportional to T/V, or $P \propto T/V$. Thus, if the temperature doubles and the volume is halved, the new pressure is four times greater than the original pressure:

$$\frac{P_1 V_1}{T_1} = \frac{P_2 V_2}{T_2}; \qquad V_2 = 0.5V_1; \ T_2 = 2T_1; \ P_2 = ?$$

$$P_2 = \frac{P_1 V_1 T_2}{T_1 V_2} = \frac{P_1 V_1 \ \times \ 2T_1}{T_1 \ \times \ 0.5V_1} = 4\,P_1$$

(b) If the temperature is halved and the volume is doubled, the new pressure is one-fourth the original pressure:

$$\frac{P_1 V_1}{T_1} = \frac{P_2 V_2}{T_2}; \qquad V_2 = 2V_1; \ T_2 = 0.5T_1; \ P_2 = ?$$

$$P_2 = \frac{P_1 V_1 T_2}{T_1 V_2} = \frac{P_1 V_1 \ \times \ 0.5T_1}{T_1 \ \times \ 2V_1} = 0.25P_1$$

Avogadro's Law and Standard Molar Volume

8.68 Avogadro's law states that equal volumes of gases at the same temperature and pressure contain equal numbers of molecules. Since the volume of space taken up by gas molecules is so much smaller than the amount of space between molecules, Avogadro's law is true regardless of the chemical identity of the gas.

8.70

$$1.0 \text{ L } \times \ \frac{1 \text{ mol}}{22.4 \text{ L}} \ \times \ \frac{6.02 \times 10^{23} \text{ molecules}}{1 \text{ mol}} = 2.7 \times 10^{22} \text{ molecules}$$

$$1.0 \text{ L } \times \ \frac{1 \text{ mol}}{22.4 \text{ L}} \ \times \ \frac{32.0 \text{ g}}{1 \text{ mol}} = 1.4 \text{ g } O_2$$

8.72

$$16.5 \text{ L } \times \ \frac{1 \text{ mol}}{22.4 \text{ L}} \ \times \ \frac{16.0 \text{ g } CH_4}{1 \text{ mol } CH_4} = 11.8 \text{ g } CH_4$$

8.74

$$V = 4.0 \text{ m } \times \ 5.0 \text{ m } \times \ 2.5 \text{ m } = 50 \text{ m}^3; \ 50 \text{ m}^3 \ \times \ \frac{10^3 \text{ L}}{1 \text{ m}^3} = 5.0 \times 10^4 \text{ L}$$

$$\frac{1 \text{ mol}}{22.4 \text{ L}} \ \times \ 5.0 \times 10^4 \text{ L} = 2230 \text{ mol gas}$$

$$\frac{0.21 \text{ mol } O_2}{1 \text{ mol gas}} \ \times \ 2230 \text{ mol gas} = 470 \text{ mol } O_2$$

$$470 \text{ mol } O_2 \ \times \ \frac{32.0 \text{ g } O_2}{1 \text{ mol } O_2} = 15{,}000 \text{ g } O_2 = 15 \text{ kg } O_2$$

The Ideal Gas Law

8.76   The ideal gas law: $PV = nRT$

8.78 $PV = nRT$; $n = PV/RT$

For Cl_2: $P = 1.0$ atm; $V = 2.0$ L; $R = 0.082 \dfrac{L \cdot atm}{mol \cdot K}$; $T = 273$ K

$$n = \frac{1.0 \text{ atm} \times 2.0 \text{ L}}{0.082 \dfrac{L \cdot atm}{mol \cdot K} \times 273 \text{ K}} = 0.089 \text{ mol } Cl_2$$

$$0.089 \text{ mol } Cl_2 \times \frac{71 \text{ g}}{1 \text{ mol } Cl_2} = 6.3 \text{ g } Cl_2$$

For CH_4: $P = 1150$ mmHg $= 1.5$ atm; $V = 3.0$ L; $R = 0.082 \dfrac{L \cdot atm}{mol \cdot K}$; $T = 300$ K

$$n = \frac{1.5 \text{ atm} \times 3.0 \text{ L}}{0.082 \dfrac{L \cdot atm}{mol \cdot K} \times 300 \text{ K}} = 0.18 \text{ mol } CH_4$$

$$0.18 \text{ mol } CH_4 \times \frac{16 \text{ g}}{1 \text{ mol } CH_4} = 2.9 \text{ g } CH_4$$

There are more molecules in the CH_4 sample than in the Cl_2 sample. The Cl_2 sample, however, weighs more because the molar mass of Cl_2 is much greater than the molar mass of CH_4.

8.80

$n = 2.3$ mol He; $T = 294$ K; $V = 0.15$ L

$$P = \frac{nRT}{V} = \frac{2.3 \text{ mol He} \times 0.082 \dfrac{L \cdot atm}{mol \cdot K} \times 294 \text{ K}}{0.15 \text{ L}} = 370 \text{ atm}$$

$$370 \text{ atm} \times \frac{14.7 \text{ psi}}{1 \text{ atm}} = 5.40 \times 10^3 \text{ psi}$$

8.82

$$n = 15.0 \text{ g } CO_2 \times \frac{1 \text{ mol}}{44 \text{ g}} = 0.341 \text{ mol } CO_2; \quad T = 310 \text{ K}; \quad V = 0.30 \text{ L}$$

$$P = \frac{nRT}{V} = \frac{0.341 \text{ mol } CO_2 \times 62.4 \dfrac{mmHg \cdot L}{mol \cdot K} \times 310 \text{ K}}{0.30 \text{ L}} = 2.2 \times 10^4 \text{ mmHg}$$

8.84

$$n = 18.0 \text{ g } O_2 \text{ x } \frac{1 \text{ mol}}{32.0 \text{ g}} = 0.563 \text{ mol } O_2; \quad T = 350 \text{ K}; \quad P = 550 \text{ mmHg}$$

$$V = \frac{nRT}{P} = \frac{0.562 \text{ mol } O_2 \text{ x } 62.4 \frac{\text{mmHg} \cdot \text{L}}{\text{mol} \cdot \text{K}} \text{ x } 350 \text{ K}}{550 \text{ mmHg}} = 22.4 \text{ L } O_2$$

Dalton's Law and Partial Pressure

8.86 Partial pressure is the pressure contribution of one component of a mixture of gases to the total pressure.

8.88

$$440 \text{ mmHg } \text{x } \frac{1 \text{ atm}}{760 \text{ mmHg}} \text{ x } \frac{160 \text{ mmHg}}{1.0 \text{ atm}} = 93 \text{ mmHg}$$

Liquids

8.90 The vapor pressure of a liquid is the partial pressure of the vapor above the liquid.

8.92 Increased pressure raises a liquid's boiling point; decreased pressure lowers a liquid's boiling point.

8.94

(a) $\dfrac{9.72 \text{ kcal}}{1 \text{ mol } H_2O} \text{ x } 3.00 \text{ mol } H_2O = 29.2 \text{ kcal of heat required.}$

(b) $\dfrac{9.72 \text{ kcal}}{1 \text{ mol } H_2O} \text{ x } \dfrac{1 \text{ mol } H_2O}{18.0 \text{ g}} \text{ x } 320 \text{ g} = 173 \text{ kcal of heat is released.}$

Solids

8.96 The atoms in a crystalline solid are arranged in a regular, orderly network. The atoms in an amorphous solid have no regular arrangement.

8.98

$$\frac{45.9 \text{ cal}}{1 \text{ g}} \text{ x } \frac{1 \text{ kcal}}{1000 \text{ cal}} \text{ x } \frac{60.0 \text{ g}}{1 \text{ mol}} \text{ x } 1.75 \text{ mol} = 4.82 \text{ kcal}$$

Chemistry in Action

8.100 Increased concentrations of CO_2 in the atmosphere, coupled with an increase in the average global temperature, are evidence for global warming.

8.102 *Systolic pressure* (the higher number) is the maximum blood pressure developed in the artery just after contraction. *Diastolic pressure* (the lower number) is the minimum pressure that occurs at the end of the heartbeat cycle. A blood pressure reading of 180/110 is an indication of high blood pressure.

8.104 The supercritical state of matter is a condition intermediate between liquid and gas, in which there is some space between molecules yet they are too close together to be truly a gas.

General Questions and Problems

8.106 As the temperature increases, the kinetic energy of gas molecules increases, and the force per unit area that they exert in colliding against the walls of a container increases, thus increasing pressure.

8.108 3.0 L of H_2 and 1.5 L of O_2 react completely. At STP, one mole of H_2 occupies 22.4 L. Thus, 3.0 L of hydrogen = 3.0/22.4 or 0.13 mol. This is also the number of moles of H_2O formed.

$$n = 0.13 \text{ mol } H_2O; \quad T = 373 \text{ K}; \quad P = 1.0 \text{ atm}$$

$$V = \frac{nRT}{P} = \frac{0.13 \text{ mol } H_2O \times 0.0821 \dfrac{L \cdot atm}{mol \cdot K} \times 373 \text{ K}}{1.0 \text{ atm}} = 4.0 \text{ L } H_2O$$

8.110

$$0.0094 \text{ mol } CO_2 \times \frac{44.0 \text{ g } CO_2}{1 \text{ mol } CO_2} = 0.41 \text{ g } CO_2$$

$$\frac{0.41 \text{ g } CO_2}{1 \text{ min}} \times \frac{60 \text{ min}}{1 \text{ hr}} \times \frac{24 \text{ hr}}{1 \text{ day}} = \frac{590 \text{ g } CO_2}{day}$$

8.112 $P = 0.975 \text{ atm}; \quad V = 1.6 \times 10^5 \text{ L}; \quad T = 375 \text{ K}$

$$n = \frac{PV}{RT} = \frac{0.975 \text{ atm} \times 1.6 \times 10^5 \text{ L}}{0.0821 \dfrac{L \cdot atm}{mol \cdot K} \times 375 \text{ K}} = 5.07 \times 10^3 \text{ mol}$$

$$\text{Density} = \frac{5.07 \times 10^3 \text{ mol}}{1.6 \times 10^5 \text{ L}} \times \frac{29 \text{ g}}{mol} = \frac{0.92 \text{ g}}{L}$$

The air in the balloon is less dense than air at STP (density = 1.3 g/L).

8.114 Divide the molar mass (molecular weight in grams) by 22.4 L to find the density in grams per liter.

Gas	Molecular Weight	Density (g/L) at STP
(a) CH_4	16.0 g/mol	0.714
(b) CO_2	44.0 g/mol	1.96
(c) O_2	32.0 g/mol	1.43

8.116

(a)

(b)

Ethylene glycol   Chloroethane

(c) Ethylene glycol has a higher boiling point than chloroethane because it forms hydrogen bonds.

8.118 (a) Since the size of a Rankine degree is the same as a Fahrenheit degree, we can use the same conversion factor as we use for °F/°C conversions.

$$\frac{9\,°R}{5\,°C} \times 273.15\,°C = 491.67\,°R$$

(b) To calculate the gas constant R, use the ideal gas law at standard temperature and pressure.

$$R = \frac{PV}{nT};\quad P = 1\ \text{atm};\quad V = 22.4\ \text{L};\quad n = 1\ \text{mol};\quad T = 491.67\,°R$$

$$R = \frac{1\ \text{atm} \times 22.4\ \text{L}}{1\ \text{mol} \times 492\,°R} = 0.0455\ \frac{\text{L} \cdot \text{atm}}{\text{mol} \cdot °R}$$

Self-Test for Chapter 8

Multiple Choice

1. Which of the following units would you be least likely to use in a chemical laboratory?
   (a) pascal   (b) pounds per square inch   (c) mmHg   (d) atmosphere

2. A fixed amount of a gas has its temperature and volume doubled. What happens to its pressure?
   (a) increases fourfold   (b) doubles   (c) stays the same   (d) is halved

3. In which of the gas laws is the amount of gas not fixed?
   (a) Boyle's law   (b) Charles's law   (c) Gay-Lussac's law   (d) Avogadro's law

4. Which of the following compounds does not exhibit hydrogen bonding?
   (a) CH_3OCH_3 (b) CH_3OH (c) HF   (d) CH_3NH_2

5. Which of the following compounds is the lowest melting?
   (a) NaI   (b) Au   (c) SiO_2 (d) sugar

6. Which term describes the change of state that occurs when a gas changes to a solid?
   (a) fusion   (b) condensation   (c) deposition   (d) sublimation

7. When does a gas obey ideal behavior?
   (a) at low density   (b) at high pressure   (c) at low temperature   (d) in a large container

8. If 22.0 g of CO_2 has a pressure of 1.00 atm at 300 K, what is its volume?
   (a) 22.4 L   (b) 12.3 L   (c) 11.2 L   (d) 9.5 L

9. What volume does the amount of gas in Problem 8 occupy at STP?
   (a) 22.4 L   (b) 12.3 L   (c) 11.2 L   (d) 9.5 L

10. What is the density of CO_2 gas in g/L at STP if one mole of gas has a volume of 22.4 L?
    (a) 44.0 g/L   (b) 11.0 g/L   (c) 6.4 g/L   (d) 1.96 g/L

Sentence Completion

1. In Boyle's law, the _____ of a gas is inversely proportional to its _____.

2. A liquid has _____ volume and _____ shape.

3. _____ law states that the total pressure of a gas mixture is the sum of the individual pressure of the components in the mixture.

4. A pressure of 760 mmHg and a temperature of 273 K are known as ___ ___ ___ .

5. _____ law says that equal volumes of gases at the same temperature and pressure contain equal numbers of molecules.

6. In a closed container, liquid and vapor are at _____.

7. Units for measuring pressure include _____, _____, _____, _____, and _____.

8. The _____ __ _____ is the heat necessary to melt one gram of a solid at its melting point.

9. In Charles's law, _____ and _____ are kept constant.

10. Gas particles move in straight lines, with energy proportional to _____.

11. The transformation of a substance from one phase to another is known as a _____ ___ _____.

12. A liquid that evaporates readily is said to be _____.

True or False

1. Molecules of ethyl alcohol exhibit hydrogen bonding.

2. All gases are similar in their physical behavior.

3. Molecules of CH_3Cl experience both dipole–dipole interactions and London forces.

4. Doubling the pressure of a gas at constant temperature doubles the volume.

5. $R = 0.082$ L atm/(mol · K) is a value for the gas constant.

6. Atoms in solids have an orderly arrangement.

7. Standard temperature and pressure are 760 mmHg and 273°C.

8. All substances become solids if the temperature is low enough.

9. The atmospheric pressure in Death Valley (282 ft below sea level) is lower than the atmospheric pressure at sea level.

10. The more liquid there is in a closed container, the higher the vapor pressure.

11. Surface tension is a liquid's resistance to flow.

Match each entry on the left with its partner on the right. Use each answer once.

1. $P_1V_1 = P_2V_2$ (a) Avogadro's law

2. Dipole–dipole attraction   (b) Gas constant

3. $P_{total} = P_{gas\ 1} + P_{gas\ 2} + ...$ (c) Force per unit area

4. 760 mmHg at 273 K   (d) Charles's law

5. Hydrogen bonding   (e) Occurs between molecules of CH_3Br

6. $V_1/n_1 = V_2/n_2$ (f) STP

7. 0.007500 mmHg   (g) Boyle's law

8. London forces   (h) Occurs between molecules of CH_3OH

9. 62.4 mmHg L/mol K   (i) Ideal gas law

10. $V_1/T_1 = V_2/T_2$ (j) Pascal

11. Pressure   (k) Dalton's law of partial pressure

12. $PV = nRT$ (l) Occurs between molecules of N_2

Chapter Outline

I. Characteristics of solutions (Sections 9.1–9.6).
   A. Mixtures and solutions (Section 9.1).
      1. Mixtures are either heterogeneous or homogeneous.
         a. Heterogeneous mixtures have nonuniform mixing.
         b. Homogeneous mixtures have uniform mixing.
      2. Homogeneous mixtures can be classified by particle size.
         a. In solutions, particles range in size from 0.1 to 2 nm.
         b. In colloids, particles range in size from 2 to 1000 nm.
      3. When a solid is dissolved in a liquid, the liquid is the solvent and the solid is the solute.
   B. The solution process (Sections 9.2–9.3).
      1. Solubility depends on the strength of attraction between solute particles and solvent, relative to the attractions in the pure substances.
      2. In predicting solubility, polar solvents dissolve polar substances, and nonpolar solvents dissolve nonpolar substances.
      3. Solvation can be either an exothermic or an endothermic process.
      4. Some ionic compounds attract water to form solid hydrates (Section 9.3).
   C. Solubility (Sections 9.4–9.6).
      1. Solubility is a dynamic process (Section 9.4).
         a. When no more of an added solute will dissolve, the solution is said to be saturated.
         b. In a saturated solution, an equilibrium is established between dissolving and crystallizing.
      2. The solubility of a substance is the maximum amount of the substance that will dissolve in a solvent.
      3. Effect of temperature on solubility (Section 9.5).
         a. The effect of temperature on the solubility of a solid solute is unpredictable.
         b. A gas is always less soluble as temperature increases.
         c. A solid that is more soluble at high temperature than at low temperature may form a supersaturated solution.
      4. Effect of pressure on solubility (Section 9.6).
         a. Increased pressure makes gas molecules more soluble in a liquid.
         b. Henry's law: $C = kP_{gas}$.
            i. The solubility of a gas in a liquid is proportional to its partial pressure over the liquid at constant T.
         c. When the partial pressure of a gas changes:
         $$\frac{C_1}{P_1} = \frac{C_2}{P_2} = k \text{ (at constant T)}$$
II. Quantitative relationships in solutions (Sections 9.7–9.10).
   A. Concentration (Section 9.7).
      1. Percent concentrations.
         a. (m/m) % concentration $= \dfrac{\text{Mass of solute (g)}}{\text{Mass of solution (g)}}$ x 100%.
         b. (v/v) % concentration $= \dfrac{\text{Volume of solute (mL)}}{\text{Volume of solution (mL)}}$ x 100%.
         c. (m/v) % concentration $= \dfrac{\text{Mass of solute (g)}}{\text{Volume of solution (mL)}}$ x 100%.

2. parts per million (ppm) $= \dfrac{\text{Mass of solute (g)}}{\text{Mass of solution (g)}} \times 10^6$.

$\phantom{\text{2. parts per million (ppm)}} = \dfrac{\text{Volume of solute (mL)}}{\text{Volume of solution (mL)}} \times 10^6$.

3. parts per billion (ppb) $= \dfrac{\text{Mass of solute (g)}}{\text{Mass of solution (g)}} \times 10^9$.

$\phantom{\text{3. parts per billion (ppb)}} = \dfrac{\text{Volume of solute (mL)}}{\text{Volume of solution (mL)}} \times 10^9$.

4. Molarity $= \dfrac{\text{Moles of solute}}{\text{Volume of solution (L)}}$.

    a. Molarity can be used as a conversion factor.

B. Dilution (Section 9.8).
   1. During dilution, the number of moles of solute remains constant, while volume changes.
   2. $M_1 \times V_1 = M_2 \times V_2$.
   3. V_1 / V_2 is known as a dilution factor.
C. Equivalents and milliequivalents (Sections 9.9–9.10).
   1. Electrolytes (Section 9.9).
      a. Substances that dissociate completely are strong electrolytes.
      b. Substances that dissociate partially are weak electrolytes.
      c. Molecular substances that don't produce ions are nonelectrolytes.
   2. The concentration of electrolytes is expressed in equivalents (Section 9.10).
      a. 1 gram-equivalent of an ion $= \dfrac{\text{molar mass of the ion}}{\text{number of charges on the ion}}$.
      b. Milliequivalents are useful when measuring ion concentrations in body fluids.
III. Properties of solutions (Sections 9.11–9.13).
   A. Effects of particles in solution—colligative properties (Section 9.11).
      1. Lowering of vapor pressure.
      2. Boiling point elevation.
      3. Freezing point depression.
      4. These effects don't depend on the identity of the particles.
   B. Osmosis (Section 9.12–9.13).
      1. When two solutions of different concentrations are separated by a semipermeable membrane, water passes through to the more concentrated side. This is known as osmosis.
      2. Osmotic pressure can be applied to establish an equilibrium between the rates of forward and reverse passage of water across the membrane.
      3. The osmotic pressure of a solution depends only on the number of particles in solution.
      4. Osmolarity = molarity × number of particles per formula unit.
      5. Two solutions that are isotonic have the same osmolarity.
         a. In cells, a hypotonic solution causes hemolysis.
         b. A hypertonic solution causes crenation.
      6. Dialysis is a process similar to osmosis except that the pores in the membrane allow small solute molecules to pass (Section 9.13).
         a. Hemodialysis is used to cleanse the blood of people whose kidneys malfunction.
         b. Colloidal particles are too large to pass through semipermeable membranes.

Solutions to Chapter 9 Problems

9.1   Orange juice is heterogeneous, and all of the other mixtures are homogeneous, although hand lotion might be heterogeneous in some cases. Apple juice and tea are solutions because they are nonfilterable and transparent to light. Hand lotion is a colloid.

9.2   Remember the rule "like dissolves like."
(a) CCl_4 and H_2O don't form solutions because CCl_4 is nonpolar and H_2O is polar.
(b) Benzene and $MgSO_4$ don't form solutions because $MgSO_4$ is ionic and benzene is nonpolar.
(c), (d) These two pairs of substances form solutions because they are chemically similar.

9.3   Glauber's salt: $Na_2SO_4 \cdot 10H_2O$

9.4   Molar mass of Glauber's salt: 322 g/mol. 322 g of Glauber's salt provides 1.00 mol of sodium sulfate.

9.5   A solution of 12.5 g KBr in 20 mL H_2O is equivalent to a solution of 62.5 g KBr in 100 mL H_2O. According to Figure 9.3, the solution is unsaturated at 60 °C. Cooling the solution to 10 °C makes the solution supersaturated.

9.6

$$\frac{C_1}{P_1} = \frac{C_2}{P_2}; P_1 = 760 \text{ mmHg}; C_1 = 0.169 \text{ g/100 mL}; P_2 = 2.5 \times 10^4 \text{ mmHg}; C_2 = ?$$

$$C_2 = \frac{C_1 P_2}{P_1} = \frac{\left(\dfrac{0.169 \text{ g}}{100 \text{ mL}}\right) \times 2.5 \times 10^4 \text{ mmHg}}{760 \text{ mmHg}} = 5.6 \text{ g } CO_2/100 \text{ mL}$$

9.7

$$\frac{C_1}{P_1} = \frac{C_2}{P_2}; P_1 = 1.00 \text{ atm}; C_1 = 0.169 \text{ g/100 mL}; P_2 = 4.0 \times 10^{-4} \text{ atm}; C_2 = ?$$

$$C_2 = \frac{C_1 P_2}{P_1} = \frac{\left(\dfrac{0.169 \text{ g}}{100 \text{ mL}}\right) \times 4.0 \times 10^{-4} \text{ atm}}{1.00 \text{ atm}} = 6.8 \times 10^{-5} \text{ g } CO_2/100 \text{ mL}$$

9.8   According to Dalton's Law (Section 8.11), the total pressure exerted by a gas is the sum of the partial pressures of the gases in the mixture. Thus the partial pressure of oxygen at a total pressure of 265 mmHg is 0.21 x 265 mmHg = 56 mmHg. The oxygen-carrying curve shows that hemoglobin is approximately 90% saturated at this partial pressure.

9.9   This is a (mass/mass) % concentration problem in which a mass of 100 g of alloy contains 15.8 g Ni. To find the mass of the alloy that contains 36.5 g Ni:

$$\text{Mass of alloy} = 36.5 \text{ g Ni} \times \frac{100 \text{ g alloy}}{15.8 \text{ g Ni}} = 231 \text{ g alloy}$$

9.10   A 7.5% (v/v) solution contains 7.5 mL of solute per 100 mL of solution.

$$500 \text{ mL solution} \times \frac{7.5 \text{ mL acetic acid}}{100 \text{ mL solution}} = 38 \text{ mL acetic acid}$$

To prepare the desired solution, measure 38 mL of acetic acid into a 500.0 mL volumetric flask and add water to the 500.0 mL mark.

9.11   1 dL = 100 mL

$$\frac{8.6 \text{ mg}}{100 \text{ mL}} \times \frac{1 \text{ g}}{1000 \text{ mg}} \times 100\% = 0.0086\% \text{ (m/v) } Ca^{2+}$$

Remember: (m/v)% specifies that the mass of solute be expressed in grams.

9.12   (a) A 16% (m/v) solution contains 16 g of solute per 100 mL of solution.

$$125 \text{ mL} \times \frac{16 \text{ g glucose}}{100 \text{ mL}} = 20 \text{ g glucose}$$

(b) A 2.0% (m/v) solution contains 2.0 g of solute per 100 mL of solution.

$$1.2 \text{ g KCl} \times \frac{100 \text{ mL } H_2O}{2.0 \text{ g KCl}} = 60 \text{ mL } H_2O$$

9.13

$$\frac{32 \text{ mg NaF}}{20 \text{ kg solution}} \times \frac{1 \text{ kg}}{10^6 \text{ mg}} \times 10^6 = 1.6 \text{ ppm}$$

9.14   For lead:

$$\frac{0.015 \text{ mg Pb}}{1 \text{ kg solution}} \times \frac{1 \text{ kg}}{10^6 \text{ mg}} \times 10^6 = 0.015 \text{ ppm}$$

$$\frac{0.015 \text{ mg Pb}}{1 \text{ kg solution}} \times \frac{1 \text{ kg}}{10^3 \text{ g}} \times 100 \text{ g} = 0.0015 \text{ mg Pb}$$

For copper:

$$\frac{1.3 \text{ mg Cu}}{1 \text{ kg solution}} \times \frac{1 \text{ kg}}{10^6 \text{ mg}} \times 10^6 = 1.3 \text{ ppm}$$

$$\frac{1.3 \text{ mg Cu}}{1 \text{ kg solution}} \times \frac{1 \text{ kg}}{10^3 \text{ g}} \times 100 \text{ g} = 0.13 \text{ mg Cu}$$

9.15

$$\frac{50.0 \text{ g}}{0.160 \text{ L}} \times \frac{1 \text{ mol}}{337 \text{ g}} = 0.927 \text{ M}$$

9.16

$$\text{moles of solute} = \text{molarity (M)} \times \text{volume} = \frac{\text{mol}}{\text{L}} \times \text{L}$$

(a) $M = \frac{0.35 \text{ mol NaNO}_3}{1 \text{ L}}$; $V = 175 \text{ mL} = 0.175 \text{ L}$

$$\text{moles} = \frac{0.35 \text{ mol}}{1 \text{ L}} \times 0.175 \text{ L} = 0.061 \text{ mol NaNO}_3$$

(b) $M = \frac{1.4 \text{ mol HNO}_3}{1 \text{ L}}$; $V = 480 \text{ mL} = 0.48 \text{ L}$

$$\text{moles} = \frac{1.4 \text{ mol}}{1 \text{ L}} \times 0.48 \text{ L} = 0.67 \text{ mol HNO}_3$$

9.17 First, find the number of moles of cholesterol in 250 mL of blood:

$$250 \text{ mL} \times \frac{0.0050 \text{ mol cholesterol}}{1000 \text{ mL}} = 0.001\ 25 \text{ mol cholesterol}$$

Next, find the molar mass of cholesterol:

$$(27 \times 12.0 \text{ g/mol C}) + (46 \times 1.0 \text{ g/mol H}) + (16.0 \text{ g/mol O}) = 386.0 \text{ g/mol}$$

Now, convert moles into grams:

$$0.001\ 25 \text{ mol cholesterol} \times \frac{386.0 \text{ g}}{1 \text{ mol}} = 0.48 \text{ g cholesterol}$$

9.18

(a) $0.065 \text{ L} \times \dfrac{0.12 \text{ mol HCl}}{1 \text{ L}} = 0.0078 \text{ mol HCl}$

(b) $0.0078 \text{ mol HCl} \times \dfrac{1 \text{ mol CaCO}_3}{2 \text{ mol HCl}} \times \dfrac{100.0 \text{ g CaCO}_3}{1 \text{ mol CaCO}_3} = 0.39 \text{ g CaCO}_3$

9.19 $V_2 = 500.0 \text{ mL}; \quad M_2 = 1.25 \text{ M}; \quad M_1 = 16.0 \text{ M}; \quad V_1 = ?$

$$V_1 = V_2 \times \frac{M_2}{M_1} = 500.0 \text{ mL} \times \frac{1.25 \text{ M}}{16.0 \text{ M}} = 39.1 \text{ mL}$$

Ballpark check: Since the final molarity is about 1/12 the initial molarity, the initial volume is about 1/12 the final volume, or about 40 mL.

9.20 $C_1 = 5.0 \text{ ppm}; \quad V_1 = 1.5 \text{ L}; \quad C_2 = 0.010 \text{ ppm}; \quad V_2 = ?$

$$V_2 = V_1 \times \frac{C_2}{C_1} = 1.5 \text{ L} \times \frac{5.0 \text{ ppm}}{0.01 \text{ ppm}} = 750 \text{ L}$$

9.21

One equivalent = molar mass of ion (g) ÷ number of charges on ion.

Ion	Molar Mass	Charge	Gram-Equivalent	Milligram-Equivalent
(a) K^+	39.1 g	+1	39.1 g	39.1 mg, or 3.91×10^{-2} g
(b) Br^-	79.9 g	−1	79.9 g	79.9 mg, or 7.99×10^{-2} g
(c) Mg^{2+}	24.3 g	+2	12.2 g	12.2 mg, or 1.22×10^{-2} g
(d) SO_4^{2-}	96.0 g	−2	48.0 g	48.0 mg, or 4.80×10^{-2} g
(e) Al^{3+}	27.0 g	+3	9.0 g	9.0 mg, or 9.0×10^{-3} g
(f) PO_4^{3-}	95.0 g	−3	31.7 g	31.7 mg, or 31.7×10^{-2} g

9.22   One gram-equivalent of Mg^{2+} = 12.2 g [Problem 9.21(c)].

$$\frac{g\ Mg^{2+}}{1\ L} = \frac{12\ g\ Mg^{2+}}{1\ Eq} \times \frac{1\ Eq}{1000\ mEq} \times \frac{3.0\ mEq}{1\ L} = \frac{0.036\ g\ Mg^{2+}}{1\ L}$$

$$\frac{0.036\ g\ Mg^{2+}}{L} \times \frac{1000\ mg}{1\ g} \times \frac{1\ L}{1000\ mL} \times 250\ mL = 9.0\ mg\ Mg^{2+}$$

9.23   For Na^+:
$$\frac{20\ mEq\ Na^+}{1.0\ L} \times \frac{23\ mg\ Na^+}{1\ mEq} \times \frac{1\ g}{1000\ mg} \times \frac{1.0\ L}{1000\ mL} \times 100\ mL = 0.046\ (m/v)\%\ Na^+$$
For K^+:
$$\frac{10\ mEq\ K^+}{1.0\ L} \times \frac{39\ mg\ K^+}{1\ mEq} \times \frac{1\ g}{1000\ mg} \times \frac{1.0\ L}{1000\ mL} \times 100\ mL = 0.039\ (m/v)\%\ K^+$$

9.24   (a) 0.67 mol of $MgCl_2$ in 0.5 kg H_2O yields 2.0 mol ions.
(b) 2.0 mol ions in 0.5 kg H_2O is equivalent to 4.0 mol ions in 1.0 kg H_2O, which raise the boiling point by 4.0 x 0.51 °C = 2.0 °C.

Boiling point = 100.0 °C + 2.0 °C = 102.0 °C

9.25   If HF were a strong electrolyte it would dissociate completely, and a solution of 1.0 mol HF would yield 2.0 mol ions, which would elevate the boiling point of water by 2.0 x 0.51 °C = 1.02 °C. Since the observed boiling point elevation is only 0.5 °C, HF must be a weak electrolyte that is only slightly dissociated.

9.26   (a) The red curve represents the pure solvent, because the solvent boils at a lower temperature than the solution.
(b) A liquid boils when its vapor pressure equals atmospheric pressure. The solvent boils at 62 °C, and the solution boils at 69 °C, an approximately 7° boiling point elevation.
(c) One mole of solute raises the boiling point approximately 3.5 °C, and the observed boiling point elevation is approximately 7 °C. Thus, the concentration of the solute is about 2 M.

9.27   Glucose is not an electrolyte. Thus 1.0 mol glucose lowers the freezing point of 1.0 kg H_2O by 1.9 °C.
Freezing point = 0.0 °C – 1.9 °C = –1.9 °C

9.28   A freezing point depression of 1.86 °C is produced by 1 mol of ions in 1 kg of water. Thus, a freezing point depression of 2.8 °C must be produced by 2.8 ÷ 1.86 = 1.5 mol of ions. Since 0.5 mol of the ionic substance produces the freezing point depression expected for 1.5 mol ions, the substance gives three ions when it dissolves.

9.29   Osmolarity = molarity x number of particles.
(a) For 0.35 M KBr, osmolarity = 0.35 M x 2 = 0.70 osmol, since KBr yields two ions (K^+ and Br^-) in solution.
(b) For 0.15 M glucose, osmolarity = 0.15 M x 1 = 0.15 osmol, since glucose yields only one particle in solution. For K_2SO_4, osmolarity = 0.05 M x 3 = 0.15 osmol, since K_2SO_4 provides three particles per mole in solution. Total osmolarity = 0.30 osmol.

9.30 (a) For the oral rehydration solution, osmolarity is equal to the sum of the osmolarities of the individual components. For each of the ionic components, the number of millimoles = the number of mEq, since each ion has one charge. Thus,

$$90 \text{ mM Na}^+ + 20 \text{ mM K}^+ + 110 \text{ mM Cl}^- = 220 \text{ mM ions}$$
$$0.090 \text{ M Na}^+ + 0.020 \text{ M K}^+ + 0.110 \text{ M Cl}^- = 0.220 \text{ M ions}$$

For glucose:

$$\frac{2.0 \text{ g glucose}}{100 \text{ mL}} \times \frac{1000 \text{ mL}}{1 \text{ L}} \times \frac{1 \text{ mol}}{180 \text{ g glucose}} = 0.11 \text{ M glucose}$$

(b) Osmolarity = molarity x number of particles. In this problem, all components yield one particle in solution.
Osmolarity = 0.22 M + 0.11 M = 0.33 osmol

Understanding Key Concepts

9.32 The boiling point of water is elevated by 0.5 °C for every mole of dissolved particles. 1 mol HCl dissolves to form 2 mol particles, which elevate the boiling point of water by 1 °C. Acetic acid exists in solution almost completely as CH_3CO_2H, and 1 mol acetic acid dissolves to form 1 mol particles, which elevate the boiling point of water by only 0.5 °C.

9.34

(a)   (b)   (c)

When a beaker of glucose solution (shaded) and a beaker of pure water (unshaded) stand for several days, the liquid levels appear as those pictured in (a). The dissolved glucose particles lower the vapor pressure of water and make evaporation slower.

Solutions and Solubility

9.36 In a homogeneous mixture (such as tea), mixing is uniform throughout because the particle size is small. In a heterogeneous mixture (such as chicken soup), mixing is nonuniform because particle size is larger.

9.38 The polarity of water enables it to dissolve many ionic solids.

9.40 Rubbing alcohol (b) and black coffee (d) are solutions.

9.42

$$C_2 = \frac{C_1 P_2}{P_1}; \quad C_1 = 51.8 \text{ g/100 mL}; \quad P_1 = 760.0 \text{ mmHg}; \quad P_2 = 225.0 \text{ mmHg}$$

$$= \frac{(51.8 \text{ g/100 mL}) \times 225.0 \text{ mmHg}}{760.0 \text{ mmHg}} = 15.3 \text{ g/100 mL}$$

Concentration and Dilution of Solutions

9.44 Depending on the solubility of the solute in the solvent, a saturated solution may be either dilute or concentrated. If a solute is only slightly soluble in a solvent, a saturated solution will be dilute. If the solute is very soluble in the solvent, a saturated solution will be concentrated. For a highly soluble solute, even a highly concentrated solution may be unsaturated.

9.46 Molarity (M) is defined as the number of moles of solute per liter of solution.

9.48

$$\frac{6.0 \text{ mL ethyl alcohol}}{100.0 \text{ mL solution}} \times 750.0 \text{ mL solution} = 45.0 \text{ mL ethyl alcohol}$$

Add water to 45.0 mL of ethyl alcohol to make a final volume of 750.0 mL.

9.50

$$250 \text{ mL solution} \times \frac{0.10 \text{ mol NaCl}}{1000 \text{ mL solution}} \times \frac{58.5 \text{ g NaCl}}{1 \text{ mol NaCl}} = 1.5 \text{ g NaCl}$$

Dissolve 1.5 g NaCl in water to a final volume of 250 mL.

9.52

(a) $0.078 \text{ mol KCl} \times \dfrac{74.6 \text{ g KCl}}{1 \text{ mol KCl}} = 5.8 \text{ g KCl}$

$\dfrac{5.8 \text{ g KCl}}{75 \text{ mL}} \times 100 \text{ mL} = 7.7 \text{ g KCl}; \dfrac{7.7 \text{ g KCl}}{100 \text{ mL}} \times 100\% = 7.7\% \text{ (m/v) KCl}$

(b) $0.044 \text{ mol sucrose} \times \dfrac{342 \text{ g sucrose}}{1 \text{ mol sucrose}} = 15 \text{ g sucrose}$

$\dfrac{15 \text{ g sucrose}}{380 \text{ mL}} \times 100 \text{ mL} = 3.9 \text{ g sucrose}; \dfrac{3.9 \text{ g}}{100 \text{ mL}} \times 100\% = 3.9\% \text{ (m/v) sucrose}$

9.54

(a) $50.0 \text{ mL} \times \dfrac{8.0 \text{ g KCl}}{100 \text{ mL}} = 4.0 \text{ g KCl} ; 4.0 \text{ g KCl} \times \dfrac{1 \text{ mol KCl}}{74.6 \text{ g KCl}} = 0.054 \text{ mol KCl}$

(b) $200.0 \text{ mL} \times \dfrac{7.5 \text{ g acetic acid}}{100 \text{ mL}} = 15 \text{ g acetic acid}$

$15 \text{ g acetic acid} \times \dfrac{1 \text{ mol acetic acid}}{60 \text{ g acetic acid}} = 0.25 \text{ mol acetic acid}$

9.56

$23 \text{ g KOH} \times \dfrac{100 \text{ mL}}{10.0 \text{ g KOH}} = 230 \text{ mL of a } 10.0\% \text{ (m/v) solution}$

$23 \text{ g KOH} \times \dfrac{1 \text{ mol}}{56.1 \text{ g KOH}} = 0.41 \text{ mol KOH}$

$0.41 \text{ mol KOH} \times \dfrac{1000 \text{ mL}}{0.25 \text{ mol KOH}} = 1600 \text{ mL of } 0.25 \text{ M solution}$

9.58

$$\frac{10 \text{ mg KCN}}{1 \text{ kg body weight}} \times \frac{1 \text{ kg}}{10^6 \text{ mg}} \times 10^6 = 10 \text{ ppm}$$

9.60

(a) $\dfrac{12.5 \text{ g NaHCO}_3}{0.350 \text{ L}} \times \dfrac{1 \text{ mol}}{84.0 \text{ g}} = 0.425 \text{ M}$

(b) $\dfrac{45.0 \text{ g H}_2\text{SO}_4}{0.300 \text{ L}} \times \dfrac{1 \text{ mol}}{98.1 \text{ g}} = 1.53 \text{ M}$

(c) $\dfrac{30.0 \text{ g NaCl}}{0.500 \text{ L}} \times \dfrac{1 \text{ mol}}{58.5 \text{ g}} = 1.03 \text{ M}$

9.62

$$0.0040 \text{ mol HCl} \times \frac{1000 \text{ mL}}{0.75 \text{ mol}} = 5.3 \text{ mL HCl}$$

9.64   First, calculate the number of moles of H_2SO_4 spilled:

$$0.450 \text{ L} \times \frac{0.50 \text{ mol H}_2\text{SO}_4}{1 \text{ L}} = 0.23 \text{ mol H}_2\text{SO}_4$$

According to the equation given in the problem, each mole of H_2SO_4 reacts with two moles of $NaHCO_3$. Thus, the 0.23 mol of H_2SO_4 spilled need to be neutralized with 0.46 mol of $NaHCO_3$.

$$0.46 \text{ mol NaHCO}_3 \times \frac{84 \text{ g}}{1 \text{ mol}} = 39 \text{ g NaHCO}_3$$

9.66

20.0% (v/v) means $\dfrac{20.0 \text{ mL concentrate}}{100.0 \text{ mL juice}}$

Thus, $100.0 \text{ mL concentrate} \times \dfrac{100.0 \text{ mL juice}}{20.0 \text{ mL concentrate}} = 500.0 \text{ mL juice}$

Since the final volume of the diluted juice is 500.0 mL, you would need to add 400.0 mL water to the original 100.0 mL of concentrate.

9.68

$$V_1 = V_2 \times \frac{C_2}{C_1}; \quad V_2 = 2.0 \text{ L}; \quad C_2 = 75 \text{ ppm}; \quad C_1 = 285 \text{ ppm}$$

$$= 2.0 \text{ L} \times \frac{75 \text{ ppm}}{285 \text{ ppm}} = 0.53 \text{ L of 285 ppm KNO}_3 \text{ solution}$$

9.70

$$V_2 = V_1 \times \frac{M_1}{M_2}; \ V_1 = 25.0 \text{ mL}; \ M_1 = 12.0 \text{ M}; \ M_2 = 0.500 \text{ M}$$

$$= 25.0 \text{ mL} \times \frac{12.0 \text{ M}}{0.500 \text{ M}} = 600 \text{ mL of } 0.500 \text{ M HCl solution}$$

Electrolytes

9.72 An electrolyte is a substance that conducts electricity when dissolved in water.

9.74 If the concentration of Ca^{2+} is 3.0 mEq/L, there are 3.0 mmol of charges due to calcium per liter of blood. Since calcium has a charge of +2, there are 1.5 mmol of calcium per liter of blood.

9.76

$$10\% \text{ (m/v)} = \frac{10 \text{ g KCl}}{100 \text{ mL}}; \quad 30 \text{ mL} \times \frac{10 \text{ g KCl}}{100 \text{ mL}} = 3.0 \text{ g KCl}$$

The molar mass of KCl is 74.6 g/mol. Thus:

$$3.0 \text{ g KCl} \times \frac{1 \text{ mol}}{74.6 \text{ g}} = 0.040 \text{ mol KCl}$$

Since one equivalent equals one mole when an ion has only one charge, there are 0.040 Eq, or 40 mEq, of K^+ in a 30 mL dose.

9.78 Use the value 100 mEq/L for the concentration of Cl^- in blood:
For Cl^- ion, 100 mEq = 100 mmol = 0.100 mol.

$$1.0 \text{ g } Cl^- \times \frac{1 \text{ mol}}{35.5 \text{ g}} \times \frac{1 \text{ L}}{0.100 \text{ mol}} \times \frac{1000 \text{ mL}}{1 \text{ L}} = 280 \text{ mL}$$

Properties of Solutions

9.80 0.20 mol NaOH contains 0.40 mol solute particles, and 0.20 mol $Ba(OH)_2$ contains 0.60 mol solute particles. Since $Ba(OH)_2$ produces more solute particles, it produces greater lowering of the freezing point when dissolved in 2.0 kg of water.

9.82 Methanol has a molar mass of 32.0 g and provides one mole of solute particles per mole of methanol.

$$10.0 \text{ °C} \times \frac{1 \text{ mol}}{1.86 \text{ °C} \times 1 \text{ kg}} \times 5.00 \text{ kg} = 26.9 \text{ mol methanol}$$

$$26.9 \text{ mol} \times \frac{32.0 \text{ g}}{1 \text{ mol}} = 861 \text{ g of methanol needed}$$

Osmosis

9.84   The inside of a red blood cell contains dissolved substances and therefore has a higher osmolarity than pure water. Water thus passes through the cell membrane to dilute the cell contents until pressure builds up and the cell eventually bursts.

9.86

Solution	Molarity	Number of Particles	Osmolarity
(a) 0.25 M KBr	0.25 M	2	0.50 osmol
0.20 M Na_2SO_4	0.20 M	3	0.60 osmol (greater)
(b) 0.30 M NaOH	0.30 M	2	0.60 osmol
3% (m/v) NaOH	0.75 M	2	1.5 osmol (greater)

9.88   The molar mass of NaCl is 58.5 g, and each mole of NaCl yields two moles of particles.

$$\frac{270 \text{ g}}{3.8 \text{ L}} \times \frac{1 \text{ mol}}{58.5 \text{ g}} \times 2 \text{ particles } = 2.4 \text{ osmol}$$

Chemistry in Action

9.90   At high altitude, P_{O2} is low, and not enough oxygen is available to cause 100% saturation of hemoglobin. In order to deliver enough oxygen to body tissues, the body compensates by manufacturing more hemoglobin, which drives the hemoglobin equilibrium to the right.

9.92   In addition to fluid replacement, sports drinks provide electrolytes to replenish those lost during exercise, they furnish soluble complex carbohydrates for slow-release energy, and they may contain vitamins to protect cells from damage.

General Questions and Problems

9.94

(a) $0.18 \times 5.0 \text{ atm} \times \dfrac{760 \text{ mmHg}}{1.0 \text{ atm}} = 680 \text{ mmHg}$

(b) $\dfrac{C_1}{P_1} = \dfrac{C_2}{P_2}$; $P_1 = 760 \text{ mmHg}$; $C_1 = 2.1 \text{ g/100 mL}$; $P_2 = 680 \text{ mmHg}$; $C_2 = ?$

$= \dfrac{(2.1 \text{ g/100 mL}) \times 680 \text{ mmHg}}{760 \text{ mmHg}} = 1.9 \text{ g/100 mL}$

9.96   Molar mass of uric acid ($C_5H_4N_4O_3$) = 168 g.

(a) (m/v)%: $\dfrac{0.067 \text{ g}}{1 \text{ L}} = \dfrac{0.0067 \text{ g}}{100 \text{ mL}}$; $\dfrac{0.0067 \text{ g}}{100 \text{ mL}} \times 100\% = 0.0067\%$ (m/v)

(b) ppm: One L of water weighs 1 kg. Thus

$\dfrac{0.067 \text{ g}}{1 \text{ L}} = \dfrac{0.067 \text{ g}}{1 \text{ kg}} \times \dfrac{1 \text{ kg}}{1000 \text{ g}}$; $\dfrac{0.067 \text{ g}}{1000 \text{ g}} \times 10^6 = 67 \text{ ppm}$

(c) $\dfrac{0.067 \text{ g}}{1 \text{ L}} \times \dfrac{1 \text{ mol}}{168 \text{ g}} = 0.000\,40 \text{ M} = 4.0 \times 10^{-4} \text{ M}$

9.98 (a) The volume of concentrated HNO_3 that contains 0.150 mol is:

$$V_2 = V_1 \times \frac{moles_2}{moles_1} = 1.0\ L \times \frac{0.15\ mol}{16\ mol} = 0.0094\ L\ HNO_3 = 9.4\ mL\ HNO_3$$

(b) The volume of a 0.20 M solution that contains 0.15 moles:

$$V_2 = V_1 \times \frac{moles_2}{moles_1} = 1.0\ L \times \frac{0.15\ mol}{0.20\ mol} = 0.75\ L$$

9.100

Component	Mass	Molar Mass	Molarity
(a) NaCl	8.6 g	58.5 g	0.147 M
(b) KCl	0.30 g	74.6 g	0.0040 M
(c) $CaCl_2$	0.33 g	111 g	0.0030 M

9.102

$$\frac{10\ mg}{5.0\ L} \times \frac{1\ L}{1000\ mL} \times \frac{1\ g}{1000\ mg} \times 100\% = 0.0002\%\ (m/v)$$

9.104

$$0.080\%\ (v/v) = \frac{0.080\ mL}{100\ mL} = \frac{0.80\ mL}{1\ L};\ \frac{0.80\ mL}{1\ L} \times 5.0\ L = 4.0\ mL\ alcohol$$

9.106 (a) $CoCl_2(s) + 6\ H_2O(g) \rightleftharpoons CoCl_2 \cdot 6H_2O(s)$

(b) Molar mass of $CoCl_2 \cdot 6H_2O = 238$ g

$$2.50\ g\ CoCl_2 \times \frac{1\ mol\ CoCl_2 \cdot 6\ H_2O}{238\ g} \times \frac{6\ mol\ H_2O}{1\ mol\ CoCl_2 \cdot 6\ H_2O} \times \frac{18.0\ g\ H_2O}{1\ mol\ H_2O} = 1.13\ g\ H_2O$$

9.108 (a) If 36.0 % of TCA is dissociated, the solution consists of 0.360 mol TCA anions, 0.360 mol H^+ cations, and 0.640 mol undissociated TCA, for a total of 1.360 mol ions and molecules in 1 kg water.

(b) The freezing point of water is depressed by 2.53 °C, resulting in a final temperature of –2.53 °C.

$$1.36\ mol \times \frac{1.86\ °C}{1\ mol} = 2.53\ °C$$

Self-Test for Chapter 9

Multiple Choice

1. 50 mL of a 1.0 M NaOH solution is diluted to 1.0 L. What is the dilution factor?
   (a) 1/50   (b) 1/20   (c) 1/10   (d) 1/2

2. Which of the following will not speed up the rate of solution of a solid?
   (a) stirring   (b) heating   (c) grinding the solid into powder   (d) increasing pressure on the solution

3. To make up 500 mL of a 5% (v/v) solution of methanol (CH_3OH; molar mass = 32 g) in water:
   (a) Dilute 25 mL of CH_3OH with water to a volume of 500 mL.
   (b) Dilute 5 mL of CH_3OH with water to a volume of 500 mL.
   (c) Add 32 g of CH_3OH to 500 g of water.
   (d) Add 25 mL of CH_3OH to 500 mL of water.

4. Which solution has the greatest osmolarity?
   (a) 0.2 M $CaCl_2$ (b) 0.3 M Na_3PO_4 (c) 0.5 M NaCl   (d) 0.8 M glucose

5. Which of the following is a colloid?
   (a) wine   (b) maple syrup   (c) milkshake   (d) salad oil

6. How many mL of a 12.0 M HCl solution are needed to make 1.0 L of 0.10 M HCl?
   (a) 120 mL   (b) 83 mL   (c) 50 mL   (d) 8.3 mL

7. Which of the following properties do not depend on the number of particles in solution?
   (a) boiling point elevation   (b) osmotic pressure   (c) heat of solution   (d) freezing point depression

8. How many grams of NaOH are needed to make 300 mL of a 0.3 M solution?
   (a) 40 g   (b) 12 g   (c) 3.6 g   (d) 1.0 g

9. How many moles of glucose are present in 250 mL of a 0.25 M solution?
   (a) 0.0625 mol   (b) 0.1 mol   (c) 0.25 mol   (d) 1.0 mol

10. How many mL of a 0.20 M solution of NaF contain 2.1 g of NaF?
    (a) 500 mL   (b) 250 mL   (c) 100 mL   (d) 50 mL

Sentence Completion

1. Two liquids soluble in each other are said to be _____.

2. An ___ ____ is the amount of an ion in grams that contains Avogadro's number of charges.

3. A weight/volume solution can be made up in a piece of glassware called a _____ _____.

4. According to Henry's law, the _____ of a gas varies with its _____ _____.

5. Two solutions that have the same osmolarity are _____.

6. Compounds that attract water from the atmosphere are called _____.

7. The formula used for calculating dilutions is _____.

8. Milk is an example of a _____.

9. _____ and _____ _____ _____ can pass through a dialysis membrane.

10. A solution that has reached its solubility limit is said to be _____.

11. An example of a nonelectrolyte is _____.

12. A solution that is hypotonic with respect to blood has a _____ osmolarity than blood plasma.

True or False

1. A solute is the liquid used to dissolve a substance.

2. It is possible to have a solution of a solid in a solid.

3. In making a volume/volume percent solution, one liquid is added to 100 mL of the other liquid.

4. All ionic compounds are soluble in water.

5. A solution of 0.10 M Na_3PO_4 has a greater osmolarity than a solution of 0.15 M NaCl.

6. Weight/weight percent is a useful way to express concentration.

7. In carrying out a dilution, the number of moles of solute remains constant.

8. The solubility of most substances increases with temperature.

9. A colloid differs from a solution in its ability to transmit light.

10. A blood cell undergoes crenation when placed in distilled water.

11. Particles dissolved in water lower the boiling point of water.

12. The amount of gas dissolved in a liquid increases with increasing pressure.

Match each entry on the left with its partner on the right.

1. Osmotic membrane   (a) Muddy water

2. V_1/V_2 (b) Molarity x number of particles

3. Solution   (c) Conducts electricity in water

4. Equivalent   (d) Vinegar

5. Suspension   (e) Crystalline compound that holds water

6. Dialysis membrane   (f) Dilution factor

7. Osmolarity   (g) Butter

8. Hypotonic   (h) Permeable only to water

9. Colloid   (i) A solution of lower osmolarity than another

10. Crenation   (j) Formula weight/number of charges

11. Hydrate   (k) Permeable to water and small molecules

12. Electrolyte   (l) Happens to cell in hypertonic solution

Chapter 10 – Acids and Bases

Chapter Outline

I. Introduction to acids and bases (Sections 10.1–10.3).
  A. Definition of acids and bases (Sections 10.1, 10.3).
    1. Arrhenius definition (Section 10.1).
      a. Acids donate H^+ ions in solution.
      b. Bases donate OH^- ions in solution.
      c. Acid + base —> salt + H_2O.
    2. Brønsted–Lowry definition (Section 10.3).
      a. A Brønsted–Lowry acid is a proton donor (an H_3O^+ donor).
        i. Some acids can donate more than one proton.
      b. A Brønsted–Lowry base is a proton acceptor.
        i. The base may be negatively charged or neutral.
      c. An acid–base reaction is one in which a proton is transferred.
      d. Products of acid–base reactions are also acids and bases.
      In the reaction $HA + B: —> A^- + BH^+$:
        i. HA and A^- are an acid–conjugate base pair.
        ii. B: and BH^+ are a base–conjugate acid pair.
  B. Many common substances are acids or bases (Section 10.2).
II. Acid/base strength (Sections 10.4–10.9).
  A. Strong/weak acids and bases (Section 10.4).
    1. Strong acids and bases are 100% dissociated in water.
    2. Weak acids and bases are less than 100% dissociated in solution.
    3. The stronger the acid, the weaker the conjugate base.
    The weaker the acid, the stronger the conjugate base.
    4. An acid–base proton transfer always favors formation of the weaker acid.
  B. Acid dissociation constants (Section 10.5).
    1. K_a is a measure of the degree to which an acid HA dissociates to H_3O^+ and A^-.
    2. K_a values for weak acids are much less than 1.
    3. Donation of each successive H^+ ion from a polyprotic acid becomes successively more difficult.
    4. Most organic acids have K_a near 10^{-5}.
  C. Water as an acid and a base (Section 10.6).
    1. Water can act both as an acid and a base.
    2. Substances that can act as both acids and bases are amphoteric.
    3. Dissociation of H_2O.
      a. $K_w = [H_3O^+][OH^-] = 1.00 \times 10^{-14}$ at 25 °C.
      b. This relationship is true for any aqueous solution.
      c. Thus, we can calculate $[H_3O^+]$ or $[OH^-]$ for any aqueous solution.
  D. Measuring acidity (Sections 10.7–10.9).
    1. pH (Sections 10.7–10.8).
      a. A pH of < 7 indicates acidity; a pH of > 7 indicates basicity.
      b. pH is the negative logarithm of $[H_3O^+]$.
      c. The pH scale is logarithmic.
      d. pH can be computed with a calculator.
    2. In the laboratory, pH can be measured with indicators or a pH meter (Section 10.9).

III. Buffers (Section 10.10).
   A. Characteristics of buffers.
      1. A buffer is the solution of a weak acid and its salt (or a weak base and its salt) at similar concentration.
      2. When a small amount of acid or base is added to a buffered solution, pH changes very little.
      3. The effective pH range of a buffer solution is determined by the K_a of the acid or base.
         a. A buffer solution works best when [HA] is close in value to [A$^-$].
         b. A buffer solution works best when [HA] and [A$^-$] are approximately ten times greater than the amount of acid or base added.
      4. The Henderson–Hasselbalch equation ($pH = pK_a + \log$ ([A$^-$]/[HA]) is useful in buffer calculations. ($pK_a = -\log K_a$)
      5. The carbonate/bicarbonate buffer system is the major regulator of the pH of body fluids.
         a. The phosphate system and proteins are two other buffer systems in the body.
IV. Equivalents of acids and bases (Sections 10.11–10.13).
   A. Normality (Section 10.11).
      1. A gram-equivalent of acid or base $= \dfrac{\text{molar mass}}{\text{number of H}^+ \text{ or OH}^- \text{ produced}}$.
      2. One equivalent of acid neutralizes one equivalent of base.
      3. Normality $= \dfrac{\text{equivalents of acid or base}}{\text{liters of solution}}$.
      4. Normality = (molarity of acid or base) × (number of H$^+$ or OH$^-$ produced).
   B. Common acid–base reactions (Section 10.12).
      1. Acid + hydroxide ion —> water + salt.
      2. Acid + carbonate or bicarbonate —> water + salt + CO_2.
      3. Acid + ammonia —> ammonium salt.
   C. Titration (Section 10.13).
      1. Titration is used to determine the acid or base concentration of a solution.
      2. In titration, a known volume of a solution of unknown acid or base concentration completely reacts with a solution of known concentration.
      3. The volume of solution of known concentration is measured, and the concentration of the unknown is calculated.
V. Acidity and basicity of salt solutions (Section 10.14).
   A. The salt of a strong base and a strong acid is neutral in solution.
   B. The salt of a strong base and a weak acid is basic in solution.
   C. The salt of a weak base and a strong acid is acidic in solution.
   D. The pH of the salt of a weak base and a weak acid can be predicted only if K_a values are known.

Solutions to Chapter 10 Problems

10.1 HCO_2H (a) and H_2S (b) are Brønsted–Lowry acids because they have protons to donate.

10.2 SO_3^{2-} (a) and F^- (c) are Brønsted–Lowry bases because they can be proton acceptors.

10.3 (a) The conjugate acid of HS^- is H_2S.
(b) The conjugate acid of PO_4^{3-} is HPO_4^{2-}.
(c) The conjugate base of H_2CO_3 is HCO_3^-.
(d) The conjugate base of NH_4^+ is NH_3.

10.4

10.5 In Table 10.1, the stronger acid is listed *higher* in the table than the weaker acid.

Stronger acids: (a) NH_4^+ (b) H_2SO_4 (c) H_2CO_3

10.6 In Table 10.1, the stronger base is listed *lower* in the table than the weaker base.

Stronger bases: (a) F^- (b) OH^-

10.7

From Table 10.1, we see that OH^- is a stronger base than PO_4^{3-} and that HPO_4^{2-} is a stronger acid than H_2O. Thus, the forward direction of the equilibrium is favored.

$HPO_4^{2-}(aq) + OH^-(aq) \rightleftharpoons PO_4^{3-}(aq) + H_2O(l)$
stronger acid   stronger base   weaker base   weaker acid

10.8

10.9   Remember that an electrostatic potential map shows the most electron-rich area of the molecule as red and the least electron-rich area as blue. In alanine, the $-NH_3^+$ group is the most electron-poor, and thus its hydrogens are the most acidic.

10.10 The value for K_a of benzoic acid is smaller than the value for citrate, indicating that benzoic acid is a weaker acid. Benzoate is thus a stronger base than citrate.

10.11 (a) Ammonia is basic.

$$[OH^-] = \frac{K_w}{[H_3O^+]} = \frac{1.0 \times 10^{-14}}{3.1 \times 10^{-12}} = 3.2 \times 10^{-3} \text{ M}$$

(b) Vinegar is acidic. Since $1 \times 10^{-14} = [H_3O^+][OH^-]$,

$$[OH^-] = \frac{K_w}{[H_3O^+]} = \frac{1.0 \times 10^{-14}}{4.0 \times 10^{-3}} = 2.5 \times 10^{-12} \text{ M}$$

10.12 (a) pH = $-\log [H^+] = -\log [3.1 \times 10^{-12}] = 11.51$
(b) pH = $-\log [H^+] = -\log [4.0 \times 10^{-3}] = 2.40$

10.13 (a) For pH = 13, $[H_3O^+] = 1 \times 10^{-13}$ M; $[OH^-] = 0.1$ M
(b) For pH = 3, $[H_3O^+] = 1 \times 10^{-3}$ M; $[OH^-] = 1 \times 10^{-11}$ M
(c) For pH = 8, $[H_3O^+] = 1 \times 10^{-8}$ M; $[OH^-] = 1 \times 10^{-6}$ M

The solution of pH = 3 is most acidic, and the solution of pH = 13 is most basic.

10.14 A solution of 0.01 M HNO_2 has a higher pH because HNO_2 is a weaker acid, and its $[H^+]$ is lower.

10.15

Solution	pH	Acidic/Basic	$[H_3O^+]$	$[OH^-]$
(a) Saliva	6.5	acidic	3×10^{-7} M	3×10^{-8} M
(b) Pancreatic juice	7.9	basic	1×10^{-8} M	1×10^{-6} M
(c) Orange juice	3.7	acidic	2×10^{-4} M	5×10^{-11} M
(d) Wine	3.5	acidic	3×10^{-4} M	3×10^{-11} M

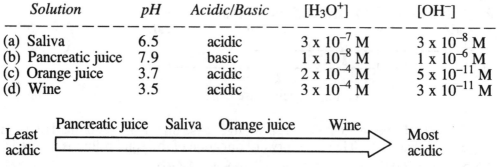

10.16 Use a calculator to determine pH. Remember that the significant figures in the answer are the digits to the right of the decimal point.

(a) $[H_3O^+] = 5.3 \times 10^{-9}$ mol/L: pH = 8.28
(b) $[H_3O^+] = 8.9 \times 10^{-6}$ mol/L: pH = 5.05

10.17 $[H_3O^+] = 2.5 \times 10^{-3}$, since HCl is a strong acid. As in the previous problem, use the EE key and the log key on your calculator, and take the negative value of the log.
$[H_3O^+] = 2.5 \times 10^{-3}$; pH = $-\log (2.5 \times 10^{-3}) = -(-2.60) = 2.60$

10.18 Refer to Worked Examples 10.13 and 10.14 in the text.
When 0.020 mol of HNO_3 is added, the HF concentration increases from 0.100 M to 0.120 M, and the F^- decreases from 0.120 M to 0.100 M because of the reaction:

$$F^-(aq) + HNO_3(aq) \longrightarrow HF(aq) + NO_3^-(aq)$$

$$pH = pK_a + \log\frac{[A^-]}{[HA]} = 3.46 + \log\frac{[0.100]}{[0.120]} = 3.46 - 0.08 = 3.38$$

10.19

$$NH_4^+(aq) + H_2O(aq) \rightleftharpoons H_3O^+(aq) + NH_3(aq)$$

$$pH = pK_a + \log\frac{[NH_3]}{[NH_4^+]} = 9.25 + \log\frac{[0.080]}{[0.050]} = 9.25 + 0.20 = 9.45$$

10.20

$$pH = pK_a + \log\frac{[HCO_3^-]}{[H_2CO_3]}; \quad 7.40 = 6.37 + \log\frac{[HCO_3^-]}{[H_2CO_3]}$$

$$\log\frac{[HCO_3^-]}{[H_2CO_3]} = 1.03; \quad \frac{[HCO_3^-]}{[H_2CO_3]} = 10.7$$

The ratio of bicarbonate ion to carbonic acid is 10.7, indicating that more than 90% of dissolved CO_2 exists as bicarbonate at pH = 7.4

10.21 You can see that there are nine HCN molecules and six CN^- molecules in the figure.

$$pH = pK_a + \log\frac{[CN^-]}{[HCN]} = 9.31 + \log\frac{[6]}{[9]} = 9.31 - 0.18 = 9.13$$

10.22, 10.23

Sample	Mass	Molar Mass	# of ions*	Gram Equivalent	# of g-Eq	Normality of 300.0 mL
(a) HNO_3	5.0 g	63.0 g	1	63.0 g	0.079	0.26 N
(b) $Ca(OH)_2$	12.5 g	74.1 g	2	37.0 g	0.338	1.13 N
(c) H_3PO_4	4.5 g	98.0 g	3	32.7 g	0.14	0.47 N

*The "number of ions" refers to the number of H^+ or OH^- ions produced for each mole of acid or base in solution.

10.24 $3 HCl(aq) + Al(OH)_3(aq) \longrightarrow 3 H_2O(l) + AlCl_3(aq)$

$2 HCl(aq) + Mg(OH)_2(aq) \longrightarrow 2 H_2O(l) + MgCl_2(aq)$

10.25 (a) $2 HCO_3^-(aq) + H_2SO_4(aq) \longrightarrow 2 H_2O(l) + 2 CO_2(g) + SO_4^{2-}(aq)$

(b) $CO_3^{2-}(aq) + 2 HNO_3(aq) \longrightarrow H_2O(l) + CO_2(g) + 2 NO_3^-(aq)$

10.26 $2 NH_3(aq) + H_2SO_4(aq) \longrightarrow (NH_4)_2SO_4(aq)$

10.27

10.28 First, write the balanced equation for the neutralization reaction:

$$HCl(aq) + NaOH(aq) \longrightarrow H_2O(l) + NaCl(aq)$$

We see from this equation that one mole of base is needed to neutralize each mole of acid.

$$\text{Moles HCl} = 58.4 \text{ mL} \times \frac{1 \text{ L}}{1000 \text{ mL}} \times \frac{0.250 \text{ mol NaOH}}{1 \text{ L}} \times \frac{1 \text{ mol HCl}}{1 \text{ mol NaOH}}$$

$$= 0.0146 \text{ mol HCl}$$

$$\frac{0.0146 \text{ mol HCl}}{20.0 \text{ mL}} \times \frac{1000 \text{ mL}}{1 \text{ L}} = 0.730 \text{ M HCl}$$

10.29 $2 NaOH(aq) + H_2SO_4(aq) \longrightarrow 2 H_2O(l) + Na_2SO_4(aq)$

Notice that two moles of base are needed to neutralize one mole of acid.

$$\text{Moles NaOH} = 50.0 \text{ mL} \times \frac{1 \text{ L}}{1000 \text{ mL}} \times \frac{0.200 \text{ mol H}_2SO_4}{1 \text{ L}} \times \frac{2 \text{ mol NaOH}}{1 \text{ mol H}_2SO_4}$$

$$= 0.0200 \text{ mol NaOH}$$

$$0.0200 \text{ mol NaOH} \times \frac{1 \text{ L}}{0.150 \text{ mol}} = 0.133 \text{ L NaOH} = 133 \text{ mL NaOH}$$

10.30 $2 KOH(aq) + H_2SO_4(aq) \longrightarrow 2 H_2O(l) + Na_2SO_4(aq)$

(a) $\text{Moles H}_2SO_4 = 16.1 \text{ mL} \times \frac{1 \text{ L}}{1000 \text{ mL}} \times \frac{0.150 \text{ mol H}_2SO_4}{1 \text{ L}} = 2.42 \times 10^{-3} \text{ mol}$

$2.42 \times 10^{-3} \text{ mol H}_2SO_4 \times \frac{2 \text{ Eq H}_2SO_4}{1 \text{ mol H}_2SO_4} = 4.84 \times 10^{-3} \text{ Eq H}_2SO_4$

(b) $\frac{0.004\ 84 \text{ mol KOH}}{0.0215 \text{ L}} = 0.225 \text{ M KOH}$

10.31

$$\text{Moles NaOH} = 9.30 \text{ mL} \times \frac{1 \text{ L}}{1000 \text{ mL}} \times \frac{0.0012 \text{ mol NaOH}}{1 \text{ L}} = 1.1 \times 10^{-5} \text{ mol NaOH}$$

$$\frac{1.1 \times 10^{-5} \text{ mol NaOH}}{0.050 \text{ L}} = 2.2 \times 10^{-4} \text{ M KOH} = 2.2 \times 10^{-4} \text{ M H}_3\text{O}^+; \text{ pH} = 3.66$$

10.32 The salt of a weak acid and a strong base produces a basic solution, the salt of a strong acid and a weak base produces an acidic solution, and the salt of a strong acid and a strong base is neutral.

Salt	Cation is from:	Anion is from:	Solution is:
(a) K_2SO_4	strong base (KOH)	strong acid(H_2SO_4)	neutral
(b) Na_2HPO_4	strong base (NaOH)	weak acid ($H_2PO_4^-$)	basic
(c) MgF_2	strong base ($Mg(OH)_2$)	weak acid (HF)	basic
(d) NH_4Br	weak base (NH_3)	strong acid (HBr)	acidic

Understanding Key Concepts

10.34 In both molecules, the most acidic hydrogen (deepest blue) is bonded to oxygen. Acetic acid is more acidic because its hydrogen is more positively polarized and less tightly held.

10.36 (a) Picture (3) represents a weak diprotic acid, which has dissociated slightly to form the HA^- anion.

(b) Picture (1) represents an impossible situation. H_2A dissociates stepwise to form HA^-. Only when virtually all H_2A has dissociated to form HA^- is A^{2-} formed by dissociation of HA^-.

Acids and Bases

10.38 In water, HBr dissociates almost completely. Water acts as a base to accept a proton, and a solution of H_3O^+ and Br^- results.

10.40 In water, KOH dissociates completely to yield K^+ and OH^- ions.

10.42 A monoprotic acid, such as HCl, has only one proton to donate, whereas a diprotic acid, such as H_2SO_4, has two protons to donate.

10.44 Strong acids: (a) $HClO_4$; (e) HI

Brønsted–Lowry Acids and Bases

10.46 Brønsted–Lowry acids: (a) HCN; (d) H_2CO_3; (f) $CH_3NH_3^+$
Brønsted–Lowry base: (b) $CH_3CO_2^-$
Neither: (c) $AlCl_3$; (e) Mg^{2+}

10.48

	(a)	(b)	(c)	(d)
Base	$ClCH_2CO_2^-$	C_5H_5N	SeO_4^{2-}	$(CH_3)_3N$
Conjugate acid	$ClCH_2CO_2H$	$C_5H_5NH^+$	$HSeO_4^-$	$(CH_3)_3NH^+$

10.50 $HCO_3^-(aq) + HCl(aq) \longrightarrow H_2O(l) + CO_2(g) + Cl^-(aq)$

$HCO_3^-(aq) + NaOH(aq) \longrightarrow H_2O(l) + Na^+(aq) + CO_3^{2-}(aq)$

$H_2PO_4^-(aq) + HCl(aq) \longrightarrow H_3PO_4(aq) + Cl^-(aq)$

$H_2PO_4^-(aq) + NaOH(aq) \longrightarrow HPO_4^{2-}(aq) + H_2O(l) + Na^+(aq)$

10.52 (a) $HCl(aq) + NaHCO_3(s) \longrightarrow H_2O(l) + CO_2(g) + NaCl(aq)$

(b) $H_2SO_4(aq) + 2\,NaHCO_3(s) \longrightarrow 2\,H_2O(l) + 2\,CO_2(g) + Na_2SO_4(aq)$

Acid and Base Strength: K_a and pH

10.54 For the reaction: $HA(aq) + H_2O(l) \rightleftharpoons H_3O^+(l) + A^-(aq)$

$$K = \frac{[H_3O^+][A^-]}{[HA][H_2O]}$$

Since $[H_2O]$ has no effect on the equilibrium, we define a new constant:

$$K_a = K[H_2O] = \frac{[H_3O^+][A^-]}{[HA]}$$

10.56 K_w is the product of the molar concentrations of H_3O^+ and OH^- in any aqueous solution and is numerically equal to 1.0×10^{-14} at 25°C.

$$K_a = \frac{[H_3O^+][OH^-]}{[H_2O]}; \quad K_a[H_2O] = K_w = [H_3O^+][OH^-]$$

10.58 A solution of 0.10 M HCl is 100% dissociated; $[H^+] = [HCl] = 0.10$, and pH = 1. A solution of 0.10 M CH_3COOH is only partially dissociated, and its pH is expected to be higher than 1.0.

10.60 $H_3PO_4(aq) + H_2O(l) \rightleftharpoons H_2PO_4^-(aq) + H_3O^+(aq)$

$$K_a = \frac{[H_2PO_4^-][H_3O^+]}{[H_3PO_4]}$$

$H_2PO_4^-(aq) + H_2O(l) \rightleftharpoons HPO_4^{2-}(aq) + H_3O^+(aq)$

$$K_a = \frac{[HPO_4^{2-}][H_3O^+]}{[H_2PO_4^-]}$$

$HPO_4^{2-}(aq) + H_2O(l) \rightleftharpoons PO_4^{3-}(aq) + H_3O^+(aq)$

$$K_a = \frac{[PO_4^{3-}][H_3O^+]}{[HPO_4^{2-}]}$$

10.62 Urine (pH = 7.9) is weakly basic, since solutions with pH greater than 7.0 are basic. The $[H_3O^+] = 1 \times 10^{-8}$

10.64 The $[H_3O^+]$ of sweat ranges from 1×10^{-4} to 2×10^{-7} — a range of three orders of magnitude.

10.66 The pH of an 0.02 M solution of a strong monoprotic acid is 1.7. The pH of a 0.02 M solution of a strong base is $14 - 1.7 = 12.3$

10.68

		$[H_3O^+]$	pH
(a)	Egg white	2.5×10^{-8} M	7.60 (iv)
(b)	Apple cider	5.0×10^{-4} M	3.30 (i)
(c)	Ammonia	2.3×10^{-12} M	11.64 (iii)
(d)	Vinegar	4.0×10^{-3} M	2.40 (ii)

Most acidic: vinegar, apple cider, egg white, ammonia   *Least acidic*

10.70 (a) pH = 4; $[H_3O^+] = 1 \times 10^{-4}$ M $[OH^-] = 1 \times 10^{-10}$ M
(b) pH = 11; $[H_3O^+] = 1 \times 10^{-11}$ M $[OH^-] = 1 \times 10^{-3}$ M
(c) pH = 0; $[H_3O^+] = 1$ M $[OH^-] = 1 \times 10^{-14}$ M
(d) pH = 1.38; $[H_3O^+] = 4.2 \times 10^{-2}$ M $[OH^-] = 2.4 \times 10^{-13}$ M
(e) pH = 7.96; $[H_3O^+] = 1.1 \times 10^{-8}$ M $[OH^-] = 9.1 \times 10^{-7}$ M

Buffers

10.72 A buffer is composed of a weak acid and its conjugate base. Any added H_3O^+ can react with the conjugate base and be neutralized, and any added OH^- can react with the acid. In either case, the ratio of acid to conjugate base changes only slightly, and the pH of a buffered solution remains nearly constant.

10.74

(a) $pH = pK_a + \log\dfrac{[CH_3CO_2^-]}{[CH_3CO_2H]} = 4.74 + \log\dfrac{[0.100]}{[0.100]} = 4.74$

(b) $CH_3CO_2^- Na^+(aq) + HNO_3(aq) \longrightarrow CH_3CO_2H(aq) + NaNO_3(aq)$.
The added acid is neutralized by sodium acetate.

$CH_3CO_2H(aq) + OH^-(aq) \longrightarrow CH_3CO_2^-(aq) + H_2O(l)$
The added base is neutralized by acetic acid.

10.76

$pH = pK_a + \log\dfrac{[CN^-]}{[HCN]} = 9.31 + \log\dfrac{[0.150]}{[0.200]} = 9.31 - 0.12 = 9.19$

10.78

$pH = pK_a + \log\dfrac{[NH_3]}{[NH_4^+]} = 9.25 + \log\dfrac{[0.10]}{[0.15]} = 9.25 - 0.18 = 9.07$

Concentrations of Acid and Base Solutions

10.80 An equivalent of an acid or base is its formula weight in grams divided by the number of H_3O^+ or OH^- ions it produces.

10.82

Sample	Molar Mass	# of H^+ or OH^-	Gram Equivalent
(a) HNO_3	63.0 g	1	63.0 g
(b) H_3PO_4	98.0 g	3	32.7 g
(c) KOH	56.1 g	1	56.1 g
(d) $Mg(OH)_2$	58.3 g	2	29.2 g

10.84 Since a 0.0050 N solution of any acid has 0.0050 equivalents per liter, 25 mL of a 0.0050 N KOH solution is needed to neutralize 25 mL of a 0.0050 N H_2SO_4. 50 mL of a 0.005 M NaOH solution is needed to neutralize 25 mL of a 0.005 M H_2SO_4 since each H_2SO_4 molecule yields two hydrogens.

10.86 (a) 0.25 mol $Mg(OH)_2$ x 2 Eq/mol = 0.50 Eq $Mg(OH)_2$

(b) Molar mass of $Mg(OH)_2$ = 58.3 g;   1 Eq $Mg(OH)_2$ = 29.2 g

$$2.5 \text{ g } Mg(OH)_2 \text{ x } \frac{1 \text{ Eq}}{29.2 \text{ g}} = 0.086 \text{ Eq } Mg(OH)_2$$

(c) Molar mass of CH_3CO_2H = 60.0 g;   1 Eq CH_3CO_2H = 60.0 g

$$15 \text{ g } CH_3CO_2H \text{ x } \frac{1 \text{ Eq}}{60 \text{ g}} = 0.25 \text{ Eq } CH_3CO_2H$$

10.88 Molar mass of $Ca(OH)_2$ = 74.1 g; 1 Eq $Ca(OH)_2$ = 37.1 g

$$\frac{5.0 \text{ g}}{0.500 \text{ L}} \text{ x } \frac{1 \text{ mol}}{74.1 \text{ g}} = 0.13 \text{ M}; \frac{0.13 \text{ mol}}{1 \text{ L}} \text{ x } \frac{2 \text{ Eq}}{1 \text{ mol}} = \frac{0.26 \text{ Eq}}{1 \text{ L}} = 0.26 \text{ N}$$

10.90 $HCl(aq) + NaOH(aq) \longrightarrow H_2O(l) + NaCl(aq)$

One mole of HCl is needed to neutralize one mole of NaOH.

$$\text{Moles HCl} = 22.4 \text{ mL x } \frac{0.12 \text{ mol NaOH}}{1 \text{ L}} \text{ x } \frac{1 \text{ L}}{1000 \text{ mL}} \text{ x } \frac{1 \text{ mol HCl}}{1 \text{ mol NaOH}}$$

$$= 0.0027 \text{ mol HCl}$$

$$\frac{0.0027 \text{ mol HCl}}{12 \text{ mL}} \text{ x } \frac{1000 \text{ mL}}{1 \text{ L}} = 0.23 \text{ M HCl}$$

10.92 $2 \, KOH(aq) + H_2SO_4(aq) \longrightarrow 2 \, H_2O(l) + K_2SO_4(aq)$

$$0.0150 \text{ L } H_2SO_4 \text{ x } \frac{0.0250 \text{ mol } H_2SO_4}{1 \text{ L } H_2SO_4} \text{ x } \frac{2 \text{ mol KOH}}{1 \text{ mol } H_2SO_4} = 0.000750 \text{ mol KOH}$$

$$\frac{0.000750 \text{ mol NaOH}}{0.0100 \text{ L NaOH}} = 0.0750 \text{ M}$$

Chemistry in Action

10.94 (a) The pH of stomach acid ranges from 2 to 3.

     (b) $NaHCO_3(aq) + HCl(aq) \longrightarrow CO_2(g) + H_2O(l) + NaCl(aq)$

     (c) Molarity of acid at pH 1.8 = 0.016 M

$$\frac{0.016 \text{ mol HCl}}{1 \text{ L}} \text{ x } 0.0150 \text{ L} = 0.000 \, 24 \text{ mol HCl}$$

$$0.000 \, 24 \text{ mol HCl } \text{ x } \frac{1 \text{ mol antacid}}{1 \text{ mol HCl}} \text{ x } \frac{84.0 \text{ g}}{1 \text{ mol antacid}} = 0.020 \text{ g} = 20 \text{ mg}$$

10.96 Bicarbonate reacts with excess H_3O^+ to form H_2CO_3, which goes on to produce H_2O and CO_2 (which is exhaled). This reaction removes H_3O^+ from the blood stream and lowers the serum $[H^+]$, raising pH.

10.98 pH of rain = 5.6; $[H_3O^+] = 3 \times 10^{-6}$ M

General Questions and Problems

10.100

     (a) The ideal gas law (Chapter 8): $PV = nRT$; $n = PV/RT$

$$P = 1.0 \text{ atm}; \quad V = 15 \text{ L HCl}; \quad R = 0.0821 \, \frac{L \cdot atm}{mol \cdot K}; \quad T = 25 \, °C = 298 \text{ K}$$

$$n = \frac{1 \text{ atm } \text{ x } 15.0 \text{ L HCl}}{0.0821 \, \dfrac{L \cdot atm}{mol \cdot K} \text{ x } 298 \text{ K}} = 0.613 \text{ mol HCl}$$

     (b) $\dfrac{0.613 \text{ mol HCl}}{0.250 \text{ L}} = 2.45 \text{ M}; \text{ pH} = -0.39$

10.102 Citric acid reacts with sodium bicarbonate to release CO_2 bubbles:

     $C_6H_5O_7H_3(aq) + 3 \, NaHCO_3(aq) \longrightarrow C_6H_5O_7Na_3(aq) + 3 \, H_2O(l) + 3 \, CO_2(g)$

Sodium bicarbonate is the antacid.

10.104

Both 50 mL of a 0.20 N HCl solution and 50 mL of a 0.20 acetic acid solution contain the same number of moles of acid – 0.010 moles. Because HCl is a strong acid, it is almost completely dissociated in water, and the H_3O^+ concentration approaches 0.20 M. Acetic acid, however, is a weak acid that is only slightly dissociated, and the H_3O^+ concentration is much lower – around 0.002 M. Since the HCl solution has a higher H_3O^+ concentration, it has a lower pH.

10.106 $2\ HCl(aq)\ +\ Ca(OH)_2(aq)\ \longrightarrow\ 2\ H_2O(l)\ +\ CaCl_2(aq)$

$$0.140\ L\ HCl\ \times\ \frac{0.150\ mol\ HCl}{1\ L\ HCl}\ \times\ \frac{1\ mol\ Ca(OH)_2}{2\ mol\ HCl}\ =\ 0.0105\ mol\ Ca(OH)_2$$

$$\frac{0.0105\ mol\ Ca(OH)_2}{30.0\ mL\ Ca(OH)_2}\ \times\ \frac{1000\ mL}{1\ L}\ =\ 0.35\ M\ Ca(OH)_2\ =\ 0.70\ N\ Ca(OH)_2$$

10.108

(a) $NH_4^+(aq)\ +\ OH^-(aq)\ \longrightarrow\ NH_3(g)\ +\ H_2O(l)$
　　　acid　　　　　base　　　　　　conjugate base　conjugate acid

(b) $PV = nRT$; $P = 755$ mmHg; $V = 2.86$ L; $T = 333$ K; $R = \dfrac{62.4\ mmHg \cdot L}{mol \cdot K}$

$$n\ =\ \frac{PV}{RT}\ =\ \frac{755\ mmHg\ \times\ 2.86\ L}{\dfrac{62.4\ mmHg \cdot L}{mol \cdot K}\ \times\ 333\ K}\ =\ 0.104\ mol\ NH_3$$

$$0.104\ mol\ \times\ \frac{53.5\ g}{1\ mol}\ =\ 5.56\ g\ NH_4Cl$$

10.110

(a)　　$Na_2O(aq)\ +\ H_2O(l)\ \longrightarrow\ 2\ NaOH(aq)$

(b) $1.55\ g\ Na_2O\ \times\ \dfrac{1\ mol\ Na_2O}{62.0\ g\ Na_2O}\ \times\ \dfrac{2\ mol\ NaOH}{1\ mol\ Na_2O}\ =\ 0.0500\ mol\ NaOH$

$$\frac{0.0500\ mol\ NaOH}{500.0\ mL}\ \times\ \frac{1000\ mL}{1\ L}\ =\ 0.100\ M\ NaOH;\ pH\ =\ 13.00$$

(c) $0.0500\ mol\ NaOH\ \times\ \dfrac{1\ mol\ HCl}{1\ mol\ NaOH}\ \times\ \dfrac{1\ L}{0.0100\ mol\ HCl}\ =\ 5.00\ L\ HCl$

$5.00\ L\ HCl = 5.00 \times 10^3\ mL\ HCl$

Self-Test for Chapter 10

Multiple Choice

1. What volume of 0.10 M H_2SO_4 will neutralize 30 mL of 0.05 M $Ca(OH)_2$?
   (a) 30 mL   (b) 15 mL   (c) 10 mL   (d) 6.0 mL

2. Which of the following salts is acidic in solution?
   (a) NH_4Br (b) $NaBr$ (c) NH_4CN (d) $NaCN$

3. KCN is the salt of a:
   (a) strong acid and strong base   (b) strong acid and weak base   (c) weak acid and strong base
   (d) weak acid and weak base

4. A solution has a pH of 9. What is the value of $[OH^-]$?
   (a) 5   (b) 10^{-9} (c) 9   (d) 10^{-5}

5. Which of the following is a diprotic acid?
   (a) CH_3CO_2H (b) $Ba(OH)_2$ (c) H_2SO_3 (d) H_3PO_4

6. Look at Table 10.2 and decide which base is a weaker base than F^-:
   (a) $H_2PO_4^-$ (b) HCO_3^- (c) CN^- (d) NH_3

7. Which of the following substances turns phenolphthalein red?
   (a) urine   (b) milk of magnesia   (c) blood   (d) coffee

8. Which of the following bases is an Arrhenius base?
   (a) $NaOH$ (b) $Ca_3(PO_4)_2$ (c) NH_3 (d) LiF

9. In the reaction $Mg(OH)_2(aq) + 2\ HBr(aq) \longrightarrow 2\ H_2O(l) + MgBr_2(aq)$, what is the conjugate acid of $Mg(OH)_2$?
   (a) HBr (b) H_2O (c) $MgBr_2$ (d) can't tell

10. How many water molecules are produced in the balanced neutralization reaction of $H_3PO_4 + Mg(OH)_2$?
    (a) 2   (b) 3   (c) 4   (d) 6

Sentence Completion

1. One _____ of an acid reacts with one _____ of a base.

2. Phenolphthalein turns _____ in basic solution.

3. H_2CO_3 is a _____ acid.

4. The anion of a weak acid is a _____ base.

5. _____ is the splitting apart of an acid into a proton and an anion.

6. An Arrhenius base yields _____ when dissolved in water.

7. _____ is the reaction of an acid with a base.

8. _____ is the measure of a solution's acidity.

9. To completely neutralize 10.0 mL of 1.0 M H_3PO_4, you need _____ mL of 1.0 M NaOH.

10. CH_3CO_2H and $CH_3CO_2^-$ are known as a _____ acid–base pair.

11. The buffer system of blood is the _____ / _____ system.

12. Substances that can act as either acids or bases are _____.

True or False

1. 30.0 mL of 0.10 M H_2SO_4 is neutralized by 30.0 mL of 0.10 M NaOH.

2. A change of one pH unit is a tenfold change in $[H_3O^+]$.

3. H_2SO_4 / HSO_4^- is a good buffer system.

4. All bases are negatively charged.

5. Bicarbonate ion neutralizes more acid than carbonate ion.

6. If the pH of a solution is 7.0, $[OH^-] = 10^{-7}$.

7. Water can act as both an acid and a base.

8. According to the Brønsted definition, an acid is a substance that dissolves in water to give H_3O^+ ions.

9. Ammonia reacts with an acid to yield ammonium hydroxide.

10. Whether an acid or a base is strong or weak depends on its percent dissociation in water.

11. The reaction $H_2O + H_2PO_4^- \longrightarrow H_3O^+ + HPO_4^{2-}$ proceeds in the direction written.

12. One equivalent of $Ca(OH)_2$ equals 37 g.

Match each entry on the left with its partner on the right.

1. Strong acid   (a) $[H_3O^+]$ $[OH^-]$

2. 1 M HCl   (b) Cl^-

3. $[H_3O^+] = 10^{-8}$ (c) pH = 6

4. Alkalosis   (d) HCl

5. K_w (e) 1 N acid

6. Weak base   (f) CH_3CO_2H

7. Strong base   (g) $[OH^-] = 10^{-6}$

8. Salt   (h) Blood pH lower than 7.35

9. $[H_3O^+] = 10^{-6}$ (i) $CH_3CO_2^-$

10. Weak acid   (j) Na_2SO_4

11. 1 M H_3PO_4 (k) 3 N acid

12. Acidosis   (l) Blood pH higher than 7.35

Chapter Outline

I. Introduction to radioactivity (Sections 11.1–11.3).
   A Nuclear reactions (Section 11.1).
     1. A nuclear reaction occurs when a nuclide spontaneously changes to a different nuclide.
     2. Nuclear reactions differ from chemical reactions in several ways.
       a. Nuclear reactions produce different elements.
       b. Different isotopes have the same behavior in chemical reactions but different behavior in nuclear reactions.
       c. The rate of a nuclear reaction is unaffected by a change in temperature.
       d. A nuclear reaction is the same whether an atom is in a compound or is elemental.
       e. The energy change in a nuclear reaction is immense.
   B. The discovery and nature of radioactivity (Section 11.2).
     1. Radioactivity was discovered by Becquerel and the Curies.
     2. Three types of radiation may be emitted:
       a. α radiation: He^{2+} nuclei with low penetrating power.
       b. β radiation: electrons (e^{-}) with medium penetrating power.
       c γ radiation: high-energy light waves with very high penetrating power.
   C. Stable and unstable isotopes (Section 11.3).
     1. All elements have radioactive isotopes.
     2. Most radioisotopes are made in particle accelerators: These are known as artificial radioisotopes.
     3. Radioisotopes have the same chemical properties as their nonradioactive isotopes.
II. Nuclear decay (Sections 11.4–11.7).
   A. Nuclear emissions (Section 11.4).
     1. Alpha emission.
       a. After α emission, the atomic number of the resulting isotope decreases by 2, and the mass number decreases by 4.
     2. Beta emission.
       a. In β emission, a neutron decomposes to a proton and an electron.
       b. The electron is emitted, and the proton is retained.
       c. The atomic number of the resulting isotope increases by 1, and the mass number is unchanged.
     3. Gamma (γ) emission.
       a. Gamma (γ) emission usually accompanies α or β emission and doesn't affect either mass number or atomic number.
     4. Positron emission.
       a. Positron emission occurs when a proton is converted to a neutron and an ejected positron (positive electron).
       b. The mass number of the nucleus is unchanged, but the atomic number decreases by 1.
     5. Electron capture (EC).
       a. EC occurs when a nucleus captures an electron from the surrounding electron cloud, converting a proton into a neutron.
       b. The mass number of the nucleus is unchanged, but the atomic number decreases by 1.

B. Half-life (Section 11.5).
    1. Half-life is the amount of time it takes for half of a sample of a radioisotope to decay.
    2. Half-life doesn't depend on the amount of sample or on temperature.
    3. Each half-life sees the decay of half of what remains of the sample.
    4. Radiocarbon dating uses the decay of carbon-14 to determine the age of archeological artifacts.
C. Radioactive decay series (Section 11.6).
    1. Some heavy radioisotopes undergo a series of disintegrations until a nonradioactive product is reached.
D. Ionizing radiation (Section 11.7).
    1. Ionizing radiation is any high-energy radiation that can create reactive ions when it collides with a chemical compound.
    2. Ionizing radiation converts molecules into highly reactive ions.
    3. Ionizing radiation can injure the body.
        a. Gamma and X radiation are more harmful when radiation comes from outside the body.
        b. Alpha and β radiation are more dangerous when emitted from within the body.
    4. The intensity of radiation decreases with the square of the distance from the source.
III. Detecting radiation (Sections 11.8–11.9).
A. Devices for detecting radiation (Section 11.8).
    1. Photographic film badges.
    2. Geiger counter.
    3. Scintillation counter.
B. Units of radiation (Section 11.9).
    1. The *curie*(Ci) measures the number of disintegrations per second.
    2. The *roentgen* (R) measures the intensity of radiation.
    3. The *rad* (gray in SI units) measures the energy absorbed per gram of tissue.
    4. The *rem* and the *sievert* (SI) measure tissue damage.
IV. Artificial transmutation (Section 11.10).
A. Artificial transmutation occurs when nuclei are bombarded with high-energy particles.
B. After bombardment, a new nucleus is produced.
C. The transuranium elements were all produced via artificial transmutation.
V. Nuclear fission and nuclear fusion (Section 11.11).
A. Nuclear fission.
    1. Nuclear fission occurs when a heavy nucleus fragments after bombardment by a small particle, such as a neutron.
    2. The large amounts of energy released are due to mass-to-energy conversions and are measured by $E = mc^2$.
    3. Many different fission products can result from one bombardment.
    4. In some cases, bombardment with one neutron can cause production of more than one neutron, in addition to fragmentation.
        a. This is called a chain reaction.
        b. If the bombarded sample weighs more than a critical mass, a nuclear explosion can result.
        c. A controlled fission reaction can be used to produce energy.
B. Nuclear fusion.
    1. If two light nuclei are made to collide, a nuclear fusion reaction occurs that produces a combined nucleus plus energy.
    2. Nuclear fusion reactions occur in stars.

Solutions to Chapter 11 Problems

11.1 For α emission, subtract 2 from the atomic number of radon and 4 from the mass number:

$$^{222}_{86}Rn \rightarrow \, ^{4}_{2}He + \, ^{218}_{84}?$$

Then look in the periodic table for the element with atomic number 84:

$$^{222}_{86}Rn \rightarrow \, ^{4}_{2}He + \, ^{218}_{84}Po$$

11.2 Add 4 to the mass number of radon-222 to calculate the isotope of radium:

$$^{226}_{88}Ra \rightarrow \, ^{4}_{2}He + \, ^{222}_{86}Rn$$

11.3

$$^{89}_{38}Sr \rightarrow \, ^{0}_{-1}e + ?$$

The mass number of the product element stays the same, but the atomic number increases by 1, to 7. Looking in the periodic table, we find that ^{89}Y is the element formed:

$$^{89}_{38}Sr \rightarrow \, ^{0}_{-1}e + \, ^{89}_{39}Y$$

11.4

(a) $^{3}_{1}H \rightarrow \, ^{0}_{-1}e + \, ^{3}_{2}He$ (b) $^{210}_{82}Pb \rightarrow \, ^{0}_{-1}e + \, ^{210}_{83}Bi$ (c) $^{20}_{9}F \rightarrow \, ^{0}_{-1}e + \, ^{20}_{10}Ne$

11.5 For positron emission, the atomic number decreases by 1, but the mass number stays the same.

(a) $^{38}_{20}Ca \rightarrow \, ^{0}_{1}e + \, ^{38}_{19}K$ (b) $^{118}_{54}Xe \rightarrow \, ^{0}_{1}e + \, ^{118}_{53}I$ (c) $^{79}_{37}Rb \rightarrow \, ^{0}_{1}e + \, ^{79}_{36}Kr$

11.6 As in positron emission, the atomic number decreases by 1 and the mass number stays unchanged in electron capture.

(a) $^{62}_{30}Zn + \, ^{0}_{-1}e \rightarrow \, ^{62}_{29}Cu$ (b) $^{110}_{50}Sn + \, ^{0}_{-1}e \rightarrow \, ^{110}_{49}In$ (c) $^{81}_{36}Kr + \, ^{0}_{-1}e \rightarrow \, ^{81}_{35}Br$

11.7 Table 11.2 shows the changes brought about by various radioactive decay patterns. Only β emission produces a change of +1 to the atomic number and a decrease in the number of neutrons. The original element was indium ($Z = 49$), and tin ($Z = 50$) is the decay product.

$$^{120}_{49}In \rightarrow \, ^{0}_{-1}e + \, ^{120}_{50}Sn$$

11.8 17,000 ÷ 5730 = 2.97, or approximately 3 half-lives.

The percentage of $^{14}_{6}C$ is (1/2) x (1/2) x (1/2) x 100% = 12.5% of the original sample.

11.9 To determine blood volume, use the formula:

$$R_{sample} = R_{tracer}\left(\frac{V_{sample}}{V_{system} + V_{tracer}}\right)$$

Where $R_{sample} = 0.10\%$, $R_{tracer} = 100\%$, $V_{sample} = 5.00$ mL, and $V_{tracer} = 1.00$ mL
As an approximation, ignore the volume of the tracer, and rearrange the formula:

$$V_{system} = (R_{tracer} \text{ x } V_{sample}) / R_{sample} = (100\% \text{ x } 5.00 \text{ mL}) / 0.10\% = 5000 \text{ mL} = 5.0 \text{ L}$$

It is apparent that the volume of the tracer is very small, relative to the volume of the system.

11.10 Find the point on the graph that represents 50% of the sample remaining. Locate the time that corresponds to this point; this is the half-life – 3 days.

11.11

$$\frac{I_1}{I_2} = \frac{d_2^2}{d_1^2} : I_1 = 250 \text{ units}; I_2 = 25 \text{ units}; d_1^2 = (4.0 \text{ m})^2 = 16 \text{ m}^2; d_2^2 = ?$$

$$d_2^2 = \frac{d_1^2 \text{ x } I_1}{I_2} = \frac{16 \text{ m}^2 \text{ x } 250 \text{ units}}{25 \text{ units}} = 160 \text{ m}^2$$

$$d_2 = 13 \text{ m}$$

11.12

$$\frac{5 \text{ mrem}}{270 \text{ mrem}} \text{ x } 100\% = 1.9\%$$

The annual dose of radiation for most people will increase by approximately 2%.

11.13

$$\frac{44 \text{ } \mu Ci}{1 \text{ mL}} \text{ x } 3.98 \text{ mL} = 175 \text{ } \mu Ci$$

11.14 In Section 11.9, we learned that 1 Gray = 100 rad.

$$0.20 \text{ kGy x } \frac{1000 \text{ Gy}}{1 \text{ kGy}} \text{ x } \frac{100 \text{ rad}}{1 \text{ Gy}} = 2.0 \text{ x } 10^4 \text{ rad}$$

To convert the dose to rem, use the formula rem = rad x RBE, where RBE = relative biological effectiveness factor.

The dose is $2.0 \text{ x } 10^4$ rem if the radiation is primarily γ rays (RBE = 1). Since α radiation (RBE = 20) is 20 times more penetrating than γ radiation, the dose is 20 x $2.0 \text{ x } 10^4$ rad = $4 \text{ x } 10^5$ rem for α radiation

11.15

$$^{241}_{95}\text{Am} \rightarrow {}^{4}_{2}\text{He} + {}^{237}_{93}\text{Np}$$

11.16

$$^{241}_{95}\text{Am} + {}^{4}_{2}\text{He} \rightarrow 2 \text{ } {}^{1}_{0}\text{n} + {}^{243}_{97}\text{Bk}$$

11.17

$$^{40}_{18}\text{Ar} + {}^{1}_{1}\text{H} \rightarrow {}^{1}_{0}\text{n} + {}^{40}_{19}\text{K}$$

11.18 Try to estimate the value of n in the expression $0.1\% = 100\% \times (0.5)^n = 100\% \times 1/2^n$. This expression shows that the amount of radiation decreases to 1/1000 of its initial value. A table of powers of two shows that after 10 half-lives ($n = 10$) the intensity of radiation will have dropped to approximately 1/1000 of its initial activity. If a half-life is 6 hours, it will take 60 hours for the activity of the radiation to reach this level.

11.19

$$^{235}_{92}U + {}^{1}_{0}n \rightarrow 2\,{}^{1}_{0}n + {}^{137}_{52}Te + {}^{97}_{40}Zr$$

11.20

$$^{2}_{1}H + {}^{2}_{1}H \rightarrow {}^{1}_{0}n + {}^{3}_{2}He$$

Understanding Key Concepts

11.22

$$^{28}_{12}Mg \rightarrow {}^{0}_{-1}e + {}^{28}_{13}Al$$

11.24 The illustrated isotope, with six protons and eight neutrons, is ${}^{14}_{6}C$.

11.26

$$^{241}_{94}Pu \rightarrow {}^{241}_{95}Am \rightarrow {}^{237}_{93}Np \rightarrow {}^{233}_{91}Pa \rightarrow {}^{233}_{92}U$$

11.28 The half-life is approximately 3.5 years.

Radioactivity

11.30 A substance is said to be radioactive if it emits radiation by decay of an unstable nucleus.

11.32

Nuclear Reaction	*Chemical Reaction*
Involves change in an atom's nucleus	Involves change in an atom's outer-shell electrons
Usually produces a different element	Never produces a different element
Different isotopes have different behavior in a nuclear reaction	Different isotopes have the same behavior in a chemical reaction
Rate is unaffected by a change in temperature or by a catalyst	Rate changes with a change in temperature or by using a catalyst
Rate is the same, whether the atom is in a compound or uncombined	
Energy change is millions of times larger for a nuclear reaction	

11.34 Ionizing radiation causes cell damage by breaking bonds in DNA. The resulting damage may lead to mutation, cancer, or cell death.

11.36 A neutron in the nucleus decomposes to a proton and an electron, which is emitted as a β particle.

Nuclear Decay and Transmutation

11.38 A nuclear equation is balanced if the number of nucleons is the same on both sides and if the sums of the charges on the nuclei and on any other elementary particles are the same on both sides.

11.40 For an atom emitting an α particle, the atomic number decreases by 2, and the mass number decreases by 4.
For an atom emitting a β particle, the atomic number increases by 1, and the mass number is unchanged.

11.42 In nuclear fission, bombardment of a nucleus causes fragmentation in many different ways to yield a large number of smaller fragments. Normal radioactive decay of a nucleus produces an atom with a similar mass and yields a predictable product.

11.44

(a) $^{35}_{16}S \rightarrow ^{0}_{-1}e + ^{35}_{17}Cl$

(b) $^{24}_{10}Ne \rightarrow ^{0}_{-1}e + ^{24}_{11}Na$

(c) $^{90}_{38}Sr \rightarrow ^{0}_{-1}e + ^{90}_{39}Y$

11.46

(a) $^{109}_{47}Ag + ^{4}_{2}He \rightarrow ^{113}_{49}In$

(b) $^{10}_{5}B + ^{4}_{2}He \rightarrow ^{13}_{7}N + ^{1}_{0}n$

11.48

(a) $^{235}_{92}U + ^{1}_{0}n \rightarrow ^{160}_{62}Sm + ^{72}_{30}Zn + 4\,^{1}_{0}n$

(b) $^{235}_{92}U + ^{1}_{0}n \rightarrow ^{87}_{35}Br + ^{146}_{57}La + 3\,^{1}_{0}n$

11.50

$^{198}_{80}Hg + ^{1}_{0}n \rightarrow ^{198}_{79}Au + ^{1}_{1}H$

A proton is produced in addition to gold-198.

11.52 The four α decays result in a loss of 16 nucleons from the mass number and a reduction of 8 in atomic number. The β decay results in a gain of 1 in atomic number and no change in mass number. The parent isotope, which has seven more protons and a mass 16 units greater than bismuth-212, is thorium-228.

Half-Life

11.54 If strontium-90 has a half-life of 28.8 years, half of a given quantity of strontium-90 will have decayed after 28.8 years.

11.56 (a) An 80% decrease in activity takes place in 2.3 half-lives (Figure 11.4). For selenium-75, this is equivalent to 2.3 x 120 days = 280 days.

(b) 365 ÷ 120 = 3.04, or approximately 3 half-lives.

0.050 g x $(0.5)^3$ = 0.050 x 0.125 = 0.0063 g

Approximately 0.0063 grams of $^{75}_{34}Se$ will remain after a year.

11.58 If the half-life of mercury-97 is 64.1 hours:
7 days = 168 hours ; 168/64.1 = 2.6, or approximately 3 half-lives
30 days = 720 hours ; 720/64.1 = approximately 11 half-lives
5.0 ng x $(0.5)^3$ = approx. 1 ng of mercury-197 remains after 7 days.
5.0 ng x $(0.5)^{11}$ = approx. 2 x 10^{-3} ng of mercury-197 remains after 30 days.

Measuring Radioactivity

11.60 The inside walls of a Geiger counter tube are negatively charged, and a wire in the center is positively charged. Radiation ionizes argon gas inside the tube, which creates a conducting path for current between the wall and the wire. The current is detected, and the Geiger counter makes a clicking sound.

11.62 In a scintillation counter, a phosphor emits a flash of light when struck by radiation. The number of flashes are counted and converted to an electrical signal.

11.64 According to Table 11.6, any amount of radiation above 25 rems produces detectable effects in humans.

11.66

$$28 \text{ mCi} \times \frac{1 \text{ mL}}{15 \text{ mCi}} = 1.9 \text{ mL}$$

11.68

(a) $\dfrac{I_1}{I_2} = \dfrac{d_2^2}{d_1^2}$; $I_1 = 300$ rem; $d_1^2 = (2.0 \text{ m})^2 = 4.0 \text{ m}^2$; $d_2^2 = (16.0 \text{ m})^2 = 256 \text{ m}^2$; $I_2 = $?

$$I_2 = \frac{d_1^2 \times I_1}{d_2^2} = \frac{4.0 \text{ m}^2 \times 300 \text{ rem}}{256 \text{ m}^2} = 4.7 \text{ rem}$$

(b) $\dfrac{I_1}{I_2} = \dfrac{d_2^2}{d_1^2}$; $I_1 = 300$ rem; $d_1^2 = (2.0 \text{ m})^2 = 4.0 \text{ m}^2$; $d_2^2 = (25.0 \text{ m})^2 = 625 \text{ m}^2$; $I_2 = $?

$$I_2 = \frac{d_1^2 \times I_1}{d_2^2} = \frac{4.0 \text{ m}^2 \times 300 \text{ rem}}{625 \text{ m}^2} = 1.9 \text{ rem}$$

Chemistry in Action

11.70 (1) *In vivo procedures* take place inside the body and assess the functioning of organs or body systems. Determination of whole-blood volume using chromium-51 is an example.

(2) *Therapeutic procedures* are used to kill diseased tissue. For example, irradiation of a tumor with cobalt-60 is a treatment for cancer.

(3) In *boron neutron capture therapy (BNCT)*, boron-containing drugs are administered to a cancer patient and are concentrated in the tumor, which is then irradiated with a neutron beam. The boron captures a neutron and undergoes transmutation to produce a lithium nucleus and an alpha particle, which kills the tumor.

11.72 The purpose of food irradiation is to kill harmful microorganisms by exposing food to ionizing radiation, which destroys the genetic material of the microorganisms.

11.74 The body-imaging techniques CT and PET are noninvasive and yield a large array of images that can be processed by computer to produce a three-dimensional image of an organ.

General Questions and Problems

11.76 The region with no filter monitors α radiation, the region with a plastic filter monitors β radiation, and the region with a tinfoil filter monitors γ radiation. This type of badge filters the types of radiation by penetrating power.

11.78 Nuclear reactions occur spontaneously, and no substance can "react with" radioactive emissions to neutralize them.

11.80

$$\frac{I_1}{I_2} = \frac{d_2^2}{d_1^2}; \quad I_1 = 28 \text{ cpm}; \quad d_1^2 = (10 \text{ m})^2 = 100 \text{ m}^2; \quad d_2^2 = (5.0 \text{ m})^2 = 25 \text{ m}^2; \quad I_2 = ?$$

$$I_2 = \frac{d_1^2 \times I_1}{d_2^2} = \frac{100 \text{ m}^2 \times 28 \text{ cpm}}{25 \text{ m}^2} = 110 \text{ cpm}$$

11.82

(a) $^{99}_{42}\text{Mo} \rightarrow {}^{0}_{-1}\text{e} + {}^{99}_{43}\text{Tc}$ ^{99}Mo decays to Tc-99*m* by β emission.

(b) $^{98}_{42}\text{Mo} + {}^{1}_{0}\text{n} \rightarrow {}^{99}_{42}\text{Mo}$

11.84

(a) $^{238}_{94}\text{Pu} \rightarrow {}^{4}_{2}\text{He} + {}^{234}_{92}\text{U}$

(b) The metal case serves as a shield to protect the wearer from α radiation.

11.86 Embryos and fetuses are particularly susceptible to the effects of radiation because their rate of cell division is high.

11.88 Nuclear fission does not require high temperatures or holding materials long enough for nuclei to react. Drawbacks of fission include disposal of radioactive waste and issues of safety.

11.90

(a) $^{253}_{99}Es + ^{4}_{2}He \rightarrow ^{256}_{101}Md + ^{1}_{0}n$ (b) $^{250}_{98}Cf + ^{11}_{5}B \rightarrow ^{257}_{103}Lr + 4\,^{1}_{0}n$

11.92

$^{10}_{5}B + ^{1}_{0}n \rightarrow ^{7}_{3}Li + ^{4}_{2}He.$

11.94 Alpha particles are used for the bombardment.

$^{238}_{92}U + 3\,^{4}_{2}He \rightarrow ^{246}_{98}Cf + 4\,^{1}_{0}n$

Self-Test for Chapter 11

Multiple Choice

1. Bombardment of a uranium-235 atom with a neutron produces three neutrons, which can go on to bombard three more U-235 atoms. How many neutrons are produced after the fourth cycle?
    (a) 12   (b) 36   (c) 81   (d) 108

2. The product of the α emission of $^{146}_{62}Sm$ is:
    (a) $^{146}_{63}Eu$ (b) $^{144}_{61}Pm$ (c) $^{144}_{60}Nd$ (d) $^{142}_{60}Nd$

3. A half-inch-thick piece of plastic blocks 50% of radiation. How much radiation passes through a one-inch-thick piece of plastic?
    (a) 50%   (b) 25%   (c) 12%   (d) 0%

4. The *curie* measures:
    (a) amount of radioactivity   (b) ionizing intensity of radiation   (c) amount of radiation absorbed   (d) tissue damage

5. A sample of a radionuclide has a half-life of 40 days. How much radioactivity remains after 160 days?
    (a) 25%   (b) 12.5%   (c) 6.25%   (d) 0%

6. How many disintegrations per second does one microcurie of a sample emit?
    (a) 3.7×10^{10} (b) 3.7×10^{7} (c) 3.7×10^{6} (d) 3.7×10^{4}

7. If a person standing 100 m from a radiation source approaches to within 10 m of the source, how much does the intensity of the radiation change?
    (a) increases by a hundredfold   (b) increases tenfold   (c) stays the same   (d) decreases tenfold

8. Artificial transmutation was probably used to produce which one of the following radionuclides?

    (a) $^{238}_{92}U$ (b) $^{210}_{82}Pb$ (c) $^{60}_{27}Co$ (d) $^{239}_{94}Pu$

9. Which of the following radioisotopes is not medically useful?

    (a) $^{131}_{53}I$ (b) $^{14}_{6}C$ (c) $^{24}_{11}Na$ (d) $^{60}_{27}Co$

10. In an experiment by the Curies, aluminum-27 was bombarded with α particles. If each aluminum-27 atom captured one α particle and emitted one neutron, what other atom was produced?

    (a) $^{29}_{13}Al$ (b) $^{28}_{14}Si$ (c) $^{30}_{15}P$ (d) $^{31}_{15}P$

Sentence Completion

1. The change of one element to another is called _____.

2. _____ _____ causes the most tissue damage.

3. A chemical compound tagged with a radioactive atom can be used as a _____.

4. All people are exposed to _____ radiation.

5. A nuclear equation is balanced when the number of _____ is the same on both sides of the equation.

6. The age of a sample can be determined by measuring the amount of _____ it contains.

7. The _____ is a unit for measuring the number of radioactive disintegrations per second.

8. In _____ _____, an atom is split apart by neutron bombardment to give small fragments.

9. People who work around radiation sources wear _____ _____ for detection of radiation.

10. PET and CT are techniques for _____ _____.

11. Very light elements release large amounts of energy when they undergo _____ _____.

12. The _____ _____ is the size of a radioactive sample that is needed for a nuclear reaction to be self-sustaining.

True or False

1. If a sample has a half-life of 12 days, it will have decayed completely in 24 days.

2. X rays are considered to be ionizing radiation.

3. The ratio of carbon-14 to carbon-12 in the atmosphere is constant.

4.   Pierre and Marie Curie discovered radioactivity.

5.   A β particle travels at nearly the speed of light.

6.   An α particle travels at nearly the speed of light.

7.   The product of β emission has an atomic number 1 amu smaller than the starting material.

8.   A nuclear power plant can undergo a nuclear explosion in an accident.

9.   The rad is the unit most commonly used in medicine to measure radiation dosage.

10. Radiation causes injury by ionizing molecules.

11. Most of the known radioisotopes are naturally occurring.

12. Many isotopes undergo nuclear fission.

Match each entry on the left with its partner on the right.

1.   Rutherford   (a) α particle

2. $^{245}_{96}\text{Cm}$ (b) Used in cancer therapy

3. $t_{1/2}$ (c) Discovered radioactivity

4. $^{0}_{-1}\text{e}$ (d) Neutron

5.   Becquerel   (e) Used for archeological dating

6. $^{90}_{38}\text{Sr}$ (f) Discovered α and β particles

7. $^{1}_{0}\text{n}$ (g) Natural radioactive element that undergoes fission

8.   P. and M. Curie   (h) Discovered radium

9. $^{60}_{27}\text{Co}$ (i) Transuranium element

10. $^{4}_{2}\text{He}$ (j) Component of radioactive waste

11. $^{14}_{6}\text{C}$ (k) β particle

12. $^{235}_{92}\text{U}$ (l) Half-life

Chapter Outline

I. Introduction to organic chemistry (Sections 12.1–12.5).
  A. The nature of organic molecules (Section 12.1).
    1. Carbon always forms four bonds.
    2. Almost all of the bonds in organic molecules are covalent.
      a. These bonds are polar covalent bonds when carbon forms a bond to an element on the far left of the periodic table.
      b. Carbon can form multiple bonds by sharing more than two electrons.
    3. Organic molecules have specific three-dimensional shapes.
    4. In addition to hydrogen, oxygen and nitrogen are often present in organic molecules.
    5. Organic molecules are low-melting and low-boiling, relative to inorganic compounds.
    6. Organic molecules are usually insoluble in water and don't conduct electricity.
  B. Functional groups (Section 12.2).
    1. A functional group is an atom or group of atoms that has a characteristic reactivity.
    2. The chemistry of organic molecules is determined by functional groups.
    3. Functional groups fall into three categories.
      a. Hydrocarbons.
      b. Compounds with C–X single bonds, where X is electronegative.
      c. Compounds with C=O double bonds.
  C. Structures of organic molecules: alkane isomers (Sections 12.3–12.4).
    1. When hydrocarbons contain more than three carbons, there is more than one way to arrange the carbon atoms (Section 12.3).
      a. Some alkanes are straight-chain alkanes.
      b. Other alkanes are branched.
    2. Compounds with the same formula but different orders of connecting the carbon atoms are called constitutional isomers.
      a. Constitutional isomers have different structures and different properties.
    3. Drawing structures (Section 12.4).
      a. Condensed structures are simpler to draw than structural formulas.
        i. In condensed structures, C—H and C—C single bonds are implied rather than drawn.
        ii. Vertical bonds are often shown for clarity.
        iii. Occasionally, parentheses are used to show a row of —CH_2— groups.
      b. In line structures C and H don't appear.
        i   Each C–C bond is represented as a line
        ii. The beginning or end of a line represents a carbon atom.
        iii. Any atom other than C or H must be shown.
  D. The shapes of organic molecules (Section 12.5).
    1. The groups around a C—C bond are free to assume an infinite number of conformations.
    2. Molecules adopt the least crowded conformation.
    3. Two structures with identical connections between atoms are identical, no matter how they are drawn.
II. Alkanes (Sections 12.6–12.8).
  A. Naming alkanes (Section 12.6).
    1. Straight-chain alkanes.
      a. Count the carbons.
      b. Find the root name.
      c. Add -ane to the root name.

2. Alkyl groups.
   a. Remove a hydrogen from an alkane and replace -ane with -yl.
   b. More than one alkyl group can be formed from some alkanes.
      i.   Isopropyl and propyl are the two groups that can be formed from propane.
      ii. Four groups can be formed from butane.
      iii. Alkyl groups can be substituents on a straight chain.
3. Substitution patterns.
   a. Primary carbon: $R–CH_3$.
   b. Secondary carbon: $R–CH_2–R'$.
   c. Tertiary carbon:
   $$\begin{matrix} & R' \\ & | \\ R–&CH–R \end{matrix}$$
   d. Quaternary carbon:
   $$\begin{matrix} & R' \\ & | \\ R–&C–R' \\ & | \\ & R'' \end{matrix}$$
4. Naming branched-chain alkanes.
   a. Name the main chain by finding the longest continuous chain of carbons and naming it.
   b. Number the carbons in the main chain, starting from the end nearer the first branch point.
   c. Identify and number each branching substituent according to its point of attachment to the main chain.
   d. Write the name as a single word.
B. Properties of alkanes (Section 12.7).
   1. The boiling points and melting points of alkanes increase with the number of carbons.
   2. Alkanes are insoluble in water but are soluble in nonpolar organic solvents.
   3. Alkanes are colorless and odorless.
   4. Alkanes are flammable.
   5. Alkanes with four or fewer carbons are gases, those from C_5 to C_{15} are liquids, and those with more than 15 carbons are solids.
C. Reactivity of alkanes (Section 12.8).
   1. Alkanes are very unreactive.
   2. Reactions that alkanes undergo:
      a. Combustion: alkane $+ O_2 —> CO_2 + H_2O$.
      b. Halogenation: alkane $+ X_2 —>$ halogenated alkane $+$ HCl.
III. Cycloalkanes (Sections 12.9–12.10).
A. Properties of cycloalkanes (Section 12.9).
   1. Cycloalkanes contain rings of carbon atoms.
   2. Cyclopropane and cyclobutane are more reactive than other cycloalkanes.
   3. Cyclohexane exists in a chairlike conformation.
   4. Cycloalkanes have properties similar to those of acyclic alkanes.
   5. Free rotation is not possible around the carbon–carbon bonds of a cycloalkane ring.
B. Drawing and naming cycloalkanes (Section 12.10).
   1. Drawing cycloalkanes.
      a. The cycloalkane ring is represented as a polygon.
   2. Naming cycloalkanes.
      a. Use the cycloalkane as the parent.
      b. Number the substituents.
         i. Start numbering at the group that has alphabetical priority.
         ii. Proceed around the ring to give to the second group the lowest possible number.

Solutions to Chapter 12 Problems

12.1

(a)

carboxylic acid

alcohol

Lactic acid

(b)

ester

C—C double bond

Methyl methacrylate

(c)

carboxylic acid

aromatic ring   amine

Phenylalanine

12.2

(a)

an aldehyde

(b)

a ketone

(c)

a carboxylic acid

12.3

(a)

C_7H_{16} Heptane

(b)

C_9H_{20} Nonane

12.4

12.5

(a)

CH₃CH₂CH₂CH₂CH₃

Pentane

(b)

CH₃
|
CH₃CHCH₂CH₃

2-Methylbutane

(c)

CH₃
|
CH₃CCH₃
|
CH₃

2,2-Dimethylpropane

12.6   *Step 1:* Find a straight carbon chain and draw it as a zigzag line.
Step 2: Add groups to the appropriate carbons, remembering that atoms other than carbon and hydrogen must be indicated.

Condensed Structure	*Straight-chain Backbone*	*Line-bond Structure*

(a)

CH₂CH₃
|
CH₃CHCCH₂CH₂CH₃
|
CH₂OH

(b)

CH₂CH₃ CH₃
| |
CH₃CHCHCH₂CHCH₃
|
CH₃CHCH₂CH₃

(c)

Br   Cl
| |
CH₃C—CHCH₂CH₂CHCH₂CH₃
| |
H₃C CH₂CH₂CH₃

Notice that it is sometimes necessary to change the direction of a group to keep two groups from bumping into each other.

12.7 Reverse the steps in the previous problem.
Step 1: Draw a chain of carbons that is the same length as the longest chain in the line structure.
Step 2: Add condensed groups to the condensed backbone.

| Line Structure | Condensed Backbone | Condensed Structure |

12.8

(a) CH_3CH_2CHO

(b) CH_3COCH_3

(c) $CH_3CH_2CO_2H$

12.9 All three structures have the same molecular formula (C_7H_{16}). Structures (a) and (c) are conformers.

12.10 To solve this problem in a systematic way, use the following method:

(a) Draw the C_7H_{16} isomer having no branches, and replace one of the $-CH_2-$ hydrogens with a $-CH_3$. There are three different isomers:

$$CH_3CH_2CH_2CH_2CH_2\overset{\overset{\displaystyle CH_3}{|}}{C}HCH_3 \qquad CH_3CH_2CH_2CH_2\overset{\overset{\displaystyle CH_3}{|}}{C}HCH_2CH_3 \qquad CH_3CH_2CH_2\overset{\overset{\displaystyle CH_3}{|}}{C}HCH_2CH_2CH_3$$

(b) Continue with the C_6 isomer having no branches, and replace the different kinds of hydrogens with –CH_3 groups, making sure that you don't draw the same isomer.

Line structures:

12.11

12.12

(a)

2,6-Dimethyloctane

(b)

$$CH_3-CH_2-CH_2-CH_2-\underset{3|}{\overset{\overset{\displaystyle CH_2-CH_3}{|}}{C}}-CH_2-CH_3$$
$$\underset{}{\overset{|}{CH_2-CH_3}}$$

CH$_2$—CH$_3$ ⟵ 3-ethyl group

longest chain—a heptane

CH$_2$—CH$_3$ ⟵ 3-ethyl group

(numbers: 7 6 5 4 3| 2 1)

3,3-Diethylheptane

12.13 To answer this problem, draw the straight-chain hydrocarbon corresponding to the parent name, and replace —H's with the groups indicated.

(a)

$$\underset{p\ \ \ s\ \ \ \ s\ \ \ t\ \ \ s\ \ \ p}{CH_3CH_2CH_2\overset{\overset{\displaystyle p\ CH_3}{|}}{CH}CH_2CH_3}$$

3-Methylhexane

(b)

$$\underset{p\ \ \ s\ \ \ \ s\ \ \ s\ \ |\ \ t\ \ \ s\ \ \ p}{CH_3CH_2CH_2CH_2\overset{\overset{\displaystyle p\ CH_3}{\overset{t}{|}}}{CH}\underset{\underset{P\ CH_3}{|}}{CH}CH_2CH_3}$$

3,4-Dimethyloctane

(c)

$$\underset{p\ \ \ \ t\ \ \ \ s\ \ \ \ |\ p}{CH_3\overset{\overset{\displaystyle p\ CH_3}{|}}{CH}CH_2\underset{\underset{q\ \ \ \ \ P\ CH_3}{}}{\overset{\overset{\displaystyle p\ CH_3}{|}}{C}}CH_3}$$

2,2,4-Trimethylpentane

Where p = primary, s = secondary, t = tertiary, and q = quaternary

12.14 There are many answers to this question. For example,

(a)

$$\underset{t}{CH_3CH_2\overset{\overset{\displaystyle CH_3}{|}}{CH}CH_3}$$

2-Methylbutane

(b)

$$CH_3\overset{\overset{\displaystyle H_3C\ \ CH_3}{|\ \ \ |}}{\underset{t\ \ \ \ |q}{CH}\ C}CH_3$$
$$\underset{}{\overset{|}{CH_3}}$$

2,2,3-Trimethylbutane

12.15

(a)

H$_3$C CH$_3$ H H

2,2-Dimethylpentane

(b)

H H H$_3$C CH$_3$ H H

2,3,3-Trimethylpentane

12.16

$$2\ CH_3CH_3\ +\ 7\ O_2\ \longrightarrow\ 4\ CO_2\ +\ 6\ H_2O$$

12.17

Six different mono- and disubstitution products can be formed from the reaction of propane with chlorine.

12.18

(a)

1-Ethyl-4-methylcyclohexane

The parent ring is a cyclohexane. The two substituents are an ethyl group and a methyl group. The ethyl group receives the smaller number because it has alphabetical priority.

(b)

CH₃ |
CH₃CH₂ ⟶ CHCH₃

1-Ethyl-3-isopropylcyclopentane

The parent ring is a cyclopentane. The two substituents are an ethyl group and an isopropyl group. The ethyl group receives the smaller number because it has alphabetical priority.

12.19

(a)

CH₂CH₃
CH₂CH₃

1,1-Diethylcyclohexane

(b)

CH₃

H₃C   CH₃

1,3,5-Trimethylcycloheptane

12.20

(a) Ethylene and propylene are the starting materials for industrial chemicals and plastics.

(b) Synthetic rubber is less sticky and safer for driving than natural rubber.

12.21

Propylcyclohexane

Understanding Key Concepts

12.22

(a)

CH₃CH₂CH with CH₃ and CH₃

12 hydrogens

(b)

CH₃CH=C with CH₃ and CH₃

10 hydrogens

(c)

HC≡CCH with CH₃ and CH₃

8 hydrogens

12.24 In a line drawing, a carbon is assumed to be at the intersection of lines.

(a)   (b)

12.26

(a)

CH₃CH₂CHCHCH₃ with CH₃ and CH₃

2,3-Dimethylpentane

(b)

CH₃CHCH₂CH₂CHCH₃ with CH₃ and CH₃

2,5-Dimethylhexane

12.28 In one of the isomers (b), the methyl groups are on the same side of the ring, and in the other isomer (a), they are on opposite sides.

(a)   (b)

opposite sides   same side

Organic Molecules and Functional Groups

12.30 Functional groups are groups of atoms within a molecule that have a characteristic chemical behavior. They are important because most of the chemistry of organic compounds is determined by functional groups. The reactivity of a functional group is similar in all compounds in which it occurs.

12.32 A polar covalent bond is a covalent bond in which electrons are shared unequally, being more attracted to one atom than the other. For example, the electrons in the C—Br bond of bromomethane are attracted more strongly to the electronegative bromine than to carbon.

12.34

(a)

(b)

12.36 There are many possible answers to each of these questions. For example,

(a)

$$CH_3CH_2CH_2CH_2CH$$

aldehyde

(b)

$$CH_3CH_2CH_2C-OCH_2CH_3$$

ester

(c)

$$HS-CH_2CH_2C-NH_2$$

amide
thiol

Alkanes and Isomers

12.38 For two compounds to be isomers, they must have the same molecular formula but different structures.

12.40 A primary carbon is bonded to one other carbon; a secondary carbon is bonded to two other carbons; a tertiary carbon is bonded to three other carbons; and a quaternary carbon is bonded to four other carbons.

12.42 There are many possible answers to this question and the following question. For example:

(a)

2,3-Dimethylbutane

(b)

Cyclopentane

12.44

(a)

CH₃CH₂CH₂CH₃   CH₃CHCH₃
                  |
                  CH₃

(b)

CH₃CH₂CH₂CH₂OH   CH₃CH₂CHCH₃   CH₃CHCH₂OH   CH₃CHCH₂OH
                        | | |
                        OH   CH₃   CH₃

(c)

CH₃CH₂OCH₂CH₃   CH₃CH₂CH₂OCH₃   CH₃CHOCH₃
                                        |
                                        CH₃

12.46

(a)

CH₃CH₂CH₂CH₂OH   CH₃CH₂CHCH₃   CH₃CHCH₂OH   CH₃CCH₃
                        | | |
                        OH   CH₃   OH CH₃

(b)

CH₃CH₂CH₂NH₂   CH₃CHCH₃   CH₃CH₂NCH₃   CH₃NCH₃
                     | | |
                     NH₂   H   CH₃

(c)

CH₃CH₂CH₂CCH₃   CH₃CH₂CCH₂CH₃   CH₃CHCCH₃
         ‖   ‖   ‖
         O   O   O CH₃

12.48

(a)

CH₃CH₂CH₃   and   CH₃CH₂   are identical.
                           |
                           CH₃

(b)

CH₃—N—CH₃   and   CH₃CH₂—N—H   are isomers.
      | |
      H   H

(c)

$$CH_3CH_2CH_2-O-CH_3 \quad \text{and} \quad CH_3CH_2CH_2-\overset{\overset{O}{\|}}{C}-CH_3 \quad \text{are unrelated.}$$

(d)

$$CH_3-\overset{\overset{O}{\|}}{C}-CH_2CH_2\overset{\overset{CH_3}{|}}{C}HCH_3 \quad \text{and} \quad CH_3CH_2-\overset{\overset{O}{\|}}{C}-CH_2CH_2CH_2CH_3 \quad \text{are isomers.}$$

(e)

$$CH_3CH=CHCH_2CH_2-O-H \quad \text{and} \quad CH_3CH_2\overset{\overset{}{|}}{\underset{\overset{}{CH_3}}{C}H}-\overset{\overset{O}{\|}}{C}-H \quad \text{are isomers.}$$

12.50 All three structures have a carbon atom with five bonds.

(a)

$$CH_3=CHCH_2CH_2OH$$

5 bonds

(b)

$$CH_3CH_2CH=\overset{\overset{O}{\|}}{C}CH_3$$

5 bonds

(c)

$$CH_2CH_2CH_2C\equiv\overset{\overset{CH_3}{|}}{C}CH_3$$

3 bonds   5 bonds

Alkane Nomenclature

12.52

(a)

$$CH_3CH_2CH_2CH_2\overset{\overset{CH_2CH_3}{|}}{C}H\overset{}{C}HCH_2CH_3$$
$$\underset{\overset{|}{CH_3}}{}$$

4-Ethyl-3-methyloctane

(b)

$$CH_3CH_2CH_2\overset{\overset{CH_3CHCH_3}{|}}{C}HCH_2\overset{}{C}HCH_3$$
$$\underset{\overset{|}{CH_2CH_3}}{}$$

5-Isopropyl-3-methyloctane

(c)

$$CH_3\overset{\overset{CH_3}{|}}{\underset{\overset{|}{CH_3}}{C}}CH_2CH_2CH_2\overset{\overset{CH_3}{|}}{C}HCH_3$$

2,2,6-Trimethylheptane

(d)

$$CH_3CH_2CH_2\overset{\overset{CH_2CH_2CH_2CH_3}{|}}{\underset{\overset{|}{CH_3CHCH_3}}{C}}CH_3$$

4-Isopropyl-4-methyloctane

(e)

$$CH_3\overset{\overset{CH_3}{|}}{\underset{\overset{|}{CH_3}}{C}}CH_2\overset{\overset{CH_3}{|}}{\underset{\overset{|}{CH_3}}{C}}CH_3$$

2,2,4,4-Tetramethylpentane

(f)

$$CH_3CH_2\overset{\overset{CH_3CH_2 \quad CH_3}{| \qquad |}}{\underset{\overset{| \qquad |}{CH_3CH_2 \quad CH_3}}{C}}CH_2CH$$

4,4-Diethyl-2-methylhexane

(g)

$$CH_3(CH_2)_7\overset{\overset{CH_3}{|}}{\underset{\overset{|}{CH_3}}{C}}-CH_3$$

2,2-Dimethyldecane

12.54

(a)

4-*tert*-Butyl-3,3,5-trimethylheptane

(b)

2,4-Dimethylpentane

(c)

4,4-Diethyl-3-methyloctane

(d)

3-Isopropyl-2,3,6,7-tetramethylnonane

(e)

3-Isobutyl-1-isopropyl-5-methylcycloheptane

(f)

1,1,3-Trimethylcyclopentane

12.56

(a)

1-Ethyl-3-methylcyclobutane

(b)

1,1,3,3-Tetramethylcyclopentane

(c)

1-Ethyl 3-propylcyclohexane

(d)

4-Butyl-1,1,2,2-tetramethylcyclopentane

12.58   *Structure*   *Error*

(a)

$$CH_3$$
$$|$$
$$CH_3CCH_2CH_2CH_3$$
$$|$$
$$CH_3$$

2,2-Dimethylpentane

The prefix *di-* must appear when two substituents are the same.

(b)

$$CH_3 \quad CH_3$$
$$| \qquad |$$
$$CH_3CHCH_2CHCH_3$$

2,4-Dimethylpentane

You must choose the longest carbon chain as the parent name.

(c)

$$CH_3$$
$$|$$
$$CH_3CHCH_2-\diamondsuit$$

Isobutylcyclobutane

This compound is an alkyl-substituted cycloalkane. Choose the cycloalkane as the parent name.

12.60

$$CH_3CH_2CH_2CH_2CH_2CH_2CH_3$$

Heptane

$$CH_3$$
$$|$$
$$CH_3CH_2CH_2CH_2CHCH_3$$

2-Methylhexane

$$CH_3$$
$$|$$
$$CH_3CH_2CH_2CHCH_2CH_3$$

3-Methylhexane

$$CH_3$$
$$|$$
$$CH_3CH_2CH_2CCH_3$$
$$|$$
$$CH_3$$

2,2-Dimethylpentane

$$H_3C \quad CH_3$$
$$| \qquad |$$
$$CH_3CH_2CHCHCH_3$$

2,3-Dimethylpentane

$$CH_3 \quad CH_3$$
$$| \qquad |$$
$$CH_3CHCH_2CHCH_3$$

2,4-Dimethylpentane

$$CH_3$$
$$|$$
$$CH_3CH_2CCH_2CH_3$$
$$|$$
$$CH_3$$

3,3-Dimethylpentane

$$CH_2CH_3$$
$$|$$
$$CH_3CH_2CHCH_2CH_3$$

3-Ethylpentane

$$CH_3 \quad CH_3$$
$$| \qquad |$$
$$CH_3CH-CCH_3$$
$$|$$
$$CH_3$$

2,2,3-Trimethylbutane

Reactions of Alkanes

12.62

$$CH_3CH_2CH_3 + 5\,O_2 \longrightarrow 3\,CO_2 + 4\,H_2O$$

12.64

General Questions and Problems

12.66

(a)

Testosterone

(b)

Thienamycin

12.68 Testosterone has 4 tertiary carbons, indicated on the structure shown in Problem 12.66(a).

12.70 Since "like dissolves like," lipstick, which is composed primarily of hydrocarbons, is more soluble in the hydrocarbon petroleum jelly than in water.

12.72 Pentane has a higher boiling point than neopentane because London forces, which must be overcome in boiling, are greater for linear than for more spherical or nonlinear compounds with the same number of carbons.

Chemistry in Action

12.74 A chemical feedstock is a simple organic chemical used as the starting material in many organic reactions.

Mastering Reactions

12.76

$$CH_3-CH_2-\overset{..}{\underset{..}{O}}-H + H^+ \rightleftharpoons CH_3-CH_2-\overset{H}{\underset{\overset{|}{+}}{O}}-H$$

Self-Test for Chapter 12

Multiple Choice

1. Which of the following functional groups doesn't contain a carbon–oxygen double bond?
   (a) ether   (b) aldehyde   (c) ketone   (d) ester

2. In which of the following alkanes are carbons not tetrahedral?
   (a) ethane   (b) propane   (c) cyclopropane   (d) cyclohexane

3. How many products can result from chlorination of ethane? (Include products with more than one chlorine.)
   (a) 2   (b) 4   (c) 6   (d) 9

4. How many branched-chain isomers of C_6H_{14} are there?
   (a) 2   (b) 3   (c) 4   (d) 5

5. Which of the following condensed structures doesn't represent a cycloalkane?
   (a) C_3H_6 (b) C_4H_{10} (c) C_5H_{10} (d) C_6H_{12}

6.

$$CH_3CH_2\overset{\overset{\displaystyle CH_3}{|}}{\underset{\underset{\displaystyle CH_2CH_3}{|}}{C}}CH_2\overset{\overset{\displaystyle CH_3}{|}}{C}HCH_3$$

The correct name for the above structure is:
   (a) 3-ethyl-3,5-dimethylhexane   (b) 3-methyl-3-*sec*-butylpentane
   (c) 2,4-dimethyl-4-ethylhexane   (d) 4-ethyl-2,4-dimethylhexane

7. How many secondary carbons are in the structure shown in Problem 6?
   (a) 1   (b) 2   (c) 3   (d) 4

8. Which of the following structures is incorrectly drawn?

   (a) $CH_3CH_2CH_2$ CH_3
   $\quad\quad CH_3CH_2CCH_2CH_2CCH_3$
   $\quad\quad\quad\quad\quad\quad CH_3$

   (b) CH_3 $CH_2CH_2CH_3$
   $\quad CH_3CCH_2CH_2CHCH_3$
   $\quad\quad CH_3$

   (c) CH_3 CH_3
   $CH_3CH_2CHCH_2CHCH_3$

   (d) CH_3 CH_3
   $CH_3CH_2CH_2CHCHCHCH_3$
   $\quad\quad\quad\quad CH_3$

9. How many moles of O_2 are necessary for the complete combustion of one mole of C_6H_{12}?
   (a) 4   (b) 6   (c) 9   (d) 10

10. Which alkyl group has a quaternary carbon when part of a hydrocarbon?
    (a) *tert*-butyl   (b) isobutyl   (c) *sec*-butyl   (d) butyl

Sentence Completion

1. C_{20} to C_{36} alkanes are known as _____.

2. Alkynes are compounds that contain _____ bonds.

3. Alcohols and ethers are functional groups that contain _____.

4. Mixtures of hydrocarbons can be separated by _____.

5. A _____ _____ is a shorthand way of drawing a chemical structure.

6. A _____ carbon is bonded to four other carbons.

7. Organic compounds generally have _____ melting points than inorganic compounds.

8. Cycloalkanes are compounds that contain carbon atoms joined in a _____.

9. Organic molecules are named by the _____ system.

10. Compounds with the same formula but different structures are called _____.

11. _____ is the reaction of an alkane with oxygen.

12. A straight-chain alkane is _____ boiling than a branched-chain alkane.

True or False

1. Cyclohexane and hexane are isomers.

2. A molecule with the formula C_5H_{12} can have the root name pentane, butane, or propane.

3. A cyclohexane ring is flat.

4. The correct name of the following alkane is 1,3-dimethylpentane.

$$\begin{array}{cc} CH_3 & CH_3 \\ | & | \\ \end{array}$$
$$CH_3CH_2CHCH_2CH_2$$

5. The compound 2,3-dimethylbutane has only primary and tertiary carbons.

6. Acyclic alkanes and cycloalkanes have similar chemical reactivity.

7. The C—Cl bond in CH_3Cl is ionic.

8. The compound 1,4-dimethylcyclohexane is correctly named.

9. Alkanes with one to four carbons exist as gases at room temperature.

10. Compounds with many functional groups are more reactive than compounds with few functional groups.

11. 2-Methylpentane and 3-methylpentane have nearly identical boiling points.

12. At room temperature, an alkane exists in a single conformation.

Match each entry on the left with its partner on the right.

1.   RCH=O   (a) Contains polar covalent bonds

2. C_5H_{12} (b) Butyl group

3. $CH_3CH(CH_3)_2$ (c) Ketone

4. $CH_3CH_2CH_2CH_3$ (d) Natural gas

5. $CH_3CH_2CH_2-$ (e) Formula of methylcyclobutane

6. $R_2C=O$ (f) Branched-chain alkane

7. CH_2Cl_2 (g) An alkene

8. $C_{30}H_{62}$ (h) Propyl group

9. C_5H_{10} (i) Aldehyde

10. $CH_3CH_2CH_2CH_2-$ (j) Formula of 2-methylbutane

11. $CH_3CH=CH_2$ (k) A solid

12. CH_4 (l) Straight-chain alkane

Chapter Outline

I. Alkenes and alkynes (Sections 13.1–13.7).
   A. Introduction (Section 13.1).
      1. Alkenes are compounds that have double bonds (—C=C—).
      2. Alkynes are compounds that have triple bonds (—C≡C—).
   B. Naming alkenes and alkynes (Section 13.2).
      1. Find the longest chain containing the double or triple bond and name the parent compound by adding *-ene* or *-yne* to the root.
      2. Number the carbons in the main chain, beginning at the end nearer the multiple bond.
         a. If the bond is an equal distance from each end, begin numbering at the end nearer the first branch point.
         b. Cyclic alkenes are named cycloalkenes, and the double-bond carbons are carbons 1 and 2.
      3. Write out the full name.
         a. Number the substituents, and list them alphabetically.
         b. Indicate the position of the multiple bond by giving it the number of the first carbon in the bond.
         c. If more than one double bond is present, use the endings *-diene, -triene, -tetraene.*
   C. Cis–trans isomerism in alkenes (Section 13.3).
      1. Atoms attached to a double bond lie in a plane.
      2. If each end of the bond is bonded to two different groups, isomerism can result.
         a. When the larger groups are on the same side of the bond, the isomer is cis.
         b. When the larger groups are on opposite sides of the bond, the isomer is trans.
   D. Properties of alkenes and alkynes (Section 13.4).
      1. Nonpolar, insoluble in water, flammable.
      2. Alkane-like in physical properties.
      3. Alkenes show cis–trans isomerism.
      4. Both alkenes and alkynes react at the multiple bond to form addition products.
   E. Organic reactions (Sections 13.5–13.7).
      1. Types of organic reactions (Section 13.5).
         a. Addition reactions occur when two reactants add to form a single product.
         b. Elimination reactions occur when a reactant splits into two products.
         c. Substitution reactions occur when two reactants exchange parts.
         d. Rearrangement reactions occur when a single reactant undergoes a rearrangement of bonds to yield an isomeric product.
      2. Reaction of alkenes and alkynes (Section 13.6).
         a. Addition reactions (Section 13.6).
            i. Alkene + H_2 —> alkane (hydrogenation).
               Alkyne + 2 H_2 —> alkane.
            ii. Alkene + X_2 —> dihaloalkane (X = halogen) (halogenation).
            iii. Alkene + HX —> alkyl halide.
               Direction of addition: X is bonded to the more substituted carbon (Markovnikov's rule).
            iv. Alkene + H_2O —> alcohol (hydration).
               Addition also follows Markovnikov's rule.
         b. Mechanism of addition reactions, using HBr addition as an example.
            i. H^+ adds to the alkene to form a carbocation.
            ii. Br^- adds to the carbocation to form the product.

3. Alkene polymers (Section 13.7).
   a. Simple alkenes of the type $H_2C=CHZ$ (monomer) can add to each other in long chains.
   b. The reaction is started by an initiator, which adds to an alkene to form a reactive intermediate.
   c. The reactive intermediate starts the growth of the chain.
   d. The product is a chain-growth polymer.
   e. Varying –Z varies the properties of the polymer.
   f. Properties of polymers also depend on chain length and degree of branching.

II. Aromatic compounds (Sections 13.8–13.10).
   A. Structure of benzene (Section 13.8).
      1. Benzene is a flat, six-membered ring containing three double bonds.
         a. All carbons in benzene are equivalent.
         b. The structure of benzene is an average of the two conventional structures.
         c. This phenomenon is known as resonance.
      2. Despite having double bonds, benzene is less reactive than alkenes.
      3. Aromatic compounds are nonpolar, water-insoluble, volatile, and flammable.
      4. Some aromatic compounds are toxic and carcinogenic.
   B. Naming aromatic compounds (Section 13.9).
      1. Use "benzene" as the parent name.
      2. For monosubstituted benzenes, the name of the substituent is followed by *-benzene* (no number needed).
      3. For disubstituted benzenes:
         a. Ortho-disubstituted benzenes have substituents in the 1,2 positions of the ring.
         b. Meta-disubstituted benzenes have substituents in the 1,3 positions of the ring.
         c. Para-disubstituted benzenes have substituents in the 1,4 positions of the ring.
      4. Many aromatic compounds have trivial names.
   C. Reactions of aromatic compounds (Section 13.10).
      Aromatic compounds undergo substitution reactions.

   a. Aromatic ring + HNO_3 $\xrightarrow{H_2SO_4}$ Nitroaromatic ring

   b. Aromatic ring + X_2 $\xrightarrow{FeX_3}$ Haloaromatic ring

   c. Aromatic ring + SO_3 $\xrightarrow{H_2SO_4}$ Aromatic sulfonic acid

Solutions to Chapter 13 Problems

13.1

(a) 2-methyl → CH_3

$CH_3CH_2CH_2CH=CHCHCH_3$
  7   6   5   4   3 2 1

2-Methyl-3-heptene

(b)

  6   5 4 3 2 1
$H_2C=CHCH_2CH_2C=CH_2$

2-methyl ⟶ CH_3

2-Methyl-1,5-hexadiene

(c)

3-Methyl-3-hexene

(d)

3-Ethyl-6-methyl-4-octyne

13.2

(a)

$$CH_3$$
$$CH_3CH_2CH_2CH_2CHCH=CH_2$$

3-Methyl-1-heptene

(b)

$$CH_3$$
$$H_3C-C-C\equiv C-CH_3$$
$$CH_3$$

4,4-Dimethyl-2-pentyne

(c)

$$CH_3$$
$$CH_3CH_2CH=CHCHCH_3$$

2-Methyl-3-hexene

(d)

1,3,3-Trimethylcyclohexene

13.3

(a)

2,3-Dimethyl-1-pentene

(b)

2,3-Dimethyl-2-hexene

13.4   (a) Attached to C3: $-H$, $-CH_2CH_3$
           Attached to C4: $-H$, $-CH_2CH_2CH_3$
Since each of the double-bond carbons has two different groups attached to it, 3-heptene
exists as cis–trans isomers:

$$CH_3CH_2CH_2 \qquad CH_2CH_3$$
$$C=C$$
$$H \qquad\qquad H$$

cis-3-Heptene

$$CH_3CH_2CH_2 \qquad H$$
$$C=C$$
$$H \qquad\qquad CH_2CH_3$$

trans-3-Heptene

(b) Attached to C2: $-CH_3$, $-CH_3$
      Attached to C3: $-H$, $-CH_2CH_2CH_3$
Since the two groups attached to C2 are identical, 2-methyl-2-hexene does not exist as
cis–trans isomers:

$$CH_3CH_2CH_2 \qquad CH_3$$
$$C=C$$
$$H \qquad\qquad CH_3$$

2-Methyl-2-hexene

(c) Attached to C2: $-H$, $-CH_3$
     Attached to C3: $-H$, $-CH_2CH(CH_3)_2$

Since each carbon has two different groups attached to it, 5-methyl-2-hexene exists as cis–trans isomers:

      cis-5-Methyl-2-hexene   *trans*-5-Methyl-2-hexene

13.5

      cis-3,4-Dimethyl-3-hexene   *trans*-3,4-Dimethyl-3-hexane

13.6

(a)   (b)

      cis-4-Methyl-2-hexene   *trans*-5,6-Dimethyl-3-heptene

13.7

(a) CH_3Br + $NaOH$ $\longrightarrow$ CH_3OH + $NaBr$

This reaction is a substitution because two reagents exchange parts to give two different products.

(b) $H_2C{=}CH_2$ + HCl $\longrightarrow$ CH_3CH_2Cl

This reaction is an addition because two reactants combine to give one product.

(c) CH_3CH_2Br $\longrightarrow$ $H_2C{=}CH_2$ + HBr

In this elimination reaction, two products are formed from one reactant.

13.8   (a) The reaction is a rearrangement.
       (b) There are 28 hydrogens present in 11-*cis*-retinal.
       (c) One aldehyde and 5 carbon–carbon double bonds are present in 11-*cis*-retinal.

13.9

(a)

(b)

(c)

(d)

13.10

(a)

(b)

(c)

(d)

13.11

In the major product, hydrogen adds to the alkene carbon that already has a hydrogen bonded to it.

13.12

13.13

13.14

13.15

(a)

(b)

(c)

The products are formed in approximately equal amounts.

13.16

CH₃
|
CH₃CH₂C=CHCH₃
3-Methyl-2-pentene

or

CH₂
‖
CH₃CH₂CCH₂CH₃
2-Ethyl-1-butene

$+$ H₂O $\longrightarrow$

CH₃
|
CH₃CH₂CCH₂CH₃
|
OH

13.17 To draw a vinyl polymer: (1) Orient the monomer unit so that the CH₂= end is on the left. (2) Draw the functional group(s) at the other end of the molecule pointing up (or up and down). (3) Break the double bond, and draw a single bond extending from each carbon. (4) Connect a monomer unit to each of the new bonds.

13.18 Reverse the steps in the previous problem to identify the monomer unit of a polymer. (1) Break the bond between the carbon containing the functional group(s) and the —CH$_2$— group to its right. (2) draw a double bond between the two carbons that once formed the carbon chain of the polymer.

(a)

(1)   (2)

(b)

(1)   (2)

13.19

(a) *m*-Ethylphenol   (b) *m*-Chlorotoluene   (c) 1-Ethyl-3-isopropylbenzene

13.20

(a) *p*-Diiodobenzene   (b) *o*-Nitrotoluene   (c) *m*-Xylene

(d) *p*-Nitrophenol

13.21

(a) *o*-Isopropylphenol   (b) *p*-Bromoaniline

13.22

(a)

(b)

(c)

13.23

ortho   meta   para

Understanding Key Concepts

13.24

(a)

2,5-Dimethyl-2-heptene

(b)

13.26

(a)

m-Isopropylphenol

(b)

o-Bromobenzoic acid

13.28

(a)

4,4-Dimethyl-1-hexyne → 3,3-Dimethylhexane

(b)

2,7-Dimethyl-4-octyne → 2,7-Dimethyloctane

Naming Alkenes, Alkynes, and Aromatic Compounds

13.30 Alkenes, alkynes, and aromatic compounds are said to be unsaturated because they have carbon–carbon multiple bonds to which hydrogen can be added.

13.32

Family:	Alkene	Alkyne	Aromatic Compound
Name Ending:	*-ene*	*-yne*	*-benzene*

13.34 There are many possible answers to this question. For example,

(a)

(b)

$CH_3CH_2CH_2C{\equiv}CH$ $CH_3CH_2C{\equiv}CCH_3$ $CH_3\overset{\overset{\displaystyle CH_3}{|}}{C}HC{\equiv}CH$

(c)   (d)

13.36

(a)

$CH_3CH{=}CHCH_2CH_3$

2-Pentene

(b)

2,5-Dimethyl-3-hexyne

(c)

3,4-Diethyl-3-hexene

(d)

$CH_3\overset{\overset{\displaystyle H}{|}}{C}{=}C{-}\overset{}{C}{=}CHCH_3$ with CH_3 and CH_3 substituents

2,4-Dimethyl-2,4-hexadiene

(e)

3,6-Dimethylcyclohexene

(f)

4-Ethyl-1,2-dimethylcyclopentene

13.38

(a)

CH_3CH_2 and H on $C{=}C$ with H and CH_3

trans-2-Pentene

(b)

CH_3CH_2 and CH_3 on $C{=}C$ with H_3C and CH_2CH_3

trans-3,4-Dimethyl-3-hexene

(c)

$H_2C{=}CH\overset{\overset{\displaystyle CH_3}{|}}{C}{=}CH_2$

2-Methyl-1,3-butadiene

(d)

$CH_3CH_2CH_2$ and H on $C{=}C$ with H and CH_2CH_3

trans-3-Heptene

(e)

$O_2N{-}\langle\rangle{-}CH_3$

p-Nitrotoluene

(f)

o-Chlorophenol (Cl and OH on benzene ring)

(g)

1,2-Dimethylcyclobutene

(h)

$CH_3CH_2CH_2\overset{\overset{\displaystyle CH_3}{|}}{C}HCH{=}CH\overset{\overset{\displaystyle CH_2CH_3}{|}}{\underset{\underset{\displaystyle CH_2CH_3}{|}}{C}}CH_2CH_3$

3,3-Diethyl-6-methyl-4-nontene

13.40

CH₃CH₂CH₂CH₂C≡CH   CH₃CH₂CH₂C≡CCH₃   CH₃CH₂C≡CCH₂CH₃
       1-Hexyne   2-Hexyne   3-Hexyne

$$CH_3CH_2CHC\equiv CH \quad CH_3CHCH_2C\equiv CH \quad CH_3CHC\equiv CCH_3 \quad CH_3CC\equiv CH$$

3-Methyl-1-pentyne   4-Methyl-1-pentyne   4-Methyl-2-pentyne

3,3-Dimethyl-1-butyne

13.42

1-Pentene   *trans*-2-Pentene   *cis*-2-Pentene

2-Methyl-1-butene   3-Methyl-1-butene   2-Methyl-2-butene

Alkene Cis–Trans Isomers

13.44 For an alkene to show cis–trans isomerism, each carbon of the double bond must be bonded to two different groups.

13.46 Only 2-pentene exists as cis–trans isomers:

cis-2-Pentene   *trans*-2-Pentene

13.48

(a)

(b)

(c)

cis-3-Heptene   *cis*-4-Methyl-2-pentene   *trans*-2,5-Dimethyl-3-hexene

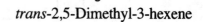

13.50 (a) These compounds are identical:

(b) These compounds are also identical:

Kinds of Reactions

13.52 In a substitution reaction, two reactants exchange parts to give two new products. In an addition reaction, two reactants add together to form a single product, with no atoms left over.

13.54 The conversion of 2-methyl-2-pentene to 1-hexene would be a rearrangement because it is the conversion of a single reactant into a single product by the reorganization of bonds.

13.56

(a)

This reaction is a substitution because two reactants exchange parts to give two new products.

(b)

This is a rearrangement.

Reactions of Alkenes and Alkynes

13.58

13.60

13.62

Addition of HBr to 4-methyl-1-pentyne might form either of the two bromoalkenes pictured above.

13.64

Reactions of Aromatic Compounds

13.66

13.68

General Questions and Problems

13.70

OH

C—OH   Salicylic acid

13.72

Structure	Error

(a)

CH₃CH=CHCH₂CHCH₃ with CH₃ branch

5-Methyl-2-hexene

Numbering should start from the end nearer the double bond.

(b)

CH₃CH₂CH₂CHC≡CCH₃ with CH₃ branch

4-Methyl-2-heptyne

The methyl group can't be bonded to carbon 1.

(c)

CH₃C=CH₂ with CH₃CHCH₃ branch

2,3-Dimethyl-1-butene

The longest chain containing the double bond should be used as the base name.

(d)

O₂N—(benzene ring)—NO₂ with NO₂

1,2,4-Trinitrobenzene

Substituents should receive the lowest possible numbers.

(e)

(cyclohexene ring with two CH₃ groups)

3,4-Dimethylcyclohexene

The double bond receives the lowest number. (For cyclic alkenes, the double bond receives no number but is understood to be between carbons 1 and 2.)

(f)

H₂C=CHC=CHCH₃ with CH₃ branch

3-Methyl-1,3-pentadiene

The double bonds should receive the lowest possible numbers.

13.74 None of the reagents that add to alkenes react with alkanes such as cyclohexane. Thus, you can mix a reagent such as Br₂ with a sample from each bottle. The mixture of cyclohexene and Br₂ turns from reddish-brown to colorless, but the mixture of cyclohexane and Br₂ remains colored.

13.76

Cl—(benzene ring)—Cl   *p*-Dichlorobenzene

13.78

Cinnamaldehyde

The other addition product does not form.

13.80

$$CH_3CH_2CH=CHCH_3 \xrightarrow{HBr} \underset{\underset{Br \quad H}{|\quad|}}{CH_3CH_2CH-CHCH_3} + \underset{\underset{H \quad Br}{|\quad|}}{CH_3CH_2CH-CHCH_3}$$

2-Pentene

The products are formed in equal amounts because each end of the double bond has the same number of hydrogens and the two intermediate carbocations are formed in approximately equal amounts.

13.82

3,4,4-Trimethyl-2-pentene

or

2-Ethyl-3,3-dimethyl-1-butene

$$\xrightarrow[\underset{catalyst}{H_2SO_4}]{H_2O}$$

Chemistry in Action

13.84 The rod cells are responsible for vision in dim light, and the cone cells are responsible for vision in bright light and for color vision.

13.86 Since naphthalene is white, it must absorb color in the ultraviolet range.

13.88 A polycyclic aromatic compound is a compound that has two or more benzene-like rings joined to share a common bond.

Mastering Reactions

13.90

2-Methylpropene   carbocation intermediate   2-Chloro-2- methylpropane

13.92

resonance forms   Br major   Br

Addition of H^+ produces a carbocation that can be represented as two resonance forms. Br^- adds to produce the observed alkene.

Self-Test for Chapter 13

Multiple Choice

1. Which of the following polymers is a hydrocarbon?
    (a) Teflon (b) poly(vinyl chloride) (c) Lucite (d) polystyrene

2.
    $$CH_2CH_3$$
    $$CH_3CH=CHCHCH_3$$
    The name of this compound is:
    (a) 3-methyl-4-hexene (b) 4-methyl-2-hexene (c) 2-ethyl-3-pentene (d) 3-ethyl-2-pentene

3. Which of the following statements about the reaction of benzene with Br_2 is true?
    (a) The reaction is catalyzed by iron. (b) The reaction is an addition reaction. (c) Two different products are formed.   (d) When bromine is added to benzene, the bromine color disappears.

4. Reaction of a hydrocarbon with 2 H_2 gives a product with the formula C_6H_{12}. Which of the following is the original hydrocarbon?
    (a) benzene (b) 3-methyl-1,3-pentadiene (c) 1,4-cyclohexadiene (d) 2-hexyne

5. Which of the following molecules shows cis–trans isomerism?
    (a) 2-hexene (b) 2-hexyne (c) 2-methyl-2-pentene (d) 2-ethyl-1-hexene

6. Which of the following statements about carbocations is true?
    (a) A carbocation has seven electrons in its outer shell.   (b) Two different carbocations can be formed in the reaction of HBr with 3-hexene.   (c) A carbocation is an intermediate in the reaction of HBr with an alkene.   (d) Carbocations are stable ions.

7. How many isomers with the formula C_5H_8 can be drawn? (Don't include isomers with rings or cis–trans isomers.)
    (a) 5 (b) 7 (c) 9 (d) 11

8. Which of the following is probably not a monomer in a polymerization reaction?
    (a) $H_2C=CHCN$ (b) $H_2C=CHCH_3$ (c) $CH_3CH=C(CH_3)_2$ (d) $H_2C=CCl_2$

9. If toluene reacted with one mole of Cl_2, and each of the products of the reaction reacted with one mole of Cl_2, how many different products could be formed? (Not all of these can be formed in the laboratory.)
    (a) 3 (b) 4 (c) 5 (d) 6

10. Which of the following alkenes is not a starting material for 3-bromo-3-methylhexane?
    (a) 2-ethyl-1-pentene (b) 3-methyl-2-hexene (c) 3-methyl-3-hexene (d) 4-methyl-2-hexene

Sentence Completion

1. The name of $CH_3CH_2CH_2CH_2C{\equiv}CCH_3$ is _____.

2. Addition of hydrogen to an alkene or alkyne is known as _____.

3. A benzene ring with substituents at the 1 and 4 positions is said to be _____ disubstituted.

4. In the addition of HX to an alkene, the H becomes attached to the carbon that already has ____ H's, and the X becomes attached to the carbon that has _____ H's.

5. Ethanol can be produced by the _____ of ethylene.

6. In the nitration of benzene, H_2SO_4 is used as a _____.

7. The intermediate formed during the addition of HBr to an alkene is called a _____.

8. Compounds with double or triple bonds are said to be _____.

9. _____ is another name for methylbenzene.

10. The reaction of Br_2 with benzene is an example of a _____ reaction.

11. _____ _____ _____ are aromatic compounds consisting of two or more rings joined together by a common bond.

12. Simple alkenes are made by _____ _____ of natural gas and petroleum.

True or False

1. Cis–trans isomers have identical physical properties.

2. Addition of one equivalent of H_2 to an alkyne yields an alkene.

3. Aromatic compounds are less reactive than alkenes.

4. The product of addition of HBr to 1-butene is 1-bromobutane.

5. The reaction of HBr with an alkene is known as halogenation.

6. A compound with the formula C_4H_6 can be either an alkyne or an alkene.

7. 1-Methylcyclohexene can exhibit cis–trans isomerism.

8. Mixing an alkene with water causes the hydration of the double bond.

9. Addition of HBr to an alkene is a two-step reaction.

10. Benzene and 1-butene react with Br_2 under the same reaction conditions.

11. Only aromatic compounds with more than one ring are carcinogenic.

12. Two different compounds result from the reaction of HBr with 2-pentene.

Match each entry on the left with its partner on the right.

1. HNO_3, H_2SO_4 (a) Alkene without cis–trans isomers

2. H_2O, H_2SO_4 (b) Used to hydrogenate an alkene

3. $CH_3C\equiv CH$ (c) Polycyclic aromatic hydrocarbon

4.   Hydroxybenzene   (d) Addition reaction

5. H_2, Pd   (e) Used to nitrate aromatic compounds

6. $(CH_3)_2CH^+$ (f) Substitution reaction

7.   Propene + Br_2 (g) Exhibits cis–trans isomerism

8.   Naphthalene   (h) Teflon monomer

9.   2-Methylpropene   (i) Alkyne

10. Benzene + Br_2 (j) Phenol

11. 2-Butene   (k) Used to hydrate an alkene

12. $CF_2=CF_2$ (l) Carbocation

Chapter Outline

I. Compounds containing oxygen (Sections 14.1–14.8).
   A. Introduction (Section 14.1).
      1. In all of these compounds, oxygen forms a single bond to either carbon or hydrogen.
      2. Alcohols (R—OH), phenols (Ar—OH), and ethers (R—O—R) are examples of these compounds.
         a. Many alcohols resemble water in their physical properties.
         b. Alcohols (and phenols) can form hydrogen bonds, which raise their boiling points.
   B. Alcohols (Sections 14.2–14.5).
      1. Common alcohols are methanol, ethanol, isopropanol, ethylene glycol, and glycerol (Section 14.2).
      2. Naming alcohols (Section 14.3).
         a. Find the longest chain containing the hydroxyl group, and name the chain by replacing the -e ending of the corresponding alkane with -ol.
         b. Number the carbon atoms in the main chain, beginning at the end nearer the –OH group.
         c. Write the name.
            i. Place the number of the —OH group immediately before the parent compound name.
            ii. Number all other substituents according to their positions and list them alphabetically.
         d. Diols are often known as glycols.
         e. Alcohols can be classified according to the number of substituents bonded to the —OH carbon.
            i. If there is one substituent (RCH_2OH), the alcohol is primary.
            ii. If there are two substituents (R_2CHOH), the alcohol is secondary.
            iii. If there are three substituents (R_3COH), the alcohol is tertiary.
      3. Properties of alcohols (Section 14.4).
         a. Hydrogen bonding makes alcohols higher boiling than other compounds of similar mass.
         b. Hydrogen bonding also makes smaller alcohols miscible with water, as well as with organic solvents.
            i. Alcohols of higher mass aren't soluble.
            ii. Diols (glycols) are even more soluble than alcohols of similar mass.
         c. Alcohols are weak acids.
      4. Reactions of alcohols (Section 14.5).
         a. Dehydration: alcohol $\xrightarrow{\text{H}_2\text{SO}_4}$ alkene + H_2O
            If more than one product is possible, the product with the more substituted double bond will be favored.
         b. Oxidation:
            i. Primary alcohol $\xrightarrow{[O]}$ aldehyde $\xrightarrow{[O]}$ carboxylic acid
            ii. Secondary alcohol $\xrightarrow{[O]}$ ketone
            iii. Tertiary alcohol $\xrightarrow{[O]}$ no reaction

    C. Phenols (Sections 14.6–14.7).
        1. Properties of phenols (Section 14.6).
            a. Phenols are named by replacing *-benzene* with *-phenol*.
            b. The properties of phenols are influenced by hydrogen bonding.
                i. Many phenols are water-soluble.
                ii. Phenols are higher boiling than alkylbenzenes.
            c. Phenols are commonly used as disinfectants.
        2. Acidity of alcohols and phenols (Section 14.7).
            a. Alcohols and phenols are weak acids.
                i. Methanol and ethanol are as acidic as water.
                ii. Dissociation of alcohols in water, or reaction of alcohols with sodium metal, produces an alkoxide anion ($^-$OR).
            b. Phenols are more acidic than water.
                i. K_a of phenol is 1.0×10^{-10}.
                ii. Phenols are soluble in dilute aqueous NaOH.
    D. Ethers (Section 14.8).
        1. Names and properties of ethers.
            a. Ethers have two organic groups bonded to the same oxygen.
            b. Ethers are named by identifying the two groups and adding the word "ether."
                i. Some cyclic ethers have common names (ethylene oxide, 1,4-dioxane).
                ii. An —OR group is an alkoxy group.
            c. Properties of ethers.
                i. Ethers are low-boiling and don't form hydrogen bonds.
                ii. Ethers are unreactive.
                iii. Ethers are good solvents for organic compounds.
                iv. Ethers are volatile and flammable.
                v. Ethers are only slightly soluble in water.
                vi. Ethers form explosive peroxides on standing.
        2. Some common ethers.
            a. Diethyl ether is commonly used as a solvent but was formerly an anesthetic.
            b. Ether groups occur in many essential oils.
II. Thiols and disulfides (Section 14.9).
    A. Thiols.
        1. Thiols are the sulfur analogs of alcohols (R—SH).
        2. Naming thiols is similar to naming alcohols, except that the suffix *-thiol* is added to the parent name.
        3. Thiols are important biologically because they occur in proteins.
        4. Thiols stink!
    B. Disulfides.
        1. Reaction of a thiol with a mild oxidizing agent produces a disulfide (RS—SR).
        2. The reverse reaction occurs when a disulfide is treated with a reducing agent.
III. Halogen-containing compounds (Section 14.10).
    A. Haloalkanes are named by considering the halogen as a substituent on a parent alkane.
    B. A few haloalkanes are named by naming the alkyl group and then naming the halide.
    C. Haloalkanes don't occur frequently in nature but are widely used in industry and agriculture.

Solutions to Chapter 14 Problems

14.1

(a)

CH₃CH₂CHCH₃
        |
        OH

an alcohol

(b)

⬡—OH

an alcohol

(c)

⌬—OH

a phenol

(d)

⌬—CH₂OH

an alcohol

(e)

⌬—OCH₃

an ether

(f)

CH₃CHOCH₂CH₃
   |
   CH₃

an ether

14.2 Even though ethers can't form hydrogen bonds with each other, they can form hydrogen bonds with water: the ether oxygen lone-pair electrons can hydrogen bond with the hydrogens of water.

14.3

(a)

      CH₃
       |
CH₃CHCH₂CH₂CH₂OH

4-Methyl-1-pentanol
primary alcohol

(b)

HO—ˢ   ᵗ—CH₃
            OH

1-Methyl-1,3-cyclopentanediol
secondary, tertiary alcohol

(c)

               CH₃
                |
CH₃CH₂CH₂CHCHCH₃
             |
             OH

2-Methyl-3-hexanol
secondary alcohol

(d)

                  OH
                  |
CH₃CH₂CH₂CH₂CHCH₂CH₃

3-Heptanol
secondary alcohol

(e)

—OH   2,3-Diethylcyclohexanol
       secondary alcohol

14.4

(a)

      CH₃
       |
H₃C—C—OH
       |
      CH₃

2-Methyl-2-propanol
(*tert*-Butyl alcohol)
tertiary alcohol

(b)

OH

3-Methyl-2-pentanol
secondary alcohol

(c)

CH₃CH₂CHCH₂CH₂CHCH₃ with CH₂OH above and Cl below

5-Chloro-2-ethyl-1-hexanol
primary alcohol

(d)

cyclopentane ring with two —OH groups

1,2-Cyclopentanediol
secondary alcohol

14.5   See Problems 14.3 and 14.4.

14.6

Highest boiling: HOCH₂CHCH₂OH, CH₃CHCH₂OH, CH₃CH₂CH₂OH, CH₃CH₂CH₃ *Lowest boiling*
                        OH   OH

14.7   *Most soluble:* (b) > (c) > (a) *Least soluble*

(a)

CH₃(CH₂)₁₀CH₂OH

The hydrocarbon part makes this alcohol water-insoluble.

(b)

OH
CH₃CH₂CHCH₃

Water-soluble.

(c)

CH₃CH₂OCH₃

An ether – slightly water-soluble.

14.8

(a)

CH₃CH—CH₂ (with H and OH circled)   →(H₂SO₄)→   CH₃CH=CH₂ + H₂O

(b)

cyclohexane with H and OH circled   →(H₂SO₄)→   cyclohexene + H₂O

(c)

CH₂—CH—CHCHCH₃ (with H, OH, H, CH₃)   →(H₂SO₄)→   H₂C=CHCH₂CHCH₃ (CH₃) + CH₃CH=CHCHCH₃ (CH₃) + H₂O
                                                        minor   major

14.9

(a)

OH   OH
CH₃CHCHCH₃   *or*   CH₃CH₂CCH₃   →(H₂SO₄)→   CH₃CH=CCH₃ + H₂O
     CH₃   CH₃   CH₃

14.10

14.11

(a)

(b)

(c)

14.12

(a)

(b)

(c)

14.13

(a)

14.18

BHA and BHT inhibit free-radical chain reactions by donating an –H to the free radical, interrupting the chain reaction.

14.19

(a)

$$2\ CH_3CH_2CH_2SH \xrightarrow{[O]} CH_3CH_2CH_2S-SCH_2CH_2CH_3 + H_2O$$

(b)

14.20

(a)   (b)

1-Chloro-1-ethylcyclopentane   3-Bromo-5-methylheptane

Understanding Key Concepts

14.22

14.24

Alcohols, Ethers, and Phenols

14.26 *Alcohols* have an —OH group bonded to an alkane-like carbon atom.
Ethers have an oxygen atom bonded to two carbon atoms.
Phenols have an —OH group bonded to a carbon of an aromatic ring.

an alcohol   an ether   a phenol

14.28 Alcohols contain —OH groups, which can form hydrogen bonds to each other. Since extra energy (heat) must be supplied to break these hydrogen bonds, alcohols have higher boiling points than ethers, which can't form hydrogen bonds.

14.30

Prednisone

14.32, 14.36

(a)

2-Methyl-2-propanol
tertiary alcohol

(b)

2-Methyl-1-propanol
primary alcohol

(c)

1,2,4-Butanetriol
* primary alcohol
# secondary alcohol

(d)

2-Methyl-2-phenyl-
1-propanol
primary alcohol

(e)

3-Methylcyclohexanol
secondary alcohol

(f)

3-Ethyl-3-methyl-2-hexanol
secondary alcohol

14.34

(a)

2,4-Dimethyl-2-heptanol

(b)

2,2-Dimethoxycyclohexanol

(c)

5-Ethyl-5-methyl-1-heptanol

(d)

3,4-Diethyl-2-hexanol

(e)

2,3,-Dimethyl-5-phenylcyclooctanol

(f)

3,3-Diethyl-1,6-heptanediol

14.36 See Problem 14.32.

14.38

Compound	Boiling Point	Reason
Hexanol	Highest	Forms hydrogen bonds
Dipropyl ether	Middle	Polar, but doesn't form hydrogen bonds
Hexane	Lowest	Nonpolar

Reactions of Alcohols

14.40 A ketone is formed on oxidation of a secondary alcohol:

A secondary alcohol   A ketone

14.42 A carboxylic acid is formed when a primary alcohol is oxidized with an excess of oxidizing agent.

a primary alcohol   an aldehyde   a carboxylic acid

14.44 Phenols are more acidic than alcohols and are converted into their sodium salts on reaction with NaOH. Thus, the phenol dissolves in aqueous NaOH but the alcohol doesn't.

14.46

(a)

CH₂CH₃ ... OH, H₂SO₄ → CH₂CH₃ ... CH₂CH₃ + H₂O

(b)

(top) H₂SO₄ → + H₂O

or

H₂SO₄ → + H₂O

(c)

$$CH_3CH_2CH_2CH_2\overset{OH}{\underset{C_6H_5}{C}}CH_3 \xrightarrow{H_2SO_4} CH_3CH_2CH_2CH=C\overset{CH_3}{\underset{C_6H_5}{}} + H_2O$$

or

$$CH_3CH_2CH_2\overset{OH}{C}HCHCH_3 \xrightarrow{H_2SO_4} CH_3CH_2CH_2CH=C\overset{CH_3}{\underset{C_6H_5}{}} + H_2O$$

The product shown is the major product because three groups are attached to the double bond.

(d)

OH ... H₂SO₄ → + H₂O

(e)

$$HOCH_2CH_2CH_2CH_2CH_2OH \xrightarrow{xs\ H_2SO_4} H_2C=CHCH_2CH=CH_2 + 2\ H_2O$$

This is the only route that gives the desired product cleanly.

(f)

or

14.48

(a)

(b)

(c)

(d)

(e)

(f)

Thiols and Disulfides

14.50 The most noticeable characteristic of thiols is their nasty odor.

14.52

Cysteine   Cysteine disulfide

14.54 Propanol is high boiling because its —OH groups can form hydrogen bonds. The —SH groups of ethanethiol don't form hydrogen bonds, and thus ethanethiol has a lower boiling point, as does chloroethane, which also doesn't form hydrogen bonds.

General Questions and Problems

14.56 Straight-chain alcohol isomers of $C_5H_{12}O$:

1-Pentanol   2-Pentanol   3-Pentanol

Straight-chain ether isomers of $C_4H_{10}O$:

Ethyl propyl ether   Methyl butyl ether

14.58 Alcohols become less soluble with increasing hydrocarbon chain length because the effect of the lengthening water-insoluble hydrocarbon chain becomes more important than the effect of the polar hydroxyl group.

14.60 An antiseptic kills microorganisms on living tissue; a disinfectant is toxic and is used only to kill microorganisms on surfaces.

14.62

(a)   (b)

Br—⬡—Br   BrCH=CCH₂CH₃
                                              |
                                              Br

p-Dibromobenzene   1,2-Dibromo-1-butene

(c)

OCH₃

CH₂CH₂CH₃

m-Propylanisole
or
m-Methoxypropylbenzene

(d)

Br

Br

1,1-Dibromocyclopentane

(e)

OH   OH
| |
CH₃CCH₂CCH₃
| |
CH₃ CH₃

2,4-Dimethyl-2,4-pentanediol

(f)

HO OH   OH
| | |
CH₃CH₂CHCHCH₂CHCH₃
        |
        CH₃

4-Methyl-2,4,5-heptanetriol

(g)

Br   CH₃
| |
CH₃C≡CCHCH₂CCH₃
       |
       CH₃

4-Bromo-6,6-dimethyl-2-heptyne

(h)

Cl

I

1-Chloro-2-iodocyclobutane

14.64

CH₃   CH₃
| |
CH₃C=CHCH₂CH₂C=CHCH₂OH   →[O]→
3,7-Dimethyl-2,6-octadien-1-ol

CH₃   CH₃ O
| | ‖
CH₃C=CHCH₂CH₂C=CHC—H
                 Citral

14.66

CH₃CH₂OH + 3 O₂ ⟶ 2 CO₂ + 3 H₂O

Chemistry in Action

14.68 At a blood alcohol concentration of 80–300 mg/dL, speech becomes slurred. At a blood alcohol concentration above 600 mg/dL, death may result.

14.70 In the "breathalyzer test," a person breathes into a tube containing $K_2Cr_2O_7$ (yellow-orange). If alcohol is present in the breath, it is oxidized by $K_2Cr_2O_7$, which is reduced to a Cr(III) compound (blue-green). The color change can be measured accurately enough to indicate blood alcohol concentration.

14.72 Vitamin E appears to be a phenolic antioxidant.

14.74 Minimum alveolar concentration (MAC) is defined as the concentration of anesthetic in inhaled air that results in anesthesia in 50% of patients.

Mastering Reactions

14.76

(a)

(b)

Self-Test for Chapter 14

Multiple Choice

1. Which of the following alcohols yields an aldehyde on oxidation?
   (a) 2-hexanol (b) 2-methyl-2-hexanol (c) 2-methyl-1-hexanol (d) p-chlorophenol

2. Which of the following compounds is least acidic?
   (a) p-chlorophenol (b) 2-butanol (c) HCl (d) acetic acid

3. How many alcohols of the formula $C_4H_{10}O$ are primary alcohols?
   (a) 1 (b) 2 (c) 3 (d) 4

4. Which of the following is known as wood alcohol?
   (a) CH_3OH (b) CH_3CH_2OH (c) $CH_3CH_2CH_2OH$ (d) $HOCH_2CH_2OH$

5.
$$\begin{array}{cc}
\text{HO} & \text{CH}_2\text{CH}_2\text{CH}_3 \\
| & | \\
\end{array}$$
$$\text{CH}_3\text{CHCH}_2\text{CHCH}_2\text{CH}_3$$
   What is the name of the compound shown?
   (a) 4-propyl-2-hexanol (b) 4-ethyl-6-heptanol (c) 4-ethylheptanol (d) 4-ethyl-2-heptanol

6. Which of the following is not a property of alcohols?
   (a) weakly acidic (b) flammable (c) react with acids (d) low-boiling

7. Which of the following is not a product of dehydration of 2,3-dimethyl-3-pentanol?
   (a) 2,3-dimethyl-1-pentene (b) 2,3-dimethyl-2-pentene (c) 3,4-dimethyl-2-pentene
   (d) 2-ethyl-3-methyl-1-butene

8. Which of the following is a cyclic ether?
   (a) enflurane (b) ethylene oxide (c) methoxybenzene (anisole) (d) methyl cyclohexyl ether

9. An alcohol of the formula $C_5H_{12}O$ forms a carboxylic acid on oxidation yet can't be dehydrated by acid. What is its name?
   (a) 1-pentanol (b) 2-methyl-2-butanol (c) 2,2-dimethyl-1-propanol (d) 2-methyl-1-butanol

10. Which reagent doesn't react with alcohols?
    (a) Na (b) H_2SO_4 (c) $KMnO_4$ (d) NaOH

Sentence Completion

1.   The common name for methanol is ___ ____.

2.   Dialcohols are often called _____.

3.   Aromatic compounds called _____ react with NaOH to give salts.

4.   The dehydration of an alcohol yields an _____.

5.   Compounds called _____ are noted for their foul odors.

6.   _____ can be used to oxidize an alcohol.

7.   Ethers are _____ boiling than alcohols of similar molecular weight.

8.   _____ is a phenol used as a food additive.

9.   The major product of alcohol dehydration has the _____ number of alkyl groups attached to the double-bond carbons.

10.   A _____ _____ is a reactive intermediate containing an unpaired electron.

11.   On prolonged contact with air, an ether forms a _____.

12.   _____ is another name for a chlorofluorocarbon.

True or False

1.   Phenols can form hydrogen bonds.

2.   An aldehyde can be formed by oxidation of a secondary alcohol.

3.   Two different alkenes result from dehydration of 2-pentanol.

4.   Another name for phenol is carbonic acid.

5.   Phenols are more acidic than alcohols.

6.   Another name for a thiol is a mercaptan.

7.   Phenol, isopropyl alcohol, and chloroethane are all antiseptics.

8.   Oxidation is the removal of two hydrogen ions.

9.   Several halogenated alkanes are used as anesthetics.

10.   Under careful reaction conditions, a primary alcohol is oxidized to an aldehyde.

11.   Isopropyl alcohol is more toxic than methyl alcohol.

12.   Hydrogen bonding accounts for both boiling-point elevation and water solubility.

Match each entry on the left with its partner on the right (use each answer once).

1. CCl_3F

2. $(CH_3)_2CHS-SCH(CH_3)_2$

3. $CH_3CH(OH)CH_2CH_2CH_3$

4. $CH_3CH_2OCH_3$

5. CH_3OH

6. CH_3SH

7. $(CH_3)_3C-OH$

8. $CH_3CH_2OOCH_3$

9. $(CH_3)_3CCOCH_3$

10. $CH_3(CH_2)_{10}CH_2OH$

11. $CH_3CH(OH)CH_2OH$

12. C_6H_5OH

(a) Peroxide

(b) Thiol

(c) Phenol

(d) Alcohol that is not water soluble

(e) Tertiary alcohol

(f) Forms two alkenes on dehydration

(g) Disulfide

(h) Ether

(i) Glycol

(j) Chlorofluorocarbon

(k) Oxidation product of 3,3-dimethyl-2-butanol

(l) Formed from CO and H_2

Chapter Outline

I. General characteristics of amines (Sections 15.1–15.3).
    A. Classification of amines (Section 15.1).
        1. Amines are classified by the degree of substitution at nitrogen.
            a. Primary amines have the structure RNH_2.
            b. Secondary amines have the structure R_2NH.
            c. Tertiary amines have the structure R_3N.
            d. Quaternary ammonium salts have the structure $R_4N^+ X^-$.
        2. The groups bonded to nitrogen may be alkyl or aryl groups and may also contain functional groups.
    B. Naming amines.
        1. Primary amines are named by identifying the alkyl group attached to nitrogen and adding the suffix -amine.
        2. Secondary and tertiary amines.
            a. If the groups are identical, the prefix di- or tri- is added to the name that would be given if the amine were primary.
            b. If the groups are different, the compound is named as an N-substituted derivative of a primary amine.
        3. The simplest aromatic amine is aniline.
        4. When the amino group is a substituent, the prefix amino- is used.
    C. Properties of amines (Section 15.2).
        1. Amines are basic.
        2. Primary and secondary amines form hydrogen bonds to each other.
        3. Amines can form hydrogen bonds with water.
        4. Simple amines are water-soluble.
        5. Amines have unpleasant odors.
        6. Amines are an important class of biomolecules.
    D. Heterocyclic amines (Section 15.3).
        1. In some nitrogen-containing compounds, nitrogen is part of a ring.
        2. Heterocyclic compounds may be aromatic or nonaromatic.
II. Reactions of amines (Sections 15.4–15.5).
    A. Acid–base reactions of amines (Section 15.4).
        1. Aqueous amines are weak bases that can accept a proton to form ammonium ions.
            a. Nonaromatic amines are stronger bases than aromatic amines.
        2. Amines can react with acids to form ammonium salts.
            a. Ammonium cations of alkylamines are named by replacing the ending -amine by the ending -ammonium.
            b. For cations of heterocyclic amines, -e is replaced by -ium.
        3. Ammonium salts react with hydroxide ion to yield an amine plus water.
        4. In the body, many amines are present as ammonium ions.
    B. Amine salts (Section 15.5).
        1. Amine salts are composed of an ammonium ion (the cation) and an anion.
        2. Most amine salts are much more soluble in water than the amines from which they were derived.
        3. Sometimes amine salts are written as amine·HX.
        4. An amine can be regenerated from an amine salt by reaction with base.
        5. Amine salts can be formed by reaction of an amine with an alkyl halide.

6. If four alkyl groups are bonded to nitrogen, the compound is a quaternary ammonium salt.
   a. Quaternary ammonium salts are usually neither acidic or basic.
III. Alkaloids: amines in plants (Section 15.6).
   1. Many alkaloids are toxic and physiologically active.
   2. Familiar alkaloids are coniine, atropine, solanine, and morphine.

Solutions to Chapter 15 Problems

15.1

(a)

$CH_3(CH_2)_4CH_2NH_2$

primary amine

(b)

$CH_3CH_2CH_2NHCH(CH_3)_2$

secondary amine

(c)

$CH_3\overset{\displaystyle CH_3}{\underset{\displaystyle CH_3}{C}}-NH_2$

primary amine

(d)

secondary amine

(e)

tertiary amine

15.2

(a)

$(CH_3CH_2CH_2)_2NH$

Dipropylamine

(b)

$N-CH_3$
CH_2CH_3

N-Ethyl-N-methylcyclopentylamine

(c)

$-NH-$

N-Isopropylaniline

15.3

(a)

$CH_3CH_2CH_2CH_2CH_2CH_2CH_2CH_2NH_2$

Octylamine

(b)

$CH_3CH_2CH_2CH_2CH_2\overset{\displaystyle CH_3}{N}H$

N-Methylpentylamine

(c)

CH_2CH_3
$-NH$

N-Ethylaniline

(d)

$\overset{\displaystyle NH_2}{C}H_2CH_2\overset{\displaystyle OH}{C}HCH_3$

4-Amino-2-butanol

15.4 Due to the possibility of confusing patients, drug companies do not make their MSDS readily available.

15.5

$$CH_3$$
$$H_3C-\overset{\overset{+}{N}}{\underset{CH_3}{|}}-CH_3$$

Tetramethylammonium ion

The atoms of tetramethylammonium ion form sixteen bonds (12 C—H bonds and 4 C—N bonds) that contain 32 valence electrons. Four neutral carbon atoms, 12 hydrogen atoms, and one nitrogen atom have a total of 33 valence electrons. Since the ion has one electron fewer than the neutral atoms, the ion has a +1 charge.

15.6

$$CH_3CH_2CH_2CH_2NHCH_2CH_3$$

N-Ethylbutylamine

15.7

Lowest Boiling ⟶ *Highest Boiling*

$$CH_3$$
$$CH_3\overset{|}{N}CH_2CH_3 \quad < \quad CH_3CH_2CH_2CH_2NH_2 \quad < \quad CH_3CH_2CH_2CH_2OH$$
$$\text{(a)} \qquad\qquad\qquad \text{(c)} \qquad\qquad\qquad \text{(b)}$$

Alcohol (b), is highest boiling because —OH bonds of alcohols are more polar and form stronger hydrogen bonds than —NH bonds of amines. Amine (a) is lowest boiling because molecules of (a), a tertiary amine, don't form hydrogen bonds to each other.

15.8   In Section 8.2, we learned that a hydrogen bond forms between an electron lone pair of an electronegative atom and a hydrogen bonded to a second electronegative atom. To draw the structures: (1) draw the amine, including the lone pair electrons; (2) form hydrogen bonds between: (i) the amine lone pair and a hydrogen atom of water, and (ii) the amine hydrogens bonded to —N and an electron lone pair of water. In (b), only hydrogen bonds of type (i) can form.

(a)   (b)

15.9

(a)

$$CH_3NH_2 \qquad\qquad CH_3CH_2NH_2 \qquad\qquad CH_3NHCH_3 \qquad\qquad CH_3\overset{|}{N}CH_3$$

Methylamine   Ethylamine   Dimethylamine CH_3

Trimethylamine

Amines that are gases at room temperature.

(b)

Pyridine

A heterocyclic amine

(c)

 —NH₂

Aniline

A compound with an amine group
on an aromatic ring

15.10

(a)

Pyrimidine

C_4H_4N

(b)

Purine

$C_5H_4N_4$

15.11 In a heterocyclic compound containing nitrogen, nitrogen must form part of the ring. Thus, compounds (a) and (d) are heterocyclic nitrogen compounds.

(a)

HN⟩—CH₂CH₂NH₂

heterocyclic nitrogen
compound

(b)

⟨⟩—NH₂

(c)

HO—⟨⟩—CH₂CHCO₂⁻
                    |
                   NH₃⁺

(d)

HO—⟨⟩ CH₂CH₂NH₃⁺

heterocyclic nitrogen
compound

15.12

(a)

(b)

15.13–15.14

(a)

N-Methylisopropylamine   N-Methylisopropylammonium bromide

(b)

Aniline   Anilinium chloride

(c)

Piperidine   Piperidinium chloride

(d)

tert-Butylammonium ion   *tert*-Butylamine

15.15 Review Section 15.4 to choose the stronger base.
 Basicity: nonaromatic amine > ammonia > aromatic amine

(a) Ethylamine is a stronger base than ammonia.

(b) Triethylamine (nonaromatic amine) is a stronger base than pyridine (aromatic amine).

15.16

(a)

Epinephrine
amine

ammonium ion

(b)

Amphetamine
amine

ammonium ion

15.17–15.18

(a)

$$CH_3CH_2CH_2CH_2\overset{\overset{\displaystyle CH_2CH_3}{|}}{\underset{\underset{\displaystyle CH_2CH_3}{|}}{N}}H^+ \; Br^-$$

Butyldiethylammonium bromide
or N,N–Diethylbutylammonium bromide
salt of a tertiary amine

(b)

$$(CH_3CH_2CH_2CH_2)_4N^+ \; OH^-$$

Tetrabutylammonium hydroxide

salt of a quaternary amine

(c)

$$CH_3CH_2CH_2NH_3^+ \; I^-$$

Propylammonium iodide
salt of a primary amine

(d)

$$CH_3\overset{\overset{\displaystyle CH_3}{|}}{\underset{\underset{\displaystyle CH_3}{|}}{C}}HNH_2^+ \; Cl^-$$

Isopropylmethylammonium chloride
salt of a secondary amine

15.19

$$CH_3CH_2CH_2CH_2NH_3^+ \; Cl^-(aq) + NaOH\,(aq) \longrightarrow CH_3CH_2CH_2CH_2NH_2 + H_2O\,(l) + NaCl\,(aq)$$

15.20 Benadryl has the general antihistamine structure illustrated below. Attached to the central skeleton ($-Z-CH_2CH_2N-$) of Benadryl are two methyl groups bonded to nitrogen (R = $-CH_3$) and two phenyl groups (R' = R" = C_6H_5-) bonded to Z (Z = $-CHO-$).

Benadryl

general antihistamine structure

15.21

Benzylammonium chloride

15.22 The most common solubility switches present in biomolecules are carboxylic acid/carboxylate ion, ammonium ion/amine, and interconversions of phosphates, diphosphates, and triphosphates with their protonated forms.

Understanding Key Concepts

15.24

Lysine   NH₂

(a) Both amine groups (as well as the carboxylic acid group) can participate in hydrogen bonding.
(b) Lysine is likely to be water-soluble because it can form hydrogen bonds with water.

15.26

An O$-$H bond of water is broken, and a N$-$H bond is formed in the reaction to form OH$^-$, an ammonium ion and an amine. The electrons remain with their original atoms.

15.28

(a)

(b)

(c)

(d)

Amines and Ammonium Salts

15.30

(a)
$CH_3CH_2CH_2CH_2CH_2NCH_3$

N-Methylpentylamine

(b)

N-Ethylcyclobutylamine

(c)
$CH_3CH_2CH_2$—————NH_2

p-Propylaniline

15.32

(a)

N-Ethyclopentylamine
secondary amine

(b)
—NH_2

Cycloheptylamine
primary amine

15.34 Diethylamine is a stronger base than diethyl ether because amines are more basic than ethers.

15.36

(a)

CH₃CH₂CHCH₃
|
CH₃NH₂⁺ NO₃⁻

N-Methyl-2-butylammonium nitrate
(salt of a secondary amine)

(b)

Pyridinium chloride
(salt of a tertiary amine)

(c)

CH₃CHCH₃
|
CH₃CH₂CH₂CH₂CH₂CH₂NH⁺ Cl⁻
|
CH₂CH₂CH₂CH₃

N-Butyl-*N*-isopropylhexylammonium chloride
(salt of a tertiary amine)

15.38

Cocaine

15.40

Quinine hydrochloride

The nonaromatic nitrogen is protonated first because it is more basic.

Reactions of Amines

15.42

(a)

(b)

(c)

15.44 Choline doesn't react with HCl because its nitrogen atom isn't basic.

General Questions and Problems

15.46 Decylamine is much less soluble in water than ethylamine because it resembles a hydrocarbon more than it resembles an amine.

15.48

PABA

15.50

Acyclovir — related to purine

15.52

	Amines	*Alcohols*
(a)	Foul smelling	Pleasant smelling
(b)	Basic	Not basic
(c)	Lower boiling, due to weaker hydrogen bonds, but higher boiling than ethers or alkyl halides	Higher boiling, due to strong hydrogen bonds

15.54

(a)

CH₃CHCH₂CH₂CH=CHCH₃

6-Methyl-2-heptene

(b)

p-Isopropylphenol

(c)

$(CH_3CH_2CH_2CH_2)_2NH$

Dibutylamine

15.56 Molecules of hexylamine can form hydrogen bonds to each other. Heat must be supplied to break these hydrogen bonds, and thus the boiling point of hexylamine is higher than that of triethylamine, a tertiary amine whose molecules don't hydrogen-bond to each other.

15.58

Baeocystin

Indole

Baeocystin is related to indole.

15.60 Pyridine is soluble in water because the ring nitrogen can form hydrogen bonds with water. No hydrogen bonding is possible for benzene.

Chemistry in Action

15.62 OSHA requires MSDS for occupational use of hazardous chemicals. You might need a MSDS for NaCl if your job involved working with large amounts of NaCl on a daily basis.

15.64

Promazine

Promazine hydrochloride

The nitrogen that is not part of a ring is protonated because it is more basic.

15.66 (a) Forensic toxicologists deal with the effects of toxic agents as they apply to criminal cases, especially cases involving drug abuse and intentional poisonings.
(b) When working with a new toxin, a researcher needs to know the structure of the toxin, its mode of action at the molecular level, and a mechanism to reverse its effects.

Self-Test for Chapter 15

Multiple Choice

1. Which of the following amines is heterocyclic?
   (a) aniline (b) cyclohexylamine (c) pyridine (d) amphetamine

2. Which of the following amines is a secondary amine?
   (a) *N*-methylaniline (b) histamine (c) triethylamine (d) codeine

3. The name of the compound shown below is:
   (a) ethylcyclopentylamine (b) cyclopentylethylamine (c) *N*-cyclopentylethylamine
   (d) *N*-ethylcyclopentylamine

4. An amine and its ammonium salt differ in all respects except:
   (a) charge (b) solubility (c) carbon skeleton (d) basicity

5. Which of the following amines has the highest boiling point?
   (a) triethylamine (b) hexylamine (c) tetramethylammonium chloride (d) dipropylamine

6. Which of the following is an alkaloid?
   (a) atropine (b) amphetamine (c) pyrimidine (d) aniline

7. How many isomers of the formula $C_4H_{11}N$ are secondary amines?
   (a) 2 (b) 3 (c) 4 (d) 5

8. All of the following amines have a heterocyclic ring except:
   (a) nicotine (b) caffeine (c) morphine (d) aniline

9. Propylamine and trimethylamine differ in all respects except:
   (a) formula weight (b) boiling point (c) solubility in water (d) melting point

10. Which of the following is a quaternary ammonium salt?
    (a) anilinium chloride (b) triethylpropylammonium chloride (c) pyridinium chloride
    (d) trimethylammonium chloride

Sentence Completion

1. When the $-NH_2$ group is a substituent, _____ is used as a prefix.

2. Tetramethylammonium bromide is a _____ amine salt.

3. _____ contains nitrogen heterocyclic rings derived from either purine or pyrimidine.

4. _____ is the science devoted to poisons.

5. A _____ has a nitrogen atom contained in a ring.

6. _____ are a class of amines derived from plants.

7. Simple amines are water-soluble because of _____ _____.

8. Most amines can be made water-soluble by conversion to _____ salts.

9. Nitric oxide is a molecule that is a ____ _____ because it has an unpaired electron.

10. Ammonia is less basic than _____ _____.

True or False

1. Amine groups in biomolecules are usually protonated in body fluids.

2. Ammonium salts are water-soluble.

3. Tertiary amines are higher boiling than primary or secondary amines.

4. Morphine and codeine are alkaloids.

5. Quaternary ammonium salts are acidic.

6. Caffeine is a heterocyclic amine.

7. Heroin is a naturally occurring alkaloid.

8. The physical properties of low-molecular-weight amines and ammonia are similar.

9. NO is responsible for elevating blood pressure.

10. The correct name for $CH_3CH_2CH_2CH_2NHCH_3$ is methylbutylamine.

Match each item in the left column with its partner on the right (use each answer once).

1. Trimethylamine

2. Atropine

3. Piperidine

4. Tetramethylammonium chloride

5. Alanine

6. Dimethylamine

7. Pyridoxine

8. Cadaverine

9. Serotonin

10. Methylamine

11. Pyridine

12. Aniline

(a) Amino acid

(b) Vitamin

(c) Primary aromatic amine

(d) Tertiary amine

(e) Aromatic heterocycle

(f) Neurotransmitter

(g) Primary amine

(h) Nonaromatic heterocycle

(i) Quaternary ammonium salt

(j) Secondary amine

(k) Diamine

(l) Alkaloid

Chapter Outline

I. Characteristics of aldehydes and ketones (Sections 16.1–16.4).
  A. The carbonyl group (Section 16.1).
    1. Carbonyl groups are polarized, with carbon having a partial positive charge and oxygen having a partial negative charge.
    2. Carbonyl groups are planar, with a 120° bond angle.
    3. Carbonyl compounds can be divided into two groups:
      a. In aldehydes and ketones, the carbonyl carbon is bonded to atoms that don't attract electrons strongly.
      b. In carboxylic acids, esters, anhydrides, and amides, the carbonyl carbon is bonded to nitrogen or oxygen.
  B. Naming aldehydes and ketones (Section 16.2).
    1. Aldehydes are named by replacing the suffix of the parent compound with -al.
      a. For substituted aldehydes, the carbon chain is numbered with the aldehyde carbon as carbon 1.
      b. Aldehydes with common names are formaldehyde, acetaldehyde and benzaldehyde.
    2. Ketones are named by replacing the suffix of the parent compound with -one.
      a. Numbering starts at the end nearer the carbonyl carbon.
      b. Ketones with common names include acetone and acetophenone.
      c. Sometimes ketones are named by naming the two alkyl groups, followed by the word "ketone."
  C. Properties of aldehydes and ketones (Section 16.3).
    1. Aldehydes and ketones are moderately polar.
    2. Aldehydes and ketones don't hydrogen-bond with each other.
    3. Aldehydes and ketones are soluble in organic solvents.
    4. Simple aldehydes and ketones are water-soluble because they can hydrogen-bond with water.
    5. Aldehydes and ketones have distinctive odors.
    6. Aldehydes and ketones are flammable.
  D. Common aldehydes and ketones (Section 16.4).
    1. Formaldehyde.
      a. Formaldehyde is an irritating component of smog.
      b. Formaldehyde is used as a disinfectant and as a preservative.
      c. Formaldehyde-containing polymers are used in building materials.
    2. Acetaldehyde.
    3. Acetone.
      a. Acetone is a commonly used organic solvent.
      b. Acetone is a product of fat metabolism.
II. Reactions of aldehydes and ketones (Sections 16.5–16.7).
  A. Oxidation (Section 16.5).
    1. Aldehydes can be oxidized to carboxylic acids.
      a. Tollens' reagent converts aldehydes to carboxylic acids and leaves a shiny silver residue on the flask.
      b. Benedict's reagent leaves a brick-red precipitate.
    2. Ketones don't react with most oxidizing agents.

B. Reduction (Section 16.6).
  1. Reducing agents reduce aldehydes to primary alcohols and ketones to secondary alcohols in a two-step reaction.
    a. Hydride ion adds to the carbonyl carbon.
    b. Hydrogen ion adds to the carbonyl oxygen.
  2. In the body, the coenzyme NADH is the reducing agent.
C. Formation of hemiacetals and acetals (Section 16.7).
  1. Hemiacetals.
    a. An alcohol can add to an aldehyde or ketone to form a hemiacetal.
      i. The negatively polarized alcohol oxygen adds to the positively polarized carbonyl carbon.
      ii. The reaction is reversible: Hemiacetals easily revert to an aldehyde or ketone.
    b. Although hemiacetals are often too unstable to isolate, the hemiacetals of sugars are stable.
  2. Acetals.
    a. Hemiacetals can react with a second molecule of an alcohol to form an acetal.
    b. Acetals are stable and can be isolated.
  3. Acetal hydrolysis.
    a. Aqueous acid reacts with acetals to regenerate the original aldehyde or ketone, plus alcohol.

Solutions to Chapter 16 Problems

16.1

16.1

(a) Prostaglandin E₁ — ketone

(b) Testosterone — ketone

(c) Vanillin — aldehyde

(d) $C_4H_9COCH_3$ ketone

(e) C_4H_9CHO aldehyde

16.2

(d)

(e)

16.3

(a)

$$CH_3CH_2CH_2CH_2CH_2CH_2CH_2CH$$ (with =O)

Octanal

(b)

Methyl phenyl ketone

(c)

$$CH_3CH_2CHCH_2CH_2CH$$ (with CH₃ and =O)

4-Methylhexanal

(d)

$$H_3C-C-C-CH_3$$ (with H₃C, H₃C substituents and =O)

tert-Butyl methyl ketone

16.4

(a)

$$CH_3CH_2CH_2CH_2CH$$ (with =O)

Pentanal

(b)

$$CH_3CH_2CCH_2CH_3$$ (with =O)

3-Pentanone
(Diethyl ketone)

(c)

$$CH_3CH_2CHCH_2CH_2CH$$ (with CH₃ and =O)

4-Methylhexanal

(d)

$$CH_3CH_2CH_2CCH_2CH_2CH_3$$ (with =O)

4-Heptanone
(Dipropyl ketone)

16.5

(a)

$$CH_3CH_2CH_2CH_2C-CN$$ (with OH and H)

(b)

$$CH_3CH_2CCH_2CH_3$$ (with HO and CN)

16.6

$$CH_3CHCH_2CCH_2CH_3$$ (with CH₃ and =O)
$$C_7H_{14}O$$

5-Methyl-3-hexanone
a ketone

$$CH_3CHCH_2CH_2CH$$ (with CH₃ and =O)
$$C_6H_{12}O$$

4-Methylpentanal
an aldehyde

16.7

(a)

$$CH_3CH_2CCH_2CH_3$$ (with =O)

polar; flammable;
liquid; b.p.<150 °C

(b)

$$CH_3CH_2C-H$$ (with =O)

polar; flammable;
liquid; b.p.<150 °C

(c)

$$CH_3CH_2CH_2CH_2CH_3$$

nonpolar; flammable;
liquid; b.p.<150 °C

16.8 Alcohols are higher boiling than aldehydes and ketones of similar molecular weight because hydrogen bonding takes place between alcohol molecules, raising their boiling points. Aldehydes and ketones, however, are higher boiling than alkanes of similar molecular weight because aldehydes and ketones are polar and show dipole–dipole interactions, which elevate their boiling points relative to the boiling points of alkanes.

16.9

16.10

16.11 First, draw the aldehyde or ketone so that the C=O group is vertical. Next, break the double bond, and add one hydrogen to the carbon and one to the oxygen. Finally, redraw the product as a condensed structure.

16.12 If the target alcohol is primary, start with an aldehyde. If the target alcohol is secondary, start with a ketone.

16.13 To identify a hemiacetal, look for a carbon with single bonds to two different oxygens. If one group bonded to the carbon is —OH and the other is —OR (R = organic group), the compound is a hemiacetal.

(a)

This compound is a hemiacetal.

(b)

OH   OH
| |
CH₃CH—CHCH₃

This compound is not a hemiacetal.

(c)

This compound is not a hemiacetal.

(d)

This compound is a hemiacetal
(the hemiacetal carbon is starred).

16.14

(a)

(d)

16.15

(a)

(b)

16.16

(a)

(b)

(b diagram)

16.17 Follow the instructions for Worked Example 16.5. If one carbon is bonded to two –OR groups, the compound is an acetal.

(a)   (b)   (c)   (d)

neither acetal   neither acetal   acetal   hemiacetal
nor hemiacetal   nor hemiacetal

16.18

$$70 \text{ kg} \times \frac{0.1 \text{ mg}}{1 \text{ kg}} \times \frac{1 \text{ cap}}{4 \text{ mg}} = 1.75 \text{ caps, or approx. 2 caps}$$

16.19 Find the two –OR groups that form the acetal. Remove them and replace them with =O to form the original aldehyde or ketone. Add –H to the –OR groups to form the original alcohol.

Understanding Key Concepts

16.20 (a) The hydride ion is added to the carbonyl carbon. The carbon end of the polar C=O bond has a partial positive charge, and thus reaction with negatively charged reagents occurs at carbon.

(b) The top arrow (reaction to the right) represents reduction, and the bottom arrow (reaction to the left) represents oxidation.

16.22 In a solution of an aldehyde in water, hydrogen bonds form between the oxygen atoms of the aldehyde and the hydrogen atoms of water. Molecules of aldehyde don't form hydrogen bonds with each other, and the hydrogen atoms bonded to the aldehyde carbon don't take part in hydrogen bonding.

16.24 In solution, glucose exists primarily in the cyclic hemiacetal form shown below because it is more stable in this form.

Aldehydes and Ketones

16.26

16.28

(a)

CH₃CH₂CCH₃

ketone

(b)

amide

ketone   amide

(c)

CH₃CH₂-O-CH₂-CH

aldehyde

(d)

OCH₃
|
CH₃CH₂C-OCH₃
|
OCH₃

no carbonyl group

(e)

ester (lactone)

(f)

O
||
CH₃CCH₂CH₂OH

ketone

Structure (c) is an aldehyde, and structures (a), (b), and (f) are ketones.

16.30

(a)

O
||
CH₃CH₂CHCHCH
|
CH₃

3-Methylpentanal

(b)

O
||
ClCH₂CH₂CHCH
|
OH

4-Chloro-2-hydroxybutanal

(c)

O
||
H₃C-⟨benzene⟩-CH

p-Methylbenzaldehyde

(d)

CH₂CH₃

2-Ethylcycloheptanone

(e)

O
||
CCH₃

Cyclopropyl methyl ketone

(f)

O
||
CCH₃

Acetophenone

16.32

(a)

CH₃
|
CH₃CH₂CCHO
|
CH₃

2,2-Dimethylbutanal

(b)

CHO
|
CH₃CH₂CH₂CCH₃
|
OH

2-Hydroxy-2-methylpentanal

(c)

CHO

3-Methylbutanal

(d)

O

4-Methyl-3-hexanone

(e)

CH₃
HO   O

3-Hydroxy-2-methylcyclohexanone

16.34 (a) The name 1-pentanone is incorrect because a ketone group can't occur at the end of a carbon chain. Correct name: pentanal.
(b) The methyl group should have the lowest possible number. Correct name: 2-methyl-3-pentanone.
(c) Numbering must start at the end of the carbon chain that is closer to the ketone functional group. Correct name: 2-butanone.

Reactions of Aldehydes and Ketones

16.36 A *hemiacetal* is produced when an aldehyde reacts with an alcohol in a 1:1 ratio. No second product is formed.

16.38 Remember that only aldehydes react with Tollens' reagent. Ketones are not oxidized.

16.40

16.42

(a)

(b)

(c)

(d)

16.44

5-Hydroxyhexanal

16.46

16.48

The hemiacetal group is derived from an aldehyde because the hemiacetal carbon has a hydrogen atom bonded to it.

General Questions and Problems

16.50

   p-Methoxybenzaldehyde

16.52 The portion of the odor due to aldehyde is less stable because aldehydes are easily oxidized to carboxylic acids.

16.54

(a)

2-Methyl-3-pentanone

(b)

$CH_2=CHCH_2CH_2CH=CH_2$

1,5-Hexadiene

(c)

m-Bromotoluene

(d)

4,5,5-Trimethyl-3-hexanone

16.56

(a)

2,4-Dinitroacetophenone

(b)

2,4-Dihydroxycyclopentanone

(c)

CH₃C—CH₃ with CH₃ above and OCH₃ below

2-Methoxy-2-methylpropane

(d)

$CH_3CH—CH—CHCH_3$ with CH₃ above, CH₃ OH CH₃ below

2,3,4-Trimethyl-3-pentanol

16.58

(a)

(b)

(c)

(d)

16.60 Treat samples of the two compounds with Tollens' reagent. The aldehyde reacts to yield a silver mirror, but the alcohol doesn't react.

16.62 2-Heptanone is less soluble in water than 2-butanone because 2-heptanone has a longer hydrocarbon chain.

Chemistry in Action

16.64 The cyanohydrin that decomposes to form HCN is nontoxic and is stable inside the millipede's body.

16.66 (a) There are several advantages to using *in vitro* testing for acute toxicity. *In vitro* testing is relatively inexpensive, and many more tests can be performed for the same cost. In addition, animals don't have to be sacrificed for *in vitro* testing.
(b) Since *in vitro* testing is performed on cultured cells that are identical, the results of testing may not be reliable for organisms that have many different kinds of cells.

16.68

$$\frac{334 \ \mu g}{1 \ kg} \times \frac{1 \ mg}{10^3 \ \mu g} \times \frac{1 \ kg}{2.205 \ lb} \times 200 \ lb = 30.3 \ mg$$

Mastering Reactions

16.70

Self-Test for Chapter 16

Multiple Choice

1. Which of the following alcohols can't be produced by reduction of an aldehyde or ketone?
   (a) 2-pentanol   (b) cyclohexanol   (c) 2-methyl-2-pentanol   (d) 2-methyl-1-butanol

2. The term "LD_{50}" refers to:
   (a) 50% of the amount of a substance that will kill a population   (b) the amount of a substance
   that will kill 50% of a population   (c) the name of a substance, 50% of which will kill a
   population   (d) none of the above

3. 3-Pentanone is unlikely to undergo which of the following reactions?
   (a) oxidation   (b) reduction   (c) acetal formation   (d) hemiacetal formation

4. Vanillin contains all of the following functional groups except:
   (a) aldehyde   (b) ether   (c) aromatic ring   (d) ketone

5. How many ketone isomers of the formula $C_6H_{12}O$ are there?
   (a) 4   (b) 5   (c) 6   (d) 7

6. Which of the following aldehydes is least soluble in water?
   (a) propanal   (b) benzaldehyde   (c) formaldehyde   (d) acetaldehyde

7. Which of the following compounds undergoes reaction with Tollens' reagent?
   (a) 3-methyl-3-pentanol   (b) glucose   (c) acetone   (d) cyclohexanone dimethyl acetal

8. The main difference between aldehydes and ketones is:
   (a) reactivity   (b) solubility   (c) flammability   (d) polarity

9. Formaldehyde is used for all of the following except:
   (a) polymers   (b) disinfectant   (c) preservative   (d) food additive

10. Which of the following statements about 3-heptanone is true?
    (a) It undergoes reaction with Benedict's reagent.   (b) It forms a cyclic acetal with 1,3-
    propanediol.   (c) It is soluble in water.   (d) It is a solid at room temperature.

Sentence Completion

1. Aldehydes, esters, and ketones are all _____ compounds.

2. The shiny product of oxidation of an aldehyde by Tollens' reagent is _____.

3. _____ is a reaction that converts an acetal to an aldehyde or a ketone.

4. A carbonyl group is polarized, with a partial _____ charge on carbon and a partial _____ charge on oxygen.

5. _____ is a ketone that is widely used as a solvent.

6. Chronic exposure to the aldehyde _____ can cause symptoms resembling those of alcoholism.

7. Bonds to the carbonyl carbon of esters and amides are _____ polar than the bonds to the carbonyl carbon of ketones and aldehydes.

8. The conversion of an aldehyde or ketone into an alcohol is said to be a _____ reaction.

9. Formaldehyde is widely used as a _____.

10. The initial product of reaction between a ketone or aldehyde and an alcohol is called a _____.

11. _____ reagent is used to detect sugar in urine.

12. _____ can be detected on the breath during starvation.

True or False

1. Glucose contains an acetal link.

2. A bombardier beetle protects itself by secreting benzoquinone.

3. Ketones are oxidized by Tollens' reagent to carboxylic acids.

4. The reduction of aldehydes and ketones is carried out by using NaOH.

5. An acetal is an alternative name for an ester.

6. Only aldehydes form acetals.

7. An aldehyde group always occurs at the end of a carbon chain.

8. In the chemical industry, formaldehyde is used to synthesize polymers.

9. NAD^+ reduces ketones and aldehydes to alcohols.

10. Acetaldehyde results from the oxidation of ethanol.

11. Both aldehydes and ketones can be reduced to alcohols.

12. Aldehydes and ketones are not capable of forming hydrogen bonds.

Match each entry on the left with its partner on the right (use each answer once).

1. $AgNO_3$, NH_3, H_2O (a) Reagent used to form an acetal

2. $CH_3CH_2COCH_3$ (b) Reduces carbonyl groups to alcohols

3. CH_3CH_2COOH (c) An amide

4. CH_3OH, H^+ catalyst   (d) Product of an aldehyde plus Tollens' reagent

5. CH_3CH_2OH (e) Tollens' reagent

6. $CH_3CH_2COOCH_3$ (f) Colored product of Benedict's test

7. $CH_3CH(OH)CH_3$ (g) Formaldehyde

8. NADH   (h) Product of aldehyde reduction

9. CH_3CHO (i) Yields secondary alcohol when reduced

10. Cu_2O (j) Ester

11. HCHO   (k) Can be oxidized to a ketone

12. CH_3CONH_2 (l) Product of primary alcohol oxidation

Chapter Outline

I. Properties and names of carboxylic acids and derivatives (Section 17.1).
  A. General characteristics.
    1. Groups bonded to the carbonyl carbon are polar.
      a. In carboxylic acids, —OH is bonded to the carbonyl carbon.
      b. In amides, —NH_2 is bonded to the carbonyl carbon.
      c. In esters, —OR is bonded to the carbonyl carbon.
    2. All of these functional groups undergo carbonyl group substitution reactions.
  B. Carboxylic acids.
    1. Properties.
      a. All have high boiling points.
      b. Carboxylic acids can form hydrogen bonds with each other.
      c. Smaller carboxylic acids are water-soluble.
      d. Volatile carboxylic acids have sharp odors.
    2. Naming carboxylic acids.
      a. For simple carboxylic acids, the -*e* of the corresponding alkane is replaced by -*oic acid*.
      b. Many simple carboxylic acids have common names.
      c. In some cases, the carbon next to the —COOH group is referred to as the α carbon.
      d. The group remaining when a carboxylic acid loses —OH is an acyl group.
      e. For dicarboxylic acids, -*dioic acid* replaces the -*e* of the corresponding alkane.
      f. Unsaturated carboxylic acids are named by using -*enoic acid*.
  C. Esters.
    1. Properties.
      a. Esters are lower boiling than carboxylic acids.
      b. Esters have pleasant odors.
      c. Simple esters are liquids.
    2. Naming esters.
      Ester names have two parts.
      a. The —OR fragment has the name of the alkyl group R.
      b. The remaining portion is the name of the parent carboxylic acid, with -*ate* replacing -*oic acid*.
  D. Amides.
    1. Properties.
      a. Amides are higher boiling than carboxylic acids; most are solids.
      b. Amides are not basic.
    2. Naming amides.
      a. An amide has the name of the parent acid, with -*amide* replacing -*oic acid*.
      b. If nitrogen is substituted, the alkyl substituents are specified, preceded by *N*- (to indicate that the substituents are bonded to nitrogen).
II. Carboxylic acids (Sections 17.2–17.4).
  A. Common carboxylic acids (Section 17.2).
    1. Acetic acid.
      a. Acetic acid is a common laboratory solvent.
      b. Acetic acid is formed from fermentation of fruit in the presence of ample O_2.
    2. Citric acid.

B. Acidity of carboxylic acids (Section 17.3).
  1. Carboxylic acids are weak acids, with $pK_a \sim 10^{-5}$.
  2. Carboxylate anions are given the name of the parent carboxylic acid, with *-ate* replacing *-oic acid*.
  3. Carboxylic acids react with base to give carboxylic acid salts.
    a. The amount of salt or acid present in solution depends on pH.
    b. Carboxylic acid salts are much more soluble in water than the parent acids.
C. Reactions of carboxylic acids (Section 17.4).
  1. Ester formation.
    a. carboxylic acid + alcohol $\xrightleftharpoons[\text{catalyst}]{H^+}$ ester + H_2O
    b. Esterification reactions are reversible.
  2. Amide formation.
    a. Carboxylic acid + ammonia (or an amine) —> amide + H_2O

III. Esters, amides, and carboxylic acid anhydrides (Sections 17.5–17.7).
  A. Aspirin and other over-the-counter carboxylic acid derivatives (Section 17.5).
    1. Aspirin.
      a. Aspirin is a salicylic acid ester.
      b. Aspirin causes pain relief, reduces fever, and reduces inflammation.
      c. Aspirin's side effects include gastric bleeding and gastric upset.
    2. Acetaminophen is an amide that can be used in place of aspirin.
    3. Ibuprofen is a carboxylic acid that is a nonsteroidal antiinflammatory drug.
    4. Benzocaine (ester) and lidocaine (amide) are used as topical anesthetics.
  B. Hydrolysis of esters and amides (Section 17.6).
    1. Esters.
      a. Ester + H_2O $\xrightarrow{\text{acid catalyst}}$ carboxylic acid + alcohol
      b. Ester + H_2O $\xrightarrow{\text{base}}$ carboxylate anion + alcohol
    2. Amides.
      a. Amide + H_2O $\xrightarrow{\text{acid or base}}$ carboxylic acid + amine (or ammonia)
  C. Polyesters and polyamides (Section 17.7).
    1. Nylons are polyamides formed in the reaction of a diacid with a diamine.
    2. Polyesters result from the reaction of a diacid with a dialcohol.

IV. Phosphoric acid derivatives (Section 17.8).
  A. Structure of phosphate esters.
    1. Phosphoric acid has three ionizable hydrogens and can form three different anions.
    2. Phosphates can react with alcohols at one, two, or three oxygens.
    3. Mono- and diphosphate esters are present in the body as anions.
  B. Phosphate esters in the body.
    1. In the body, phosphate esters exist as anions.
    2. In the body, phosphate esters can form anhydrides.
      a. Diphosphates and triphosphates are the anhydrides that occur in living things.
      b. Triphosphate esters are used for energy storage in the body.

Solutions to Chapter 17 Problems

17.1

17.2

17.3

17.4

17.5

17.6 (a) CH₃OCH₃ (b) CH₃COOH (c) CH₃CH₂CH₃

Low boiling. / Polar, but doesn't / form hydrogen bonds.

Highest boiling. / Forms strongest / hydrogen bonds.

Lowest boiling. / Nonpolar - Doesn't / form hydrogen bonds.

17.7 *More soluble*   *Less soluble*   *Reason*

(a) CH$_3$CH$_2$CH$_2$COOH   C$_8$H$_{17}$COOH   The large hydrocarbon part of C$_8$H$_{17}$COOH makes it insoluble in water.

(b) (CH$_3$)$_2$CHCOOH   CH$_3$CH$_2$COOCH(CH$_3$)$_2$ Carboxylic acids form stronger hydrogen bonds with water.

17.8

(a)

CH$_3$CH$_2$CH$_2$CO—

(b)

CH$_3$CH$_2$CH$_2$CNHCH(CH$_3$)$_2$

(c)

CH$_3$CH$_2$CH$_2$CN(CH$_2$CH$_3$)$_2$

(d)   Cyclopentyl butyrate   *N*-Isopropylbutyramide   *N*,*N*-Diethylbutyramide

17.9

(a)   (b)

tert-Butyl 2-bromobutanoate   *N*,*N*-Dimethyl-*o*-nitrobenzamide

17.10

(a)   (b)

CH$_3$CHCH$_2$CH$_2$CNH$_2$ CH$_3$CH$_2$C—NCH$_2$CH$_3$
4-Methylpentanamide   *N*-Ethyl-*N*-methylpropanamide

17.11

17.12

(a)

CH₃COOCH₃

ester (ii)

(b)

RCONHR

amide (i)

(c)

C₆H₅COOH

carboxylic acid (iii)

(d)

$$CH_3CH_2\overset{\displaystyle O}{\overset{\|}{C}}N(CH_3)_2$$

amide (i)

(e)

CH₃CH₂CH₂CONH₂

amide (i)

(f)

$$HOOCCH_2\overset{\displaystyle CH_3}{\overset{|}{C}H}CH_3$$

carboxylic acid (iii)

17.13

(a)

amide (C₆H₅CONH₂)

(b)

carboxylic acid (CH₃CH₂COOH)

(c)

ester (CH₃COOCH₂CH₃)

17.14

(a)

$$CH_3\overset{\displaystyle HO}{\overset{|}{C}H}\overset{\displaystyle O}{\overset{\|}{C}}-OH + NaOH \longrightarrow CH_3\overset{\displaystyle HO}{\overset{|}{C}H}\overset{\displaystyle O}{\overset{\|}{C}}-O^- \ Na^+ + H_2O$$

(b)

$$2 \ CH_3CH_2CH_2\overset{\displaystyle H_3C}{\underset{\displaystyle CH_3}{\overset{|}{C}}}\overset{\displaystyle O}{\overset{\|}{C}}-OH + Ca(OH)_2 \longrightarrow \left[CH_3CH_2CH_2\overset{\displaystyle H_3C}{\underset{\displaystyle CH_3}{\overset{|}{C}}}\overset{\displaystyle O}{\overset{\|}{C}}-O^- \right]_2 Ca^{2+} + 2 \ H_2O$$

17.15

Potassium salicylate

Disodium oxalate

17.16 When potassium acetate and disodium glutarate are dissolved in water, acetate ion, glutarate ion, potassium ion, and sodium ion are present; the first two are organic ions.

17.17

Hydroxyacetic acid   2-Hydroxypropanoic acid   *o*-Hydroxybenzoic acid

17.18 Redraw the structures so that the alcohol hydroxyl group and the —OH group of the carboxylic acid are facing each other. Remove water, and draw the ester bond.

17.19

(a)

(b)

17.20 Use the technique shown in Problem 17.18 to draw the amide product.

(a)

(b)

17.21

17.22

17.23

17.24 Moisture in the air causes hydrolysis of the ester bond of aspirin, yielding acetic acid.

17.25

(a)

p-Nitrobenzoic acid   2-Propanol

(b)

Phenol   2-Cyclopentene-carboxylic acid

(c)

2-Aminopropanoic acid   Ethanol

17.26

(a)

2-Butenoic acid   Methylamine

(b)

p-Nitrobenzoic acid

Dimethylamine

17.27

Nomex

17.28 As in Problems 17.18–17.20, draw the reacting partners so that the atoms involved in the reaction face each other. Remove one molecule of water for each bond formed.

17.29

17.30

Copyright © 2013 Pearson Education, Inc.

17.31

Understanding Key Concepts

17.32 (a) At physiological pH (7.4), pyruvic acid exists as the pyruvate anion, and lactic acid exists as the lactate anion.

(b)

Pyruvic acid   Lactic acid

(c) Hydrogen bonds between the carboxylate oxygen and water are shown. In addition, the carbonyl oxygens can also hydrogen-bond with water. For lactate, hydrogen bonding takes place between the hydroxyl hydrogen and water (shown), as well as between molecules of lactate. You would expect pyruvate and lactate to have comparable solubility in water.

17.34

(a) Glycerate and phosphate are connected by a phosphate ester linkage.

(b)

17.36

(a)

(b)

(c)

2-Amino-4-hydroxypentanoic acid
(2-Amino-4-hydroxyvaleric acid)

lactone

17.38 The hydrolyzed bonds are indicated on the structure.

17-Hydroxylinolenic acid   Glutamic acid   Ammonia

The charge of the products depends on whether the hydrolysis was carried out under acidic or basic conditions.

Carboxylic Acids

17.40

17.42

CH₃CH₂CH₂COOH

Butanoic acid

$$CH_3CHCOOH$$ with CH₃ above

2-Methylpropionic acid

17.44

(a)

CH₃CHCHCH₂COH (with OH, O, and CH₃ substituents)

3-Hydroxy-4-methylpentanoic acid

(b)

HOOC(CH₂)₇COOH

Nonanedioic acid

(c)

Cl—(cyclohexane ring)—COOH

4-Chlorocyclohexanecarboxylic acid

(d)

H₂N—(benzene ring)—C—OH (with O)

p-Aminobenzoic acid

17.46

(a)

CH₃CH₂CHCH₂CO⁻ K⁺ (with CH₂CH₃ substituent)

Potassium 3-ethylpentanoate

(b)

(benzene ring)—CO⁻ NH₄⁺

Ammonium benzoate

(c)

[CH₃CH₂CO⁻]₂ Ca²⁺

Calcium propanoate

17.48

(a)

CH₃CH₂CHCHCH₂COH (with CH₃ and CH₃ substituents)

3,4-Dimethylhexanoic acid

(b)

(benzene ring)—CH₂—COH

Phenylacetic acid

(c)

O₂N and O₂N substituents on benzene ring—COH

3,4-Dinitrobenzoic acid

(d)

CH₃CH₂CH₂CO⁻ ⁺NH(CH₂CH₃)₃

Triethylammonium butanoate

17.50

O   OH O
|| | ||
HOCCH₂CH—COH   Malic acid

17.52

H   COO⁻ NH₄⁺
 \   /
  C=C   Diammonium fumarate
 /   \
NH₄⁺ ⁻OOC   H

Esters and Amides

17.54 There are many answers to this question. Here are some possibilities:

(a)

O
||
CH₃CH₂CH₂CH₂CNH₂

Pentanamide

O
||
CH₃CH₂CNHCH₂CH₃

N-Ethylpropanamide

O
||
HCNCH₂CH₃
 |
 CH₂CH₃

N,N-Diethylformamide

(b)

O
||
CH₃CH₂CH₂CH₂COCH₃

Methyl pentanoate

O
||
CH₃CH₂COCH₂CH₂CH₃

Propyl propanoate

O
||
HCOCH₂CH₂CH₂CH₂CH₃

Pentyl formate

17.56

(a)

O   CH₃
|| |
CH₃COCH₂CH₂CHCH₃

3-Methylbutyl acetate
(3-Methylbutyl ethanoate)

(b)

CH₃   O
 | ||
CH₃CHCH₂CH₂COCH₃

Methyl 4-methylpentanoate

(c)

O
||
CH₃CO—⬡

Cyclohexyl acetate
(Cyclohexyl ethanoate)

(d)

OH

Phenyl o-hydroxybenzoate

17.58

(a) 3-Methylbutyl acetate

(b) Methyl 4-methylpentanoate

(c) Cyclohexyl acetate

(d) Phenyl *o*-hydroxybenzoate + H₂O

17.60

(a) 2-Ethylbutanamide

(b) *N*-Phenylbenzamide

(c) *N*-Ethyl-*N*-methylbenzamide

(d) 2,3-Dibromohexanamide

17.62

(a)

2-Ethylbutanamide

(b)

N-Phenylbenzamide + H₂O

(c)

N-Ethyl-*N*-methylbenzamide

(d)

CH₃CH₂CH₂CHCHC⁻OH + H⁻NH₂ ⟶ CH₃CH₂CH₂CHCHCNH₂ + H₂O

2,3-Dibromohexanamide

Reactions of Carboxylic Acids and Their Derivatives

17.64

17.66

17.68

Polyesters and Polyamides

17.70

Phosphate Esters and Anhydrides

17.72

The products of hydrolysis are dihydroxyacetone and hydrogen phosphate anion.

17.74

Acetyl phosphate

17.76

A cyclic phosphate diester

A cyclic phosphate diester is formed when one phosphate forms ester bonds with two hydroxyl groups in the same molecule.

General Questions and Problems

17.78

$$
\underset{\substack{\text{N,N-Dimethylformamide} \\ \textbf{A}}}{\overset{\overset{\displaystyle O}{\|}}{HC-N(CH_3)_2}}
\qquad
\underset{\substack{\textit{N}\text{-Methylacetamide} \\ \textbf{B}}}{\overset{\overset{\displaystyle O}{\|}}{CH_3C-NHCH_3}}
\qquad
\underset{\substack{\text{Propanamide} \\ \textbf{C}}}{\overset{\overset{\displaystyle O}{\|}}{CH_3CH_2C-NH_2}}
$$

A is the lowest boiling isomer. Since no hydrogens are bonded to nitrogen, no hydrogen bonding between molecules of **A** can take place. Hydrogen bonding can occur between molecules of **B**, and thus **B** is higher boiling than **A**. **C** is the highest boiling isomer.

17.80

CH₃CH₂CNH₂
Propanamide

CH₃COCH₃
Methyl acetate

Propanamide and methyl acetate are both soluble in water because both are polar molecules and can hydrogen bond with water. Propanamide is higher boiling because molecules of propanamide can form hydrogen bonds with each other.

17.82

Chemistry in Action

17.84

CCl₃COH   Trichloroacetic acid   CH₃CHCOH   Lactic acid
                                         |
                                         OH

Trichloroacetic acid is a strong acid used for chemical peeling of the skin and for removing scars and wrinkles. Lactic acid is a weaker acid used for wrinkle removal and skin moisturizing.

17.86 Kevlar is a polyamide formed from *p*-benzenedicarboxylic acid and *p*-diaminobenzene. Because it is an amide, it can be hydrolyzed by strong acids and bases.

Self-Test for Chapter 17

Multiple Choice

1. Which of the following amides does not form hydrogen bonds?
   (a) benzamide   (b) formamide   (c) *N*-methylformamide   (d) *N,N*-dimethylformamide

2. Which of the following statements about phosphoric acid anhydrides is untrue?
   (a) Energy is released when triphosphate anhydrides react with water.
   (b) Both mono- and dianhydrides occur in the body.
   (c) Hydrolysis of phosphate ester anhydrides yields caustic products.
   (d) Two molecules of water are necessary to completely hydrolyze a triphosphate anhydride.

3. Which class of compounds is lowest boiling?
   (a) carboxylic acid esters   (b) amides   (c) carboxylic acids   (d) carboxylic acid salts

4. The common name of an *-enoic* acid is:
   (a) succinic acid   (b) benzoic acid   (c) oxalic acid   (d) acrylic acid

5. Amide bonds occur in all of the following except:
   (a) nylon   (b) Dacron   (c) urea   (d) proteins

6. In the reaction $CH_3COOH + CH_3OH \rightleftharpoons CH_3COOCH_3 + H_2O$, the yield of CH_3COOCH_3 can be improved by:
   (a) distilling off the CH_3COOCH_3 (b) removing the water   (c) using more CH_3COOH and CH_3OH (d) all of the above

7. Reaction of methanol with oxalic acid in the presence of an acid catalyst forms:
   (a) methyl oxalate   (b) dimethyl oxalate   (c) methyl acetate   (d) reaction doesn't occur

8. Polypropylene and nylon resemble each other in which respect?
   (a) They are both polymers.   (b) They are both hydrocarbons.   (c) Concentrated acid will dissolve them.   (d) An initiator is needed for polymerization to occur.

9. Which of the following compounds is an α-amino acid?

   (a)
   $$H_2NCH_2CH_2\overset{\displaystyle O}{\overset{\|}{C}}OH$$
   (b)
   $$H_2N\overset{\displaystyle O}{\overset{\|}{C}}CH_2CH_3$$
   (c)
   $$H_2NCH_2\overset{\displaystyle O}{\overset{\|}{C}}OCH_3$$
   (d)
   $$H_2NCH_2\overset{\displaystyle O}{\overset{\|}{C}}OH$$

10. How many amides of the formula C_3H_7NO can be drawn?
    (a) 3   (b) 4   (c) 5   (d) 6

Sentence Completion

1. The most common general reaction of carboxylic acids, esters, and amides is called a _____ ___ _____ reaction.

2. Kevlar is a type of _____.

3. A carboxylic acid can be dissolved in water by converting it into its _____ ____.

4. The reaction of a carboxylic acid with an alcohol in the presence of an acid catalyst is called an _____ reaction.

5. In carboxylic acids, esters, and amides, the carbonyl-group carbon is bonded to an atom that strongly _____ electrons.

6. Carboxylic acids are named by using the name ending ___ ____.

7. $CH_3CH_2COOCH_2CH_2CH_3$ is named _____ _____.

8. Many flavors and fragrances are due to _____.

9. _____ is the transfer of a $-PO_3{}^{2-}$ group from one molecule to another.

10. Long-chain carboxylic acids can be found in nature as components of _____.

11. The reaction of an ester with aqueous NaOH to yield a salt and an alcohol is called a _____ reaction.

12. Malonic acid is also known as _____ acid.

True or False

1. A carboxylic acid salt is more soluble in water than a carboxylic acid.

2. A *saponification* reaction is the acid-catalyzed hydrolysis of an ester.

3. Amides and amines are both basic.

4. A carboxylic acid is higher boiling than an ester of the same molecular weight.

5. Basic hydrolysis of ethyl acetate yields acetic acid and ethanol.

6. The compound $HCON(CH_3)_2$ is named dimethylformamide.

7. Nitrate esters are important in living systems.

8. Acetic acid is about 1% dissociated in a 1 M aqueous solution.

9. Carboxylic acids are either solids or liquids at room temperature.

10. Esterification can be brought about by treating a carboxylic acid with an alcohol in the presence of NaOH.

11. Pyrophosphoric acid is a phosphate ester.

12. Propanamide is higher boiling than methyl acetate.

Match each entry on the left with its partner on the right.

1. $CH_3COOH + CH_3OH + HCl$ (a) Amide hydrolysis

2. $HOOCCH_2COOH$ (b) Ester hydrolysis

3. $(CH_3COO^-)_2Mg^{2+}$ (c) Thioester

4. $CH_3COOCH_3 + NaOH, H_2O$ (d) *-enoic* acid

5. HCOOH   (e) Phosphate ester

6. $CH_3CH=CHCOOH$ (f) Dioic acid

7. $CH_3CONH_2 + NaOH, H_2O$ (g) Amide

8. CH_3OPO_3H (h) Polyester

9. Nylon   (i) Formic acid

10. Dacron   (j) Ester formation

11. Acetyl-SCoA   (k) Acid salt

12. Lidocaine   (l) Polyamide

Chapter Outline

I. Introduction to biochemistry and proteins (Sections 18.1–18.2).
  A. Biochemistry (Section 18.1).
    1. Biochemistry is the study of the structure and function of biomolecules.
    2. The principal classes of biomolecules are proteins, carbohydrates, lipids, and nucleic acids.
    3. Biomolecules range in size from small organic molecules to polymers with millions of subunits.
    4. The three-dimensional shape of biomolecules is critical to their ability to function.
  B. Proteins (Section 18.2).
    1. Proteins are polymers of amino acids.
    2. The bonds that form between amino acids are amide bonds (peptide bonds).
      a. Two amino acids bond together to form a dipeptide.
      b. Three amino acids bond together to form a tripeptide.
      c. A chain with 10–100 amino acids is a polypeptide.
      d. The atoms that form a peptide bond have a planar relationship.
    3. There are four levels of protein structure.
      a. "Primary structure" refers to the sequence of amino acids that form peptide bonds.
      b. "Secondary structure" refers to the organization of polypeptide chains into a regular pattern.
      c. "Tertiary structure" refers to the overall shape of the protein molecule.
      d. "Quaternary structure" refers to the organization of proteins composed of several polypeptide chains.
    4. Proteins have numerous functions in living things.
      a. Among these functions are structure, support, storage, transport, and control of biochemical reactions.
II. Amino acids (Sections 18.3–18.6).
  A. Structure of amino acids (Section 18.3).
    1. Twenty amino acids commonly occur in nature.
      a. All twenty are α-amino acids.
      b. Nineteen of the twenty amino acids are primary amines.
    2. In this book, each amino acid is represented by a three-letter code.
    3. Amino acids are classified as neutral, acidic, or basic.
      a. Of the common amino acids, fifteen are neutral, three are basic, and two are acidic.
    4. Amino acid side chains are classified as hydrophilic (polar) or hydrophobic (nonpolar).
      a. Hydrophobic side chains cluster in the middle of a protein.
      b. Hydrophilic side chains are positioned on the surface of the protein.
  B. Acid–base properties of amino acids (Section 18.4).
    1. Amino acids exist as dipolar zwitterions.
      a. Amino acids have properties similar to salts: They are high-melting and soluble in water.
      b. Amino acids can react as acids or bases.
    2. The pH at which the number of positive charges on an amino acid equals the number of negative charges is called the isoelectric point (pI).
      a. Neutral amino acids have pIs in the range 5.0–6.5.
      b. Acidic amino acids are negatively charged at physiological pH.

C. Chirality and amino acids (Sections 18.5–18.6).
   1. Chirality (Section 18.5).
      a. Chirality is the property of handedness.
      b. An object that lacks a plane of symmetry is chiral.
   2. Molecular handedness (Section 18.6).
      a. A carbon that is bonded to four different atoms or groups of atoms is a chiral carbon atom.
      b. The two mirror-image forms of a chiral molecule are enantiomers, or optical isomers.
         i.   Optical isomers are one kind of stereoisomer.
         ii. Optical isomers are identical in all properties except for their effect on polarized light.
      c. All amino acids except for glycine are chiral.
      d. Only one of a pair of enantiomeric amino acids occurs naturally.
III. Proteins (Sections 18.7–18.12).
  A. Primary protein structure (Sections 18.7–18.8).
    1. The repeating chain of peptide bonds and α carbons is known as the protein backbone (Section 18.7).
      a. The atoms that form the peptide bond lie in a plane.
      b. The amino-terminal end of the peptide is written on the left, and the carboxy-terminal end is on the right.
      c. A peptide is named by listing the residues in order, from left to right.
    2. Protein function is dependent on the exact sequence of amino acids in protein primary structure.
    3. Primary structure is responsible for the shape of a protein molecule.
      a. In sickle-cell anemia, a change in only one amino acid is responsible for the disease.
    4. Several types of interactions determine protein shape (Section 18.8).
      a. Noncovalent interactions.
         i.   Hydrogen bonds can occur between atoms on the protein backbone.
         ii. Hydrogen bonds can occur between side-chains of amino acids or between side-chain amino acids and the polypeptide backbone.
         iii. Ionic interactions can occur between ionized acidic and basic amino acids; these are called salt bridges.
         iv. Hydrophobic interactions occur between nonpolar side chains.
      b. Covalent interactions. The thiol groups of cysteine residues form disulfide bonds.
  B. Secondary protein structure (Section 18.9).
    1. Secondary structure refers to the ordered relationships of backbone atoms resulting from hydrogen bonding.
    2. There are two types of secondary structures.
      a. The α-helix is a right-handed coil formed by hydrogen bonds between an N—H group and a carbonyl group four amino acids away.
      b. The β-sheet occurs when polypeptide chains line up next to each other, and hydrogen bonds form between adjacent chains.
    3. Fibrous and globular proteins show examples of secondary structure.
      a. Some fibrous proteins are composed almost entirely of α-helices.
      b. Globular proteins have smaller regions of α-helix and β-sheet secondary structure.
    4. The parts of the polypeptide chain not involved in a secondary structural element are called random coil segments.
  C. Tertiary protein structure (Section 18.10).
    1. Tertiary structure.
      a. Tertiary structure describes the overall shape of proteins.

      b. The interactions responsible for tertiary structure may be between amino acids many units apart.

      c. Interactions described in Section 18.8 give each protein its unique three-dimensional shape.

  2. Examples.

      a. Ribonuclease—a globular protein.

          i. Hydrophobic side-chains congregate in the middle, and hydrophilic side chains are distributed on the outside.

      b. Myoglobin—a globular protein.

          i. Myoglobin has eight α-helix segments.

         ii. A heme group is embedded within the polypeptide chain.

D. Quaternary structure (Section 18.11).

  1. Quaternary structure describes the noncovalent interactions between the polypeptide chains of proteins that consist of more than one chain.

  2. Examples:

      a. Hemoglobin consists of four polypeptide chains held together by hydrophobic interactions.

      b. Collagen is formed by several tropocollagen strands overlapping lengthwise.

  3. Classification of proteins.

      a. Fibrous proteins are insoluble and are composed of fibers and sheets.

      b. Globular proteins are water-soluble and have chains folded into compact shapes.

      c. Simple proteins contain only amino acids.

      d. Conjugated proteins contain one or more non-amino acid units.

E. Chemical properties of proteins (Section 18.12).

  1. Hydrolysis.

      a. Polypeptide amide bonds can be cleaved by acid or enzymes to yield amino acids.

  2. Denaturation.

      a. Denaturation disturbs a protein's shape without disrupting primary structure.

      b. Denaturation changes the properties of proteins.

      c. Denaturation can be caused by various agents.

          i. Heat disturbs side-chain interactions.

         ii. Mechanical agitation.

        iii Detergents disrupt the interactions of hydrophobic side chains.

        iv. Organic compounds disrupt hydrogen bonds.

         v. pH changes disrupt salt bridges.

        vi. Inorganic salts disrupt salt bridges.

  3. Occasionally, denatured proteins can undergo renaturation.

Solutions to Chapter 18 Problems

18.1   Amino acids containing an aromatic ring: phenylalanine, tyrosine, tryptophan

Phenylalanine   Tyrosine   Tryptophan

Amino acids containing sulfur: cysteine, methionine

Cysteine   Methionine

Amino acids that are alcohols: serine, threonine, tyrosine (a phenol)

Serine   Threonine   Tyrosine

Amino acids with alkyl group side chains: alanine, valine, leucine, isoleucine

Alanine   Valine   Leucine   Isoleucine

18.2

Alanine

18.3

COO⁻
|
H--C
/ ＼NH₃⁺
(CH₃)₂CH

Serine   Valine

The serine side chain has a polar hydroxyl group; the valine side chain has a nonpolar isopropyl group.

18.4

(a)

$$H_2N-CH-C-OH$$
|
$$CH-OH$$
|
$$CH_3$$

α-amino acid
(Threonine)

(b)

$$H_2N-C-CH_2CH_2CH_3$$

not an α-amino acid
(amide)

(c)

$$CH_3CH_2CHCH_2-NH_2$$
|
$$OH$$

not an α-amino acid
(amino alcohol)

(d)

$$HO-C-CHCH_2CH(CH_3)_2$$
|
$$NH_2$$

α-amino acid
(Leucine)

18.5

	Side-Chain Functional Groups:	Hydrogen Bonding?
(a) Phe, Thr		no
(b) Asn, Ser		yes
(c) Thr, Tyr		yes
(d) Gly, Trp		no

Amino acids that have amine, amide, alcohol, or phenol groups are capable of hydrogen bonding to other amino acids having these groups. Only in (b) and (c) do both amino acids have groups that can participate in hydrogen bonding. Other combinations of hydrogen bonds can be drawn in (b) and (c).

18.6

18.7

H₃N⁺—CH—C(=O)—OH
|
CH₂
|
CH₂
|
C—OH
‖
O   at low pH

Glutamic acid

H₂N—CH—C(=O)—O⁻
|
CH₂
|
CH₂
|
C—O⁻
‖
O   at high pH

At low pH, both of the carboxylic acid groups and the amino group are protonated. At high pH, the carboxylic acid groups exist as carboxylate anions and the amino group is not protonated.

18.8   In the zwitterionic form of an amino acid, the —NH₃⁺ group is an acid (because it can donate H⁺), and the —COO⁻ group is a base (because it can accept H⁺).

18.9   Chiral: (a) chair   (b) jar (because of the screw top)   (d) scissors

18.10 Handed: wrench, shoe, corkscrew
Not handed: thumb tack, pencil, eraser

Many other answers are possible.

18.11

$$NH_2$$
|
H₃C—C—CH₃
|
H

2-Aminopropane

$$NH_2$$
|
CH₃CH₂—*C—CH₃
|
H

2-Aminobutane

2-Aminopropane is achiral because no carbon has four different groups bonded to it. 2-Aminobutane is chiral because four different groups are bonded to carbon 2 (—H, —CH₃, —NH₂ and —CH₂CH₃).

18.12

(a)

Cl
|
CH₃CH₂CCH₂CH₃
|
H

achiral

(b)

Cl
|
CH₃CH₂CH₂*CCH₃
|
H

chiral

(c)

CH₃   CH₃
| |
CH₃CHCH₂*CCH₂CH₃
|
H

chiral

The starred carbon atoms in (b) and (c) each have four different groups bonded to them.

18.13 Threonine and isoleucine each have two chiral carbon atoms (starred in the following structures).

Threonine   Isoleucine

18.14

The starred carbon in the second isomer is chiral because four different groups (—H, —Cl, —Br, —CH₃) are bonded to it.

18.15

Serine   Valine   Valine   Serine

18.16 (a) Gly–Ser–Tyr   Tyr–Ser–Gly   Ser–Tyr–Gly
            Gly–Tyr–Ser   Tyr–Gly–Ser   Ser–Gly–Tyr

(b)

Gly–Ser–Tyr   Gly–Tyr–Ser

18.17 Ile–Arg–Val   Arg–Ile–Val   Val–Arg–Ile
        Ile–Val–Arg   Arg–Val–Ile   Val–Ile–Arg

18.18

(a)

Leu–Asp

Leucine (Leu)
neutral

Aspartate (Asp)
polar, acidic

(b)

Tyr–Ser–Lys

Tyrosine (Tyr)
All residues in (b) are polar

Serine (Ser)

Lysine (Lys)
basic

18.19

Tyr–Ser–Lys

18.20 Chymotrypsin breaks peptide bonds on the carboxylate side of aromatic amino acids. Table 18.3 shows that Phe, Tyr and Trp are the three aromatic acids that are found in proteins. Vasopressin contains Phe and Tyr, and three fragments result from treatment of vasopressin with chymotrypsin.

Asp–Tyr⌡Phe⌡Glu–Asn–Cys–Pro–Lys–Gly

↓ Chymotrypsin

Asp–Tyr + Phe + Glu–Asn–Cys–Pro–Lys–Gly

18.21 (a) Glutamine and serine interact through *hydrogen bonds* between the terminal —NH$_2$ group of glutamine and the —OH of serine.

(b) Isoleucine and proline are pulled together through *hydrophobic interactions* between the alkyl side chain of isoleucine and the ring portion of proline.

(c) A *salt bridge* occurs between the negatively charged aspartate carboxyl group and the terminal amine group of lysine.

(d) The alkyl side chain of alanine and the aromatic ring of phenylalanine are held together by *hydrophobic interactions*.

18.22 (a) Hydrogen bonds from side chains: tyrosine, asparagine, serine.

(b) Hydrophobic group interactions: alanine, isoleucine, valine, leucine.

18.23 In an α-helix, a carbonyl oxygen forms a hydrogen bond with an amide hydrogen 12 atoms away. Thus, 11 backbone atoms lie between the atoms that take part in an α-helix hydrogen bond.

18.24 (a) Hydrogen bonding is responsible for sheet formation.

(b) Hydrogen bonding takes place between an amide hydrogen and an amide carbonyl oxygen on an adjacent chain.

18.25 The secondary structure of proteins is stabilized by hydrogen bonds between amide nitrogens and carbonyl oxygens of the polypeptide backbone. Tertiary structure is stabilized by hydrogen bonds between groups on the side chains of amino acids.

18.26 In α-keratin, pairs of α-helixes twist together into small fibrils that are twisted into larger bundles. In tropocollagen, three coiled chains wrap around each other to form a triple helix.

18.27 (a) This statement describes tertiary structure, which is stabilized by hydrogen bonds, hydrophobic interactions, salt bridges, and disulfide bonds between side chains on the same polypeptide chain.

(b) This statement describes secondary structure (α-helix), which is stabilized by hydrogen bonds between amide hydrogen atoms and carbonyl oxygen atoms on the polypeptide backbone.

(c) This statement describes quaternary structure, which is stabilized by hydrophobic interactions, hydrogen bonds, and salt bridges.

Understanding Key Concepts

18.28 Peptides that contain neither acidic nor basic amino acids have a net charge of +1 at pH = 2 because both the N-terminal amino group and the C-terminal carboxylic acid group are protonated. At pH = 11, these peptides have a net charge of –1, because the N–terminal group is uncharged and the C-terminal group is a carboxylate anion.

(a) Val

(b) Arg

(c) Tyr–Ser

(d) Glu–Asp

at pH = 2

at pH = 11

(e) Gln–Ala–Asn

at pH = 2

at pH = 11

(f) Met–Trp–Cys

18.30

Hydrogen bonds in an α-helix are indicated by dashed lines.

18.32 (a) Leu, Phe, Ala, or any amino acid with a nonpolar side chain might be found in the part of the protein that lies within the cell membrane.

(b),(c) Asp, Lys, Thr, or any amino acid with a hydrophilic side chain might be found in the part of the protein that either lies outside the cell membrane or inside the cell membrane.

Amino Acids

18.34

(a) Valine (Val)   (b) Serine (Ser)   (c) Glutamic acid (Glu)

18.36

(a) Cysteine (Cys)

(b) Tyrosine (Tyr)

18.38 At a neutral pH (pH = 5 – 8), an amino acid with a pI less than 5 is negatively charged, and an amino acid with a pI greater than 8 is positively charged. Otherwise, an amino acid has no net charge at neutral pH and is neutral. Asparagine (pI = 5.4) and proline (pI = 6.3) are neutral. Lysine (pI = 9.7) is positively charged.

18.40

(a) This structure represents aspartic acid at pH = 3, its isoelectric point. (low pH)

(b) This structure represents aspartic acid at pH = 13. (high pH)

(c) This structure represents aspartic acid at pH = 1 (low pH)

At neutral pH, a structure with two carboxylates and a protonated amino group predominates.

Handedness in Molecules

18.42 A chiral object is one that has handedness. Examples include a glove and a car.

18.44 Chiral: (a) mayonnaise jar (because of screw threads), (b) screw
Achiral: (c) brick

18.46 2-Bromo-2-chloropropane has a symmetry plane and is achiral. 2-Bromo-2-chlorobutane and 2-bromo-2-chloro-3-methylbutane don't have symmetry planes and are chiral because each has a carbon atom bonded to four different atoms or groups of atoms. A star indicates a chiral carbon atom.

(a)

2-Bromo-2-chloropropane
achiral

(b)

2-Bromo-2-chlorobutane
chiral

(c)

2-Bromo-2-chloro-3-methylbutane
chiral

18.48

Leucine

Peptides and Proteins

18.50 A simple protein is composed only of amino acids. A conjugated protein consists of a simple protein associated with one or more nonprotein molecules.

18.52

Type of Protein	Function	Example
Enzymes:	Catalyze biochemical reactions	Ribonuclease
Hormones:	Regulate body functions	Insulin
Storage proteins:	Store essential substances	Myoglobin
Transport proteins:	Transport substances through body fluids	Serum albumin
Structural proteins:	Provide shape and support	Collagen
Protective proteins:	Defend the body against foreign matter	Immunoglobulins
Contractile proteins:	Do mechanical work	Myosin and actin

18.54 (a) *Primary structure* refers to the sequence of connection of amino acids in a protein.
(b) *Secondary structure* refers to the orientation of segments of the protein chain into a regular pattern, such as an α-helix or a β-sheet, by hydrogen bonding between backbone atoms.
(c) *Tertiary structure* refers to the coiling and folding of the entire protein chain into a three-dimensional shape as a result of interactions between amino acid side chains.
(d) *Quaternary structure* refers to the aggregation of several protein chains to form a larger structure.

18.56 The disulfide bonds between two cysteine residues help to stabilize a protein's tertiary structure by drawing parts of the polypeptide chain together.

18.58 (a) *Hydrophobic interactions* occur between hydrocarbon side chains of amino acids. In a protein, these side chains cluster in the center of the molecule to exclude water, and are responsible for the nearly spherical tertiary shape of globular proteins. Alanine and isoleucine take part in hydrophobic interactions.

(b) *Salt bridges* occur between negatively charged and positively charged amino acid side chain groups. They can stabilize the tertiary structure of a protein by connecting two distant parts of a polypeptide chain or by pulling the protein backbone together in the middle of the chain. They can also stabilize quaternary structure by bringing together two polypeptide chains. Lysine and aspartate can form salt bridges.

18.60 When a protein is denatured, its three-dimensional structure is disrupted, and its ability to catalyze reactions is impaired. Primary structure is not affected by denaturation.

18.62 Val–Met–Leu   Met–Val–Leu   Leu–Met–Val
Val–Leu–Met   Met–Leu–Val   Leu–Val–Met

18.64 Amino acids with polar side chains (aspartate and histidine, for example) are likely to be found on the outside of a globular protein, where they can form hydrogen bonds with water and with each other. Amino acids with nonpolar side chains (alanine and valine, for example) are likely to be found on the inside of globular proteins, where they can escape from water.

18.66

N-terminal
amino acid

Tyr – Gly – Gly – Phe – Met

C-Terminal
amino acid

Properties and Reactions of Amino Acids and Proteins

18.68

(a)

(b)

18.70

18.72 A peptide rich in Lys and Asp residues is more soluble in water than a peptide rich in Ala and Leu residues. The side chains of Lys and Asp are polar and are better solvated by water than the nonpolar, hydrophobic side chains of Ala and Leu.

Chemistry in Action

18.74 People need a daily source of protein in the diet because the human body doesn't store the protein or the amino acids needed for its continuous synthesis of proteins. The body does store fats and carbohydrates.

18.76 Food from animal sources is more likely to contain complete protein than food from plant sources because the proteins in animals contain all of the common amino acids.

18.78

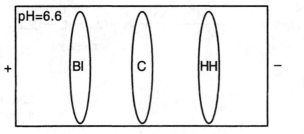

At pH = 6.6, collagen (isoelectric point = 6.6) has as many positive charges as negative charges and does not migrate. Bovine insulin (pI = 5.4) is negatively charged and migrates to the positively charged electrode. Human hemoglobin (pI = 7.1) is positively charged and migrates to the negative electrode.

18.80 During long sieges, people were unable to find fresh fruit and vegetables to eat. Fresh produce contains vitamin C, which is necessary for the synthesis of collagen. Without vitamin C, collagen is defective, and scurvy results.

18.82 A change in protein secondary structure from α-helix to β-pleated sheet alters the shape of the prion and causes groups that were close together in the normal prion to be farther apart in the altered prion. This change disrupts hydrogen bonds and salt bridges that were present in the normal prion and results in the formation of new tertiary interactions.

General Questions and Problems

18.84 Protein digestion is the hydrolysis of peptide bonds to form amino acids. Protein denaturation is the disruption of secondary, tertiary, or quaternary structure without disrupting peptide bonds.

18.86 (a) Bradykinin:

Arg——Pro———Pro———Gly——Phe

—Ser———Pro———Phe———Arg

(b) The rigid proline rings introduce kinks and bends in bradykinin and prevent hydrogen
bonds from forming (because proline has no hydrogens to form hydrogen bonds).

18.88

Oxytocin

18.90 Amino acids that can form hydrogen bonds contain the following functional groups: amine, alcohol, amide, and carboxylic acid (carboxylate). These amino acids are arginine, aspartic acid, asparagine, glutamic acid, glutamine, histidine, lysine, serine, threonine, and tyrosine. Shown below is hydrogen bonding between asparagine and serine.

Hydrogen bonds between the amino acids and water:

18.92 Polar, hydrophilic amino acids that can form hydrogen bonds with water are found on the outside of globular proteins. Examples: (b) Glu, (e) Ser.
Nonpolar amino acids that have small side chains are found in fibrous proteins. Examples: (a) Ala, (f) Val. Phe and Leu are nonpolar but are too bulky to be often found in fibrous proteins.

18.94 If an aspartate residue were substituted for a glutamate residue, a health problem might not occur because both amino acids have similar physical properties and chemical behavior.

18.96 Pineapple that is canned has been heated to inactivate enzymes. Thus, no enzymatic hydrolysis occurs when canned pineapple is added to gelatin.

18.98 If a diabetic took insulin orally, digestive enzymes would catalyze its hydrolysis, and the individual amino acids would be absorbed as food.

18.100 A combination of grains, legumes, and nuts in each meal provides all of the essential amino acids.

Self-Test for Chapter 18

Multiple Choice

1. Which level of protein structure doesn't involve hydrogen bonds?
   (a) primary (b) secondary (c) tertiary (d) quaternary

2. Which of the following amino acids has a hydrophobic side chain?
   (a) asparagine (b) threonine (c) histidine (d) phenylalanine

3. The isoelectric point of an amino acid is 7.6. Which of the following statements about it is untrue?
   (a) At pH = 7.6, the number of positive charges equals the number of negative charges.
   (b) It is a basic amino acid.
   (c) At pH = 5.5, both the carboxylic acid group and the amine group are protonated.
   (d) It forms salt bridges when it is part of a polypeptide chain.

4. Which of the following organic molecules is chiral?
   (a) 1-pentanol (b) 2-pentanol (c) 3-pentanol (d) 2-methyl-2-butanol

5. How many tetrapeptides can be formed from alanine, lysine, and two valines?
   (a) 6 (b) 12 (c) 18 (d) 24

6. Which of the following is an amino acid with a nitrogen heterocyclic ring?
   (a) histidine (b) threonine (c) tyrosine (d) cysteine

7. Addition of heavy metal ions to a protein disrupts which structural element?
   (a) hydrogen bonds (b) primary structure (c) hydrophobic interactions (d) disulfide bonds

8. A table in which proteins are described as collagens and immunoglobulins classifies them by
   (a) size (b) shape (c) function (d) the type of nonprotein associated with them

9. In a nucleoprotein, the protein is conjugated with:
   (a) carbohydrate (b) metal ions (c) RNA (d) lipids

10. Substitution of one amino acid for another in a polypeptide chain disrupts:
    (a) secondary structure (b) tertiary structure (c) isoelectric point (d) all or none of the above, depending on the amino acids involved

Sentence Completion

1. The isoelectric point of a neutral amino acid is near pH = _____.

2. Two molecules that differ only in the arrangement of groups around a chiral carbon atom are called _____.

3. Amino acids exist as dipolar ions called _____.

4. The repeating chain of amide bonds in a peptide is called the _____.

5. A disulfide bond between two cysteines in the same chain produces a _____ in the peptide.

6. A protein bonded to a carbohydrate is called a _____.

7. _____ structure refers to how the entire protein is folded and coiled into a specific three-dimensional shape.

8. In the secondary structure called a _____ _____, polypeptide chains line up in a parallel arrangement held together by hydrogen bonds.

9. The tripeptide Ser-Gln-Lys contains side chains that are _____.

10. The amino acids methionine and cysteine are the only two that contain the element _____.

11. A chain with fewer than 50 amino acids is called a _____.

12. _____ interactions pull nonpolar side chains together to exclude water.

True or False

1. All amino acids have at least one chiral carbon atom.

2. Tyrosine and valine can react to form a dipeptide.

3. Protein denaturation disrupts the primary structure of a protein.

4. Lysylalanine is identical to alanyllysine.

5. Some amino acids have an isoelectric point near 10.

6. Simple proteins are more common than conjugated proteins.

7. β-Sheets and α-helices occur mostly in fibrous proteins.

8. Amino acids are quite water-soluble.

9. Proteins, as well as amino acids, have isoelectric points.

10. Both fibrous and globular proteins are water-soluble.

11. Proteins may be classified by biological function.

12. 2-Butanol has a chiral carbon atom.

Match each entry on the left with its partner on the right.

1. Isoleucine

2. Insulin

3. Glycylglycine

4. Glycine

5. β-Sheet

6. Aspartic acid

7. Collagen

8. Cysteine

9. Albumin

10. Arginine

11. Proline

12. Tryptophan

(a) Achiral amino acid

(b) Secondary structure

(c) Fibrous protein

(d) Amino acid that is a secondary amine

(e) Amino acid with hydrocarbon side chain

(f) Globular protein

(g) Peptide hormone

(h) Basic amino acid

(i) Aromatic amino acid

(j) Dipeptide

(k) Acidic amino acid

(l) Can form disulfide bridges

Chapter Outline

I. Introduction to enzymes (Sections 19.1–19.3).
   A. Catalysis by enzymes (Section 19.1).
      1. Enzymes are globular proteins that catalyze biochemical reactions.
         a. The active site is the region of the enzyme where catalysis takes place.
         b. The reactant in an enzyme-catalyzed reaction is called the substrate.
         c. Some enzymes are specific for one particular substrate, whereas others catalyze reactions involving a number of substrates.
         d. Most enzymes are specific with respect to stereochemistry.
      2. Enzymes affect only the rate of reaction and not the position of equilibrium.
      3. The catalytic efficiency of an enzyme is measured by its turnover number.
   B. Enzyme cofactors (Section 19.2).
      1. Many enzymes include protein portions and nonprotein portions that are called cofactors.
      2. The cofactors, called coenzymes, are either metal ions or small organic molecules.
      3. Enzymes can obtain from cofactors chemically reactive groups not available as side chains.
      4. Some cofactors are covalently bonded; others serve as cosubstrates.
   C. Enzyme classification (Section 19.3).
      1. Classes of enzymes.
         a. Oxidoreductases catalyze oxidation–reduction reactions.
         b. Transferases catalyze the transfer of a specific group from one substrate to another.
         c. Hydrolases catalyze the hydrolysis of substrates.
         d. Isomerases catalyze the isomerization of substrates.
         e. Lyases catalyze the addition or elimination of small molecules.
         f. Ligases catalyze the bonding of two substrate molecules.
      2. Naming enzymes.
         a. The first part of the name identifies the substrate.
         b. The second part of the name identifies the enzyme subclass.
II. Enzyme function (Sections 19.4–19.6).
   A. How enzymes work (Section 19.4).
      1. Models for representing enzyme action.
         a. The shape of the active site is complementary to the shape of the substrate.
            i. This description of enzyme–substrate is called the lock-and-key model.
         b. A more modern interpretation of enzyme–substrate interaction is the induced-fit model.
            i. In this model, an enzyme is flexible enough to change shape to fit the spatial requirement of the substrate.
           ii. The enzyme and substrate induce each other to change shape.
      2. Mechanism of enzyme catalysis.
         a. An enzyme–substrate complex is formed when the substrate migrates to the active site, and atoms that will take part in the reaction are held in place (proximity effect).
         b. Reactants are positioned at the exact distance necessary for reaction to occur (orientation effect).
         c. The active site provides the kinds of functional groups necessary for catalysis (catalytic effect).
         d. The activation energy for reaction is lowered by introducing strain into the bonds of the substrate (energy effect).

C. Effect of concentration on enzyme activity (Section 19.5).
  1. When substrate concentration varies, and enzyme concentration remains constant:
    a. Additional substrate increases the rate until all active sites are occupied.
    b. At this point, reaction rate becomes constant.
    c. The enzyme is said to be saturated.
  2. Under most conditions, reaction rate is controlled by enzyme efficiency.
    a. The upper limit to reaction rate is about 10^8 collisions per mole per second.
  3. When substrate concentration is high, and enzyme concentration varies:
    a. Additional enzyme increases the reaction rate.
    b. The increase in reaction rate is directly proportional to enzyme concentration.
D. Influence of temperature and pH on enzymes (Section 19.6).
  1. Temperature.
    a. All enzymes have an optimum temperature for greatest catalytic efficiency. In the human body, this temperature is 37°C.
    b. At temperatures above 50–60°C, enzymes denature.
  2. pH.
    a. Enzymes also have an optimum pH.
    b. If pH is too high or too low, enzymes lose their ability to catalyze reactions.
III. Enzyme regulation (Sections 19.7–19.9).
  A. General strategies of control (Section 19.7).
    1. Activation is any process that increases the action of an enzyme.
    2. Inhibition is any process that slows or stops the action of an enzyme.
  B. Feedback and allosteric control.
    1. Feedback control.
      a. The product of a series of reactions is an inhibitor for the first reaction.
      b. This strategy keeps excessive amounts of products from accumulating.
    2. Allosteric control.
      a. Most enzymes are regulated by allosteric control.
      b. Allosteric enzymes have more than one polypeptide chain.
      c. Allosteric enzymes have catalytic sites and regulatory sites.
      d. Binding of a positive regulator increases reaction rate.
      e. Binding of a negative regulator decreases reaction rate.
  C. Enzyme inhibition (Section 19.8).
    1. Reversible uncompetitive inhibition.
      a. An inhibitor binds to the enzyme at a site other than the active site and changes the shape of the enzyme.
      b. The enzyme is a less effective catalyst, and reaction rate is slowed.
      c. The inhibitor doesn't compete with the substrate.
    2. Reversible competitive inhibition.
      a. In competitive inhibition, a substrate that resembles the normal substrate occupies the enzyme's active site.
      b. Competitive inhibition is reversible.
        i. The degree of inhibition can be regulated by controlling the amounts of substrate and inhibitor.
        ii. Increasing the concentration of substrate displaces inhibitor from the active site.
    3. Irreversible inhibition.
      a. The inhibitor bonds covalently to the active site, and the enzyme is irreversibly inhibited.
  D. Covalent modification and genetic control (Section 19.9).
    1. Zymogens.
      a. Some enzymes (zymogens) are synthesized in a form that differs from their catalytic form.
      b. Zymogens are activated by enzymatic addition or removal of a part of the zymogen.

c. Enzymes that might injure the body if constantly present in their active form are synthesized as zymogens.
2. Phosphorylation/dephosphorylation.
a. Phosphate groups can be added to serine and threonine side chains to activate certain enzymes.
3. Genetic control.
a. Synthesis of some enzymes is regulated by genes.
b. Genetic control is used for enzymes needed only at certain stages of development.
IV. Vitamins and minerals (Section 19.10).
A. Vitamins are small organic molecules that must be supplied in the diet.
B. Vitamins are classified by solubility.
1. Water-soluble vitamins are either coenzymes or precursors to coenzymes.
a. Water-soluble vitamins include vitamin C and the B vitamins.
2. Fat-soluble vitamins are stored in the body's fatty tissues.
a. Vitamin A is important for vision.
b. Vitamin D regulates calcium absorption.
c. Vitamin E is an antioxidant.
d. Vitamin K is involved in blood clotting.
C. Antioxidants.
1. Antioxidants include vitamins C, E, β-carotene, and selenium.
2. Antioxidants quench free radicals, suspected of being the source of many diseases.
D. Minerals.
1. Many transition metals are needed as micronutrients and enzyme cofactors.
2. Other minerals are needed in greater amounts for structural and metabolic purposes.

Solutions for Chapter 19 Problems

19.1 Ribonuclease catalyzes a maximum of 100 (10^2) reactions per second.

19.2 There are two reasons: (1) The enzyme might catalyze reactions within the eye if it were not removed. (2) Saline is sterile and is isotonic with body fluids.

19.3 Most vitamin/mineral supplements contain the listed metal ion cofactors (iron, zinc, copper, manganese, molybdenum, vanadium, cobalt, and nickel), as well as selenium and boron.

19.4 (a) NAD$^+$ contains niacin; coenzyme A contains pantothenic acid; FAD contains riboflavin.
(b) The other cofactors are minerals.

19.5 (a) Alcohol dehydrogenase catalyzes the removal of two —H from an alcohol.
(b) Aspartate transaminase catalyzes the transfer of an amino group from aspartate to a second substrate.
(c) Tyrosine–tRNA synthetase catalyzes the synthesis of tyrosine–tRNA from tyrosine and its tRNA, coupled with ATP hydrolysis.
(d) Phosphohexose isomerase catalyzes the isomerization of a phosphohexose.

19.6 (a) The enzyme is named urease. (b) The enzyme is cellulase.

19.7 Hexokinase belongs to the transferase class. It catalyzes the transfer of a phosphoryl group to a hexose.

19.8 In this lyase reaction, water adds to fumarate (substrate) to give L-malate (product).

19.9 Reaction (a) might be catalyzed by a decarboxylase because it involves a loss of CO_2. Reaction (b) isn't catalyzed by a decarboxylase.

19.10 Acidic, basic, and polar side chains can take part in catalytic activity and in holding the substrate in the active site. Nonpolar side chains can take part in holding the substrate in the active site but are not likely to be involved in catalytic activity.

19.11 If an enzyme is saturated with substrate, substrate molecules are bound to all of the active sites. (a) Increasing the substrate concentration has no effect on the rate because there are no empty sites where the added substrate can bind. (b) Adding more enzyme increases the rate because more enzyme–substrate complexes can form.

19.12 The rate of the reaction shown in Figure 19.7a is greater at 35 °C than at 25 °C. The rate is greater at 35 °C than at 45 °C.

19.13 The rate of the reaction catalyzed by pepsin is much greater at pH = 2 than at pH = 4.

19.14 Two strategies keep the enzyme active: (1) Use of chaperonins, enzymes that return a protein to its active form; (2) The protein itself is rigid and resists heat denaturation.

19.15 CPK, AST, and LDH_1 leak from damaged heart vessels.

19.16 (a) L-Isoleucine most likely inhibits enzyme E1.
(b) If product A inhibited E1, no isoleucine would form. Thus, product A can't be an inhibitor in the sequence shown.

19.17

(a)   (b)

p-Aminobenzoate

Structure (b) is a possible competitive inhibitor for the enzyme that has *p*-aminobenzoate (PABA) as a substrate because it resembles PABA both in shape and in the type of functional groups present.

19.18 A product of an enzyme-catalyzed reaction that resembles the substrate might be a competitive inhibitor for the enzyme.

19.19 Ritonavir acts on HIV protease by irreversible inhibition because it bonds to the active site of the enzyme.

19.20 (a) *Competitive inhibition* by use of a drug can regulate an overactive enzyme.
(b) *Covalent modification* by phosphorylation–dephosphorylation can regulate enzymes that are needed for quick energy. Alternatively, *feedback control* can regulate glucose production. When glucose levels are adequate, glucose inhibits the enzyme that catalyzes its formation. When glucose levels drop, the enzyme is no longer inhibited, and glucose is formed.
(c) *Covalent modification*, either by activation of a zymogen or by phosphorylation–dephosphorylation, is a type of enzyme regulation that occurs when an enzyme must be quickly activated.
(d) *Genetic control* regulates enzymes that are needed only during certain stages of development.

19.21 Vitamin A is fat-soluble because it has a long hydrocarbon chain. Vitamin C is water-soluble because it has polar hydroxyl groups.

19.22 The difference among these compounds occurs at the functional group at the end of the hydrocarbon chain. In retinal, a $-CHO$ group (aldehyde) replaces the $-CH_2OH$ group; in retinoic acid, the $-CH_2OH$ group becomes a $-COOH$ group.

19.23 Vitamins can be enzyme cofactors; some are antioxidants; they aid absorption of calcium and phosphate ions; they are used in synthesis of visual pigments; they are involved in the synthesis of blood-clotting factors.

19.24 Vitamins C and E, and ß-carotene (Vitamin A) function as antioxidants. These vitamins scavenge damaging free radicals.

19.25 Selenium is the most toxic micronutrient, causing damage to the respiratory tract and hair loss. Nevertheless, it is an enzyme cofactor that is a necessary micronutrient in small quantities.

Understanding Key Concepts

19.26

---- hydrogen bonds

ııııı salt bridges

19.28 The enzyme in Problem 19.27 will most likely not use D-lactate as a substrate because most enzymes are "handed" and catalyze the reaction of only one enantiomer of a pair of enantiomers. It is possible that D-lactate might act as a competitive inhibitor of the enzyme.

19.30 (a) Increasing the substrate concentration at constant inhibitor concentration increases the rate when substrate concentration is low. Very soon, however, a maximum rate is reached, and adding more substrate does not change the rate of reaction. This maximum rate is always lower than the rate of the uninhibited reaction.
(b) Decreasing the inhibitor concentration at constant substrate concentration increases the rate of reaction. As inhibitor concentration is decreased, more inhibitor dissociates from the enzyme, leaving active enzyme that is free to react with substrate.

19.32 (a) Feedback inhibition   (b) Irreversible inhibition   (c) Genetic control
(d) Uncompetitive inhibition

Structure and Classification of Enzymes

19.34 (a) A *dehydrogenase* catalyzes the removal of two –H to form a double bond.
(b) A *decarboxylase* catalyzes the replacement of a carboxyl group by –H.
(c) A *lipase* catalyzes the hydrolysis of ester groups in lipids.

19.36 (a) Amylase   (b) Peroxidase   (c) DNAse

19.38 An enzyme is a large three-dimensional molecule with a catalytic site into which a substrate can fit. Enzymes are specific in their action because only one or a few molecules have the appropriate shape and functional groups to fit into the catalytic site.

19.40 (a) A *hydrolase* catalyzes this reaction, which is the hydrolysis of a peptide bond.
(b) A *lyase* catalyzes this reaction.
(c) An *oxidoreductase* catalyzes the introduction of a double bond into a molecule by removal of H_2.

19.42 (a) A *dehydrase* catalyzes the loss of water from a substrate to give a double bond.
(b) A *transmethylase* catalyzes the transfer of a methyl group between substrates.
(c) A *reductase* catalyzes the reduction of a substrate.

19.44 A urease is a hydrolase because it catalyzes the hydrolysis of urea to ammonia and carbonic acid.

19.46 (a) Riboflavin (B_2)   (b) Pantothenic acid (B_5) (c) Niacin (B_3)

Enzyme Function and Regulation

19.48 In the lock-and-key model of enzyme action, the active site of an enzyme has a specific shape (lock) into which only a specific substrate (key) can fit. In the induced-fit model, the shape of the active site changes to accommodate the substrate.

19.50 The amino acid residues involved in the active site can be brought close to each other by protein folding without being near each other in the polypeptide chain.

19.52 To function in the very acidic environment of the stomach, an enzyme must be active at a low pH. To function in the intestine, an enzyme must have high catalytic activity at a pH near neutral. Each enzyme has an optimum pH for catalysis, and an enzyme that is most active at neutral pH will not be active in a strongly acidic environment.

19.54 At a high substrate concentration relative to enzyme concentration, the rate of reaction triples if the concentration of enzyme is tripled.

19.56 (a) Raising the temperature of the enzyme-catalyzed reaction from 37 °C to 60 °C drastically decreases the rate of reaction and possibly denatures the enzyme..
(b) Lowering the pH of the enzyme-catalyzed reaction from 7 to 3 will probably decrease the rate of reaction, since most enzymes have their optimum rates at close to neutral pH. However, if the enzyme has a rate optimum near 3, then the decrease in pH will increase the rate of reaction.
(b) Adding an organic solvent denatures the enzyme, stopping the reaction.

19.58 (a) *Competitive inhibition* occurs when the structure of a second substrate closely resembles that of the normal substrate for an enzyme. The second substrate can occupy the active site and inhibit binding at the active site of the usual substrate. Competitive inhibition is usually reversible.

Uncompetitive inhibition occurs when an inhibitor binds to the enzyme at a location other than the active site. The conformation of the enzyme changes, and the enzyme is inactivated or its catalytic ability is reduced. Noncompetitive inhibition is reversible.

Irreversible inhibition occurs when a molecule covalently bonds to the active site of an enzyme. The active site is thus irreversibly inactivated, and enzyme activity stops.

(b) In competitive inhibition, the inhibitor bonds noncovalently to the active site. In uncompetitive inhibition, the inhibitor binds noncovalently with a group away from the active site. In irreversible inhibition, the inhibitor forms a covalent bond at the active site.

19.60 Graph C represents the activity of Eco R1 after EDTA has been added. When EDTA is first added, the rate levels off as EDTA chelates the Mg^{2+} ions. When all Mg^{2+} has been removed, the enzyme is no longer active and the rate approaches zero.

19.62 Lead poisons enzymes by bonding to cysteine residues or by displacing an essential metal from an active site. Bonding to cysteine is irreversible and denatures the enzyme.

19.64 Papain is effective as a meat tenderizer because it catalyzes the hydrolysis of peptide bonds and partially digests the proteins in the meat and softens tough connective tissue.

19.66 Allosteric enzymes have two types of binding sites – one type of site is for catalysis of the enzymatic reaction and one type of site is for regulation of the reaction. Having two kinds of sites allows for greater regulation and control of enzyme activity.

19.68 Feedback inhibition occurs when the end product of a series of reactions is an inhibitor for an earlier reaction. When this product accumulates, it inhibits an enzyme that catalyzes an earlier step in the series, and the rate of product formation slows down. When the amount of product decreases, inhibition stops, and product formation is resumed.

19.70 A zymogen is an enzyme that is synthesized in a form different from its active form and is activated when needed by removal of a covalently bonded portion of the enzyme. Some enzymes are secreted as zymogens because they would digest or otherwise injure the body if they were secreted in their active form.

Vitamins

19.72 Vitamins are small essential organic molecules that the body can't manufacture and that must be obtained in trace amounts from the diet.

19.74 Vitamin C (water-soluble) is excreted in the urine and must be replenished daily, whereas vitamin A (fat-soluble) can be stored in fatty tissue.

19.76 Calcium and phosphorus are both components of bone.

Chemistry in Action

19.78 Enzymes from thermophiles that break down starch to form glucose allow the reaction to be run at higher temperatures, increasing the reaction rate and yield without undergoing denaturation.

19.80 Creatine phosphokinase (CPK) gives the earliest indication of a heart attack. The levels of lactate dehydrogenase (LDH) isoenzymes confirm a heart attack after several days.

19.82 A mild ACE inhibitor allows for more careful control of blood pressure. If a very potent ACE inhibitor were used to control blood pressure, blood pressure might drop drastically and cause serious medical problems. If pit viper peptide were modified so that it caused irreversible inhibition of ACE, it would be a more powerful inhibitor, but it would also be a more dangerous drug. A possible modification to pit viper peptide might be the inclusion of an —SH group near proline that binds irreversibly to the zinc atom at the active site.

19.84 Vitamin A: 0%; Vitamin C: 0%; Calcium: 4%; Iron: 6% This food is not a good source of vitamins and minerals.

19.86 Listings for vitamin A, vitamin C, iron, and calcium are mandatory on food labels because they are considered to be of greatest importance in maintaining good health.

General Questions and Problems

19.88

19.90

$$1.6 \text{ mg riboflavin} \times \frac{100 \text{ mL apple juice}}{0.014 \text{ mg riboflavin}} = 11,000 \text{ mL} = 11 \text{ L apple juice}$$

19.92 Because competitive inhibition is reversible, addition of a large amount of the normal substrate will reverse the binding of the inhibitor, and the rate of reaction of the normal substrate will return to its usual value. The effects of uncompetitive inhibition can't be reversed by addition of excess substrate.

19.94 If valine replaced serine, the enzyme would be inactivated because the —OH functional group of serine is essential for enzyme activity. If aspartate replaced glutamate, the effect would probably be minor because both amino acids have the same functional groups.

Self-Test for Chapter 19

Multiple Choice

1. A subclass of enzyme that catalyzes cleavage of peptide bonds is a:
    (a) lipase (b) dehydrase (c) protease (d) reductase

2. Which of the following is an enzyme cofactor?
    (a) thiamine (b) tocopherol (c) hexokinase (d) trypsin

3. The ability of enzymes to bring reactants together is known as the:
    (a) orientation effect (b) catalytic effect (c) proximity effect (d) energy effect

4. Fat-soluble vitamins serve all of the following functions except:
    (a) promotion of bone growth (b) acting as an antioxidant (c) aiding night vision
    (d) preventing anemia

5. Which of the following enzymes probably requires a coenzyme that is reduced during reaction?
   (a) transferase   (b) oxidase   (c) isomerase   (d) dehydrase

6. The most likely control mechanism for reactions that occur during embryonic development is:
   (a) feedback control   (b) genetic control   (c) zymogens   (d) allosteric control

7. Snake venom probably causes its effects by:
   (a) noncompetitive inhibition   (b) competitive inhibition   (c) allosteric control
   (d) irreversible inhibition

8. Why does the rate of enzymatic reactions decrease as temperature is lowered?
   (a) Salt bridges are disrupted.   (b) The shape of the active site is changed.   (c) Reactions are slower at lower temperatures.   (d) The enzyme begins to denature.

9. If an enzyme is saturated, adding more substrate will:
   (a) increase reaction rate   (b) have no effect on reaction rate   (c) decrease reaction rate
   (d) have varying effects, depending on the enzyme

10. In which of the following types of enzyme regulation can adding large amounts of substrate restore an enzyme's reaction rate to its maximum value?
    (a) feedback inhibition   (b) irreversible inhibition   (c) uncompetitive inhibition
    (d) competitive inhibition

Sentence Completion

1.   An enzyme called a _____ catalyzes the isomerization of a chiral center.

2.   _____ are enzymes that have slightly different structures but that catalyze the same reaction.

3.   Vitamin __ is necessary for the synthesis of blood-clotting factors.

4.   In the _____ - _____ model of enzyme action, an enzyme can change its shape slightly to fit different substrates.

5.   In _____ inhibition, an inhibitor changes the shape of an enzyme by binding at a location other than the active site.

6.   If the temperature becomes too high, enzymes begin to _____.

7.   The catalytic activity of an enzyme is measured by its _____ _____.

8.   A type of covalent modification of an enzyme involves addition or removal of a _____ group.

9.   The _____ effect is responsible for bringing substrate and catalytic sites together.

10.   The upper limit of any enzyme's rate of reaction is ___collisions per mole per second.

11.   An _____ enzyme has more than one chain and has binding sites for both substrate and regulator.

12.   An enzyme that is synthesized in a form different from its active form is called a _____.

True or False

1. 98.6°F is the optimum temperature for most enzymes.

2. In an enzyme–substrate complex, the substrate is in its lowest energy shape.

3. Uncompetitive inhibition is irreversible.

4. A dehydrogenase catalyzes the loss of H_2O from a substrate.

5. At the active site, the enzyme and substrate are held together by covalent bonds.

6. Vitamins may be small organic molecules or inorganic ions.

7. Chymotrypsinogen is a zymogen.

8. β-Carotene is the active form of vitamin A.

9. Copper, cobalt, and selenium are essential enzyme cofactors.

10. Heavy metals cause irreversible inhibition of enzymes.

11. As enzyme concentration is increased, the reaction rate eventually levels off.

12. The side chains of serine and threonine are sites of covalent modification.

Match each entry on the left with its partner on the right.

1. Papain   (a) Deficiency causes anemia

2. Vitamin D   (b) Occurs away from an enzyme's active site

3. Competitive inhibition   (c) Nonspecific enzyme

4. Kinase   (d) Catalyzes hydrolysis of ester groups in lipids

5. Alanine transaminase   (e) Protein part of enzyme, plus cofactor

6. Cofactor   (f) Deficiency causes scurvy

7. Uncompetitive inhibition   (g) Transfers a phosphate group between substrates

8. Vitamin B_6 (h) Fat-soluble vitamin

9. Lipase   (i) Occurs at an enzyme's active site

10. Vitamin C   (j) Metal ion or small organic molecule

11. Active enzyme   (k) Specific enzyme

12. Lyase   (l) Catalyzes loss of small molecule from substrate

Chapter 20   The Generation of Biochemical Energy

Chapter Outline

I. Energy and cells (Sections 20.1–20.3).
 A. Energy requirements for living things (Section 20.1).
  1. Energy must be released from food gradually.
  2. Energy must be stored in a readily accessible form.
  3. The rate of release of energy from storage must be finely controlled.
  4. Just enough energy must be released as heat to maintain body temperature.
  5. Energy in a form other than heat must be available to drive reactions that aren't spontaneous at body temperature.
 B. Free energy and biochemical reactions (Section 20.2).
  1. In favorable chemical reactions, free energy is released.
   a. Favorable reactions occur when heat is released and/or disorder increases.
   b. These reactions are described as exergonic.
   c. In favorable reactions, the products are more stable than the reactants.
   d. Favorable reactions have a negative value for ΔG.
  2. Free energy must be provided for unfavorable chemical reactions to take place.
   a. Unfavorable reactions are described as endergonic.
   b. Energy must be supplied in order for endergonic reactions to proceed.
   c. In unfavorable reactions, the products are less stable than the reactants.
   d. Unfavorable reactions have a positive value for ΔG.
 C. Cells and their structure (Section 20.3).
  1. Simple organisms have prokaryotic cells.
  2. More complicated organisms have eukaryotic cells.
   a. These cells have membrane-enclosed nuclei and organelles.
  3. Structure of eukaryotic cells.
   a. Everything between the cell membrane and the nuclear membrane is the cytoplasm.
   b. The fluid of the cytoplasm is the cytosol.
   c. The most important organelles are the mitochondria.
    i. Mitochondria consist of a smooth outer membrane and a folded inner membrane.
    ii. The space between the two membranes is the intermembrane space.
    iii. The space enclosed by the inner membrane is the mitochondrial matrix.
    iv. Most of the energy-producing reactions of the cell begin in the mitochondrial matrix.
II. Metabolism (Sections 20.4–20.7).
 A. Overview of metabolism (Section 20.4).
  1. A sequence of reactions in metabolism is known as a metabolic pathway.
   a. Pathways may be linear, cyclic, or spiral.
   b. Pathways that break molecules apart are known as catabolic pathways.
   c. Pathways that build molecules are known as anabolic pathways.
  2. Catabolism consists of four phases.
   a. Digestion occurs in the mouth and small intestine.
   b. Small molecules are degraded in the cell to yield acetyl-CoA.
   c. Acetyl groups are oxidized to yield CO_2, H_2O, and energy.
   d. Some of the energy is transferred to ATP and reduced coenzymes.

B. Strategies of metabolism (Sections 20.5–20.7).
  1. ATP and energy transfer (Section 20.5).
    a. ATP contains two phosphoric anhydride bonds and a phosphate ester bond.
    b. Hydrolysis of one phosphate anhydride bond provides –7.3 kcal/mol (–30.5 kJ/mol) of energy.
    c. Synthesis of ATP from ADP and phosphate requires +7.3 kcal/mol (–30.5 kJ/mol) of energy.
    d. Synthesis of ATP occurs when there is energy to store, and hydrolysis of ATP occurs when energy is needed.
  2. Metabolic pathways and coupled reactions (Section 20.6).
    a. In any reaction, the amount of energy consumed or released is the same, no matter what the path.
    b. The overall energy change for a series of reactions can be found by adding up the free energy changes for the individual steps.
    c. A reaction that is energetically unfavorable can take place if it is coupled with a reaction that is energetically favorable.
      i. The phosphorylation of glucose can take place by coupling with the conversion of ATP to ADP.
      ii. ATP can be synthesized by coupling with the transfer of a phosphoryl group from phosphoenolpyruvate.
  3. Oxidized and reduced coenzymes (Section 20.7).
    a. Many biochemical reactions are redox reactions.
      i. Oxidation may be loss of electrons, loss of hydrogen, or addition of oxygen.
      ii. Reduction may be gain of electrons, gain of hydrogen, or removal of oxygen.
      iii. Reductions and oxidations always occur together.
    b. Common redox coenzymes are NAD^+, $NADP^+$ and FAD (written in the oxidized form).
      i. NAD^+ and $NADP^+$ are used to oxidize alcohols to carbonyl compounds.
      ii. FAD catalyzes the formation of a double bond.
    c. The energy stored in $FADH_2$, $NADH/H^+$, and $NADPH/H^+$ is passed on to ATP.
III. Metabolic pathways (Sections 20.8–20.10).
  A. The citric acid cycle (Section 20.8).
    1. Oxidation of two-carbon acyl groups from acetyl-CoA to CO_2 occurs in the citric acid cycle.
    2. The citric acid cycle is a closed loop of eight reactions in which the product of step 8 is a reactant in step 1.
    3. The cycle operates only if:
      a. Acetyl groups are available.
      b. NAD^+ and FAD are in their oxidized form.
      c. Oxygen is available.
    4. A summary of steps:
      a. Steps 1, 2: Preparation.
        i. Acetyl-CoA + oxalate —> citrate.
        ii. Citrate is isomerized to isocitrate.
      b. Steps 3, 4: Oxidative decarboxylation.
        i. Isocitrate is oxidized and decarboxylated to form α-ketoglutarate, with reduction of NAD^+.
        ii. α-Ketoglutarate is decarboxylated to form succinyl-CoA and reduced NAD^+.
      c. Step 5: Phosphorylation.
        i. Succinyl-CoA + GDP —> succinate + HSCoA + GTP.
      d. Step 6: Oxidation of succinate.
        i. Succinate + FAD —> fumarate + $FADH_2$.

    e. Steps 7, 8: Regeneration of oxaloacetate.
       i. Fumarate + H_2O —> malate.
       ii. Malate + NAD^+ —> oxaloacetate + NADH/H^+.
  5. Net result of citric acid cycle:
    a. Production of four reduced coenzyme molecules.
    b. Conversion of an acetyl group to two CO_2 molecules.
    c. Production of one GTP.
B. The electron transport chain and production of ATP (Section 20.9).
  1. The end product of the electron transport chain is water in the reaction:
      $O_2 + 4\,e^- + 4\,H^+$ —> $2\,H_2O$
  2. The reactions of the electron transport chain are coupled to oxidative phosphorylation.
  3. Enzymes for electron transport are embedded in the inner mitochondrial membrane.
  4. Features of the electron transport chain:
    a. Hydrogen and electrons from NADH and $FADH_2$ enter the respiratory chain from the mitochondrial matrix.
    b. Electrons pass from weaker to stronger electron acceptors.
    c. Some of the energy released is used to transport H^+ into the intermembrane space.
    d. The H^+ concentration gradient creates a potential energy difference that is crucial for ATP synthesis.
    e. H^+ ions can return to the complex only by passing through a channel that is part of the ATP synthase complex.
       i. The energy that they release drives the phosphorylation of ATP.
  5. Various cofactors, including iron–sulfur clusters and cytochromes, are involved in electron transport.
  6. Ultimately, electrons are passed on to oxygen, which combines with H^+ to form H_2O.
  7. The energy needed for ATP synthesis is provided by the passage of H^+ ions through the ATP synthase enzyme complex.
  8. The passage of electrons from one mol NADH produces from 2.5 to 3 mol ATP.
C. Harmful oxygen by-products and antioxidants (Section 20.10).
  1. Oxygen can be consumed in other redox reactions besides electron transport.
  2. The products of these reactions may be H_2O_2, the $\cdot OH^-$ radical, or superoxide ion $\cdot O_2^-$.
  3. People are protected from the harmful effects of these species by several enzymes, as well as by antioxidants and vitamins A, C and E.

Solutions to Chapter 20 Problems

20.1 Use two facts to solve this problem:
    (1) A reaction with a negative ΔG is exergonic, and a reaction with a positive ΔG is endergonic.
    (2) A reaction with a larger negative ΔG releases more energy than a reaction with a smaller negative ΔG.

    Thus, reactions (a) and (c) are exergonic, and reaction (b) is endergonic. Reaction (a) releases the most energy, because its ΔG has a larger negative value than the ΔG's of the other reactions.
    L-Malate $\longrightarrow$ Fumarate + H_2O ΔG = + 0.9 kcal/mol (+3.77 kJ/mol)

20.2 The amount of energy produced by both processes is the same.

20.3 (a) Oxidation of glucose is exergonic, and photosynthesis is endergonic.
    (b) Sunlight provides the energy for the endergonic pathway.

20.4 (a) Carbohydrates are digested in the mouth, stomach, and small intestine to yield sugars, which are degraded in the cytosol to pyruvate via glycolysis. Pyruvate is converted to acetyl-CoA, which enters the citric acid cycle and is oxidized to CO_2. The reduced coenzymes that are generated by oxidation of acetyl-CoA enter the electron-transport chain and are used in the production of ATP by oxidative phosphorylation.
(b) The products of amino acid catabolism can enter the central metabolic pathway as pyruvate, as acetyl-CoA, and as citric acid cycle intermediates.

20.5

Acetyl phosphate

20.6 This strategy ensures that an exergonic reaction occurs only when the energy it releases is needed.

20.7

Glycerol   Glycerol 1-phosphate

20.8 If a metabolic pathway that breaks down a molecule is exergonic, the reverse of that pathway (synthesis) *must* be endergonic. The only way to synthesize the product is to couple the energetically unfavorable reactions with other reactions that are energetically favorable in a pathway that differs from the reverse of the breakdown pathway.

20.9 Together, the soda + hamburger contain 660 Calories. If jogging consumes 10 Calories/minute, it would take 660 Calories ÷ 10 Calories/minute = 66 minutes to burn off these calories.

20.10 Acetyl phosphate + H_2O $\longrightarrow$ Acetate + $HOPO_3^{2-}$ + H^+ $\Delta G = -10.3$ kcal/mol
                                                                                                    (= −43.1 kJ/mol)

ADP + $HOPO_3^{2-}$ + H^+ $\longrightarrow$ ATP + H_2O $\Delta G = +7.3$ kcal/mol
                                                                                              (= +30.5 kJ/mol)

Acetyl phosphate + ADP $\longrightarrow$ Acetate + ATP $\Delta G = -3.0$ kcal/mol
                                                                                   (= −12.6 kJ/mol)

The reaction is favorable because ΔG is negative.

20.11 All of these are found in FAD. The part of the structure on the right is ADP (b), which contains a phosphate anhydride bond (d). The part of the structure on the left contains a substituted benzene ring [(c), top]. There are five heterocyclic rings (a) - the three in ADP and the two rings of $FADH_2$ that are not benzene rings.

20.12 The hydrogen atoms removed are circled. The reactions are catalyzed by oxidoreductases.

Step 3:

Step 6:

Step 8:

20.13 Citrate and isocitrate are the anions of tricarboxylic acids.

20.14 Reduced coenzymes are produced in steps 3, 4, 6, and 8.

20.15 FAD is the coenzyme involved with the formation of a carbon–carbon double bond; NAD^+ is involved with the formation of a carbonyl double bond.

20.16 Citrate is a tertiary alcohol, and isocitrate and malate are secondary alcohols.

20.17 Isocitrate has two chiral carbon atoms.

20.18 Steps 1–4 correspond to the first stage, and Steps 5–8 correspond to the second stage.

20.19 The pH is higher in the mitochondrial matrix because the $[H^+]$ is higher in the intermembrane space.

20.20 *Similarities:* both involve the reaction of glucose, oxygen, carbon dioxide, and water; both take place in organelles (chloroplasts, mitochondria); both involve large, metal-ion-containing molecules (chlorophyll, heme); both involve electron transfer; both involve similar coenzymes.

Differences: photosynthesis captures energy, whereas electron transport releases energy; photosynthesis requires light, whereas oxidative phosphorylation doesn't.

20.21 O_2 is the final electron acceptor. When H^+ ions move from a region of high concentration to a region of low concentration, energy is released that is used in ATP synthesis.

Understanding Key Concepts

20.22 (a) Exergonic reaction:

Succinyl phosphate + H_2O $\longrightarrow$ Succinate + $HOPO_3^{2-}$ + H^+

(b) Endergonic reaction:

ADP + $HOPO_3^{2-}$ + H^+ $\longrightarrow$ ATP + H_2O ΔG = +7.3 kcal/mol (+30.5 kJ/mol)

20.24 When ATP "drives" a reaction, energy from ATP hydrolysis is used to allow another reaction to proceed. In this case, the reaction that forms fatty acid-CoA from a fatty acid and coenzyme A is endergonic and is unfavorable in the absence of ATP. When the energy from hydrolysis of ATP is used to drive the reaction, the formation of fatty acid-CoA can take place. Coupling is the metabolic strategy in which the energy from an energetically favorable reaction can be used to allow an energetically unfavorable reaction to take place.

20.26

Isocitrate   α-Ketoglutarate

(a) The coenzyme NAD^+ is involved with reaction **A**.
(b) CO_2 is evolved and an H^+ is added in reaction **B**.
(c) The product of Step **A** is a β–keto acid because its ketone group is two carbons away from the carboxylic acid group bonded to the middle carbon.
(d) Isocitrate dehydrogenase is an oxidoreductase.

20.28 Metals are better oxidizing and reducing agents. Also, they can accept and donate electrons in one-electron increments.

Free Energy and Biochemical Reactions

20.30 An endergonic reaction requires energy, and an exergonic reaction releases energy.

20.32 Enzymes only increase the rate of reaction and have no effect on either the magnitude or the sign of ΔG.

20.34 Reactions (a) and (b) are exergonic; reaction (c) is endergonic. Reaction (b) proceeds farthest toward products at equilibrium because it has the largest negative value for ΔG.

Cells and Their Structure

20.36 All of the traits listed can be characteristic of eukaryotic cells; (a), (c), and (d) are specifically eukaryotic characteristics. Traits (b) and (e) are characteristic of prokaryotes.

20.38 Organelles are subcellular structures that perform specialized tasks within the cell.

20.40 Cristae, the folds of the inner mitochondrial membrane, provide extra surface area for electron transport and ATP production to take place.

Metabolism

20.42 Metabolism refers to all reactions that take place inside cells. Digestion is a part of metabolism in which food is broken down into small organic molecules.

20.44 Acetyl-CoA is formed from the catabolism of all three major classes of food.

Strategies of Metabolism

20.46 An ATP molecule transfers a phosphoryl group to another molecule in exergonic reactions.

20.48

1,3-Bisphosphoglycerate + H_2O $\longrightarrow$
    3-Phosphoglycerate + $HOPO_3^{2-}$ + H^+ $\Delta G = -11.8$ kcal/mol
                                                        $(-49.4$ kJ/mol$)$
ADP + $HOPO_3^{2-}$ + H^+ $\longrightarrow$ ATP + H_2O $\Delta G = +7.3$ kcal/mol
                                                        $(+30.5$ kJ/mol$)$

1,3-Bisphosphoglycerate + ADP $\longrightarrow$
    3-Phosphoglycerate + ATP $\Delta G = -4.5$ kcal/mol
                                    $(-18.8$ kJ/mol$)$

The reaction is favorable because ΔG is negative.

20.50 The hydrolysis of fructose 6-phosphate ($\Delta G = -3.3$ kcal/mol) is not favorable for phosphorylating ADP ($\Delta G = +7.3$ kcal/mol) because the overall value of ΔG ($+4.0$ kcal/mol) is positive. Any of the reactions in Table 20.1 that have a value of ΔG greater than -7.3 kcal/mol can be coupled with the phosphorylation of ADP to produce a favorable reaction.

20.52 (a) NAD^+ is reduced when a molecule is dehydrogenated.
(b) NAD^+ is an oxidizing agent because it oxidizes substrates and is itself reduced.
(c) NAD^+ oxidizes secondary alcohols to ketones.
(d) After dehydrogenation, NAD^+ becomes $NADH/H^+$.
(e)

The Citric Acid Cycle

20.54 The citric acid cycle takes place in cellular mitochondria.

20.56 The two acetyl-CoA carbons are oxidized to CO_2 in the citric acid cycle.

20.58 Three molecules of NADH/H$^+$ and one molecule of FADH$_2$ are produced in each turn of the citric acid cycle.

20.60 Step 3 (isocitrate → α-ketoglutarate), Step 4 (α-ketoglutarate → succinyl-CoA) and Step 8 (malate → oxaloacetate) store energy as NADH.

The Electron Transport Chain/Oxidative Phosphorylation

20.62 One complete citric acid cycle produces four reduced coenzymes, which enter the electron transfer chain and ultimately generate ATP.

20.64 The ultimate products of the electron transport chain are water, energy in the form of ATP, and the oxidized coenzymes FAD and NAD$^+$.

20.66 (a) FAD = flavin adenine dinucleotide
(b) CoQ = coenzyme Q
(c) NADH/H$^+$ = reduced nicotinamide adenine dinucleotide, plus hydrogen ion
(d) Cyt c = Cytochrome c

20.68 *First* – – – – – – – – – – – – – – – – – –> *Last*
NADH, coenzyme Q, cytochrome c

20.70 If FADH$_2$ and NADH weren't reoxidized, the body's supply of the oxidized forms of these coenzymes would be depleted, and the citric acid cycle would stop.

20.72 In oxidative phosphorylation, reduced coenzymes are oxidized, and ADP is phosphorylated.

20.74 The energy to drive oxidative phosphorylation is supplied by the movement of H$^+$ ions from the intermembrane space to the mitochondrial matrix through channels that are part of the ATP synthase enzyme complex embedded in the inner mitochondrial membrane.

20.76 When ATP production is decoupled, oxygen consumption increases because the proton gradient disappears, more water is formed, and more oxygen is used.

20.78 A seal has more brown fat because it needs to generate more body heat than a cat does.

Chemistry in Action

20.80 Bacteria use H$_2$S because no light is available for the usual light-dependent reaction of H$_2$O that provides O$_2$ and electrons.

20.82 (no answer)

20.84 Daily activities such as walking use energy, and thus the body requires a larger caloric intake than that needed to maintain basal metabolism.

20.86 The light-dependent reaction of photosynthesis occurs in the chloroplasts and is used to produce O_2, NADPH, and ATP. The NADPH and ATP are used in the light-independent reaction to produce carbohydrate molecules from water and carbon dioxide.

20.88 Refrigeration slows the breakdown of carbohydrates by decreasing the rate of respiration.

General Questions and Problems

20.90

20.92 NAD^+ and FAD are associated with oxidoreductases.

20.94 This reaction requires FAD because it involves the removal of two hydrogen atoms to introduce a double bond. The enzyme involved is an oxidoreductase (dehydrogenase).

20.96 Energy from combustion is released to the surroundings as heat and is wasted. Energy from metabolic oxidation is released in several steps and is stored in each step so that it is available for use in other metabolic processes.

20.98 The enzymes superoxide dismutase and catalase and vitamins E, C, and A can inactivate these reactive oxygen species.

20.100 The cells that need the most energy have the most mitochondria. In order, from fewest to most mitochondria per cell: adipose tissue, skin cells, skeletal muscle, heart muscle.

20.102 The intermembrane space is more acidic because it has a higher $[H^+]$ concentration.

20.104 *Least oxidized–––––––––> Most oxidized*
      succinate, fumarate = malate, oxaloacetate

Self-Test for Chapter 20

Multiple Choice

1. Which of the following oxygen by-products isn't produced in the human body?
   (a) $\cdot O_2^-$ (b) O_3 (c) $HO\cdot$ (d) H_2O_2

2. The hydrolysis of which of the following substrates can be coupled with the reaction ADP + phosphate —> ATP to produce an energetically favorable reaction?
   (a) glucose 6-phosphate (b) glucose 1-phosphate (c) creatine phosphate
   (d) fructose 6-phosphate

3. Which of the following cofactors isn't held in a fixed position in electron transport?
   (a) coenzyme Q (b) FMN (c) iron–sulfur clusters (d) cytochrome a

4. Which of the following reactions is an oxidation?
   (a) Fe^{3+} —> Fe^{2+} (b) CH_3COOH —> CH_3CHO
   (c) $CH_3CH_2CH_2COOH$ —>$CH_3CH=CHCOOH$ (d) CH_3COOCH_3—> $CH_3COOH + CH_3OH$

5. All of the following statements about electron transport are true except:
   (a) A concentration gradient is established between the inner membrane and the mitochondrial matrix. (b) Electrons are passed from weaker electron acceptors to stronger electron acceptors. (c) A greater amount of energy is produced from oxidation of NADH than from oxidation of $FADH_2$. (d) Some of the enzyme cofactors in the electron transport chain are mobile.

6. All of the following reactions are oxidations except:
   (a) isocitrate —> α-ketoglutarate (b) α-ketoglutarate —> succinyl-SCoA
   (c) succinate —> fumarate (d) fumarate —> malate

7. Which of the following citric acid cycle enzymes is an isomerase?
   (a) citrate synthetase (b) aconitase (c) succinyl-CoA synthetase (d) fumarase

8. Which coenzyme is not an oxidizing agent?
   (a) FAD (b) Coenzyme Q (c) Acetyl-CoA (d) NAD^+

9. All of the following reactions have positive ΔG except:
   (a) photosynthesis (b) hydrolysis of acetyl-CoA (c) formation of ATP from ADP
   (d) formation of glucose 6-phosphate

10. Which of the following metabolic pathways doesn't occur in mitochondria?
    (a) oxidative phosphorylation (b) ATP synthesis (c) citric acid cycle (d) degradation of carbohydrates

Sentence Completion

1. _____ cells are found in higher organisms.

2. A → B → C is known as a _____ _____.

3. ATP is synthesized from _____ and _____.

4. A reaction that requires energy in order to take place is said to be energetically _____.

5. The citric acid cycle is also known as the _____ and as the _____ - _____ cycle.

6. α-Ketoglutaric acid reacts with acetyl-CoA to yield _____ and _____.

7. Reactions that use the coenzyme _____ remove two hydrogens from an alcohol to yield a ketone.

8. A complete citric acid cycle yields _____ molecules of ATP.

9. _____ is the material that fills the interior of a cell.

10. _____ is a fast-acting enzyme that catalyzes the decomposition of reactive oxygen species.

11. The reaction succinate —> fumarate is catalyzed by _____ _____ .

12. _____ _____ is the minimal amount of energy required to stay alive.

True or False

1. ATP is a higher-energy molecule than ADP.

2. Both prokaryotic and eukaryotic cells are found in higher organisms.

3. Anabolism is the breakdown of high-energy molecules.

4. In a reaction that is energetically unfavorable, the energy of the products is less than the energy of the reactants.

5. The third and fourth stages of digestion take place in the mitochondria.

6. A reaction that is energetically unfavorable can use ATP as an energy source.

7. $FADH_2$ donates two electrons to cytochrome c in the respiratory chain.

8. FAD removes two hydrogens from a carbon chain to yield a double bond.

9. Release of heat and increase of order contribute to making a reaction favorable.

10. ATP is synthesized only in the respiratory chain.

11. In the synthesis of ATP from ADP, a phosphate ester bond is formed.

12. The reactions of the citric acid cycle may be exergonic or endergonic.

Match each entry on the left with its partner on the right.

1. Mitochondrion

2. Oxidative phosphorylation

3. Isocitrate

4. Anabolic reaction

5. Succinyl-CoA → succinate

6. Citric acid cycle

7. Malate → oxaloacetate

8. Catabolic reaction

9. Respiratory chain

10. Cytochrome

11. Succinate → fumarate

12. Organelle

(a) Uses energy

(b) Yields one molecule of H_2O

(c) Releases energy

(d) Site of energy production in cell

(e) Reduces NAD^+ to $NADH/H^+$

(f) Tricarboxylic acid

(g) Contains an iron atom

(h) Subcellular structure

(i) Reduces FAD to $FADH_2$

(j) ATP synthesis

(k) Yields 2 molecules of CO_2

(l) Yields acetyl-CoA plus ATP

Chapter 21   Carbohydrates

Chapter Outline

I. General information about carbohydrates (Sections 21.1–21.3).
    A. Classification of carbohydrates (Section 21.1).
        1. By complexity.
            a. Monosaccharides don't yield smaller molecules when hydrolyzed.
            b. Disaccharides are composed of two monosaccharides.
            c. Polysaccharides are composed of a large number of monosaccharides.
        2. By carbonyl group.
            a. Aldoses contain an aldehyde carbonyl group.
            b. Ketoses contain a ketone carbonyl group.
        3. By number of carbons in a monosaccharide unit.
            a. Prefixes (*tri-*, *tetra-*, *penta-*) indicate the number of carbons in the monosaccharide.
    B. Handedness (Section 21.2–21.3).
        1. General characteristics of handed molecules (Section 21.2).
            a. Compounds having a carbon bonded to four different groups are chiral.
                i.   A compound with a chiral carbon can exist in either a right-handed form (D) or a left-handed form (L).
                ii. These two forms are called enantiomers.
                iii. An "optically active" compound rotates the plane of plane-polarized light.
                iv. Enantiomers rotate the plane of plane-polarized light to the same extent but in opposite directions.
            b. Compounds having *n* chiral centers can have 2^n possible stereoisomers.
                i.   Some of these isomers are enantiomers.
                ii. Stereoisomers that are not mirror images are diastereomers.
                iii. Some chiral compounds have fewer than the predicted number of stereoisomers because of symmetry.
        2. D and L sugars (Section 21.3).
            a. Stereoisomers can be drawn as Fischer projections.
                i.   In these projections, the chiral carbon is drawn as the intersection of two perpendicular lines.
                ii. Bonds that point out of the page are shown as horizontal lines.
                iii. Bonds that point back into the page are vertical lines.
                iv. In sugars, the carbonyl group is at or near the top of a Fischer projection.
            b. Monosaccharides are divided into two families.
                i.   In D sugars, the —OH group bonded to the chiral carbon farthest from the carbonyl group points to the right.
                ii. In L sugars, the —OH group bonded to the chiral carbon farthest from the carbonyl group points to the left.
                iii. Most of the carbohydrates that occur naturally are D stereoisomers.
            c. Fischer projections of molecules with more than one chiral carbon are drawn by stacking the chiral centers on top of each other.
            d. The enantiomer of a Fischer projection can be drawn by reversing the horizontal substituents on each chiral carbon.
            e. The designations D and L are unrelated to the sign of the direction of rotation.
II. Monosaccharides (Sections 21.4–21.6).
    A. Structure of monosaccharides (Section 21.4).
        1. Monosaccharides with five or more carbons usually exist as cyclic internal hemiacetals, formed between a hydroxyl group and the carbonyl group.

        a. The hemiacetal carbon (C1) can have two stereoisomeric forms.

        b. Stereoisomers that differ in configuration only at the hemiacetal carbon are called anomers and are diastereomers.

    2. Fischer projections can be converted to cyclic Haworth projections.

        a. In a Haworth projection of the β anomer, the —CH$_2$OH group and the anomeric —OH group are on the same side of the ring.

        b. In a Haworth projection of the α anomer, the —CH$_2$OH group and the anomeric —OH group are on opposite sides of the ring.

        c. Groups that are on the left in a Fischer projection point up in a Haworth projection.

        d. Groups that are on the right in a Fischer projection point down in a Haworth projection.

        e. The —CH$_2$OH group at C6 points up in D sugars.

    3. In solution, glucose exists as a mixture of open chain glucose (0.02%), the α anomer (36%), and the β anomer (64%).

        a. Any mixture of glucose anomers achieves the same percent of anomers in solution.

        b. This phenomenon is called mutarotation.

B. Important monosaccharides (Section 21.5).

    1. Glucose is the most important monosaccharide in human metabolism.

    2. Galactose.

        a. Galactose differs from glucose only in the configuration at C4.

        b. Galactose is a component of the disaccharide lactose.

        c. Galactosemia is an inherited disorder of galactose metabolism.

    3. Fructose.

        a. Fructose is a component of the disaccharide sucrose.

        b. Fructose is a ketohexose.

    4. Ribose and 2-deoxyribose.

        a. These monosaccharides are aldopentoses.

        b. In 2-deoxyribose, the —OH group at C2 is replaced by –H.

        c. Both of these sugars occur as components of nucleic acids.

C. Reactions of monosaccharides (Section 21.6).

    1. Reaction with oxidizing agents.

        a. Aldoses can be oxidized to carboxylic acids.

        b. In basic solution, ketoses can also be oxidized to carboxylic acids.

           i. Ketoses and aldoses are in equilibrium with an intermediate enediol.

        c. Carbohydrates that react with oxidizing agents are called reducing sugars.

    2. Reaction with alcohols.

        a. Hemiacetals react with alcohols to form acetals that are called glycosides.

        b. The bond between the anomeric carbon atom and the oxygen of the —OR group is a glycosidic bond.

    3. Formation of a bond between two monosaccharides.

        a. Glycosidic bonds can form between two monosaccharides or between a monosaccharide and another molecule.

           i. These bonds may have either α or β orientation.

           ii. Glycosides are not reducing sugars.

        b. Bonds between monosaccharides in more complex carbohydrates are also glycosidic bonds.

           i. The bond is described by specifying the positions of the connected carbon atoms and by using α or β to indicate the orientation.

        c. Hydrolysis is the cleavage of a glycosidic bond.

    4. The alcohol groups of monosaccharides can react with phosphate groups to form phosphate esters.

III. Important disaccharides (Section 21.7).
  A. Maltose.
    1. Maltose consists of two glucose molecules joined by an α-1,4 glycosidic bond.
    2. Maltose occurs in prepared foods and occurs in the body as a product of starch digestion.
    3. Maltose is a reducing sugar.
  B. Lactose.
    1. Lactose consists of a β-D-glucose molecule joined to a β-D-galactose molecule by a β-1,4 glycosidic linkage.
    2. Lactose is a reducing sugar.
    3. Lactose occurs in milk.
    4. Lactose intolerance is a metabolic disorder in which lactose can't be digested.
  C. Sucrose.
    1. Sucrose consists of an α-D-glucose molecule joined to a β-D-fructose molecule by a glycosidic bond connecting the two anomeric carbons.
    2. Sucrose isn't a reducing sugar.
    3. Sucrose is the most common disaccharide.
IV. Important biomolecules derived from carbohydrates (Section 21.8).
  A. Chitin is a polymer of N-acetyl-D-glucosamine that occurs in the shells of shellfish and in insects.
  B. Cartilage and tendons consist of protein fibers and polysaccharides composed of β-D-glucuronic acid and N-acetyl-D-glucosamine or galactose derivatives.
  C. Hyaluronate and chondroitin 6-sulfate are present in joints, tendons and cartilage.
  D. Heparin is a polysaccharide that contains sulfate groups and that functions as an anticoagulant.
  E. Glycoproteins contain carbohydrates bonded to proteins and have important functions at cell surfaces.
V. Polysaccharides (Section 21.9).
  A. Polysaccharides consist of hundreds to thousands of monosaccharides connected by glycosidic bonds.
  B. Cellulose.
    1. Cellulose consists of thousands of β-D-glucose units connected by β-1,4 glycosidic bonds.
    2. Chains of cellulose fibers can form hydrogen bonds.
    3. Humans can't digest cellulose.
  C. Starch.
    1. Starch consists of glucose units joined by α-1,4 glycosidic bonds.
    2. There are two kinds of starch.
      a. Amylose consists of hundreds of glucose units joined by α-1,4 glycosidic bonds and is soluble in hot water.
      b. Amylopectin is much larger than amylose, also contains α-1,6 branches every 25 units, and is insoluble in water.
      c. Starch is digested in the small intestine by α-amylase.
  D. Glycogen.
    1. Glycogen resembles amylopectin but is larger and has more branches.
    2. In humans and animals, glycogen is used for carbohydrate storage.

Solutions to Chapter 21 Problems

21.1   The classification of a monosaccharide consists of three parts:
(1) the prefix *aldo-* (if the carbonyl group is an aldehyde) or *keto-* (if the carbonyl group is a ketone);
(2) a number prefix, such as *tri-, tetr-, pent-, hex-* (to show the number of carbons in the monosaccharide);
(3) the suffix *-ose*, which indicates that the compound is a sugar).

(a)

$$\underset{5}{HOCH_2} - \overset{OH}{\underset{4}{CH}} - \overset{OH}{\underset{3}{CH}} - \overset{OH}{\underset{2}{CH}} - \overset{O}{\underset{1}{CH}}$$

An aldopentose

(b)

$$\underset{3}{HOCH_2} - \overset{O}{\underset{2}{C}} - \underset{1}{CH_2OH}$$

A ketotriose

(c)

$$\underset{4}{HOCH_2} - \overset{OH}{\underset{3}{CH}} - \overset{OH}{\underset{2}{CH}} - \overset{O}{\underset{1}{CH}}$$

An aldotetrose

21.2

$$HOCH_2 - \overset{OH}{CH} - \overset{OH}{CH} - \overset{OH}{CH} - \overset{O}{CH}$$

An aldopentose

$$HOCH_2 - \overset{OH}{CH} - \overset{OH}{CH} - \overset{OH}{CH} - \overset{O}{C} - CH_2OH$$

A ketohexose

21.3   An aldoheptose has five chiral carbon atoms. Using the fact that a molecule with n chiral carbons has 2^n stereoisomers, we calculate that an aldoheptose has a maximum of $2^5 = 32$ stereoisomers.

21.4

If the monosaccharide shown on the left were to look in the mirror, it would see monosaccharide (d), its enantiomer.

21.5   The bottom carbon is not chiral. The orientations of the hydroxyl groups bonded to the chiral carbons must be shown in order to indicate which stereoisomer is pictured.

21.6 The enantiomers are mirror images. The –OH bonded to the chiral carbon farthest from the carbonyl group points to the right in the D enantiomer and to the left in the L enantiomer.

(a)   (b)

A D-aldopentose   An L-aldopentose   An L-ketohexose   A D-ketohexose

21.7 An enzymatic path would produce only the target enantiomer. This would provide the desired product without need for separation of enantiomers and would eliminate the need to test both enantiomers.

21.8 First, coil D-talose into a circular shape:

Next, rotate around the indicated single bond between C4 and C5 so that the —CH₂OH group (C6) points up.

Finally, form a hemiacetal bond between the aldehyde and the —OH group at C5.

β-anomer

α-anomer

21.9   Reverse the series of steps shown in Problem 21.8. First, break the hemiacetal bond.

Rotate around the single bond between C4 and C5 so that the hydroxyl group on C5 points down.

Uncoil D-idose to arrive at the Fischer projection.

D-Idose

21.10 (a) Rings **1** and **4** (5 carbons) are amino sugars. (b) Ring **3** (4 carbons) is an unmodified sugar. (c) Ring **2** (6 carbons) is a nonsugar.

21.11

← anomeric carbon (2)

The drawing represents the β anomer because the —OH group bonded to the anomeric carbon is on the same side of the ring as carbon 6.

21.12 Chiral carbons are starred. Remember that anomeric carbons and all other carbons bonded to four different groups are chiral.

(a)   (b)   (c)

α-D-Fructose   α-D-Ribose   β-D-2-Deoxyribose

21.13

L-Fucose   α-D-Galactose   β-D-Galactose

(a) L-Fucose is an α anomer because the anomeric hydroxyl group is on the opposite side of the hemiacetal ring from carbon 6.
(b) L-Fucose is missing a hydroxyl group on carbon 6.
(c) The —OH group at carbon 2 that is below the plane of the ring in D-galactose is above the plane of the ring in L-fucose. The —OH groups that are above the plane of the ring in D-galactose are below the plane of the ring in L-fucose.
(d) 6-Deoxy-L-galactose is a correct name for L-fucose.

21.14 *N*-acetyl-D-glucosamine, D-galactose, and L-fucose are found in all blood types.

21.15

α-D-Ribose   + CH₃OH $\xrightarrow[\text{catalyst}]{H^+}$ Methyl α-D-riboside   +   H₂O

+

β-D-Ribose   Methyl β-D-riboside

The two products are acetals because reaction with methanol occurs at the hemiacetal hydroxyl group, producing a compound with two —OR groups.

20.16 Cellobiose has a β-1,4 glycosidic link.

21.17

21.19 Starch, a polysaccharide, is an example of a complex carbohydrate in the diet. Glucose and fructose are simple carbohydrates found in the diet. Soluble and insoluble fiber are complex carbohydrates that can't be hydrolyzed to simple carbohydrates, and most of them pass undigested through the body.

21.20 Glutamine and asparagine are the two amino acids with side-chain amide groups.

21.21 The two subunits of heparin are joined by an α-1,4 glycosidic link.

21.22 Starch has so few hemiacetal units per molecule (only the one at the end of a very long chain) that a positive reducing-sugar reaction with Tollens' reagent or Benedict's reagent is undetectable.

21.23 The spherical particles of glycogen are compact and easily available as a source of glucose. The chains of cellulose serve as structural components of plants.

21.24 This is irreversible inhibition, which is effective because it permanently inactivates an enzyme's active site. This inhibits the synthesis of bacterial cell walls, which are composed of modified sugar polymers (peptidoglycans).

Understanding Key Concepts

21.26 (a) The two fructose molecules are diastereomers and anomers; they are stereoisomers that aren't mirror images. (b) D-Galactose and L-galactose are enantiomers. (c) L-Allose and D-glucose are diastereomers.

21.28 (a) (b) None of the three monosaccharides are identical, and none are enantiomers.

21.30 Monosaccharides **B** and **C** are the components of lactose, but **B** and **C** would have to be connected **C–B**, instead of **B–C**, in order for lactose to be part of the trisaccharide.

21.32 In solution, an equilibrium exists between open-chain glucose and its cyclic hemiacetal forms. The open-chain form reacts with the oxidizing agent, and, according to Le Châtelier's principle, the equilibrium shifts to produce more of the open-chain form, which is also oxidized. Ultimately, all of the glucose is oxidized to gluconate.

Classification and Structure of Carbohydrates

21.34 The family-name ending for a sugar is *-ose*.

21.36

(a)	(b)	(c)	(d)
Threose	Ribulose	Xylose	Tagatose
an aldotetrose	a ketopentose	an aldopentose	a ketohexose

21.38 A repeating unit of heparin has nine chiral carbons.

21.40

oxygen missing here

a four-carbon deoxy sugar

21.42 *Glucose*, the most important monosaccharide in living organisms, is the principal energy source for metabolism.

Galactose can also serve as an energy source and is a component of compounds needed in brain tissue.

Fructose is a component of sucrose and can be metabolized as glucose.

Ribose occurs in nucleic acids and forms part of CoA and ATP.

Handedness in Carbohydrates

21.44 L-Glucose and D-glucose are mirror images (enantiomers).

21.46

The reduction product of D-erythrose has a symmetry plane and is achiral.

21.48 A polarimeter measures the degree of rotation of plane-polarized light by a solution of an optically active compound.

21.50 Equimolar solutions of enantiomers rotate light to the same degree but in opposite directions.

Reactions of Carbohydrates

21.52 A sugar must have an aldehyde carbonyl group or a group that can isomerize to an aldehyde in order to be a reducing sugar.

21.54 Most sugars exist in the cyclic hemiacetal form, in which a sugar hydroxyl group has added to the sugar carbonyl group in the same molecule. *Anomer* is the name given to each of the two stereoisomers formed. Anomers differ in the orientation of substituents at the hemiacetal carbon.

21.56 The α form of D-gulose is shown, because the anomeric —OH group at C1 is on the opposite side of the hemiacetal ring from the —CH_2OH group at C6.

21.58

β-D-Altrose   α-D-Altrose

21.60

D-Fructose   Sorbitol   Mannitol

21.62

D-Ribose   Ribonic acid

21.64 A *glycoside* is the acetal product that results from reaction of the hemiacetal —OH group of a carbohydrate with an alcohol.

21.66

The product in this problem has a cyclic hemiacetal carbon and is in equilibrium with an open-chain aldehyde that is a reducing sugar. The glycosides in Problem 21.65 are acetals and are not in equilibrium with an aldehyde.

Disaccharides and Polysaccharides

21.68 Lactose and maltose have hemiacetal linkages that give positive Tollens' test results. Sucrose has no hemiacetal group and is thus unreactive toward Tollens' reagent.

21.70 Amylose and amylopectin are both components of starch and both consist of long polymers of α-D-glucose linked by α-1,4 glycosidic bonds. Amylopectin is much larger and has α-1,6 branches every 25 units or so along the chain.

21.72 Gentiobiose contains both an acetal grouping and a hemiacetal grouping. Gentiobiose is a reducing sugar because it has a hemiacetal group on the right-hand monosaccharide unit. A β-1,6 linkage connects the two monosaccharides.

21.74 Trehalose is a nonreducing sugar because it contains no hemiacetal linkages. The two D-glucose monosaccharides are connected by an α-1,1 acetal link

21.76 Amylopectin is the major component of starch, which is used for carbohydrate storage in plants, and glycogen is used for carbohydrate storage in animals.

Chemistry in Action

21.78 Enzyme-catalyzed reactions are usually stereospecific and produce only one enantiomer of the compound of interest.

21.80 People with type O blood can receive blood only from other donors that have type O blood. People with type AB blood can give blood only to other people with type AB blood because antibodies to AB blood are present in the blood of people having any of the other blood types.

21.82 Pectin and vegetable gum are two kinds of soluble fiber, which can be found in fruits, barley, oats, and beans.

21.84 Most of a plant cell wall is composed of cellulose (a polymer of β-D-glucose) in a matrix of pectin, lignin, and hemicellulose.

21.86 Penicillin inhibits the enzyme that synthesizes peptidoglycan polypeptide bridges. Since mammals don't contain this enzyme, penicillin doesn't harm mammalian cells.

General Questions and Problems

21.88 As in the previous problem, the α and β forms are not enantiomers because they are not mirror images.

21.90

Raffinose

21.92 1,3,4-Trihydroxy-2-butanone has one chiral carbon and exists as a pair of enantiomers.

1,3,4-Trihydroxy-2-butanone

21.94 Enzymes produced by the bacteria in yogurt predigest most of the lactose, making it possible for lactose-intolerant people to eat yogurt without symptoms.

21.96

Dulcitol

$$\begin{array}{c} CH_2OH \\ H \!-\!\!\!-\!\!\!- OH \\ HO \!-\!\!\!-\!\!\!- H \\ HO \!-\!\!\!-\!\!\!- H \\ H \!-\!\!\!-\!\!\!- OH \\ CH_2OH \end{array}$$ plane of symmetry

Dulcitol is optically inactive because it has a plane of symmetry and thus doesn't have an enantiomer.

21.98

$$42 \text{ g } \times \frac{4.0 \text{ kcal}}{\text{g}} = 170 \text{ kcal}; \; 170 \text{ kcal} \times \frac{4.18 \text{ kJ}}{\text{kcal}} = 710 \text{ kJ}$$

21.100

Carbohydrate	Example	Source
monosaccharide	fructose	fruit
disaccharide	sucrose	sugar cane
polysaccharide	cellulose	all plants

21.102 Hydrogen bonds between chains stabilize cellulose and make it rigid and insoluble.

Self-Test for Chapter 21

Multiple Choice

1. One of these disaccharides is not a reducing sugar. Which one?
   (a) sucrose   (b) maltose   (c) lactose   (d) cellobiose

2. Which one of the following bonds doesn't occur in common polysaccharides?
   (a) α-1,4 bonds   (b) α-1,6 bonds   (c) β-1,4 bonds   (d) β-1,6 bonds

3. The compound shown is:
   (a) The α anomer of a ketopentose   (b) the α anomer of an aldohexose   (c) the β anomer of an aldopentose   (d) the β anomer of a ketohexose

4. Oxidation of the aldotetroses pictured in Section 21.2 can be controlled to produce dicarboxylic acids known as tartaric acids. How many stereoisomeric tartaric acids are there?
   (a) 1   (b) 2   (c) 3   (d) 4

5. *N*-Acetyl-D-glucosamine is a component of all of the following, except:
   (a) chitin   (b) blood group determinants   (c) tendons   (d) heparin

6. Humans can't digest cellulose because:
   (a) Its molecules are too big.   (b) Humans don't produce enzymes to digest polysaccharides.
   (c) Humans can't digest branched polysaccharides.   (d) Human enzymes that digest carbohydrates can only hydrolyze α glycosidic bonds.

7. Which blood group is the "universal donor"?
   (a) A   (b) B   (c) AB   (d) O

8. Which of the following polysaccharides consists of only α-1,4 glycosidic bonds?
   (a) amylopectin   (b) cellulose   (c) amylose   (d) glycogen

9. Which of these errors of carbohydrate metabolism is not life-threatening?
   (a) galactosemia   (b) lactose intolerance   (c) diabetes mellitus   (d) blood-group incompatibility

10 How many stereoisomers does an open-chain 2-ketopentose have?
   (a) 2   (b) 4   (c) 6   (d) 8

Sentence Completion

1. An object that has handedness is said to be _____.

2. Starch molecules are digested by enzymes called _____.

3. The two mirror image forms of a chiral molecule are called _____.

4. A reaction between an aldehyde carbonyl group and an alcohol hydroxyl group in the same molecule yields a _____ _____.

5. *Levulose* is another name for _____.

6. _____ and _____ are two kinds of starch.

7. The reaction of a monosaccharide with an alcohol yields a _____.

8. _____ is used for food storage in animals.

9. D-Glucose can be classified as a _____.

10. 3-Pentanol is an _____ molecule.

11. A _____ is a stereoisomer that is not an enantiomer.

12. _____ have important functions at cell surfaces.

True or False

1. All naturally-occurring carbohydrates are chiral.

2. Glucose is a reducing sugar.

3. In an L sugar, the —OH on the carbon nearest to the carbonyl group points to the left.

4. Humans can digest polysaccharides containing β-1,4 acetal links but not α-1,4 acetal links.

5. Achiral objects possess a plane of symmetry.

6. Crystalline glucose is a mixture of α anomer, β anomer, and open-chain forms.

7. Sucrose contains both acetal and hemiacetal groups.

8. Amylopectin and glycogen contain 1,4 and 1,6 acetal links.

9. An acetal is an ester.

10. Maltose is a disaccharide composed of glucose and galactose.

11. Two diastereomers rotate plane-polarized light in equal amounts but in opposite directions.

12. Not all compounds with n chiral carbons have 2^n stereoisomers.

Match each entry on the left with its partner on the right.

1. Maltose

2. Cellulose

3. Methyl glucoside

4. Ribose

5. Fructose

6. Glycogen

7. Dextrose

8. Glucose

9. Sucrose

10. Lactose

11. Glyceraldehyde

12. Amylose

(a) Aldohexose

(b) Glucose

(c) Aldotriose

(d) Glucose + fructose

(e) Glucose + glucose

(f) Polysaccharide of α-D-glucose

(g) Galactose + glucose

(h) Aldopentose

(i) Ketohexose

(j) Acetal

(k) Animal starch

(l) Polysaccharide of β-D-glucose

Chapter Outline

I. Introduction to carbohydrate metabolism (Sections 22.1–22.2).
    A. Digestion of carbohydrates (Section 22.1).
       1. Digestion is the breakdown of food into small molecules.
       2. The products of digestion are absorbed from the intestinal tract.
       3. Digestion of carbohydrates.
          a. α–Amylase in the mouth breaks starch into smaller polysaccharides and maltose.
          b. α–Amylase in the small intestine further breaks down polysaccharides.
          c. Disaccharides are broken down to monosaccharides in the small intestine.
    B. Overview of glucose metabolism (Section 22.2).
       1. *Glycolysis* is the conversion of glucose to pyruvate; it occurs when energy is needed.
       2. *Glycogenesis* is the synthesis of glycogen from glucose; it occurs when excess glucose is present.
       3. The *pentose phosphate pathway* supplies other monosaccharides; it occurs when these are in short supply.
       4. *Glycogenolysis* is the breakdown of glycogen to glucose units; it occurs when the body needs glucose.
       5. Pyruvate has several fates:
          a. Under normal circumstances, pyruvate is converted to acetyl-CoA.
          b. When oxygen is lacking, pyruvate is converted to lactate.
          c. When the body is starved for glucose, pyruvate and other noncarbohydrates are converted to glucose via *gluconeogenesis*.
II. Glycolysis and pyruvate metabolism (Sections 22.3–22.6).
    A. Glycolysis is the breakdown of glucose to two pyruvates (Section 22.3).
       1. Glycolysis occurs in the cytosol.
    B. Steps in glycolysis:
       1. Steps 1–3: Phosphorylation.
          a. Step 1: Glucose moves into the cell and is converted to glucose 6-phosphate, with the expenditure of one ATP.
          b. Step 2: Glucose 6-phosphate is isomerized to fructose 6-phosphate.
          c. Step 3: Fructose 6-phosphate is converted to fructose 1,6-bisphosphate, with the expenditure of one ATP.
       2. Steps 4, 5: Cleavage and isomerization.
          a. Step 4: Fructose 1,6-bisphosphate is cleaved to glyceraldehyde 3-phosphate and dihydroxyacetone phosphate.
          b. Step 5: Dihydroxyacetone phosphate is isomerized to glyceraldehyde 3-phosphate.
       3. Steps 6–10: Energy generation.
          a. Step 6: Glyceraldehyde 3-phosphate is phosphorylated and oxidized to 1,3-bisphosphoglycerate: $NAD^+ \longrightarrow NADH/H^+$.
          b. Step 7: 1,3-Bisphosphoglycerate transfers a phosphate to ADP to yield 3-phosphoglycerate.
          c. Step 8: 3-Phosphoglycerate is isomerized to 2-phosphoglycerate.
          d. Step 9: 2-Phosphoglycerate is dehydrated to phosphoenolpyruvate.
          e. Step 10: Phosphoenolpyruvate transfers a phosphate group to ADP to yield ATP and pyruvate.
    C. End results of glycolysis.
       1. Conversion of glucose to 2 pyruvates.
       2. Production of 2 ATP.
       3. Production of 2 $NADH/H^+$.

D. Entry of other sugars into glycolysis (Section 23.4).
   1. Fructose is converted to fructose 6-phosphate and enters glycolysis.
   2. Mannose is converted to fructose 6-phosphate and enters glycolysis.
   3. Galactose is converted to glucose 6-phosphate and enters glycolysis.
E. Pyruvate metabolism (Section 23.5).
   1. When oxygen is available, pyruvate is converted to acetyl-CoA, with the conversion of NAD^+ to $NADH/H^+$ and the production of CO_2.
   2. Under anaerobic conditions, pyruvate is reduced to lactate, and $NADH/H^+$ is converted to NAD^+.
   3. When glucose is in short supply, pyruvate can be converted back to glucose by gluconeogenesis.
   4. In yeast, pyruvate is converted to ethanol and CO_2.
F. Energy output in complete catabolism of glucose (Section 22.6).
   1. The total energy output from glucose metabolism is the combined result of
     a. Glycolysis.
     b. Pyruvate —> acetyl-CoA.
     c. Citric acid cycle of two acetyl-CoA molecules (and passage of the resulting reduced coenzymes through the respiratory chain).
     d. Passage of two reduced coenzymes from glycolysis through the respiratory chain.
   2. The number of ATP produced depends on:
     a. The number of electrons that enter the respiratory chain from reduced coenzymes.
     b. The number of ATP produced per reduced coenzyme.
     c. An estimated 30–32 ATP are produced per mol glucose catabolized.
III. Regulation of glucose metabolism (Sections 22.7–22.9).
  A. Regulation of glucose concentration in the blood (Section 22.7).
   1. Hypoglycemia: low blood sugar.
     a. The hormone glucagon stimulates breakdown of glycogen to glucose to raise blood sugar.
   2. Hyperglycemia: high blood sugar.
     a. The hormone insulin stimulates passage of glucose into cells to be used in energy production.
  B. Fasting and starvation (Section 22.8).
   1. First, glucose is released from glycogen.
   2. Then, glucose is synthesized from proteins via gluconeogenesis.
   3. Then, fats are metabolized to acetyl-CoA, which enters the citric acid cycle.
   4. As the citric acid cycle is overloaded, acetyl-CoA is removed by formation of ketone bodies.
   5. Ultimately, the body produces 50% of ATP from ketone bodies.
   6. The body can endure this state for months.
  C. *Diabetes mellitus* (Section 22.9).
   1. There are two types of *diabetes mellitus*.
     a. In Type I (juvenile), the pancreas produces insufficient insulin.
       i. Type I diabetes is an autoimmune disease, in which insulin-producing cells are destroyed.
       ii. Type I diabetes is treated by supplying insulin.
     b. In Type II (adult-onset), insulin doesn't aid the passage of glucose across the cell membrane.
       i. Type II diabetes results when cell receptors fail to recognize insulin.
       ii. Drugs that increase insulin levels are an effective treatment.
   2. Complications of diabetes.
     a. Cataracts may result from buildup of sorbitol in the eye.
     b. Ketoacidosis is caused by buildup of acidic ketones.
     c. Hypoglycemia may be due to an overdose of insulin or to failure to eat.

IV. Other pathways of carbohydrate metabolism (Sections 22.10–22.11).
  A. Glycogen metabolism (Section 22.10).
    1. Glycogenesis.
      a. Glycogenesis occurs when glucose levels are high.
      b. The pathway to glycogen synthesis:
        i. Glucose —> Glucose 6-phosphate —> Glucose 1-phosphate —>
            Glucose-UDP —> Glycogen
    2. Glycogenolysis.
      a. Glycogenolysis occurs when there is an immediate need for energy.
      b. The pathway of glycogenolysis:
        i. Glycogen —> Glucose 1-phosphate —> Glucose 6-phosphate —> Glucose
  B. Gluconeogenesis (Section 22.11).
    1. Gluconeogenesis is the synthesis of glucose from any of several small molecules,
       including lactate, pyruvate, amino acids, and glycerol.
    2. Gluconeogenesis occurs when the body is starved for glucose.
    3. Seven of the steps of gluconeogenesis are reversals of glycolysis steps.
      a. The other three steps are too endergonic, and alternate pathways must be used.
      b. Step 1 of gluconeogenesis:
        i. Pyruvate —> Oxaloacetate —> Phosphoenolpyruvate
      c. Oxaloacetate is an intermediate that allows amino acids to enter gluconeogenesis.

Solutions to Chapter 22 Problems

22.1 (a) *Glycogenesis* is the synthesis of glycogen from glucose.
(b) *Glycogenolysis* is the release of glucose units from glycogen.
(c) *Gluconeogenesis* is the synthesis of glucose from lactate or other noncarbohydrates.

22.2 The following synthetic pathways have glucose 6-phosphate as their first reactant:

Glycogenesis: synthesis of glycogen from glucose
Pentose phosphate pathway: synthesis of five-carbon sugars from glucose
Glycolysis: conversion of glucose to pyruvate

22.3 (1) In Step 6, 1,3-bisphosphoglycerate is synthesized. In Step 7, the energy is harvested in ATP as 3-phosphoglycerate is formed.

(2) In Step 9, phosphoenolpyruvate is synthesized. In Step 10, the energy is harvested in ATP as pyruvate is formed.

22.4 The following steps of glycolysis are isomerizations:
Step 2: Glucose 6-phosphate → Fructose 6-phosphate
Step 5: Dihydroxyacetone phosphate → Glyceraldehyde 3-phosphate
Step 8: 3-Phosphoglycerate → 2-Phosphoglycerate

22.5

Glucose 6-phosphate   Fructose 6-phosphate

22.6 (a) Pyruvate is oxidized to a greater extent than glucose because it has two carbon–oxygen double bonds.
(b) Oxidation occurs in Step 6, in which glyceraldehyde 3-phosphate is oxidized and phosphorylated to give 1,3-bisphosphoglycerate. NAD^+ is the oxidizing agent.

22.7 Sucrose promotes the growth of decay-producing bacteria. Honey, which contains glucose and fructose, is better for tooth health.

22.8

Fructose   Fructose 6-phosphate

Fructose 6-phosphate enters glycolysis at Step 3.

22.9

D-Glucose   D-Galactose

Glucose and galactose differ in configuration at carbon 4.

22.10 (a) The remaining energy escapes as heat.
(b) The exergonic nature of the reaction makes it very favorable in the forward direction and unfavorable in the reverse direction. Also, escape of the gaseous product drives the reaction to completion in the forward direction.

22.11 Humans have used fermentation to produce beer and wine, to leaven bread, and to make yogurt and cheese.

22.12 As starvation begins, insulin starts to decrease as glucagon starts to increase, while liver glycogen begins a rapid decrease. After several hours, the levels of insulin and glucagon continue to change, and blood glucose drops significantly. As glycogen is used up, fatty acids and ketone bodies appear in the bloodstream. At the end of 24 hours, liver glycogen is depleted, the levels of glucose and insulin are reduced, and the levels of glucagon, free fatty acids, and ketone bodies are elevated.

22.13 To confirm a diagnosis of diabetes, a doctor would order a fasting blood glucose test and a glucose tolerance test.

22.14

Sorbitol

Sorbitol can't form a cyclic hemiacetal because it doesn't have a carbonyl group.

22.15 (a) The increase in $[H^+]$ drives the equilibrium shown in Section 22.9 to the right, causing the production of CO_2.
(b) This effect is an example of Le Châtelier's principle.

22.16 Reaction of creatine phosphate with ADP produces ATP in one step. Production of ATP from glucose or glycogen requires several steps.

22.17

Glycerol   Glycerol 3-phosphate   Dihydroxyacetone
                                                        phosphate

Understanding Key Concepts

22.18 Most of the enzymes involved with digestion are hydrolases, which catalyze the hydrolysis of bonds in large molecules to produce smaller molecules.

22.20 The energy investments made when glucose is converted to glucose 6-phosphate (Step 1) and when fructose 1-phosphate is converted to fructose 1,6-bisphosphate (Step 3) produce the phosphorylated intermediates needed in later stages of glycolysis. These intermediates take part in the reactions that ultimately repay the initial energy investment. Cleavage of fructose 1,6-bisphosphate at Step 4 generates the two three-carbon molecules whose transformations result in the formation of pyruvate.

22.22

Step	Enzyme	Class
1	Hexokinase	Transferase
2	Glucose 6-phosphate isomerase	Isomerase
3	Phosphofructokinase	Transferase
4	Aldolase	Lyase
5	Triose phosphate isomerase	Isomerase
6	Glyceraldehyde 3-phosphate dehydrogenase	Oxidoreductase, transferase
7	Phosphoglycerate kinase	Transferase
8	Phosphoglycerate mutase	Isomerase
9	Enolase	Lyase
10	Pyruvate kinase	Transferase

Transferases are the most common class of enzymes in glycolysis because several reactions involve phosphate transfers to ADP and from ATP. Ligases are not represented among the enzymes of glycolysis because ligases are involved with the synthesis of larger molecules from smaller molecules, with the expenditure of ATP. Glycolysis is a pathway for the breakdown of larger molecules to smaller molecules, with the eventual generation of ATP.

22.24 Compounds available for gluconeogenesis include pyruvate, lactate, many amino acids, glycerol, and intermediates of the citric acid cycle, especially oxaloacetate. Lactate, formed in muscle tissue, is carried in the bloodstream to the liver, where, in the cytosol of liver cells, it is converted to pyruvate. Pyruvate is transported to liver mitochondria, where gluconeogenesis takes place. Gluconeogenesis takes place when the body's supply of glucose is low.

22.26 (a) No. Molecular oxygen is not involved in any of the steps of glycolysis.
(b) Molecular oxygen is used in electron transport, where it combines with hydrogen ions and with electrons from coenzymes (reduced in the citric acid cycle) to produce water. The reoxidized coenzymes can reenter the citric acid cycle or can be used in glycolysis.

Digestion and Metabolism

22.28 Lactose + H_2O $\xrightarrow{\text{Lactase}}$ Glucose + Galactose

This process occurs in the mucous lining of the small intestine.

22.30

Type of Food Molecules	Products of Digestion
Proteins	Amino acids
Triacylglycerols	Glycerol and fatty acids
Maltose	Glucose
Sucrose	Glucose and fructose
Lactose	Glucose and galactose
Starch	Glucose

22.32 Under aerobic conditions, pyruvate forms acetyl-CoA.
Under anaerobic conditions, pyruvate forms lactate.
Under fermentation conditions, pyruvate forms ethanol and CO_2.

22.34

	Substrate(s)	Product
(a) Glycogenesis	Glucose	Glycogen
(b) Glycogenolysis	Glycogen	Glucose + chain-shortened glycogen

22.36

If the Body Needs	Fate of Intermediates in Pentose Phosphate Pathway
NADPH	Pentose phosphate intermediates are recycled to glucose 6-phosphate for further production of NADPH.
ATP	Fructose 6-phosphate and glyceraldehyde 3-phosphate (pentose phosphate intermediates) enter glycolysis.
Nucleic acid synthesis	Ribose 5-phosphate is the major product.

Glycolysis

22.38 (a) Glycolysis takes place in all of these types of cells.
(b) Gluconeogenesis takes place in the liver.
(c) (d) Glycogenesis and glycogenolysis are carried out in liver and muscle cells.

22.40 None of the ATP produced in glycolysis results from oxidative phosphorylation; all of the phosphorylations are substrate-level.

22.42 (a) Phosphorylation:

Step 1:   Glucose →   Glucose 6-phosphate

Step 3:   Fructose 6-phosphate →   Fructose 1,6-bisphosphate

Step 6:   Glyceraldehyde 3-phosphate →   1,3-Bisphosphoglycerate

Step 7:   1,3-Bisphosphoglycerate →   3-Phosphoglycerate

Step 10:   Phosphoenolpyruvate →   Pyruvate

(b) Oxidation:

Step 6:   Glyceraldehyde 3-phosphate →   1,3-Bisphosphoglycerate

(c) Dehydration:

Step 9:   2-Phosphoglycerate →   Phosphoenolpyruvate
The last two phosphorylations involve phosphate transfers *to* ADP.

22.44 *Note:* Substrate-level phosphorylation is formation of ATP as a by-product of a reaction, as opposed to formation of ATP as a byproduct of electron transport.

(a) Glycolysis of 1 mol glucose produces 2 mol ATP as a result of substrate-level phosphorylation, and a maximum of 6 mol ATP formed by oxidative phosphorylation. See the note in the previous problem. (Actually, 4 mol ATP are produced by phosphorylation, but 2 mol ATP are consumed in steps 1 and 3 of glycolysis.)

(b) Aerobic conversion of pyruvate to acetyl-CoA doesn't produce ATP by substrate-level phosphorylation but produces a maximum of 3 mol ATP by oxidative phosphorylation.

(c) In the citric acid cycle, 1 mol of acetyl-CoA produces 1 mol ATP by substrate-level phosphorylation (Step 5) and a maximum of 11 mol ATP from oxidative phosphorylation.

Most of the ATP produced in the citric acid cycle results from passage of the reduced coenzymes NADH and $FADH_2$ through the electron-transport chain.

22.46

22.48 Catabolism of one mole of sucrose produces four moles of acetyl-CoA.

Regulation of Glucose Metabolism/Metabolism in Diabetes Mellitus

22.50

Condition	Blood Sugar Level	Symptoms
Hypoglycemia	Low	Weakness, sweating, rapid heartbeat, confusion, coma, death
Hyperglycemia	High	Increased urine flow, low blood pressure, coma, death

22.52 As starvation continues, acetyl-CoA is converted to *ketone bodies* to prevent buildup in the cells.

22.54 In Type II diabetes, insulin is in good supply, but cell membrane receptors fail to recognize insulin and to allow the passage of glucose into cells.

22.56 In diabetes, excess glucose in the eyes and extremities is converted to sorbitol, which can't be transported out of cells. This elevated sorbitol level changes the osmolarity of tissues and causes cataracts and gangrene.

22.58 Muscle cells, unlike liver cells, lack an enzyme that converts glucose 6-phosphate to glucose, which can pass into the bloodstream. Consequently, the glucose 6-phosphate product of glycogenolysis in muscle cells enters directly into glycolysis.

22.60 The exact reverse of an energetically favorable reaction must be energetically unfavorable. Since glycogenolysis is an energetically favorable hydrolysis, its exact reverse must be energetically unfavorable. Thus, glycogenesis must occur by an alternate pathway, which involves more steps.

Glucose Anabolism

22.62 Lactate and pyruvate are two molecules that can serve as starting materials for glucose synthesis. Other small molecules may also enter into gluconeogenesis.

22.64 Several steps of the exact reverse of the energetically favorable conversion of glucose to pyruvate are energetically unfavorable.

22.66 Three steps of gluconeogenesis are not the exact reverse of steps of glycolysis –Steps 1, 3, and 10. All of these steps involve phosphate transfers.

22.68 The Cori cycle is needed when muscle glucose is depleted and when oxygen is in short supply.

Chemistry in Action

22.70 Plaque is composed of glycoproteins from saliva, bacteria, dextran, and polysaccharide storage granules released by the bacteria.

22.72 In an environment rich in sucrose, bacteria associated with tooth decay secrete an enzyme that transfers glucose units from digested sucrose to the dextran polymer. The residual fructose is metabolized to lactate, which lowers pH. The resulting acidic environment in the mouth dissolves minerals in teeth, leading to cavities.

22.74 Fermented products include beer, wine, cheese, yogurt, sour cream, and buttermilk.

22.76 The fasting level of glucose in a diabetic is 140 mg/dL or greater, as compared to an average level of 90 mg/dL for a nondiabetic.

22.78 The response curve of a prediabetic person to a glucose challenge lies between the curve for a diabetic person and the curve for a non-diabetic person.

22.80 *First used* — — — — — — — — — — — — — — —>   *Last used*
ATP, creatine phosphate, glucose, glycogen, fatty acids from triacylglycerols

General Questions and Problems

22.82 Kinase enzymes are associated with phosphoryl group transfers.

22.84 Glucose obtained from the hydrolysis of glycogen is phosphorylated by reaction with inorganic phosphate ion and enters the glycolysis pathway as glucose 6-phosphate. Thus, one fewer ATP is needed (at Step 1), and one more ATP is produced.

22.86 In the absence of oxygen, the pyruvate product of catabolism of glucose in wine is fermented by yeast enzymes to ethanol and CO_2, which increased the pressure in the bottle and popped the lid.

22.88 Reaction (a) consumes energy, and reaction (b) releases energy.

22.90 (1) Lactate in the bloodstream is transported to the liver, where it can be converted to pyruvate, which can be converted to glucose via gluconeogenesis. The glucose can be returned to the muscles for energy. (2) Buildup of lactate in muscle tissue lowers pH, which causes physiological problems.

22.92 (a) Glycolysis predominates when glucose is in good supply and energy is needed. (b) Gluconeogenesis predominates when glucose is in short supply and during fasting and early stages of starvation.

Self-Test for Chapter 22

Multiple Choice

1. The synthesis of glucose from small molecules is called:
   (a) glycolysis   (b) glucogenesis   (c) gluconeogenesis   (d) glycogenesis

2. Which one of the following substances can cross cell membranes?
   (a) glucose 6-phosphate   (b) ATP   (c) glucose   (d) acetyl-CoA

3. The synthesis of glycogen occurs in the:
   (a) liver and bloodstream   (b) liver and muscles   (c) liver and pancreas   (d) muscles and pancreas

4. The exact reverse of which of the following steps of glycolysis also occurs in gluconeogenesis?
   (a) glucose —> glucose 6-phosphate   (b) phosphoenolpyruvate —> pyruvate
   (c) fructose 6-phosphate —> fructose 1,6-bisphosphate
   (d) 3-phosphoglycerate —> 2-phosphoglycerate

5. When the body needs to synthesize nucleic acids:
   (a) The oxidative phase of the pentose phosphate path is bypassed.   (b) The synthesis of NADPH is increased.   (c) Glucose 6-phosphate enters glycolysis.   (d) Three-, four-, or seven-carbon sugars are produced.

6. After several weeks of starvation, the body's principal energy source is:
   (a) protein   (b) fat   (c) carbohydrate   (d) all three

7. Type I *diabetes mellitus* is a disorder of:
   (a) insufficient insulin production   (b) faulty glucose metabolism   (c) autoimmune response
   (d) all three

8. Which of the following is not a route for pyruvate metabolism in the human body?
   (a) conversion to acetyl-CoA   (b) reduction to lactate   (c) fermentation to alcohol
   (d) reformation of glucose

9. Glycogenesis resembles glycogenolysis in that:
   (a) Both require the coenzyme UTP.   (b) Both occur when glucose is in good supply.
   (c) Both are stimulated by the hormone epinephrine.   (d) Both involve glucose 6-phosphate as an intermediate.

10. Which of the following monosaccharides doesn't enter glycolysis?
    (a) ribose   (b) mannose   (c) galactose   (d) fructose

Sentence Completion

1. The _____ – _____ pathway is another name for glycolysis.

2. Step __ of glycolysis involves an oxidation and a phosphorylation.

3. _____ _____ _____ catalyzes the formation of acetyl-CoA from pyruvate.

4. _____ aids in the passage of blood glucose across cell membranes.

5. The first step of glycogenolysis is the formation of ____ ____.

6. Steps ___ and ____ are known as the energy investment part of glycolysis.

7. The metabolic response to ____ ____ resembles starvation.

8. _____ and _____ supply the energy for gluconeogenesis.

9. When pyruvate is converted to acetyl-CoA, one molecule of _____ is lost.

10. The isomerization of glucose 6-phosphate to fructose 6-phosphate is catalyzed by ___ ___ __.

11. The hormone _____ stimulates breakdown of glycogen.

12. _____ may be due to an overdose of insulin.

True or False

1. The pentose phosphate pathway is important because it produces NADH.

2. Fructose, galactose, and mannose can all enter the glycolysis pathway.

3. Conversion of glucose 6-phosphate to fructose 6-phosphate requires ATP.

4. Glycogenesis is the exact reverse of glycogenolysis.

5. Hyperglycemia is a high level of blood glucose.

6. The reactions of glycolysis occur in the mitochondria.

7. 36 ATP molecules are produced for each glucose that passes through the glycolysis pathway.

8. Glucagon is the storage form of glucose.

9. All four transformations of pyruvate occur in the human body.

10. Cleavage of fructose 1,6-diphosphate yields two molecules of glyceraldehyde 3-phosphate.

11. Pyruvate is converted to lactate under anaerobic conditions.

12. Each conversion of glyceraldehyde 3-phosphate to pyruvate requires two ATPs.

Match each entry on the left with its partner on the right.

1. Glycolysis
2. Hyperglycemia
3. Enolase
4. Glycogenolysis
5. UDP-glucose
6. Ribose 5-phosphate
7. Gluconeogenesis
8. Ethanol
9. Hypoglycemia
10. Glycogenesis
11. Lactate
12. Aldolase

(a) Formed by fermentation of pyruvate

(b) Formed from pyruvate under anaerobic conditions

(c) Intermediate in glycogen synthesis

(d) Synthesis of glucose from pyruvate

(e) Catalyzes the cleavage of fructose 1,6-diphosphate

(f) Low blood sugar

(g) Synthesis of glycogen from glucose

(h) Product of pentose phosphate pathway

(i) Catalyzes loss of water from 2-phosphoglyceric acid

(j) Breakdown of glycogen to glucose

(k) High blood sugar

(l) Breakdown of glucose to pyruvate

Chapter Outline

I. Structure and classification of lipids (Section 23.1).
    A. Lipids are defined by solubility in nonpolar solvents.
    B. Classification of lipids.
        1. Waxes.
        2. Triacylglycerols.
        3. Glycerophospholipids.
        4. Sphingolipids.
        5. Sterols and eicosanoids.
II. Fatty acids and their esters (Sections 23.2–23.4).
    A. Fatty acids (Section 23.2).
        1. Fatty acids are long-chain carboxylic acids.
           a. A shorthand notation indicates the length of the chain (C_n).
        2. Fatty acids are classified by the number of double bonds they have.
           a. Fatty acids with no double bonds are saturated and are described as $C_n:0$).
           b. Fatty acids with one double bond are monounsaturated ($C_n:1$).
           c. Fatty acids with more than one double bond are polyunsaturated $C_n:>1$).
    B. Waxes are esters of long-chain alcohols with fatty acids.
    C. Fats and oils.
        1. Fats and oils are mixtures of esters of glycerol with three fatty acids and are known as triacylglycerols.
        2. Properties of fats and oils (Section 23.3).
           a. Hydrophobic.
           b. Uncharged.
           c. Melting point is determined by the length of the fatty acid side chains and the number of double bonds.
              i. Solid fats have saturated fatty acid side chains and are higher melting.
              ii. Liquid fats have unsaturated fatty acid side chains and are lower melting.
        3. Reactions of triacylglycerols (Section 23.4).
           a. Hydrogenation.
              i. Control of hydrogenation determines the consistency of a fat.
           b. Hydrolysis.
              i. In the body, enzymes catalyze hydrolysis of triacylglycerols.
              ii. In the laboratory, strong aqueous base is used.
              iii. The resulting fatty acid salts are called soaps.
              iv. Soaps clean because the polar end dissolves in water and the nonpolar end dissolves in grease.
              v. Soap molecules cluster together in water to form micelles; grease is trapped in the middle of a micelle.
III. Cell membrane lipids (Sections 23.5–23.6).
    A. Phospholipids (Section 23.5).
        1. Glycerophospholipids.
           a. Glycerophospholipids are esters of glycerol with two fatty acids and a phosphate group that is bonded to one of a number of different compounds containing an –OH group.
           b. The phospholipid with choline as a phosphate ester is a lecithin.
              i. Lecithins are components of cell membranes.
              ii. Lecithin is often used as an emulsifying agent.

    2. Sphingolipids and other membrane lipids.
      a. Sphingolipids are derivatives of the amino alcohol sphingosine.
      b. Sphingolipids consist of:
        i. An amide bond between a fatty acid and sphingosine.
        ii. A phosphate ester also bonded to choline.
      c. Sphingomyelins are sphingolipids that are constituents of the coating around nerve fibers.
  B. Glycolipids resemble sphingolipids, except that the phosphate group at C1 is replaced by a carbohydrate.
    1. Cerebrosides, found in cell membranes, have a monosaccharide at C1.
    2. Gangliosides have a small polysaccharide at C1.
      a. Gangliosides are components of neurotransmitters and receptors.
  C. Sterols have a central structure consisting of four fused rings. (Section 23.6).
    1. Cholesterol.
      a. Cholesterol serves as a starting material for steroid hormones.
      b. Cholesterol is a component of cell membranes that helps maintain the structure of the membrane.
    2. Bile acids are synthesized from cholesterol and aid in digestion of fats.
    3. Steroid hormones.
      a. Mineralcorticoids regulate fluid balance.
      b. Glucocorticoids regulate glucose metabolism and inflammation.
      c. Sex hormones regulate reproduction and secondary sex characteristics.
IV. Cell membranes (Sections 23.7–23.8).
  A. Structure of cell membranes (Section 23.7).
    1. Cell membranes are composed of two parallel layers of phospholipids, called a *lipid bilayer*.
    2. The nonpolar tails are clustered in the middle, and the polar heads point inward and outward.
    3. The fluid-mosaic model of a cell membrane explains the more complex structural details.
      a. Glycolipids and cholesterol are in the lipid part and provide membrane structure.
      b. Glycoproteins (20%) mediate the action of cell contents with the outer environment.
        i. Some proteins form channels to allow specific molecules to enter or leave.
        ii. Glycoproteins that extend through the bilayer are called integral proteins.
        iii. Glycoproteins that are partially embedded are peripheral proteins.
        iv. The carbohydrate portions act as receptors for enzymes and neurotransmitters.
      c. The membrane is fluid and doesn't rupture.
        i. Fluidity of the membrane increases with the amounts of saturated and unsaturated fatty acids in the lipid portion.
  B. Transport across cell membranes (Section 23.8).
    1. Passive transport.
      a. Simple diffusion.
        i. Gases and small nonpolar molecules diffuse through the bilayer.
        ii. Small hydrophilic molecules pass through channels formed by integral proteins.
      b. Facilitated diffusion.
        i. Facilitated diffusion is passive transport, but proteins help solutes to pass across the membrane.
    2. Active transport.
      a. Ions and other substances that maintain concentration gradients inside and outside the cell move by active transport.
      b. Active transport requires an expenditure of energy and involves changing the shape of an integral protein.

V. Eicosanoids (Section 23.9).
   A. General information.
      1. Eicosanoids are derivatives of 20-carbon unsaturated fatty acids.
      2. Eicosanoids are synthesized from arachidonic acid.
      3. Eicosanoids are short-term messengers.
   B. There are two classes of eicosanoids.
      1. Prostaglandins.
         a. Prostaglandins consist of a five-membered ring with two side chains.
         b. Biological effects include blood pressure lowering, stimulation of uterine contractions, and lowering the extent of gastric secretions.
      2. Leukotrienes mediate inflammatory and allergic responses.

Solutions to Chapter 23 Problems

23.1 The circled groups can be used to identify lipid families.

(a)

an eicosanoid

(b)

a glycerophospholipid

(c)

a wax

23.2

from C_{20} carboxylic acid   from C_{32} alcohol

23.3

Glyceryl trioleate

23.4 Although the two treats contain a similar number of calories, the ice cream cone contains a higher percentage of both saturated and unsaturated fat. The cookies (36% fat) also have a percentage of fat closer to the nutritional guidelines (30% fat) and are the better choice.

23.5 (a) Butter has the largest percentage of saturated fatty acids.
(b) Soybean oil has the largest percentage of polyunsaturated fatty acids.
(c) Soybean oil has the largest percentage of linoleic acid.

23.6

Arachidonic acid

23.7 The starred carbon of the triacylglycerol pictured below is bonded to four different groups and is chiral. (Whenever two different fatty acids are bonded to carbon 1 and carbon 3 of glycerol, carbon 2 is chiral.)

$$
\begin{array}{l}
CH_2-O-\overset{\overset{\displaystyle O}{\|}}{C}-R'' \\
{}^*CH-O-\overset{\overset{\displaystyle O}{\|}}{C}-R' \\
CH_2-O-\overset{\overset{\displaystyle O}{\|}}{C}-R
\end{array}
$$

23.8 London forces bind the nonpolar segments of lipids together. These forces are generally weak, but when there are many such interactions, their total contribution is relatively large. Lipids don't mix with water because the hydrogen bonds between water molecules are stronger than the forces between lipid molecules or between water molecules and lipid molecules.

23.9   Glyceryl trioleate (Problem 23.3)

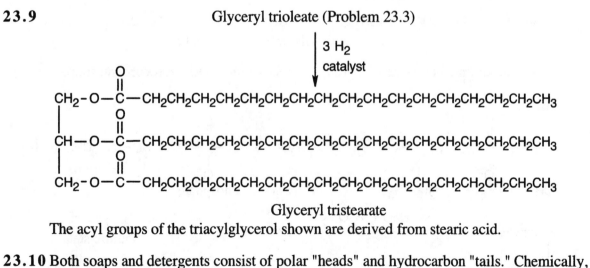

Glyceryl tristearate

The acyl groups of the triacylglycerol shown are derived from stearic acid.

23.10 Both soaps and detergents consist of polar "heads" and hydrocarbon "tails." Chemically, most detergents and all soaps have anionic polar groups. Detergents are preferred for cleaning because they don't form scum.

23.11

23.12 Lecithins emulsify fats in the same way as soaps dissolve grease: The fats are coated by the nonpolar part of a lecithin, and the polar part of lecithins allows fats to be suspended in aqueous solution.

23.13

(a)

R' is an unsaturated hydrocarbon group, and R is a saturated hydrocarbon group.

(b)

23.14

Choline — Phosphate

Hydrophilic head

A sphingomyelin

Hydrophobic tails

23.15

A glycerophospholipid

23.16

CH₃(CH₂)₁₂—CH=CH—CH—OH
R—C—NH—CH
CH₂-O—P—OCH₂-C—COO⁻

The illustrated structure is a phospholipid (a) because it contains a phosphate group. It is a sphingolipid (c) because it has a sphingosine backbone. It is a lipid (e) because it is soluble in nonpolar solvents. It contains a phosphate ester group (f).

23.17 Butter contains cholesterol (unhealthy), and solid margarine may contain trans fatty acids (unhealthy).

23.18 Integral membrane proteins must be hydrophobic to remain in the hydrophobic environment of a cell membrane. They must contain many amino acids with nonpolar side chains and must be folded so that the hydrophilic regions face outward.

23.19 You would predict that NO would cross a lipid bilayer by simple diffusion because it is small and relatively nonpolar.

23.20 Glucose 6-phosphate has a charged phosphate group and can't pass through the hydrophobic lipid bilayer.

23.21 The inner and outer surfaces of the lipid bilayer are in different environments and serve different functions. For example, the outer surface must receive signals from the cell's surroundings and must contain groups that allow the cell to be identified. The inner surface must include groups needed to pass messages to other parts of the cell.

23.22

The carboxylic acid group and the hydroxyl group are capable of forming hydrogen bonds. The molecule has both polar and nonpolar regions.

Understanding Key Concepts

23.24 Three of the fatty acids in the table shown in the previous problem are C_{18} fatty acids (stearic acid, oleic acid, and linoleic acid). When the triacylglycerols are hydrogenated, the unsaturated fatty acids are converted to stearic acid. The composition of the triacylglycerols after hydrogenation can be found by adding the percentages of C_{18} fatty acids.

Triacylglycerol	Percent C_{16} Fatty Acids	Percent C_{18} Fatty Acids
Triacylglycerol A	21.4%	75.3%
Triacylglycerol B	12.2%	87.5%
Triacylglycerol C	11.2%	85.1%

After hydrogenation, triacylglycerol B would be composed of 12.2% palmitic acid and 87.5% stearic acid. The hydrogenation product of triacylglycerol B closely resembles the hydrogenation product of triacylglycerol C because they have similar percentages of C_{16} fatty acids and C_{18} fatty acids.

23.26 Because the membrane is fluid, rather than rigid, it is able to flow together after an injury instead of shattering.

Waxes, Fats, and Oils

23.28 A lipid is a naturally occurring organic molecule that dissolves in nonpolar solvents.

23.30 A C_{18} fatty acid is a straight-chain carboxylic acid.

$$CH_3CH_2CH_2CH_2CH_2CH_2CH_2CH_2CH_2CH_2CH_2CH_2CH_2CH_2CH_2CH_2CH_2C \overset{O}{\underset{OH}{\|}}$$ Stearic acid

23.32 *Saturated fatty acids* are long-chain carboxylic acids that contain no carbon–carbon double bonds.
Monounsaturated fatty acids contain one carbon–carbon double bond.
Polyunsaturated fatty acids contain two or more carbon–carbon double bonds.

23.34 An essential fatty acid can't be synthesized by the human body and must be part of the diet.

23.36 The unsaturated fatty acid (linoleic acid) is lower melting because its double bonds introduce kinks that prevent it from solidifying.

23.38 Fats are composed of triacylglycerols containing both saturated and unsaturated fatty acids and are solids at room temperature. Oils are made up of triacylglycerols containing mainly unsaturated fatty acids and are liquids at room temperature.

23.40

$$CH_2{-}O{-}\overset{\overset{O}{\|}}{C}{-}CH_2CH_2CH_2CH_2CH_2CH_2CH_2CH_2CH_2CH_2CH_3$$
$$CH{-}O{-}\overset{\overset{O}{\|}}{C}{-}CH_2CH_2CH_2CH_2CH_2CH_2CH_2CH_2CH_2CH_2CH_3$$
$$CH_2{-}O{-}\overset{\overset{O}{\|}}{C}{-}CH_2CH_2CH_2CH_2CH_2CH_2CH_2CH_2CH_2CH_2CH_3$$

Glyceryl trilaurate

23.42 A wax serves as a protective coating for fruits, berries, leaves, animal fur, and feathers.

23.44

$$CH_3(CH_2)_{13}CH_2\overset{\overset{O}{\|}}{C}{-}OCH_2(CH_2)_{14}CH_3$$

Cetyl palmitate

23.46

Chemical Reactions of Lipids

23.48 Hydrogenation converts unsaturated fatty acids to saturated fatty acids.

23.50 The reaction is a saponification.

23.52

Glyceryl tristearate is higher melting than the original lipid because it has no double bonds and can solidify more easily.

Phospholipids, Glycolipids, and Cell Membranes

23.54 A triacylglycerol is an ester of glycerol and three fatty acids; a phospholipid contains a phosphate group. There are two main kinds of phospholipids. A *glycerophospholipid* is an ester of glycerol 3-phosphate, two fatty acids, and an amino alcohol bonded to the phosphate group. A *sphingolipid* is an amide of sphingosine and a fatty acid, and has an amino alcohol bonded to a phosphate group, which is attached to C1 of sphingosine.

23.56 A sphingomyelin and a cerebroside are similar in that both have a sphingosine backbone. The difference between the two occurs at C1 of sphingosine. A sphingomyelin has a phosphate group bonded to an amino alcohol at C1; a cerebroside has a glycosidic link to a monosaccharide at C1.

23.58 Glycerophospholipids are more soluble in water than triacylglycerols because they have an ionic phosphate group that is solvated by water.

23.60 In a soap micelle, the polar hydrophilic heads are on the exterior, and the hydrophobic tails cluster in the center. In a membrane bilayer, hydrophilic heads are on both the exterior and interior surfaces of the membrane, and the region between the two surfaces is occupied by hydrophobic tails.

23.62 Glycolipids, cholesterol, and glycoproteins are present in cell membranes in addition to phospholipids.

23.64

a cerebroside

23.66

a glycerophospholipid

23.68 Active transport requires energy because it is a process in which substances are transported across a membrane in a direction opposite to their tendency to diffuse.

23.70 (a) NO moves into cells by simple diffusion.
(b) Fructose, like glucose, is transported into cells by facilitated diffusion.
(c) Ca^{2+} probably crosses a cell membrane through protein pores. (It is also possible that active transport is used.)

Sterols

23.72 Cholesterol is a component of cell membranes and is the starting material for the synthesis of steroid hormones and bile acids.

23.74 Male sex hormones: androsterone, testosterone.
Female sex hormones: estradiol, estrone.

Eicosanoids

23.76 Eicosanoids are called "local hormones" because they are synthesized near their site of action.

23.78 Arachidonic acid is synthesized from linolenic acid, an essential fatty acid.

23.80 Leukotrienes are responsible for triggering asthmatic attacks, inflammation and allergic reactions, and thus it is desirable to inhibit their synthesis.

23.82 By transferring its acetyl group, aspirin inhibits the enzyme that is responsible for the first step in the conversion of arachidonic acid to prostaglandins.

Chemistry in Action

23.84 In addition to fats and oils, other foods with high lipid content are meat, fish, poultry, dairy products, nuts, seeds, whole-grain cereals, and prepared foods.

23.86 Detergents and soaps both have hydrocarbon "tails" and polar "heads," and both form micelles, in which the hydrocarbon "tails" surround greasy dirt and aggregate in the center of a cluster. The polar "heads" protrude into the aqueous medium and make the cluster soluble.

23.88 (a), (b) Margarine contains more monounsaturated and polyunsaturated fatty acids.
(c) Butter contains fewer trans fatty acids.

General Questions and Problems

23.90 Glyceryl trioleate (b), a sphingomyelin (c), a cerebroside (e), and a lecithin (f) are saponifiable lipids.

23.92

$$
\begin{array}{l}
\text{CH}_2\text{-O}-\overset{\overset{\displaystyle O}{\|}}{C}-(\text{CH}_2)_{12}\text{CH}_3 \\[4pt]
\text{CH}-\text{O}-\overset{\overset{\displaystyle O}{\|}}{C}-(\text{CH}_2)_7\text{CH}=\text{CHCH}_2\text{CH}=\text{CHCH}_2\text{CH}=\text{CHCH}_2\text{CH}_3 \\[4pt]
\text{CH}_2\text{-O}-\overset{\overset{\displaystyle O}{\|}}{C}-(\text{CH}_2)_{12}\text{CH}_3
\end{array}
$$

or

$$
\begin{array}{l}
\text{CH}_2\text{-O}-\overset{\overset{\displaystyle O}{\|}}{C}-(\text{CH}_2)_{12}\text{CH}_3 \\[4pt]
\text{CH}-\text{O}-\overset{\overset{\displaystyle O}{\|}}{C}-(\text{CH}_2)_{12}\text{CH}_3 \\[4pt]
\text{CH}_2\text{-O}-\overset{\overset{\displaystyle O}{\|}}{C}-(\text{CH}_2)_7\text{CH}=\text{CHCH}_2\text{CH}=\text{CHCH}_2\text{CH}=\text{CHCH}_2\text{CH}_3
\end{array}
$$

23.94 (a) tallow = beef fat   (b) cooking oil = plant oil   (c) lard = pork fat

23.96 Cholesterol acetate is saponifiable because it has an ester bond.

Cholesterol acetate

23.98   Sphingomyelins, cerebrosides, and gangliosides are abundant in brain tissue.

23.100   A decrease in sphingomyelin is observed in multiple sclerosis.

23.102   An itchy bump from a mosquito bite (a), and a stuffy nose after working in the rose garden (d) involve prostaglandin responses.

23.104

$$\frac{200 \text{ mg cholesterol}}{1 \text{ dL}} \times \frac{10 \text{ dL}}{1 \text{ L}} \times 5.75 \text{ L} \times \frac{1 \text{ g}}{1000 \text{ mg}} = 11.5 \text{ g cholesterol}$$

An average person has approximately 11–12 grams of cholesterol in his or her blood.

Self-Test for Chapter 23

Multiple Choice

1. Small polar molecules pass through the lipid bilayer by:
   (a) simple diffusion through the lipid bilayer (b) facilitated transfer
   (c) active transport   (d) simple diffusion through channels

2. Cholesterol is:
   (a) a male sex hormone (b) a saponifiable lipid (c) a component of cell membranes
   (d) common to plants and animals

3. Which of the following is not an effect of prostaglandins?
   (a) stimulation of allergic response (b) lowering of blood pressure (c) reduction of gastric
   secretions (d) stimulation of uterine contractions

4. Active transport requires all of the following except:
   (a) the solutes to be nonpolar organic molecules (b) the expenditure of ATP (c) the need for
   cells to maintain a concentration gradient between the inside and the outside (d) the assistance
   of integral proteins

5. Which of the following contain a glycosidic bond?
   (a) triacylglycerols (b) sphingomyelins (c) lecithins (d) cerebrosides

6. The basic hydrolysis of which of the following triacylglycerols produces only polyunsaturated
   fatty acids?
   (a) glyceryl trioleate (b) glyceryl tristearate (c) glyceryl linoleate dioleate (d) glyceryl
   trilinolenate

7. How many different triacylglycerols (including enantiomers!) can be formed from glycerol,
   two stearic acids, and one oleic acid?
   (a) 1 (b) 2 (c) 3 (d) 4

8. Which of the following molecules aren't components of glycolipids?
   (a) sphingosine (b) phosphate groups (c) fatty acids (d) sugars

9. A cell membrane is composed of all of the following except:
   (a) triacylglycerols (b) phosphoglycerides (c) sphingomyelins (d) glycolipids

10. Waxes:
    (a) are triacylglycerols   (b) can be hydrolyzed by base
    (c) contain no more than thirty carbons   (d) are only produced by plants

Sentence Completion

1. A glycolipid contains an _____ link between sphingosine and a sugar.

2. _____ is a mixture of long-chain fatty acid salts.

3. The carboxylate end of a fatty acid is _____ and the organic chain end is _____.

4. _____ and _____ are two components of cell membranes.

5. The common model of a cell membrane is called the _____ _____ model.

6. Steroid structures are based on a _____ ring system.

7. Prostaglandins are synthesized in the body from a fatty acid called _____ acid.

8. Clusters of soap molecules in water are called _____.

9. _____ are phospholipids that are abundant in brain tissue.

10. Phospholipids aggregate in a closed, sheetlike membrane called a _____ _____.

11. _____ are a group of compounds derived from 20-carbon unsaturated fatty acids.

12. _____ proteins are involved with active transport across cell membranes.

True or False

1. Lipids are defined by their physical properties, not by their structure.

2. Saturated fats are lower melting than unsaturated fats.

3. Sphingolipids contain a carboxylic acid ester group.

4. Cholesterol is synthesized by the human body.

5. Sphingosine is a component of both phospholipids and glycolipids.

6. When soap molecules are dissolved in water, they form a lipid bilayer.

7. Cholesterol is a hormone.

8. The main difference between fats and oil is in their melting points.

9. Cerebrosides are a major constituent of the coating around nerve fibers.

10. Waxes and fats are both carboxylic acid esters.

11. Leukotrienes are synthesized in the cells where they act.

12. Facilitated diffusion requires an energy investment.

Match each entry on the left with its partner on the right.

1. Decyl stearate

2. Prostaglandin

3. Choline

4. Stearic acid

5. Integral protein

6. Glyceryl trilaurate

7. Cerebroside

8. Oleic acid

9. Lecithin

10. Linoleic acid

11. Sphingomyelin

12. Peripheral protein

(a) Extends completely through the cell membrane

(b) Monounsaturated fatty acid

(c) Partially embedded in the cell membrane

(d) Phosphoglyceride

(e) Amino alcohol

(f) Saturated fatty acid

(g) Polyunsaturated fatty acid

(h) C_{20} acid with a five-membered ring

(i) Sphingolipid

(j) Fat

(k) Glycolipid

(l) Wax

Chapter Outline

I. Triacylglycerols (Sections 24.1–24.4).
   A. Digestion of triacylglycerols (Section 24.1).
     1. Triacylglycerols (TAGs) pass through the mouth unchanged.
     2. In the stomach, TAGs are broken down into small droplets.
     3. As TAGs pass into the intestines, lipases and bile are produced.
       a. Bile acids solubilize lipid droplets.
       b. Lipases hydrolyze lipids to mono- and diacylglycerols, fatty acids, and glycerol.
     4. Products of TAG digestion are absorbed through the intestinal wall.
       a. Smaller molecules are transported to the liver.
       b. Free fatty acids and acylglycerols are reconverted to triacylglycerols and packaged into lipoproteins (chylomicrons).
   B. Lipoproteins for lipid transport (Section 24.2).
     1. Triacylglycerols and fatty acids enter metabolism from three sources:
       a. Diet.
       b. Storage in adipose tissue.
       c. Synthesis in the liver.
     2. These lipids must be made soluble by association with lipoproteins.
     3. A lipoprotein is a globule of triacylglycerols and fatty acids surrounded by a layer of phospholipids.
     4. Five kinds of lipoproteins are important.
       a. Chylomicrons carry lipids in the diet through the lymphatic system into the blood.
       b. VLDLs carry TAGs from the liver to tissues for storage or energy production.
       c. IDLs carry remnants of VLDLs from peripheral tissues back to the liver for use in synthesis.
       d. LDLs carry cholesterol from the liver to tissues.
       e. HDLs carry cholesterol from cells to the liver, where it is converted to bile acids.
   C. Metabolism of triacylglycerols (Section 24.3–24.4).
     1. Overview (Section 24.3).
       a. Triacylglycerols are hydrolyzed.
         i. TAGs in the diet are hydrolyzed to glycerol and fatty acids by lipoprotein lipase in capillary walls in adipose tissue.
         ii. TAGs in adipocytes are hydrolyzed within the cells, and the fatty acids travel into the bloodstream with albumins.
       b. Glycerol is carried to the liver or kidneys.
         i. Glycerol is converted to dihydroxyacetone phosphate, which enters glycolysis or gluconeogenesis.
       c. Fatty acids have two fates.
         i. When energy is in good supply, fatty acids are converted to TAGs for storage.
         ii. When energy is needed, fatty acids are metabolized to acetyl-CoA.
       d. Acetyl-CoA is used for
         i. Generation of energy via the citric acid cycle and oxidative phosphorylation.
         ii. Biosynthesis of fatty acids.
         iii. Production of ketone bodies.
         iv. Synthesis of sterols.

2. Storage and mobilization of triacylglycerols (Section 24.4).
    a. When blood glucose levels are high, TAGs are synthesized for storage.
        i.   The glycerol 3-phosphate needed is made from dihydroxyacetone phosphate, which comes from glycolysis.
        ii. The fatty acyl-CoAs needed come from digestion or biosynthesis.
        iii. Two fatty acyl-CoA are added to glycerol 3-phosphate.
        iv. After removal of phosphate from phosphatidic acid, the third fatty acyl-CoA is added.
    b. When blood glucose levels are low, fatty acids and glycerol are released from adipocytes and enter the bloodstream.
II. Fatty acid oxidation (Sections 24.5–24.7).
    A. Steps in fatty acid oxidation (Section 24.5).
        1. Activation.
            a. Fatty acids react with HSCoA to form fatty acyl-CoA.
            b. At the same time, ATP is converted to AMP + 2 $HOPO_3^{2-}$.
        2. Transport.
            a. Fatty acyl-CoAs are transported across the mitochondrial membrane.
        3. Oxidation (β Oxidation).
            a.

            e. An n-carbon fatty acid produces n/2 acetyl-CoA.
    B. Energy from fatty acid oxidation (Section 24.6).
        1. The number of molecules of ATP produced from a fatty acid that yields n acetyl-CoA molecules is $14n - 6$.
        2. Fats produce more than twice the amount of energy per unit weight than carbohydrates do.
    C. Production of ketone bodies (ketogenesis) (Section 24.7).
        1. Ketone bodies are formed when the body produces excess acetyl-CoA.
        2. Synthesis of ketone bodies.
            a. 2 Acetyl-CoA —> acetoacetyl-CoA + ⁻SCoA.
            b. Acetoacetyl-CoA + acetyl-CoA —> 3-hydroxy-3-methylglutaryl-CoA + HSCoA.
            c. 3-Hydroxy-3-methylglutaryl-CoA —> acetyl-CoA + acetoacetate.
            d. Acetoacetate + NADH/H⁺ —> 3-hydroxybutyrate + NAD⁺.
            e. Acetoacetate —> acetone + CO_2.

3. Catabolism of ketone bodies produces much of the energy that the body needs during starvation.
4. When ketone bodies are formed faster than the body can utilize them, ketoacidosis occurs.
   a. In ketoacidosis, blood pH drops, ketone bodies are excreted in the urine, and coma and death may result.

III. Fatty acid biosynthesis (lipogenesis) (Section 24.8).
   A. Lipogenesis occurs when amino acids and carbohydrates are in good supply.
   B. Lipogenesis resembles fatty acid oxidation but isn't its exact reverse.
      1. Lipogenesis occurs in the cytosol, and intermediates are carried by ACP.
   C. Mechanism of lipogenesis.
      1. Condensation.
         a. Acetyl-CoA + HCO_3^- —> H_2O + malonyl-CoA.
         b. Malonyl-CoA + HSACP —> malonyl-ACP + HSCoA.
         c. Acetyl-CoA + HSACP —> acetyl-ACP + HSCoA.
         d. Acetyl-ACP + malonyl-ACP —> acetoacetyl-ACP + SACP + CO_2.
      2. Reduction, using NADPH/H^+.
      3. Dehydration.
      4. Reduction, using the coenzyme NADPH/H^+.
      5. Addition of acetyl-ACP units, followed by Steps 2–5, occurs until the chain is the correct length.

Solutions to Chapter 24 Problems

24.1 Both cholate and cholesterol have the tetracyclic ring structure of a sterol. Cholate has more polar functional groups (three —OH groups and one carboxylate group) and is better able to emulsify fats than cholesterol (one —OH group). The hydrophobic side of cholate interacts with TAGs, and the hydrophilic side interacts with the aqueous environment. The less polar cholesterol is more suitable for incorporation into cell membranes. Thus, the two molecules can't change roles.

24.2 Arterial plaque is a deposit of cholesterol and other lipid-containing material that forms within larger arteries. A high HDL value indicates that cholesterol is being removed to the liver, where it is converted to bile acids. A high LDL indicates that an excess of cholesterol is being transported to tissues, where it can form arterial plaque.

24.3 The enzyme *triose phosphate isomerase* catalyzes the isomerization of dihydroxyacetone phosphate to glyceraldehyde 3-phosphate, which proceeds through the last 5 steps of glycolysis to yield pyruvate.

24.4 Excess storage of fat has been linked to a development of a number of diseases, including Type II diabetes, colon cancer, stroke, and heart disease.

24.5 (a), (b) In *Step 1*, a C=C double bond is introduced, using FAD as the oxidizing agent. In *Step 3*, an alcohol is oxidized to a ketone, using NAD^+ as the oxidizing agent.
(c) In *Step 2*, water is added to a carbon–carbon double bond.
(d) In *Step 4*, HSCoA displaces acetyl-CoA, producing a chain-shortened acyl-CoA fatty acid.

24.6

(a)

$$CH_3CH_2-CH_2CH_2-CH_2CH_2-CH_2CH_2-CH_2CH_2-CH_2CH_2-CH_2CH_2-CH_2COH$$

$$\longrightarrow \quad 8 \ CH_3C-SCoA$$

Seven β oxidations are needed.

(b) Since lignoceric acid has 24 carbons, 12 acetyl-CoAs are produced as a result of 11 β oxidations.

24.7 In the citric acid cycle, Steps 6 (dehydrogenation of succinate to produce fumarate), 7 (hydration of fumarate to produce malate), and 8 (oxidation of malate to produce oxaloacetate) are similar to the first three reactions of the β oxidation of a fatty acid.

24.8 The liver stores nutrients, synthesizes important biomolecules, regulates the concentration of substances in the blood, and inactivates toxins.

24.9 The formation of 3-hydroxybutyrate from acetoacetate is a reduction (d).

24.10 (a) Acetyl-CoA provides the acetyl groups used in the synthesis of the ketone bodies. (b) Three acetyl-CoA molecules are used. (c) During prolonged starvation, the body, including the brain, uses ketone bodies as an energy source.

24.11 Seven more malonyl- ACP molecules are needed, and 8 CO_2 are released.

Understanding Key Concepts

24.12 The NADH and $FADH_2$ produced in β oxidation must be reoxidized in the electron transport system in order for β oxidation to continue. Since oxygen is required to reoxidize these reduced coenzymes in the electron transport system, β oxidation is an aerobic pathway even though oxygen isn't directly involved.

24.14

A	**B**	**C**
high blood glucose	high glucagon / low insulin	fatty acid and TAG synthesis
low blood glucose	high insulin / low glucagon	TAG hydrolysis and fatty acid oxidation

24.16 When oxaloacetate in liver is used for gluconeogenesis, less oxaloacetate is available for the citric acid cycle, and less acetyl-CoA is able to enter the cycle. Instead, there is a buildup of acetyl-CoA in the bloodstream. Heart and muscle use the excess acetyl-CoA for synthesis of ketone bodies. Buildup of ketone bodies leads to ketoacidosis, in which blood pH is lowered and the odor of acetone is noticeable in urine and on the breath. Ketoacidosis can lead to dehydration, labored breathing, and death.

24.18 During starvation, glucose is in short supply, and the body responds by producing ketone bodies as a source of energy.

Digestion and Catabolism of Lipids

24.20 Lipids make you feel full because they slow the rate of movement of food through the stomach.

24.22 Bile emulsifies lipid droplets so that they can be attacked by enzymes.

24.24

24.26 Acylglycerols, fatty acids, and protein are combined to form *chylomicrons*, which are lipoproteins used to transport lipids from the diet into the bloodstream.

24.28 Fatty acids from adipose tissue are carried in the bloodstream by albumins.

24.30 Steps 6–10 of the glycolysis pathway are necessary for converting glyceraldehyde 3-phosphate to pyruvate. These steps include an oxidation (Step 6), a phosphorylation (Step 6), two phosphate transfers to ADP (Steps 7 and 10), an isomerization (Step 8), and a dehydration (Step 9).

24.32 Nine molecules of ATP are formed in the catabolism of glycerol to yield acetyl-CoA — the 6 mentioned in Problem 24.31 and an additional 3 in the conversion of pyruvate to acetyl-CoA (Section 22.5).
A maximum of 21 molecules of ATP are released in the complete catabolism of glycerol to CO_2 and H_2O – the 9 molecules mentioned above and an additional 12 molecules formed when acetyl-CoA is metabolized in the citric-acid cycle.

24.34 An adipocyte is a cell, almost entirely filled with fat globules, in which triacylglycerols are stored and mobilized.

24.36 Fatty acid oxidation occurs primarily in heart, liver, and muscle cells.

24.38 A fatty acid is converted to its fatty acyl-CoA in order to activate it for catabolism.

24.40 Stepwise oxidation of fatty acids is known as β oxidation because the carbon β to the thioester group (two carbons away from the thioester group) is oxidized in the process.

24.42 The coenzymes NAD⁺ and FAD are required for β oxidation.

24.44 Each cycle of β oxidation produces 5 molecules of ATP (3 ATPs from the formation of the reduced coenzyme NADH and 2 ATPs from the formation of the reduced coenzyme FADH₂), plus one molecule of acetyl-CoA, which enters into the citric acid cycle to yield 12 more molecules of ATP, for a total of 17.

24.46 *Least energy/mole* ⟶ *Greatest energy/mole*

Molecule	Glucose	Sucrose	$CH_3(CH_2)_8COOH$	$CH_3(CH_2)_{12}COOH$
ATP content/mole	38 ATP	76 ATP	78 ATP	112 ATP

24.48

24.50 The number of molecules of acetyl-CoA produced from one molecule of fatty acid is half the number of carbons in the acid. The number of cycles of β oxidation is one fewer than the number of molecules of acetyl-CoA produced.

Acid	Acetyl-SCoA Produced	Number of Cycles
(a) $CH_3(CH_2)_{12}COOH$	7	6
(b) $CH_3(CH_2)_6COOH$	4	3

Fatty Acid Anabolism

24.52 The anabolic pathway for synthesizing fatty acids is called *lipogenesis*.

24.54 Acetyl-CoA is the starting material for fatty-acid synthesis.

24.56 Stearic acid has 18 carbons and is synthesized from 9 acetyl-CoA units through 8 rounds of the lipogenesis spiral.

24.58 Lipogenesis takes place in the cytosol, whereas β oxidation takes place in mitochondria.

Chemistry in Action

24.60 Total cholesterol: 200 mg/dL or lower.
LDL: 130 mg/dL or lower.
HDL: 40 mg/dL or higher.

24.62 LDL carries cholesterol from the liver to tissues; HDL carries cholesterol from tissues to the liver, where it is converted to bile and excreted.

24.64 Obese people are in danger of developing Type II diabetes, colon cancer, heart attacks and stroke.

24.66 Calorie-dense food and lack of exercise also lead to fat accumulation.

24.68 Important functions of the liver include:

(a) Synthesis of glycogen, glucose, triacylglycerols, fatty acids, cholesterol, bile acids, plasma proteins, and blood clotting factors.
(b) Catabolism of glucose, fatty acids, and amino acids.
(c) Storage of glycogen, lipids, amino acids, iron, and fat-soluble vitamins.
(d) Inactivation of toxic substances.

General Questions and Problems

24.70 An excess of carbohydrates produces an excess of acetyl-CoA. If more acetyl-CoA is produced than is needed in the respiratory chain, it is used to synthesize fatty acids, which are used to produce the triglycerides that are deposited in adipose tissue. Once carbohydrates have been catabolized to acetyl-CoA, it is not possible to resynthesize them, because animals don't have enzymes to synthesize carbohydrates from acetyl-CoA.

24.72 In β oxidation, the alcohol intermediate is chiral because the hydroxyl carbon is bonded to four different groups.

24.74 Ketosis is a condition in which ketone bodies accumulate in the blood faster than they can be metabolized. Since two of the ketone bodies are carboxylic acids, they lower the pH of the blood, producing the condition known as ketoacidosis. Symptoms of ketoacidosis include dehydration, labored breathing, and depression; prolonged ketoacidosis may lead to coma and death.

24.76 Ketones have little effect on pH, but the two other ketone bodies are acidic, and they lower the pH of urine.

24.78 Consider a carbohydrate and a fatty acid with similar molar masses. Glucose (molar mass = 180 g) yields a maximum of 38 ATP/mole; $CH_3(CH_2)_8COOH$ (molar mass = 172 g) yields a maximum of 78 ATP/mole. Thus, the energy yield per mole from a fat is about twice the yield from a sugar. There are two principal reasons for this difference. (1) A carbohydrate has fewer carbons than a fatty acid of similar molar mass and thus produces fewer moles of acetyl-CoA per mole of carbohydrate. (2) Only 2/3 of a carbohydrate's carbons are used to form acetyl-CoA; the other carbons are released as CO_2 in the transformation pyruvate —> acetyl-CoA.

24.80 The body synthesizes cholesterol when no cholesterol is present in the diet. Thus, eliminating exogenous sources of cholesterol won't eliminate cholesterol in the bloodstream. A certain amount of cholesterol is essential for membrane function and as the starting material for synthesis of steroid hormones.

24.82

$$H_2C{=}CH{-}\underset{\underset{CH_3}{|}}{C}{=}CH_2 \qquad \text{2-Methyl-1,3-butadiene}$$

Since cholesterol contains 27 carbon atoms, at least 6 molecules of 2-methyl-1,3-butadiene are needed for its synthesis.

Self-Test for Chapter 24

Multiple Choice

1. ATP is ultimately produced in all of the following steps of fatty acid catabolism except:
   (a) fatty acid activation   (b) introduction of a double bond into a fatty acid   (c) oxidation of an alcohol to a ketone   (d) entry of acetyl-SCoA into the citric acid cycle

2. An excess of ketone bodies in the blood is known as:
   (a) ketosis   (b) ketonuria   (c) ketoacidosis   (d) ketonemia

3. The reactants for TAG synthesis are:
   (a) glycerol and fatty acids   (b) glycerol 3-phosphate and fatty acids   (c) glyceraldehyde 3-phosphate and fatty acyl-SCoA   (d) glycerol and fatty acyl-SCoA

4. Production of ketone bodies occurs in:
   (a) the liver   (b) adipose tissue   (c) muscle   (d) all of the above

5. Which of the following statements about lipogenesis is false?
   (a) Synthesis occurs two carbons at a time.   (b) Formation of acyl-SACP intermediates requires ATP.   (c) The coenzyme NADPH is needed.   (d) Lipogenesis occurs when acetyl-CoA is in abundance.

6. Chylomicrons transport all of the following except:
   (a) acylglycerols   (b) small-chain fatty acids   (c) phospholipids   (d) cholesterol

7. Fatty acids from storage in adipose tissue are transported:
   (a) by chylomicrons   (b) by VLDL   (c) by serum albumin   (d) free in the bloodstream

8. Acetyl-CoA is the starting material for synthesis of all of the following except:
   (a) steroids   (b) fatty acids   (c) ketone bodies   (d) glycerol

9. β Oxidation of $CH_3(CH_2)_8COOH$ produces a maximum of how many ATPs?
   (a) 78   (b) 72   (c) 64   (d) 60

10. When glucose is in good supply, the body:
    (a) synthesizes ketone bodies from acetyl-SCoA   (b) hydrolyzes TAGs from adipocytes
    (c) breaks down fatty acids via β-oxidation   (d) synthesizes TAGs for storage

Sentence Completion

1. One _____ and one _____ are needed for each β oxidation cycle.

2. Bile acids solubilize lipids by forming _____.

3. Triacylglycerols are stored in _____.

4. TAG synthesis begins with the conversion of glycerol to _____ _____.

5. An alternate name for β oxidation is the___ - ____ _____.

6. The first step in β oxidation involves introduction of a _____ _____.

7. _____ is the presence of ketone bodies in the urine.

8. _____ is a coenzyme for fatty-acid biosynthesis.

9. _____ is a ketone body containing a hydroxyl group.

10. Chylomicrons are transported in the _____ _____ and in the bloodstream.

11. TAGs that are released from storage are said to be _____.

12. All fatty acids are synthesized from _____.

True or False

1. Bile acids are steroids.

2. TAGs are hydrolyzed by pancreatic lipases to glycerol and fatty acids.

3. Activation of fatty acids for fatty-acid oxidation requires two phosphates to be cleaved.

4. A chylomicron is a type of lipoprotein.

5. Chylomicrons carry fatty acid-CoA across the mitochondrial membrane.

6. A fatty acid with n carbons requires $n/2 - 1$ cycles of β-oxidation for complete breakdown.

7. TAGs are synthesized from glycerol and fatty acyl-CoAs.

8. HDL transports cholesterol to tissues, where it can accumulate.

9. A fatty acid with a molecular weight similar to that of glucose yields more ATPs per molecule than glucose.

10. Fatty acid synthesis occurs in mitochondria.

11. The terminal $-CH_3$ group of a fatty acid comes from malonyl-SCoA.

12. Most naturally-occurring fatty acids have an even number of carbon atoms.

Match each entry on the left with its partner on the right.

1. Chylomicron

2. Lipogenesis

3. LDL

4. Acetone

5. Malonyl-CoA

6. Fatty-acid spiral

7. Micelle

8. Lipoprotein lipase

9. HDL

10. Albumin

11. Bile

12. Acetoacetate

(a) Lipoprotein rich in cholesterol

(b) Protein that carries fatty acids in the bloodstream

(c) Solubilizes fats

(d) Hydrolyzes TAG in adipose tissue

(e) Lipoprotein that aids in lipid transport of fats in the diet

(f) Lipoprotein rich in protein

(g) Starting material in lipogenesis

(h) Acidic ketone body

(i) Fatty-acid biosynthesis

(j) Breakdown of fatty acids into acetyl-SCoA

(k) Formed from bile and lipids

(l) Nonacidic ketone body

Chapter 25 Nucleic Acids and Protein Synthesis

Chapter Outline

I. Nucleic acids (Sections 25.1–25.4).
  A. Introduction (Section 25.1).
    1. When a cell isn't dividing, its nucleus consists of chromatin, a tangle of fibers composed of protein and DNA.
    2. Just before dividing, the DNA is duplicated.
    3. During division, chromatin organizes itself into chromosomes, each of which is a huge DNA molecule.
    4. The chromosomes are made up of genes, individual segments of DNA that contain instructions for synthesizing a single protein.
    5. The human body has 23 pairs of chromosomes.
  B. Composition of nucleic acids (Section 25.2).
    1. Nucleic acids are polymers of nucleotides.
      a. DNA and RNA are the two types of nucleic acids.
    2. Nucleotides consist of:
      a. A heterocyclic base.
        i. The bases for DNA are the purines adenine and guanine, and the pyrimidines cytosine and thymine.
        ii. For RNA, uracil replaces thymine.
      b. A pentose.
        i. For RNA, the pentose is D-ribose.
        ii. For DNA, the pentose is D-2-deoxyribose.
        iii. The pentose is connected to the base by a β-*N*-glycosidic bond to the anomeric carbon.
      c. A phosphate group.
        i. The phosphate group is attached at C5 of the pentose.
    3. The combination of sugar + base is known as a nucleoside.
      a. Nucleosides are named by replacing the -*ine* of the base name by -*osine* for purines and -*idine* for pyrimidines.
      b. If the pentose is 2-deoxyribose, the prefix *deoxy* is added to the name.
      c. To indicate position, numbers without primes are used for bases, and numbers with primes are used for the pentose.
      d. Nucleosides have important biochemical functions other than as components of nucleic acids.
    4. Nucleotides.
      a. Nucleotides are named by adding "5'-monophosphate" to the nucleoside name.
      b. Nucleotides can form di- and triphosphates.
        i. ATP plays an important role in biochemical energetics.
  C. The structure of nucleic acid chains (Section 25.3).
    1. Nucleotides are joined by phosphate ester bonds between the 5' phosphate and the 3' —OH group of the sugar of the next nucleotide.
    2. Vast numbers of nucleotides can be connected by these bonds to form immense polynucleotides.
    3. The structure and function of nucleic acids depends on the sequence of nucleotides.
    4. The sequence is described by starting at the 5' end and identifying the bases by one-letter abbreviations.

    D. Base pairing in DNA (Section 25.4).
        1. In DNA, two polynucleotide strands coil around each other in a double helix.
            a. The sugar–phosphate backbone is on the outside.
            b. The bases are inside.
        2. The two strands run in opposite directions.
        3. The two strands are held together by hydrogen bonding between bases.
            a. A and T form two hydrogen bonds to each other.
            b. C and G form three hydrogen bonds to each other.
        4. The two strands are complementary.
            a. A and T always occur in DNA in the same percentage.
            b. C and G always occur in DNA in the same percentage.
II. The function of nucleic acids (Sections 25.5–25.10).
    A. The central dogma of molecular genetics (Section 25.5).
        1. The function of DNA is to store genetic information.
        2. The function of RNA is to read and decode DNA and use the information to synthesize proteins.
        3. Nucleic acids take part in three major processes.
            a. Replication is the process in which DNA makes a copy of itself.
            b. Transcription is the process in which RNA reads the genetic message.
            c. Translation is the process in which the genetic message is used to make proteins.
    B. Replication of DNA (Section 25.6).
        1. Mechanism of replication.
            a. The double helix partially unwinds, with the assistance of helicase enzymes.
                i. Unwinding occurs simultaneously at many locations.
            b. Bases line up and form hydrogen bonds with their complements.
            c. DNA polymerase catalyzes bond formation between the 5' phosphate group on the arriving nucleotide and the 3' —OH of the old strand.
        2. Two identical new copies of the double helix are formed.
        3. Because strand growth occurs in one direction (5' —> 3'), only one strand of DNA is synthesized continuously (the leading strand).
            a. The other strand (the lagging strand) is synthesized in segments (Okazaki fragments), beginning at the replication fork.
            b. DNA ligase attaches the segments of the lagging strand.
         4. The copying of DNA requires several hours, involves many replication forks, and proceeds virtually without error.
    C. RNA (Section 25.7).
        1. Structure of RNA.
            a. RNA resembles DNA but has the following differences;
                i. The pentose is ribose.
                ii. Uracil replaces thymine.
            b. RNA chains are shorter than DNA chains.
            c. RNA chains may be single stranded or double stranded.
        2. Types of RNA.
            a. Ribosomal RNA has a molecular mass of 5×10^6 amu and occurs in ribosomes, which are the site of protein synthesis.
            b. Messenger RNA reads DNA and carries the message to the ribosomes.
            c. Transfer RNA delivers amino acids to the growing protein chain.
    D. Transcription (Section 25.8).
        1. mRNA is synthesized by transcription of DNA.
            a. RNA polymerase recognizes a control segment of DNA that precedes the nucleotides to be transcribed.
            b. A small section of DNA unwinds.
            c. Complementary bases are attached.

d. Transcription stops when RNA polymerase recognizes a "stop" nucleotide sequence.
e. All RNA is synthesized in the same way, although we will focus on mRNA in this description.
2. Only one DNA strand is transcribed — the template strand.
a. The other strand is the information strand.
b. mRNA is a copy of the information strand (with U replacing T).
3. Not all genes are continuous strands of DNA.
a. The coding sections of DNA (exons) are interrupted by noncoding sections (introns).
b. In the final mRNA, the intron sections are cut out.
E. Translation (Sections 25.9–25.10).
1. The genetic code (Section 25.9).
a. A sequence of three mRNA bases codes for a specific amino acid.
b. The codes are written in the 5' —> 3' direction.
c. Each amino acid is represented by one or more codes.
d. There are 64 codons; 61 code for amino acids, and 3 are "stop" codons.
2. Transfer RNA (Section 25.10).
a. The message carried by mRNA is decoded by tRNA.
b. Each amino acid is transported by its own tRNA to the ribosome.
c. Amino acids are bonded to tRNA by an ester bond between the —COOH group of an amino acid and C3' of ribose at the end of the tRNA.
d. Each tRNA has an anticodon that corresponds to a codon sequence on mRNA.
3. Protein synthesis.
a. Initiation.
i. The first AUG codon on the 5' end of mRNA is a "start" codon (which also codes for methionine).
ii. When the Met tRNA comes together with the mRNA codon and occupies one of the two binding sites in the ribosome, elongation can start.
iii. If Met isn't the first amino acid in the protein, it is removed after protein synthesis.
b. Elongation.
i. A tRNA with an anticodon complementary to the second mRNA codon occupies the second binding site.
ii. An enzyme in the ribosome catalyzes peptide bond formation and breaks the bond between the first amino acid and its tRNA.
iii. This tRNA leaves the ribosome.
iv. The ribosome shifts one position along the mRNA chain (translocation).
v. The second site is free to accept the next tRNA.
vi. A single mRNA can be read by many ribosomes.
c. Termination.
i. A "stop" codon signals the end of translation.
ii. An enzyme called "releasing factor" frees the polypeptide chain from the last tRNA, and the mRNA is released from the ribosome.

Solutions to Chapter 25 Problems

25.1

2'-Deoxythymidine

25.2 D-Ribose has one more oxygen atom than 2-deoxy-D-ribose. This added oxygen allows D-ribose to form an additional hydrogen bond. The hydroxyl hydrogen can also take part in hydrogen bonding.

β-D-Ribose
($C_5H_{10}O_5$)

β-2-Deoxy-D-ribose
($C_5H_{10}O_4$)

25.3

2'-Deoxyadenosine 5'-monophosphate

25.4

Guanosine 5'-triphosphate (GTP)

25.5 dUMP — 2'-Deoxyuridine 5'-monophosphate
UMP — Uridine 5'-monophosphate
CDP — Cytidine 5'-diphosphate
AMP — Adenosine 5'-monophosphate
ATP — Adenosine 5'-triphosphate

25.6 G-A-U-C-A = guanine-adenine-uracil-cytosine-adenine. The pentanucleotide comes from RNA because it contains uracil.

25.7

25.8 (a) Original strand: 5' T-A-T-A-C-T-G   3'
          Complement: 3' A-T-A-T-G-A-C   5'

(b) Original strand: 5' G-A-T-C-G-C-T-C-T   3'
          Complement: 3' C-T-A-G-C-G-A-G-A   5'

25.9

Adenine   Uracil

25.10 The phosphate groups cause the DNA molecule to be negatively charged.

25.11 (a) A longer strand of DNA has a higher "melting temperature" because larger molecules have greater numbers of hydrogen bonds.

(b) A strand of DNA containing a higher percentage of C/G base pairs has a higher "melting temperature." A C/G base pair has three hydrogen bonds, whereas an A/T pair has only two hydrogen bonds. A DNA strand with a higher percent of C/G base pairs has more hydrogen bonds, and more heat is required to separate the two strands.

25.12 Okazaki fragments are segments of DNA synthesized by using the lagging strand as a template. The fragments are later joined by a DNA ligase enzyme.

25.13 In spliceosomes, introns from hnRNA are removed to yield mRNA; in ribosomes, proteins are synthesized, using mRNA as a template. Each process uses a different RNA enzyme.

25.14 (a) DNA template strand: 5' C-A-T–G-C-T-C-T--A-C-A-G 3'

mRNA complement: 3' G-U-A-C-G-A-G-A-U-G-U-C 5'

(b) DNA template strand: 3' T-A-T-T-A–G–C-G-A-C-C-G 5'

mRNA complement   5' A-U-A-A-U-C-G-C-U-G-G-C 3'

25.15 *Amino Acid*   *Possible Codons*   (5' –> 3')

(a) Val	GUU GUC GUA GUG
(b) Phe	UUU UUC
(c) Asn	AAU AAC
(d) Gly	GGU GGC GGA GGC
(e) Met	AUG

25.16 The sequence guanine-adenine-guanine (GAG) codes for the amino acid glutamic acid.

25.17   *Codon*   *Amino Acid*

(a) AUC	Ile
(b) GCU	Ala
(c) CGA	Arg
(d) AAG	Lys

25.18 Six mRNA base triplets code for leucine: UUA, UUG, CUU, CUC, CUA, CUG. Many possible mRNA strands could code for this tripeptide if different codons were used for each Leu. Six of them are listed below:

5' UUAUUGCUU 3'   5' UUAUUGCUC 3'   5' UUAUUGCUA 3'
5' UUAUUGCUG 3'   5' UUACUUCUC 3'   5' UUACUUCUA 3'

25.19 Viruses consist of a strand of nucleic acid wrapped in a protein coat. Unlike higher organisms, viruses can't replicate or manufacture protein independent of a host cell.

25.20–25.21

mRNA sequence:	5' CUC—AUU—CCA—UGC—GAC—GUA 3'
Amino-acid sequence:	Leu——Ile——Pro——Cys—–Asp——Val
tRNA anticodons:	3' GAG UAA GGU ACG CUG CAU 5'

25.22 Rapid variation in virus antigens make it difficult to develop a universal influenza vaccine.

Understanding Key Concepts

25.24

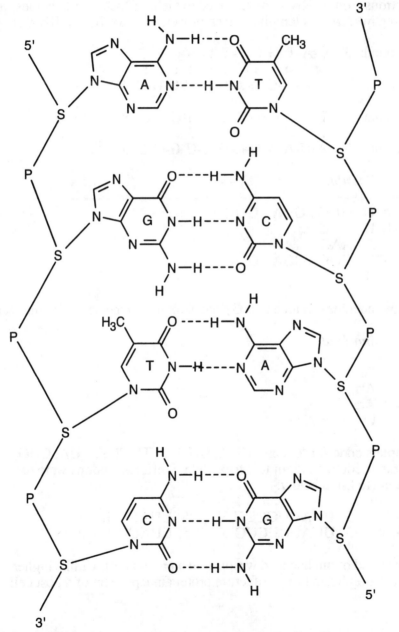

The sequence of the left chain: 5' –A–G–T–C– 3'.
The sequence of the right chain: 3' –T–C–A–G– 5'.

25.26 The sugar–phosphate backbone is found on the exterior of the DNA double helix. Since the phosphate groups are negatively charged, histone proteins should have a large number of positively charged amino acids, such as lysine, arginine, and histidine, on their surfaces.

25.28 Each amino acid has more than one mRNA codon.
Codons for Gln: CAA, CAG
Codons for His: CAC, CAU
Codons for Pro: CCC, CCU, CCA, CCG
Codons for Gly: GGG, GGU, GGA, GGC
Using the first codon listed:

(a) 5' $\boxed{C|A|A}$ $\boxed{C|A|C}$ $\boxed{C|C|C}$ $\boxed{G|G|G}$ 3' mRNA

(b) 3' $\boxed{G|T|T}$ $\boxed{G|T|G}$ $\boxed{G|G|G}$ $\boxed{C|C|C}$ 5' DNA template strand

(c) 5' $\boxed{C|A|A}$ $\boxed{C|A|C}$ $\boxed{C|C|C}$ $\boxed{G|G|G}$ 3' DNA informational strand

The upper strand of DNA is the template for the synthesis of mRNA, and its sequence of bases is the complement of the sequence of bases that make up the pro-TRH gene (with T replacing U). The lower strand is the informational strand.

(d) To find the number of DNA sequences, multiply the numbers of different codons for each amino acid.
2 x 2 x 4 x 4 = 64 possible DNA sequences code for the first four amino acids in pro-TRH.

Structure and Function of Nucleic Acids

25.30 Ribose is the sugar in RNA, and deoxyribose is the sugar in DNA. The —OH group at carbon 2 of ribose is replaced by —H in deoxyribose.

25.32 The purine bases (two fused heterocyclic rings) are adenine and guanine. The pyrimidine bases (one heterocyclic ring) are cytosine, thymine (in DNA), and uracil (in RNA).

25.34 DNA is the largest nucleic acid, mRNA is intermediate in size, and tRNA is the smallest of the three nucleic acids.

25.36 *Similarities:* Replication, transcription, and translation are all polymerizations in which a nucleic acid is used as a template for the synthesis of another biopolymer. In all of these processes, hydrogen bonding is used to bring the subunits into the correct position for bond formation and to determine the order of assembly.
Differences: In replication, DNA makes a copy of itself. In transcription, DNA is used as a template for the synthesis of mRNA. In translation, mRNA is used as a template for the synthesis of proteins. Replication and transcription take place in the nucleus of cells, and translation takes place in ribosomes.

25.38 Chromatin is composed of protein and DNA.

25.40 There are 46 chromosomes (23 pairs) in a human cell.

25.42 Bases that are complementary form hydrogen bonds with each other and thus always occur in pairs. For example, adenine is always hydrogen-bonded to thymine or uracil, and guanine is always hydrogen-bonded to cytosine.

25.44 If a sample of DNA is 22% G, the percent of C is also 22%, since G and C are complementary. The sample contains 28% A and 28% T, because A and T are also complementary.

25.46 Polynucleotides are synthesized from 5' to 3'.

25.48

Water is removed in the formation of both the sugar–phosphate linkage and the sugar–base linkage.

25.50

25.52 Introns may serve a regulatory purpose, they may separate exons that can be mixed or matched, or they may merely be left over from an earlier stage of development.

Nucleic Acids and Heredity

25.54 A number of replication forks are needed when DNA is duplicated in order to increase the speed of replication of the enormous DNA chain.

25.56 A codon is a sequence of three nucleotides on mRNA that codes for a specific amino acid in protein synthesis.

25.58 A tRNA molecule is cloverleaf-shaped and contains 70–100 nucleotides. The tRNA anticodon triplet is on one "leaf," and an amino acid bonds covalently to the 3' end.

25.60 Ser, Arg, and Leu each have six codons; Ala, Gly, Pro, Val, and Thr each have four. Met and Trp each have only one codon. To an extent, these numbers are correlated with the relative abundance of these amino acids in proteins.

25.62

Codon (5' —> 3')	Amino Acid
(a) CCC	Pro
(b) GCG	Ala
(c) UUA	Leu

25.64 Codons are written (5' —> 3'), and anticodons are written (3' —>5')

(a) Val	Codons:	GUU	GUC	GUA	GUG		
	Anticodons:	CAA	CAG	CAU	CAC		
(b) Arg	Codons:	CGU	CGC	CGA	CGG	AGA	AGG
	Anticodons:	GCA	GCG	GCU	GCC	UCU	UCC
(c) Ser	Codons:	UCU	UCC	UCA	UCG	AGU	AGC
	Anticodons:	AGA	AGG	AGU	AGC	UCA	UCG

25.66

The DNA sequence of the template strand is complementary to the DNA sequence of the informational strand. The mRNA sequence is identical to the DNA sequence on the informational strand, except that U in mRNA replaces T in DNA.

Informational strand: (5' —> 3')	TAC--CCT
Template strand: (3' —> 5')	ATG--GGA
mRNA: (5' —> 3')	UAC--CCU

25.68

Informational strand: (5' —> 3')	GTC--AGT--ACG--TTA
mRNA: (5' —> 3')	GUC--AGU-ACG--UUA
Tetrapeptide:	Val----Ser----Thr----Leu

25.70 Using the first set of base pairs in Problem 25.69 to solve this problem:

Informational strand (5' —> 3'):	TAT–GGT–GGT–TTT—ATG–TAA
Template strand (3' —> 5'):	ATA–CCA–CCA–AAA—TAC–ATT

Chemistry in Action

25.72 Ribozyme activity is common among the simplest and most primitive life forms, such as viroids, leading scientists to speculate that ribozyme catalysis might have preceded enzyme catalysis.

25.74 To be effective, a drug must be powerful enough to act on viruses within cells without damaging the cells and their genetic material. Also, drugs quickly lose their effectiveness against AIDS because of the high mutation rate of the AIDS virus.

25.76 Influenza A viruses are described by a code that describes the hemagglutinins (H) and the neuraminidases (N) in the virus. The H1N1 virus was responsible for the 1918 influenza pandemic, and the H5N1 virus is present in avian flu. Since these viruses can undergo antigenic shift in host animals, there is concern when infected birds and animals harbor influenza viruses.

General Questions and Problems

25.78 To code for preproinsulin, 81 x 3 = 243 bases are needed to code for the protein's 81 amino acids. In addition, a three-base "start" codon and a three-base "stop" codon are needed, for a total of 249 bases.

25.80 If a protein doesn't have methionine as its first amino acid, the methionine is removed after protein synthesis is complete.

Self-Test for Chapter 25

Multiple Choice

1. The name for a nucleoside formed from cytosine and 2'-deoxyribose is:
   (a) deoxycytidine 5'-monophosphate (b) 2'-deoxycytidine (c) 2'-deoxycytosine
   (d) 2'-deoxycytosine 5'-monophosphate

2. Adenine and thymine are complementary because:
   (a) They are both purines. (b) They are both pyrimidines. (c) They both occur in DNA.
   (d) They form two hydrogen bonds to each other.

3. If the base sequence CAC-TTA-GGT appears on the informational strand of DNA, which sequence occurs in mRNA?
   (a) CAC-TTA-GGT (b) CAC-UUA-GGU (c) GTG-AAT-CCA (d) GUG-AAU-CCA

4. Which statement about the RNA base sequence CGG-AAA-GUU is true?
   (a) It codes for a basic tripeptide. (b) It contains a "stop" codon. (c) Changing the third codon from GUU to GUC changes the amino acids in the tripeptide. (d) The 5' end is on the right, and the 3' end is on the left.

5. Which of the following completes the initiation phase of protein synthesis?
   (a) the small subunit of a ribosome (b) the large subunit of a ribosome (c) mRNA (d) tRNA

6. The process by which the genetic message contained in DNA is read is called:
   (a) replication (b) transcription (c) translation (d) translocation

7. Which of the following heterocyclic bases contains a methyl group?
   (a) guanine (b) cytosine (c) thymine (d) uracil

8. An enzyme involved in translation is:
   (a) DNA polymerase (b) restriction endonuclease (c) RNA polymerase (d) releasing factor

9. Which of the following statements about DNA replication is untrue?
   (a) Replication is semiconservative. (b) Each DNA strand has many replication forks.
   (c) DNA ligase catalyzes bond formation between each arriving nucleotide.
   (d) Replication proceeds in the 5'—>3' direction.

10. Which heterocyclic base contains only carbon, hydrogen, and nitrogen?
    (a) adenine (b) guanine (c) cytosine (d) thymine

Sentence Completion

1. _____ is the process by which an identical copy of DNA is made.

2. The two strands of DNA have base sequences that are _____.

3. When a cell is not actively dividing, its nucleus is occupied by _____.

4. Another name for an RNA virus is a _____.

5. An _____ is a segment of a gene that does not code for protein synthesis.

6. tRNA binds to an amino acid by an _____ linkage.

7. A _____ consists of a heterocyclic amine base bonded to an aldopentose.

8. An enzyme called a _____ _____ frees the polypeptide chain from the last tRNA during protein synthesis.

9. The point of replication of a DNA chain is called the _____ _____.

10. The sugar _____ has an —H instead of an —OH at its 2' position.

11. The _____ - _____ model describes DNA as two polynucleotide strands coiled about each other in a double helix.

12. The enzyme _____ _____ catalyzes the bonding of nucleotides to form new strands of DNA.

True or False

1. There are a total of 64 codons for the 20 amino acids.

2. The amount of adenine in an organism's DNA is equal to the amount of guanine.

3. In transcription, mRNA is a copy of the informational strand of DNA.

4. An amino acid codon occurs on tRNA.

5. The codon AUG initiates protein synthesis.

6. Synthetase enzymes catalyze the formation of ester bonds between amino acids and their tRNAs.

7. The individual units of RNA and DNA are called nucleotides.

8. The two strands of the DNA double helix run in the same direction.

9. Transcription is the process by which the genetic message is decoded and used to make proteins.

10. Most human DNA contains genetic instructions.

11. Each amino acid is specified by more than one codon.

12. The correct name for the RNA nucleotide containing G is guanidine 5'-monophosphate.

Match each entry on the left with its partner on the right.

1. 5' end	(a) Enzyme used in replication
2. A-C-G	(b) Cysteine codon
3. U-G-C	(c) Forms three hydrogen bonds
4. Adenine	(d) Coded for by six codons
5. DNA ligase	(e) RNA containing both exons and introns
6. 3' end	(f) "Stop" codon
7. Leu	(g) Purine
8. Cytosine	(h) Enzyme used in transcription
9. hnRNA	(i) —OH group
10. Uracil	(j) Cysteine anticodon
11. U-G-A	(k) Pyrimidine
12. RNA polymerase	(l) Phosphate group

Chapter 26   Genomics

Chapter Outline

I.   Mapping the human genome (Section 26.1).
   A. Two research groups have collectively decoded 99% of the human genome.
      1. The Human Genome Project.
         a. The Human Genome Project is made up of 20 international not-for-profit groups.
         b. The technique:
            i.   For each chromosome, a genetic map is developed; the map shows the location of markers determined by inheritance.
            ii. A map of finer resolution (physical map) shows markers determined by other methods.
            iii. The chromosome is cut into large segments, and the resulting clones are organized into an overlapping sequence.
            iv. Each clone is fragmented into hundreds of pieces, which are labelled and separated by electrophoresis.
            v.   The sequences are assembled into a nucleotide map.
      2. Celera.
         a. Celera is a for-profit research group.
         b. The technique:
            i.   The entire genome is broken into fragments, without identifying their origin.
            ii. The fragments are copied many times, sequenced and separated.
            iii. The sequences are reassembled, using a supercomputer.
II. Characteristics of chromosomes (Sections 26.2–26.3).
   A. Chromosome structure (Section 26.2).
      1. Telomeres.
         a. Telomeres are long series of repeating DNA that are found at the ends of each chromosome.
         b. Telomeres protect the ends of chromosomes from accidents.
         c. Telomeres also prevent the ends of chromosomes from pairing with other DNA.
         d. The enzyme telomerase catalyzes the addition of telomeres to DNA.
            i.   Telomerase is more active in young cells than in older cells.
      2. Centromeres.
         a. Centromeres are constrictions that determine the shapes of chromosomes during cell division.
         b. Centromeres contain large repetitive base sequences.
      3. Other noncoding DNA.
         a. Not all of the functions of noncoding DNA are known.
            i.   Some segments are regulatory.
            ii. Other proposed functions: accommodation of DNA folding, evolutionary roles.
      4. Genes.
         a. The coding sections of a gene (exons) are interspersed with noncoding introns.
   B. Mutations and polymorphisms (Section 26.3).
      1. Mutations.
         a. An error in mRNA transcription is not serious.

b. An error in DNA replication is a mutation and is passed on each time DNA replicates.
    i. Substances that cause mutations are mutagens.
    ii. Each time mRNA is transcribed, the resulting protein will have an error.
    iii. The consequences of a mutation range from insignificant to lethal.
c. If the error occurs in a somatic cell, cancer may result.
d. If the error occurs in a germ cell, a genetic defect may be passed on to offspring.
2. Polymorphisms.
    a. Polymorphisms are variations in nucleotide sequences that are common within a given population.
    b. Replacement of one nucleotide by another in the same location is a single-nucleotide polymorphism (SNP).
        i. SNPs are responsible for most of the variation among human beings.
        ii. SNPs are responsible for many genetic diseases.
        iii. A catalog of SNPs has been developed; it now has 3.1 million SNPs.
        iv. This catalog has been used to identify SNPs responsible for abnormalities.
III. Recombinant DNA and genomics (Section 26.4–26.5).
    A. Recombinant DNA technology is used to cut a specific gene out of one organism and insert it into the DNA of another organism (Section 26.4).
        1. The second organism is usually a bacterium.
        2. Bacterial DNA is contained in plasmids, which are easy to isolate.
    B. Technique of recombinant DNA.
        1. The plasmid is cleaved by a restriction endonuclease.
            a. There are more than 200 restriction endonucleases.
            b. Cleavage occurs at a specific site in a base sequence.
            c. Each DNA strand is left with a few unpaired bases, called "sticky ends."
        2. The gene to be inserted is also cleaved by the same endonucleases and thus has complementary sticky ends.
        3. The gene and the plasmid are mixed in the presence of a DNA ligase enzyme and the gene is inserted into the plasmid.
        4. The plasmid can be reinserted into a bacterial cell, and the bacteria, which multiply rapidly, manufacture the protein.
    C. Uses of recombinant DNA technology—genomics (Section 26.5).
        1. Agriculture.
            a. Transgenic plants and animals have been bred; their DNA includes single genes that code for desirable traits.
        2. Medicine.
            a. Gene therapy might cure inherited diseases by replacing a disease-causing gene with a healthy copy of that gene.
            b. A personal genomic survey might be helpful in drug and therapeutic choices.
            c. DNA chip screening can be used to detect polymorphisms associated with diseases and drug responses.

Solutions to Chapter 26 Problems

26.1 uouo**the**dtttrr**fat**naedigo**pred**sldjflsjfxx**rat**ponxbv**ate**ugfaqq**then**qeut**bad**pag**frat**meabrrx
(The fat red rat ate the bad rat)

26.2 Look back to Table 25.4 and note that UGU codes for cysteine, and UGG codes for tryptophan. In the synthesized protein, a tryptophan would replace a cysteine. Since cysteine forms disulfide bridges, the protein's three-dimensional structure would most likely be disrupted and its function might be affected.

26.3   The sample might not be random; the donors might not be anonymous; issues of informed consent might arise.

26.4   The complementary DNA strand is drawn by pairing the bases and by reversing the labels of the two ends of the strands. The restriction enzyme cleaves the complementary strand at the same location.

$$5' \quad -A- \mathbin{/\!/} -G-A-T-C-T- \quad 3'$$
$$3' \quad -T-C-T-A-G- \mathbin{/\!/} -A- \quad 5'$$

26.5   The explanation in the previous problem applies here.

$$5' \quad -G- \mathbin{/\!/} -A-A-T-T-C- \quad 3'$$
$$3' \quad -C-T-T-A-A- \mathbin{/\!/} -G- \quad 5'$$

26.6   To be sticky, base sequences must be complementary. Draw the complement of the first sequence. If the complement you draw is identical to the second sequence, the two sequences are sticky.
(a) The pairs are sticky.
(b), (c) The pairs aren't sticky.

26.7   Taq polymerase can withstand high temperatures and doesn't need to be replaced for each PCR cycle.

26.8   If the chance of two people having an identical fingerprint match is one in 1.5 billion, around 4 people might have an identical match.

26.9   (a) The field of *comparative genomics* deals with the identification of genes that perform identical functions in mice and humans.
(b) A person working in *genetic engineering* might be involved with creating a variety of wheat that is not harmed by a herbicide that kills weeds that interfere with wheat crops.
(c) *Pharmacogenetics* is used for screening a individual's genome to choose the most appropriate pain-killing medication for that person.
(d) *Bioinformatics* is the computer analysis of base-sequence information from groups of people with and without a certain disease to discover where the disease-causing polymorphism lies.

Understanding Key Concepts

26.10   (1) A genetic map, which shows the location of markers one million nucleotides apart, is created. (2) Next comes a physical map, which refines the distance between markers to 100,000 base pairs. (3) The chromosome is cleaved into large segments of overlapping clones. (4) The clones are fragmented into 500 base pieces, which are sequenced.

26.12   *Telomeres* protect the chromosome from mutations, prevent DNA from bonding to other DNA, and are believed to play a role in human aging. *Centromeres* form the constrictions that determine the shapes of chromosomes during cell division. *Promoter sequences* regulate which genes will be turned on. *Introns* are noncoding segments that are interspersed with gene-encoding exons and whose function is unknown.

26.14 Recombinant DNA contains two or more DNA segments that do not occur together in nature. The DNA that codes for a specific human protein can be incorporated into a bacterial plasmid using recombinant DNA technology. The plasmid is then reinserted into a bacterial cell, where its protein-synthesizing machinery makes the desired protein.

The Human Genome Map

26.16 Celera broke the genome into many unidentified fragments. The fragments were multiplied and cut into 500 base pieces, which were sequenced. A supercomputer was used to determine the order of the bases. An advantage was that the order of the bases in each fragment could be found quickly, although time was needed to put the fragments in the correct order.

26.18 50% of the human genome is composed of repeat sequences.

26.20 (a) About 200 genes are identical to bacterial genes.
(b) A single gene may produce several proteins.

26.22 The clones used in DNA mapping are multiple identical copies of DNA segments from a single individual. Clone samples large enough for experimental manipulation are essential for mapping.

Chromosomes, Mutations, and Polymorphisms

26.24 The youngest cells have long telomeric sequences of DNA, and the telomeres shorten as cells age. Thus, cell age can be predicted by telomere length.

26.26 The centromere is the constriction that determines the shape of a chromosome during cell division. It is composed of noncoding and repetitive DNA.

26.28 A silent mutation is a single base change in a codon that specifies the same amino acid as does the unmutated codon.

26.30 Some mutations occur as point mutations, and others occur as frameshift mutations.

26.32 A SNP can result in the change in identity of an amino acid inserted into a protein at a particular location in a polypeptide chain. The effect of an SNP depends on the function of the protein and the nature of the SNP. Most of the variations between individual human beings are due to SNPs.

26.34 Analysis of an individual's DNA for SNPs would allow a physician to predict the age at which inherited diseases might become active, their severity, and the response of the individual to various types of treatment.

26.36 A change in the nature of an amino acid's side chain determines whether an amino acid will create a major or a minor alteration in the protein's shape. Similar side chains have a lesser effect than very different side chains.

26.38

	Normal Codon	Codes For	Mutated Codon	Codes For
(a)	GCU	Ala	GCC	Ala
(b)	ACU	Thr	AUU	Ile

In (a), the normal mRNA and the mutated mRNA code for the same amino acid (Ala). In (b), the mutated mRNA codes for an amino acid that has a hydrophobic side chain, whereas the normal amino acid has a hydrophilic side chain. The second mutation is more serious because the mutation changes the type of amino acid and would probably affect the shape and function of the protein.

Recombinant DNA

26.40 Proteins can be produced in greater quantity than otherwise possible.

26.42 Sticky ends are unpaired bases on each end of the cleaved DNA. Recombinant DNA is formed when the sticky ends of the DNA of interest and of the DNA of the plasmid have complementary base pairs and can be joined by a DNA ligase. If the sticky ends are not complementary, the DNA segments can't be joined.

26.44 Write out the sticky sequence for the first of the two base sequences. If the sticky sequence agrees with the second sequence shown, the two sequences are sticky.
(a) The sequence TTAGC (5' to 3') is sticky with AATCG (3' to 5'), which is the same as GCTAA (5' to 3'). Thus, the two sequences are sticky.
(b) CGTACG isn't sticky with CCTTCG.

Genomics

26.46 Pharmacogenomics is the study of the genetic basis of responses to drug treatment. Pharmacogenomics helps doctors prescribe the most effective medicine for a patient, based on the patient's genetic makeup.

26.48 Corn and soybeans have been genetically altered and improved to provide disease and herbicide resistance.

26.50 A DNA chip could be used to match a patient's DNA fragments with polymorphic sequences linked to known genetic disorders, in order to diagnose inherited diseases.

General Questions and Problems

26.52 A monogenic disease is caused by the variation in just one gene.

26.54 TATGACT is sticky with ATACTGA.

26.56 A restriction endonuclease is an enzyme that recognizes a specific DNA sequence and cleaves the DNA between two particular nucleotides in that sequence.

Chemistry in Action

26.58 If the DNA from an individual or a single ethnic group had been used, it would have been impossible to map traits due to genetic variability.

26.60 An outline of a polymerase chain reaction:
(1) A solution of DNA that is to be copied is heated so that the DNA separates into two strands.
(2) Two oligonucleotide primers, which are complementary to the ends of the segment of DNA to be copied, are attached to the DNA strands.
(3) DNA polymerase and nucleotides are added, and the segment of DNA between the primers is copied.
The process is repeated many times until a large amount of the desired DNA is produced. The steps can be carried out at an elevated temperature because a heat-stable enzyme (*Taq polymerase*) is used.

26.62 A VNTR (variable number tandem repeat) is a region of noncoding DNA that contains repeating nucleotide sequences. The number of repeats of a given VNTR varies among individuals. Comparing the VNTRs on several genes of an individual allows scientists to create a DNA fingerprint of that person.

Self-Test for Chapter 26

Multiple Choice

1. A field of study that deals with the use of computers to manage and interpret genetic information is:
    (a) genetic engineering   (b) proteomics   (c) bioinformatics   (d) gene therapy

2. Approximately how many genes are in the human genome?
    (a) 3.1 billion   (b) 1.4 million   (c) 100,000   (d) 20,000

3. Which of the following is not a characteristic of a telomere?
    (a) It has a repeating series of nucleotides.   (b) Each chromosome has one telomere.   (c) The nucleotide groups of telomeres are noncoding.   (d) A telomere protects the end of a chromosome from accidental damage.

4. Which of the following mutations is least likely to cause genetic damage?
    (a) AUC to AUA   (b) AUC to AUG   (c) GUU to GGU   (d) CAA to CGA

5. Which of the following mutations is most likely to cause genetic damage?
    (a) AUC to AUA   (b) AUC to AUG   (c) GUU to GGU   (d) CAA to CGA

6. All of the following are composed of noncoding DNA except:
    (a) telomere   (b) centromere   (c) promoter sequence   (d) exon

7. Which of the following is not a characteristic of plasmids?
    (a) They are easy to isolate.   (b) They replicate in the same way as human DNA does.
    (c) They are circular.   (d) Each cell has one plasmid.

8. A hereditary disease caused by a defect in hemoglobin is:
    (a) cystic fibrosis   (b) sickle-cell anemia   (c) Tay–Sachs disease   (d) albinism

9. In which type of map are marker locations determined by inheritance patterns?
   (a) clone map   (b) physical map   (c) chromosome   (d) genetic map

10. DNA fingerprinting uses all of the following except:
   (a) a radioactive DNA probe   (b) restriction endonuclease   (c) a fluorescent marker   (d) gel electrophoresis

Sentence Completion

1. Groups of unpaired bases at the end of a DNA chain treated with a restriction endonuclease are known as _____ ____.

2. Repeat sequences in noncoding DNA are often referred to as ____ DNA.

3. In recombinant DNA technology, plasmids are cut open with a _____ _____.

4. The heat-stable enzyme used in the polymerase chain reaction is _____.

5. The ELSI program of the National Human Genome Research Institute deals with _____.

6. Mutations may be caused by exposure to _____ _____ or to chemicals called _____.

7. An _____ is a segment of a gene that does not code for protein synthesis.

8. The replacement of one nucleotide by another in the same location along the polynucleotide chain is known as a ____ _____ _____.

9. The field of _____ is directed to the study of the complete set of proteins coded by a genome or synthesized within a given type of cell.

10. A _____ is a constriction that determines the shape of a chromosome during cell division.

11. A point mutation that doesn't change the amino acid incorporated into a protein is a _____ mutation.

12. The film result of DNA fingerprinting is an _____.

True or False

1. In a frameshift mutation, the number of inserted or deleted nucleotides is not a multiple of 3.

2. "SNP" stands for single-nucleoside polymorphism.

3. The DNA used for the Human Genome Project came from a single donor.

4. By reorganization of exons during mRNA synthesis, a gene can produce several different proteins.

5. A person working in the field of pharmacogenomics is likely to work at a company that manufactures drugs.

6. Mapping of each chromosome starts at one end and works to the other end.

7. Telomeres consist of a long series of repeats of the nucleotide sequence TTAGGG.

8. The nucleotide sequences -GAACT- and -CTGGA- are "sticky."

9. The mutation of GAU to GAG is a nonsense mutation.

10. A mutation in RNA causes little damage.

11. Telomerase is responsible for removing telomeres from DNA.

12. Human insulin can be manufactured by recombinant DNA technology.

Match each entry on the left with its partner on the right.

1. Silent mutation   a. UUG —> UAG

2. Exon   b. UUA —> CUA

3. Human Genome Project   c. Shows little telomerase activity

4. Mature somatic cell   d. Addition or loss of a nucleotide

5. Missense mutation   e. Occurs in a very small number of individuals

6. Plasmid   f. Noncoding DNA

7. Mutation   g. Uses a series of "maps" for genome mapping

8. Nonsense mutation   h. Occurs in at least 1% of population

9. Celera   i. Coding DNA

10. SNP   j. GCU —> GGU

11. Intron   k. "Shotgun" approach to DNA mapping

12. Frameshift mutation   l. Bacterial DNA

Chapter Outline

I. Introduction to protein and amino acid metabolism (Sections 27.1–27.2).
    A. Protein digestion (Section 27.1).
        1. Proteins are denatured in the stomach.
        2. In the stomach, the enzyme pepsin hydrolyzes proteins to polypeptides.
        3. In the intestine, other enzymes hydrolyze the polypeptides to amino acids.
        4. Amino acids cross the cell membrane of the intestine and are absorbed directly into the bloodstream.
            a. Active transport is required for amino acids to cross the intestinal lining and to move into cells.
    B. Overview of amino acid metabolism (Section 27.2).
        1. The amino acid pool is the collection of all free amino acids in the body.
            a. The amino acid pool is the source of amino acids for protein synthesis and of nitrogen for the synthesis of nitrogen-containing biomolecules.
        2. Amino acid catabolism occurs in two steps:
            a. Removal of nitrogen, which can be
                i.   Used for synthesis of nitrogen-containing biomolecules.
                ii. Excreted as urea.
            b. Entry of the remaining carbon atoms into metabolic pathways.
                i.   Citric acid cycle.
                ii. Gluconeogenesis.
                iii. Ketogenesis.
                iv. Lipogenesis.
II. Amino acid catabolism (Sections 27.3–27.5).
    A. Removal of the amino group (Section 27.3).
        1. Transamination.
            a. In transamination, the amino group of an amino acid and the keto group of an α-keto acid change places.
            b. Transaminase enzymes are usually specific for α-ketoglutarate as the amino group acceptor.
            c. Transamination reactions are equilibria that regulate amino acid concentration.
        2. Deamination.
            a. If the glutamate from transamination is in excess, the $-NH_3^+$ group can be removed and excreted and α-ketoglutarate regenerated.
            b. This reaction is known as oxidative deamination.
            c. Either NAD^+ or $NADP^+$ is required.
            d. The reverse reaction, reductive amination, occurs in biosynthesis.
    B. The urea cycle (Section 27.4).
        1. Because ammonia is toxic, the human body converts it to urea in order to excrete it.
        2. The reactions of the urea cycle take place in the liver.
        3. Ammonia is first converted to carbamoyl phosphate.
            $NH_4^+ + HCO_3^- + 2\ ATP \longrightarrow$ carbamoyl phosphate $+ 2\ ADP + HOPO_3^{2-} + H_2O$.
        4. Steps of the cycle:
            a. Step 1: Carbamoyl phosphate + ornithine $\longrightarrow$ citrulline $+ HOPO_3^{2-}$.
            b. Step 2: Citrulline + aspartate + ATP $\longrightarrow$ argininosuccinate $+ AMP + P_2O_7^{4-}$.
            c. Step 3: Argininosuccinate $\longrightarrow$ fumarate + arginine.
            d. Step 4: Arginine $+ H_2O \longrightarrow$ urea + ornithine.

5. Results of the cycle:
   a. Urea is eliminated.
      i. The urea carbon comes from bicarbonate, one nitrogen comes from aspartate, and the other nitrogen comes from ammonia.
   b. Four phosphate bonds are broken.
   c. Fumarate, a citric acid cycle intermediate, is produced.
      i. Fumarate is converted to oxaloacetate, which undergoes transamination to yield aspartate, which reenters the cycle. (Fumarate can also enter gluconeogenesis.)
C. Fate of the carbon atoms (Section 27.5).
   1. All amino acid carbon skeletons are either citric acid cycle intermediates or fatty acid metabolism intermediates.
   2. Glucogenic amino acids.
      a. Amino acids that are converted to pyruvate or enter the citric acid cycle as α-ketoglutarate, succinyl-CoA, fumarate, or oxaloacetate are glucogenic.
      b. These amino acids can be converted to glucose.
   3. Ketogenic amino acids.
      a. Amino acids that are converted to acetyl-CoA or acetoacetyl-CoA are known as ketogenic amino acids.
      b. These amino acids can enter either ketogenesis to form ketone bodies or fatty acid biosynthesis.
   4. Some amino acids are both glucogenic and ketogenic.
III. Biosynthesis of nonessential amino acids (Section 27.6).
  A. The human body can synthesize 11 of the 20 common amino acids.
  B. All 11 amino acids derive their amino group from glutamate.
  C. Pyruvate, oxaloacetate, α-ketoglutarate, and 3-phosphoglycerate are the precursors of all nonessential amino acids.
  D. Tyrosine is formed from phenylalanine.
    1. An inability of the body to perform this conversion is the metabolic error in phenylketonuria.

Solutions to Chapter 27 Problems

27.1 (a) False. The amino acid pool is the collection of free amino acids in the body. (b) False. Our bodies don't store nitrogen-containing compounds. (c) True. (d) False. (e) False. Glycine isn't essential because it can be synthesized in the human body.

27.2

27.3

Threonine + α-Ketoglutarate → 4-Hydroxy-2-oxopentanoate + Glutamate

27.4

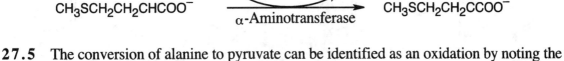

27.5 The conversion of alanine to pyruvate can be identified as an oxidation by noting the reduction of the coenzymes NAD^+ or $NADP^+$.

27.6 The three branched-chain amino acids are valine, leucine, and isoleucine.

Valine + α-Ketoglutarate → α-Keto-3-methylbutanoate + Glutamate

27.7

Arginine (a)   Ornithine (b)   (c)

27.8

The changes include deamination (1), hydrolysis (2), and oxidation (3).

27.9

27.10 Histidine and arginine are considered to be "conditional amino acids" because they are only essential to adults under certain conditions; in most cases, adults can synthesize a sufficient amount of each. They are, however essential to children.

27.11

Understanding Key Concepts

27.12

27.14

NADPH/H$^+$ can also be used as an enzyme cofactor.

The enzymes for both reactions can catalyze reaction in both directions. The product is the amino acid alanine.

27.16 An essential nutrient can't be synthesized by the body and must be provided in the diet. For example, all amino acids are "essential" in the sense that all of them are necessary for protein synthesis. The body can synthesize half of them from non-amino acid precursors; these are described as "nonessential." The other amino acids must be part of the diet.

Amino Acid Pool

27.18 The body's amino acid pool, which is the collection of free amino acids that result from diet or tissue breakdown, occurs throughout the body.

27.20 Pyruvate and 3-phosphoglycerate are glycolytic precursors of amino acids.

Amino Acid Catabolism

27.22 In a transamination reaction, a keto group of an α-keto acid and an amino group of an α-amino acid change places.

27.24

27.26 In an oxidative deamination reaction, an $-NH_3^+$ group of an amino acid (usually glutamate) is replaced by a carbonyl oxygen, and ammonium ion is eliminated. In a transamination reaction, a keto group of an α-keto acid and an amino group of an α-amino acid change places. An oxidative deamination is a redox reaction.

27.28

        Amino Acid   *α-Keto Acid*

(a)

$$CH_3CHCH_2-CH-COO^-$$
Leucine

$$CH_3CHCH_2-C-COO^-$$

Amino Acid   *α-Keto Acid*

(b)

Tryptophan

27.30 A ketogenic amino acid is catabolized to acetoacetyl-CoA or acetyl-CoA, which can be used either in the synthesis of ketone bodies or in fatty acid biosynthesis. Examples: leucine, isoleucine, lysine. (The last two are both glucogenic and ketogenic.)

The Urea Cycle

27.32 Ammonia is toxic and must be eliminated as nontoxic urea, which is water-soluble.

27.34 One nitrogen comes from carbamoyl phosphate, which is synthesized from ammonium ion produced from oxidative deamination. One nitrogen comes from aspartate.

Amino Acid Biosynthesis

27.36 Nonessential amino acids can be synthesized in one to three steps by most organisms. Plants and microorganisms synthesize essential amino acids in many more steps.

27.38 Meat, fish, and dairy products are all rich in lysine. Legumes are a good plant-based source of lysine.

27.40 Phenylketonuria (PKU) is caused by a genetic inability to convert phenylalanine to tyrosine, leading to the accumulation of phenylalanine and its metabolites in the body. PKU causes mental retardation if not detected early in life. Treatment consists of a diet restricted in phenylalanine.

27.42 All biomolecules that contain nitrogen acquire it from amino acids. These include (b) nitric oxide, (c) collagen, and (d) epinephrine.

General Questions and Problems

27.44

The enzyme that catalyzes the transamination is either isoleucine aminotransferase or alanine aminotransferase.

27.46 An amino acid can be both glucogenic and ketogenic. After catabolism, certain amino acids yield products that can enter the citric acid cycle and other products that can be intermediates of fatty acid metabolism.

27.48 Tissue is dynamic because its components are constantly being broken down and reformed. Dynamic relationships are common in protein and amino acid metabolism, where proteins are digested and resynthesized, and where amino acids are converted to other amino acids and to carbohydrate intermediates.

Energy: Fats and carbohydrates that are not stored are catabolized. Surplus amino acids must be converted to either fats or carbohydrates in order to be an energy source.

27.50 The basic scheme of the conversion of glutamate to glycogen is deamination —> gluconeogenesis —> glycogenesis.
Step 1: Glutamate (b) —> α-Ketoglutarate (e) (deamination or transamination).
Step 2: α-Ketoglutarate (e) —> Oxaloacetate (d) (citric acid cycle).
Step 3: Oxaloacetate (d) —> Phosphoenolpyruvate (f) (gluconeogenesis).
Step 4: Phosphoenolpyruvate (f) —> Glucose (a) (gluconeogenesis).
Step 5: Glucose (a) —> Glycogen (c) (glycogenolysis).
The complete sequence: (b) —> (e) —> (d) —> (f) —> (a) —> (c).

27.52 (1) The amino group is removed. (2) The amino nitrogen is either used in synthesis of new nitrogen- containing compounds or excreted as urea. (3) The remaining carbon atoms are converted into compounds that can either enter the citric acid cycle or enter ketogenesis.

27.54 Active transport of amino acids across cell membranes is achieved by several transport systems, each of which is specific for several different amino acids. An excess of one amino acid might overwhelm its transport system, making it unavailable to transport other amino acids and causing an amino acid deficiency.

Chemistry in Action

27.56

Allopurinol   Hypoxanthine   Xanthine   Uric acid

Allopurinol is identical to hypoxanthine in all but one respect: The nitrogen at position 7 of the hypoxanthine ring is at position 8 of the allopurinol ring. Just as hypoxanthine can be oxidized to xanthine, allopurinol can be oxidized to a compound similar to xanthine (alloxanthine). The product of allopurinol oxidation, however, is an inhibitor of the enzyme that converts xanthine to uric acid. Instead of producing uric acid, purine catabolism ends with the formation of the more soluble hypoxanthine and xanthine, which can be easily excreted.

Oxidation of xanthine to uric acid occurs at position 8 of the purine ring system. In allopurinol, this site is occupied by nitrogen.

27.58 A deficiency of tryptophan, "nature's Prozac," may lead to serotonin deficiency syndrome, which causes behavioral and emotional problems.

Self-Test for Chapter 27

Multiple Choice

1. Which of the following amino acids is strictly ketogenic?
   (a) proline (b) threonine (c) leucine (d) isoleucine

2. The product of transamination of valine is:
   (a) α-keto-3-methylbutanoic acid (b) α-ketobutanoic acid (c) α-keto-4-methylpentanoic acid (d) α-ketopentanoic acid

3. The amino acid proline is probably synthesized by cyclization of:
   (a) arginine (b) glutamate (c) leucine (d) threonine

4. The urea cycle takes place in the:
   (a) muscles (b) kidneys (c) bloodstream (d) liver

5. Which of the following proteases is necessary for the activation of other proteases?
   (a) pepsin (b) chymotrypsin (c) carboxypeptidase (d) trypsin

6. How many grams of protein tissue are broken down in an adult body per day?
   (a) none (b) 50 g (c) 300 g (d) 1000 g

7. Ornithine is:
   (a) a urea cycle intermediate (b) an amino acid (c) an acceptor of a carbamoyl group
   (d) all three

8. Which of the following nitrogen-containing compounds is used to treat gout?
   (a) hypoxanthine (b) xanthine (c) allopurinol (d) uric acid

9. Which of the following isn't a precursor in nonessential amino acid biosynthesis?
   (a) fumarate (b) pyruvate (c) α-ketoglutarate (d) 3-phosphoglycerate

10. Glucogenic amino acids enter gluconeogenesis via:
    (a) acetyl-CoA (b) oxaloacetate (c) α-ketoglutarate (d) fumarate

Sentence Completion

1.   In the transamination reaction of alanine and α-ketoglutarate, _____ and _____ are formed.

2.   _____ is a primary metabolic source of sulfur.

3.   Ketogenic amino acids are catabolized to _____ _____ or _____ _____.

4.   The first step in the urea cycle is the formation of _____ _____ from ammonia, CO_2, and ATP.

5.   A _____ is an enzyme that carries out peptide hydrolysis.

6.   The amino acid serine enters the citric acid cycle as _____.

7.   _____ is the key reaction in amino acid anabolism.

8.   The essential amino acid _____ is part of the urea cycle.

9.   PKU is a metabolic error in converting _____ to _____.

10.   The pain of gout is caused by an inflammatory response to _____ _____ in tissues.

11.   Liver damage is associated with a high level of the enzyme _____.

12.   The carbon in urea comes from _____.

True or False

1.   3-Phosphoglycerate is a precursor in the synthesis of nonessential amino acids.

2.   Protein digestion starts in the mouth.

3.   All ketogenic amino acids except lysine and isoleucine are also glucogenic amino acids.

4.   Essential amino acids can neither be synthesized nor catabolized in the human body.

5.   Some organisms can excrete nitrogen as ammonia without undergoing any harm.

6.   Amino acid catabolism occurs in the intestinal lining.

7.   Some intermediates in the urea cycle also occur in the citric acid cycle.

8.   The urea cycle is an endergonic process.

9.   Both nitrogens of urea come from ammonium ion.

10.   Proline is a nonessential amino acid.

11.   Each amino acid is associated with its own transaminase enzyme.

12.   Oxidative deamination is the reverse of reductive amination.

Match each entry on the left with its partner on the right.

1. Oxidative deamination

2. Ornithine

3. α-Ketoglutarate

4. Serine

5. Trypsin

6. Reductive amination

7. Leucine

8. Phenylketonuria

9. Pepsin

10. Uric acid

11. Transamination

12. Threonine

(a) Hydrolyzes proteins in the small intestine

(b) Process for synthesizing glutamate from α-ketoglutarate and NH_4^+

(c) Ketogenic amino acid

(d) End product of purine catabolism

(e) Process that transfers an amino group from an amino acid to α-ketoglutarate

(f) Nonessential amino acid

(g) Intermediate in the urea cycle

(h) Process that regenerates α-ketoglutarate from glutamate

(i) Glucogenic amino acid

(j) Intermediate in both the citric acid cycle and in amino acid metabolism

(k) Hydrolyzes proteins in the stomach

(l) Metabolic disease

Chapter 28   Chemical Messengers

Chapter Outline

I. Introduction to chemical messengers (Section 28.1).
   A. Control of vital functions is accomplished by chemical messengers.
      1. The messengers interact with the cells of a target tissue.
      2. The message is delivered by interaction between the chemical messengers and receptors.
      3. Noncovalent interactions draw messengers and receptors together.
      4. The results of the interaction are chemical changes within the target cell.
   B. Two kinds of chemical messengers are important in the body.
      1. Hormones are the chemical messengers of the endocrine system.
         a. Hormones travel through the bloodstream.
         b. The responses produced by hormones are slow but long-lasting.
      2. The chemical messengers of the nervous system are neurotransmitters.
         a. Signals travel very quickly along nerve fibers.
         b. Neurotransmitters carry the message of the signal across the gap that separates one nerve fiber from the next fiber.
         c. The effects of neurotransmitters are very short-lived.
II. Hormones (Sections 28.2–28.5).
   A. Hormones and the endocrine system (Section 28.2).
      1. The endocrine system consists of all the glands that secrete hormones.
      2. The endocrine glands are managed by the hypothalamus in three different ways.
         a. Direct neural control by a nervous system pathway from the hypothalamus.
         b. Direct release of hormones from the hypothalamus.
         c. Indirect control by release of regulatory hormones.
      3. There are three types of hormones.
         a. Polypeptide hormones.
         b. Steroid hormones.
         c. Amino acid derivatives.
      4. The signal of a hormone enters cells in either of two ways.
         a. Steroid hormones pass through the hydrophobic cell membrane.
         b. Other hormones bind with receptors in the cell wall.
   B. How hormones work: epinephrine (Section 28.3).
      1. Epinephrine carried in the bloodstream binds to a receptor on the surface of a cell.
      2. The hormone–receptor complex interacts with a nearby G protein, causing it to bind GTP.
      3. This complex activates the enzyme adenylate cyclase, which resides in the cell membrane.
      4. Adenylate cyclase catalyzes production within the cell of the second messenger, cyclic AMP.
      5. Cyclic AMP initiates reactions that activate glycogen phosphorylase, which catalyzes release of glucose from storage.
      6. After the emergency, a phosphodiesterase catalyzes hydrolysis of cyclic AMP to AMP.
   C. Types of hormones (Sections 28.4–28.5).
      1. Amino acid derivatives (Section 28.4).
         a. Many amino acid derivatives are also neurotransmitters.
            i. Examples include epinephrine, dopamine, and norepinephrine.
         b. Thyroxine is an iodine-containing hormone that regulates the synthesis of various enzymes.

2. Polypeptide hormones.
    a. TRH and TSH control the thyroid gland.
    b. Vasopressin and oxytocin are small cyclic polypeptides.
    c. Insulin regulates glucose metabolism.
3. Steroid hormones (Section 28.5).
    a. Mineralocorticoids (such as aldosterone) regulate ionic balance in cellular fluid.
    b. Glucocorticoids (such as cortisone) regulate inflammation.
    c. Sex hormones.
        i. Androgens (male hormones) include testosterone and androsterone.
        ii. Female hormones include estrogens and progestins.
    d. There are also hundreds of synthetic hormones of all types.

III. Neurotransmitters (Sections 28.6–28.10).
  A. General features of neurotransmitters (Section 28.6).
    1. A nerve impulse is transmitted along a neuron by variations in electric potential.
    2. Neurotransmitters convey the impulse across the synaptic cleft from a presynaptic neuron to a postsynaptic neuron.
    3. The impulse is transmitted down the next neuron, and the preceding process is repeated.
    4. Neurotransmitters are synthesized and stored in vesicles in the presynaptic neuron.
    5. After transmission, the neurotransmitter is inactivated in one of two ways.
        a. A chemical change inactivates the neurotransmitter.
        b. The neurotransmitter is returned to the presynaptic neuron.
    6. Most neurotransmitters are amines.
    7. Some neurotransmitters act directly, and others rely on second messengers.
  B. How neurotransmitters work: acetylcholine (ACh) (Section 28.7).
    1. Events of neurotransmission.
        a. An impulse arrives at the presynaptic neuron.
        b. The vesicles move to the cell membrane, fuse with it, and release ACh.
        c. ACh crosses the synaptic cleft and binds to receptors on the postsynaptic neuron.
        d. A change in the permeability of the postsynaptic neuron initiates the nerve impulse in that neuron.
        e. Acetylcholinesterase in the synaptic cleft catalyzes the decomposition of ACh.
        f. Choline is reabsorbed into the presynaptic neuron, and new ACh is synthesized.
    2. Interactions of drugs at ACh synapses.
        a. To have an effect a drug must connect with a receptor.
        b. Drugs that are agonists prolong the biochemical response of a receptor.
            i. Nicotine at a low dose is an example of an agonist.
        c. Drugs that are antagonists block the normal response of a receptor.
            i. Antagonists can be either competitive (tubocurarine) or irreversible (nerve gas).
  C. Histamine and antihistamines (Section 28.8).
    1. Histamine is the neurotransmitter responsible for the symptoms of allergic reactions.
    2. Antihistamines are drugs that are histamine receptor antagonists.
  D. Monoamines (Sections 28.9–28.10).
    1. Serotonin, norepinephrine, and dopamine are neurotransmitters active in the brain (Section 28.9).
    2. Since these neurotransmitters affect mood, drugs have been created to affect the concentration of these neurotransmitters at synapses.
        a. Tricyclic antidepressants (Elavil) prevent the reuptake of serotonin and norepinephrine from the synaptic cleft.
        b. MAO inhibitors (Nardil) inhibit the enzyme that breaks down monoamine neurotransmitters.
        c. SSRI antidepressants (Prozac) inhibit only the reuptake of serotonin.

3. Dopamine.
   a. Dopamine plays a role in emotion, thought and behavior through interactions with five different kinds of receptors in the brain.
   b. Dopamine levels are responsible for many types of behaviors.
      i.   An oversupply of dopamine is associated with schizophrenia.
      ii. An undersupply of dopamine is responsible for Parkinson's disease.
      iii. An ample supply of dopamine is responsible for a feeling of well-being.
   c. Drugs such as heroin, cocaine, marijuana, and alcohol increase dopamine levels.
E. Neuropeptides (Section 28.10).
   1. The brain has receptors for small polypeptides (enkephalins) that also act as receptors for opiates.
IV. Drug discovery and drug design (Section 28.11).
   A. Plants were the first source of drugs.
      1. Today, ethnobotanists seek new plant sources of drugs in remote regions.
   B. In the nineteenth century, simple drugs (benzocaine, phenacetin) were synthesized in chemical laboratories.
   C. Combinatorial chemistry generates large masses of related compounds and screens them for possible effectiveness as drugs.
   D. Supercomputers and molecular graphics are increasingly used in drug design.

Solutions to Chapter 28 Problems

28.1 Blood glucose and triacylglycerols are important metabolites whose levels reflect homeostasis. Since the concentrations of both compounds are regulated by hormones, these values also indicate the state of regulatory genes.

28.2

If you redraw the reaction shown in Figure 28.3, you can see the anion that is a by-product of the conversion of ATP to cyclic AMP. The anion (PP$_i$) is P$_2$O$_7^{4-}$.

28.3 The heterocyclic rings of caffeine and theobromine resemble the heterocyclic rings of cyclic AMP. It is possible that these two molecules could act as inhibitors to one of the enzymes that inactivates cAMP.

28.4

Glu　　　His　　　Pro

The tripeptide is Glu–His–Pro. Glutamic acid has formed a cyclic amide (lactam).

28.5

Thyroxine

Thyroxine is hydrophobic because its aromatic, hydrophobic part is larger than its zwitterionic, hydrophilic part.

28.6

Testosterone　　　　　　　　Nandrolone

Nandrolone and testosterone are identical except for the presence in testosterone of a methyl group between the first two rings that is absent in nandrolone.

28.7 Brassinolide is a steroid hormone that has a tetracyclic ring framework similar to the structure of other sterols.

28.8

(a) decarboxylation (3)
(b) acetylation (1)
(c) methylation (2)

28.9

Both structures have aromatic rings and have secondary alcohol and secondary amine functional groups. Propranolol has a naphthalene aromatic ring system and has an ether group. Epinephrine has an aromatic ring with two phenol groups. The compounds have different carbon skeletons in their side chains.

28.10 (a) Malathion, with an LD_{50} of 1000–1375 mg/kg, is the best choice because its lethal dose is highest, and it is thus the least harmful pesticide of the three. (b) Parathion, with an LD_{50} of 3–13 mg/kg, is the deadliest insecticide because its lethal dose per kilogram of body weight is smallest.

28.11 (a) Sumatripan, an agonist, prolongs the biochemical response at the serotonin receptor. (b) Ondansetron, an antagonist, blocks or inhibits the normal response at the serotonin receptor.

28.12

Tetrahydrocannabinol (THC)

THC is likely to be hydrophobic (because the phenol hydroxyl group is the only polar functional group in the molecule), and it might be expected to accumulate in fatty tissue.

28.13 (a) This structure represents an antihistamine because it has the general antihistamine structure pictured in Section 28.8.
(b) This structure represents an antidepressant. It is similar to Prozac, an SSRI, but there are noticeable differences; the aromatic rings have different substituents, and a third ring is present in the compound pictured.

Understanding Key Concepts

28.14 (a) Luteinizing hormone (LH) is a polypeptide hormone that is produced in the anterior pituitary gland.
(b) Progesterone is a steroid hormone that is produced in the ovaries.
(c) LH doesn't enter progesterone-producing cells because it is a polypeptide hormone. Instead, LH interacts on the cell surface with LH receptors that generate second messengers, which carry out the function of LH.
(d) Progesterone enters the cell directly because it is a steroid hormone and can pass through the hydrophobic cell membrane.

28.16 (a) Insulin, a polypeptide hormone, is involved in type I diabetes.
(b) In unaffected individuals, insulin is released by the pancreas. The pancreas fails to produce insulin in individuals with type I diabetes.
(c) Insulin is transported through the bloodstream to cells that need it.
(d) Insulin doesn't enter cells because it is a polypeptide hormone and can't pass through the hydrophobic cell membrane. Instead, it binds with a cell surface receptor, which generates a second messenger within the cell.

28.18 The transmission of a nerve impulse may be terminated by an enzyme that converts the neurotransmitter to an inactive form. It is also possible for the neurotransmitter to be returned to the presynaptic neuron.

Chemical Messengers

28.20 A chemical messenger is a molecule that travels from one part of the body to another location, where it delivers a signal or acts to control metabolism. The target tissue is the cell or group of cells whose activity is regulated by the messenger. A hormone receptor is the molecule with which the chemical messenger interacts if it is a hormone.

28.22 A vitamin is usually an enzyme cofactor, whereas a hormone regulates enzyme activity.

28.24 Neither a hormone nor its receptor is changed as a result of binding to each other. The binding forces between hormone and receptor are noncovalent.

Hormones and the Endocrine System

28.26 The body's endocrine system manufactures and secretes hormones, which regulate the functioning of biochemical reaction pathways.

28.28 The three major classes of hormones are polypeptide hormones, steroid hormones, and hormones that are derivatives of amino acids.

28.30 Enzymes are proteins, whereas hormones vary greatly in structure. Some hormones are polypeptides, some are proteins, some are steroids, and some are derivatives of amino acids.

28.32 Polypeptide hormones travel through the bloodstream and bind to cell receptors, which are on the outside of a cell. The receptors cause production within cells of "second messengers" that activate enzymes.

How Hormones Work: Epinephrine

28.34 Epinephrine is produced and released in the adrenal medulla.

28.36 Ephinephrine travels through the bloodstream to reach its target tissues.

28.38 The three membrane-bound proteins that transmit the epinephrine message are, in order of involvement, the hormone receptor, G protein, and adenylate cyclase.

28.40 The second messenger initiates reactions that activate glycogen phosphorylase, the enzyme responsible for releasing glucose from storage.

28.42 Epinephrine is used to treat anaphylaxis, a life-threatening allergic response whose symptoms include lowered heart rate and blood pressure and difficulty in breathing.

Hormones

28.44 Insulin is an example of a polypeptide hormone and contains 51 amino acids in two chains that are linked by disulfide bridges. It is stored in the pancreas and is released in response to high glucose levels in the blood. The hormone stimulates cells to take up glucose for use or storage.

28.46 All steroid hormones have a characteristic tetracyclic ring skeleton.

28.48 *Male sex hormones*: androsterone, testosterone.

28.50 A person who takes androgens becomes more muscular faster than a person who doesn't take androgens.

28.52 Epinephrine, norepinephrine, and dopamine can function as both hormones and as neurotransmitters.

28.54   *Hormone*   *Class*

(a)   amino acid derivative

Dopamine

(b)   Insulin   polypeptide hormone

(c)   steroid hormone

Testosterone

Neurotransmitters

28.56 A synapse is the gap between two nerve cells (neurons). Neurotransmitters released by one neuron cross the synapse to receptors on a second neuron and transmit the nerve impulse.

28.58 The signal from a neurotransmitter might be received by another nerve cell, a muscle cell, or an endocrine cell.

28.60 A nerve impulse arrives at the presynaptic end of a neuron. The nerve impulse stimulates the movement of a vesicle, containing neurotransmitter molecules, to the cell membrane. The vesicle fuses with the cell membrane and releases the neurotransmitter, which crosses the synaptic cleft to a receptor site on the postsynaptic end of a second neuron. After reception, the cell transmits an electrical signal down its axon and passes on the impulse. Enzymes then deactivate the neurotransmitter so that the neuron can receive the next impulse. Alternatively, the neurotransmitter may be returned to the presynaptic neuron.

28.62 (1) Neurotransmitter molecules are released from a presynaptic neuron in response to an impulse.(2) The neurotransmitter molecules bind to receptors on the target cell. (3) The neurotransmitter is deactivated after transmitting the message.

28.64 Enkephalins are called "neurohormones" because they are secreted in the central nervous system and have receptors in brain tissue.

Chemical Messengers and Drugs

28.66 Drugs that are agonists interact with receptors to produce or prolong the normal response of the receptor. Antagonists block or inhibit the normal response of a receptor.

28.68 Three families of drugs used to treat depression are tricyclic antidepressants, monoamine oxidase inhibitors (MAO inhibitors), and selective serotonin reuptake inhibitors (SSRI).

28.70 Chlorpheniramine counteracts allergic responses, and Zantac counteracts excess stomach acid.

28.72 Cocaine increases dopamine levels in the brain by blocking reuptake of dopamine.

28.74 Tetrahydrocannabinol (THC) increases dopamine levels in the same brain areas where dopamine levels increase after administration of heroin and cocaine.

28.76 Chlorpromazine acts as an antagonist because it blocks the dopamine signal

28.78 Endorphins are polypeptides with morphine-like activity. They are produced by the pituitary gland and have receptors in the brain.

28.80 Enkephalins and endorphins act at the same receptors as opiates.

28.82 An ethnobotanist works in remote regions of the world to learn what indigenous people have discovered about the healing power of plants.

28.84 Studies of the exact size and shape of biomolecules give scientists information about receptor sites of molecules of interest. This information allows scientists to design drugs with properties suitable for the desired drug–receptor interaction with the target biomolecule.

Chemistry in Action

28.86 Homeostasis is the maintenance of a constant internal environment in the body.

28.88 Plants must synthesize hormones in the cells where they are needed because plants don't have endocrine systems, nor do they have a continuously circulating fluid like blood.

General Questions and Problems

28.90 The hormone epinephrine is responsible for the response to imminent danger.

28.92 Both thyroxine and steroid hormones have large nonpolar regions and can cross a cell membrane to activate the synthesis of enzymes.

28.94 It is important for the second messenger (cyclic AMP) to break down rapidly after synthesis for two reasons. First, once the message has been delivered, cyclic AMP is no longer needed to activate reactions. Second, the precursor to cyclic AMP must be ready for the next signal.

28.96 When caffeine inhibits the enzymatic hydrolysis of cyclic AMP, response to a hormonal signal is prolonged.

28.98

Ethynyl estradiol · · · · · · · · · · · Norethindrone

Ethynyl estradiol and norethindrone differ only in the ring on the left. Ethynyl estradiol has a phenolic ring, and norethindrone has a ketone group and a double bond in that ring.

Estradiol · · · · · · · · · · · Progesterone

The only difference between ethynyl estradiol and estradiol is in the five-membered ring, where a –C≡CH group that is present in ethynyl estradiol is absent in estradiol. Norethindrone and progesterone differ in two respects. (1) The five-membered ring of norethindrone contains a –C≡CH group and an —OH group, whereas the five-membered group of progesterone contains a methyl ketone (acetyl) group. (2) A methyl group between the first two rings is present in progesterone and absent in norethindrone.

28.100   The first step in the conversion of tyrosine to epinephrine (substitution of —OH for —H on the aromatic ring) is catalyzed by tyrosine hydroxylase, an oxidoreductase (subclass: hydroxylase). The second step (loss of CO_2) is catalyzed by dopa decarboxylase, a lyase (subclass: decarboxylase).

28.102   Estradiol can be converted to estrone by oxidation of the —OH group in the five-membered ring.

Self–Test for Chapter 28

Multiple Choice

1. Which of the following compounds is an acetylcholine agonist?
    (a) nicotine   (b) succinylcholine   (c) tubocurarine   (d) atropine

2. Which of the following hormones regulates the balance of Na^+ and K^+ ions in cellular fluid?
    (a) androsterone   (b) progesterone   (c) aldosterone   (d) cortisone

3. Cocaine affects the brain because it:
    (a) accelerates the release of dopamine   (b) blocks reuptake of dopamine   (c) raises the level of endorphins   (d) all of the above

4. An effective antihistamine has all of the structural elements listed except:
    (a) an ethylamine skeleton   (b) a tertiary amine   (c) an ether oxygen   (d) two bulky —R groups.

5. Which of the following compounds is a neurotransmitter but not a hormone?
    (a) dopamine   (b) norepinephrine   (c) epinephrine   (d) acetylcholine

6. Which of the following compounds does not reside in the cell membrane?
    (a) cyclic AMP   (b) epinephrine receptor   (c) adenylate cyclase   (d) G protein

7. Hormones and neurotransmitters have all of the following in common except:
    (a) They both regulate reaction rates.   (b) They both can be amino acid derivatives.   (c) They both interact with receptors at target tissues.   (d) They both travel through the bloodstream.

8. Which of the following events doesn't occur in "fight or flight"?
    (a) Epinephrine crosses the cell membrane.   (b) Epinephrine stimulates production of cyclic AMP.   (c) Glucose is released from storage.   (d) Cyclic AMP is converted to ATP.

9. Control of the endocrine system occurs in the:
    (a) pancreas   (b) pituitary gland   (c) adrenal glands   (d) hypothalamus

10. Which of the following isn't a site for hormone receptors?
    (a) outer cell surface   (b) cytoplasm within the cell   (c) cell nucleus   (d) bloodstream

Sentence Completion

1. _____ is a life-threatening allergic response.

2. In direct neural control, the hypothalamus controls the release of hormones by the ____ gland.

3. Neurotransmitter molecules are stored in _____.

4. _____ is the neurotransmitter responsible for the symptoms of allergic reactions.

5. Nerves that rely on acetylcholine as their neurotransmitter are referred to as _____ nerves.

6. The hormone _____ prepares the uterus to receive a fertilized egg.

7. An _____ is a neuropeptide that acts at opiate receptors.

8. A person who studies the healing powers of plants from remote regions is a _____.

9. One neuron is separated from another by a gap called a _____ _____.

10. Heroin, alcohol, and cocaine all produce an elevated level of the neurotransmitter _____.

11. The hormone _____ contains iodine atoms.

12. After an emergency, the enzyme _____ catalyzes hydrolysis of cyclic AMP to ATP.

True or False

1. Only steroid hormones can cross the cell membrane to activate enzymes.

2. Cocaine accelerates the release of dopamine.

3. In direct release of hormones, hormones move through the bloodstream to the posterior pituitary gland, where they are stored until needed.

4. Some neurotransmitters can act directly; others use second messengers.

5. Acetylcholine is synthesized at postsynaptic neurons.

6. Choline is a quaternary ammonium ion.

7. Epinephrine reduces blood pressure and slows the heart rate.

8. An enlarged thyroid gland is a symptom of excess iodine in the diet.

9. Polypeptide hormones vary greatly in size.

10. Succinylcholine is a competitive antagonist for acetylcholine.

Match each entry on the left with its partner on the right.

1. Androgen   (a) Polypeptide hormone

2. Tricyclic antidepressant   (b) Progesterone

3. Acetylcholine agonist   (c) Cortisone

4. Natural estrogen   (d) Growth hormone

5. Second messenger   (e) Testosterone

6. Oxytocin   (f) Norethindrone

7. Regulatory hormone   (g) Cyclic AMP

8. MAO inhibitor antidepressant   (h) Amitriptyline (Elavil)

9. Synthetic estrogen   (i) Fluoxetine (Prozac)

10 Acetylcholine antagonist   (j) Phenelzine (Nardil)

11. Glucocorticoid   (k) Nicotine

12 SSRI inhibitor antidepressant   (l) Atropine

Chapter Outline

I. Water (Sections 29.1–29.2).
 A. Body water and its solutes (Section 29.1).
  1. Types of body fluids.
   a. Intracellular fluid is within cells.
   b. Extracellular fluid is outside of cells.
    i. Blood plasma.
    ii. Interstitial fluid, which fills the spaces between cells.
  2. Components of body fluids.
   a. Electrolytes (inorganic ions).
   b. Gases—O_2 and CO_2.
   c. Small organic molecules.
   d. Ionized biomolecules.
  3. All body fluids have the same osmolarity, even if they differ in composition.
  4. Movement of body fluids.
   a. Blood travels through peripheral tissues in capillaries.
    i. At the arterial end, blood pressure is higher and pushes solutes into interstitial fluid.
    ii. At the venous end, blood pressure is lower, and solutes reenter blood plasma.
    iii. Blood plasma and interstitial fluid have similar composition.
   b. Lymph capillaries collect excess interstitial fluid and other molecules too large to pass through capillary walls; this combination is called lymph.
    i. Lymph can't return to surrounding tissue.
    ii. Lymph enters the blood stream at the thoracic duct.
   c. Solutes in interstitial and intracellular fluid are exchanged by crossing cell membranes.
    i. Often, active transport is needed to maintain concentration differences.
 B. Maintenance of fluid balance (Section 29.2).
  1. The output of water and electrolytes is controlled by hormones.
  2. Receptors in the hypothalamus monitor concentration of blood solutes.
  3. If the concentration of solutes is too high, secretion of antidiuretic hormone increases.
   a. In SIADH, too much hormone keeps kidneys from excreting enough water.
   b. In *diabetes insipidus*, excessive amounts of dilute urine are excreted.
II. Blood (Sections 29.3–29.6).
 A. Components of blood (Section 29.3).
  1. Whole blood contains:
   a. Plasma.
   b. Blood cells.
  2. Blood serum is the fluid portion that remains after blood has clotted.
 B. Functions of blood.
  1. Transport.
  2. Regulation: redistribution of heat and solutes, and buffering of tissues.
  3. Defense.
   a. Immune response.
   b. Clotting.
 C. Immune response (Section 29.4).
  1. A foreign invader (antigen) is a substance that the body does not recognize as part of itself.

2. The body responds to antigens in three ways.
   a. Inflammatory responses (nonspecific).
      i. Inflammation produces swelling, warmth, and pain.
      ii. The chemical messenger histamine is released at the site of injury.
      iii. Histamine dilates capillaries and increases blood flow to the injured area, allowing clotting factors and white blood cells to pass.
      iv. Bacteria are destroyed by phagocytes (white blood cells), which can also initiate specific immune responses.
      v. Inflammation disappears when infectious agents have been removed.
   b. Cell-mediated immune response (specific).
      i. The cell-mediated immune response is under the control of T lymphocytes.
      ii. The cell-mediated immune response guards against abnormal cells due to bacteria, viruses, or cancer.
      iii. When a T cell recognizes an invader, it produces killer T cells (that destroy the invader), helper T cells (that enhance defenses), and memory T cells (that remain on guard).
   c. Antibody-mediated immune response (specific).
      i. The antibody-mediated immune response is under the control of B lymphocytes (with the assistance of T lymphocytes).
      ii. A B cell is activated when it binds to an antigen and encounters a helper T cell.
      iii. The B cells divide to produce plasma cells, which form non-cell-bound antibodies called immunoglobulins.
      iv. The antibodies find their antigens and inactivate them by one of several methods.
      v. Memory cells produce more antibodies if the same antigen reappears.
      vi. The body contains thousands of different immunoglobulins, and many have been identified.
D. Blood clotting (Section 29.5).
   1. A blood clot consists of blood cells trapped in a mesh of the protein fibrin.
      a. The process of clot formation requires many steps.
   2. The body's mechanism for halting blood loss is called hemostasis.
      a. The first event is constriction of blood vessels and formation of a plug of platelets.
      b. Then, blood clotting occurs by either of two pathways.
         i. In the intrinsic pathway, blood makes contact with the negatively charged surface of collagen.
         ii. In the extrinsic pathway, damaged tissue releases a glycoprotein called tissue factor.
      c. In either pathway, several zymogen clotting factors are released.
      d. After several steps, the enzyme thrombin catalyzes the formation of insoluble fibrin, which forms the clot.
   3. After the injury has healed, the clot is broken down by hydrolysis of its peptide bonds.
E. Red blood cells and blood gases (Section 29.6).
   1. The purpose of red blood cells (erythrocytes) is to transport blood gases.
   2. Hemoglobin is responsible for transporting O_2 and CO_2.
      a. Hemoglobin consists of four protein chains and four heme molecules.
   3. Oxygen transport.
      a. Oxygen is transported via bonding with Fe^{2+} through an unshared electron pair.
      b. The percent of heme molecules that carry oxygen is the percent saturation.
      c. The binding curve is s-shaped.
         i. The uptake of the first molecule of oxygen is more difficult than the uptake of the remaining molecules.
         ii. The release of the first O_2 is more difficult than the release of the other three.

4. CO_2 transport.
   a. CO_2 can be transported in three ways.
      i. Dissolved (about 7%).
      ii. Bonded to Hb.
      iii. As HCO_3^- in solution.
   b. Carbonic anhydrase in erythrocytes catalyzes the formation of HCO_3^- from CO_2.
   c. The HCO_3^- can be transported in blood to the lungs, where it is exhaled as CO_2.
   d. Electrolyte balance in erythrocytes is maintained by entry of one Cl^- for every HCO_3^- removed.
   e. Excess acidity is controlled by binding of H^+ to hemoglobin, with release of O_2.
5. The effects of changes in the oxygen saturation curve with changing pCO_2 and $[H^+]$ are illustrated in Figure 29.12.
6. Acidosis and alkalosis result from disruption of the body's mechanism for maintaining pH and by imbalances in CO_2 metabolism.

III. Urine (Sections 29.7–29.8).
   A. The kidney and urine formation (Section 29.7).
      1. The kidney is composed of nephrons.
      2. Blood enters the nephrons at the glomerulus, where filtration occurs.
         a. Plasma and smaller solutes are filtered into the surrounding fluid.
      3. Reabsorption recaptures water and smaller solutes.
      4. In secretion, some solutes are excreted in higher concentration than occurs in the filtrate.
      5. Some substances move by passive diffusion; others move by active transport.
      6. Hormones influence urine composition.
   B. Urine composition and function (Section 29.8).
      1. Composition of urine.
         a. The components of urine are mainly electrolytes and nitrogen-containing wastes.
         b. The concentration of these substances varies with water intake, temperature, exercise and state of health.
      2. Acid–base balance.
         a. Of the 50–100 mEq of H^+ produced in metabolism, very little appears in the urine.
         b. H^+ is produced from CO_2 in the reaction:
            i. $CO_2 + H_2O \longrightarrow H^+ + HCO_3^-$
         c. The resulting H^+ combines with either NH_3 or HPO_4^{2-} and is excreted.
         d. H^+ also combines with HCO_3^- in urine filtrate to produce CO_2, which enters the bloodstream.
      3. Fluid and Na^+ balance.
         a. The amount of H_2O reabsorbed depends on:
            i. The osmolarity of the fluid passing through the kidney.
            ii. Antidiuretic hormone-controlled membrane permeability.
            iii. The amount of Na^+ reabsorbed.
         b. Reabsorption of Na^+ is under the control of aldosterone.

Solutions to Chapter 29 Problems

29.1 When chloride concentrations are low, the reaction should proceed farther to the right, according to Le Châtelier's principle. When chloride concentrations are high, the reaction proceeds to the left. In order to move passively into a cell, a molecule cannot be charged because a cell membrane is non-polar. Therefore, the form of cisplatin shown on the left enters the cell more readily. Once inside, the equilibrium shifts to the right and forms the charged version of cisplatin, which does not cross back through the cell membrane.

29.2 (a) Interstitial fluid—(iii) Fluid that fills spaces between cells
(b) Whole blood—(ii) Fluid, solutes, and cells that together flow through veins and arteries
(c) Blood serum—(iv) Fluid that remains after clotting agents are removed from plasma
(d) Intracellular fluid—(v) Fluid within cells
(e) Blood plasma—(i) Fluid that remains when blood cells are removed

29.3 (a) The value of pH goes down because of the formation of carbonic acid from dissolved CO_2, which increases $[H_3O]^+$ and thus increases acidity.
(b) A blood gas analysis measures $[O_2]$, $[CO_2]$, and pH.

29.4 (a) Emphysema is a cause of *respiratory acidosis*. In pneumonia, the lungs have difficulty exhaling CO_2, and increased blood acidity results.
(b) Failure of the kidneys to excrete H_3O^+ results in *metabolic acidosis*.
(c) Overdose of an antacid leads to overneutralization of H_3O^+, which raises pH and leads to *metabolic alkalosis*.

29.5 (a) A panic attack causes hyperventilation, which removes CO_2 from the body, raising pH and resulting in *respiratory alkalosis*.
(b) Congestive heart failure is a cause of *respiratory acidosis*.
(c) Running a marathon can cause *metabolic acidosis*.

29.6

Heroin has two acetyl groups in the same location as the two hydroxyl groups of morphine. These relatively nonpolar acetyl groups make heroin soluble in the membrane lipids of endothelial cells and more able to pass into these cells.

Understanding Key Concepts

29.8

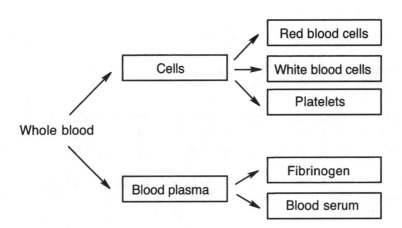

29.10 Symptoms of inflammation include swelling, redness, warmth, and pain.

29.12 *Cell-mediated immune response*, which is under the control of T cells, arises when abnormal cells, bacteria, or viruses enter cells. The invading cells are killed by T cells that destroy the invader.
Antibody-mediated immune response, which is under the control of B cells, assisted by T cells, occurs when antigenic substances enter cells. When an antigen is recognized, B cells divide to produce plasma cells, which form antibodies to the antigen. These antibodies form an antibody–antigen complex that inactivates the antigen.

Body Fluids

29.14 The three principal body fluids are intracellular fluid (64%), interstitial fluid (25%), and plasma (8%).

29.16 Substances not soluble in blood, such as lipids, are transported by blood proteins.

29.18 Blood pressure in arterial capillaries is higher than interstitial fluid pressure, and blood pressure in venous capillaries is lower than interstitial fluid pressure.

29.20 Lymph enters the bloodstream at the thoracic duct.

29.22 An excess of antidiuretic hormone causes a decrease in the water content of the urine. This excess may be caused by pulmonary or central nervous system disorders.

29.24 At 7% body mass loss, collapse is likely to occur.

29.26 *Red blood cells* transport blood gases.
White blood cells protect the body from foreign substances.
Platelets assist in blood clotting.

29.28 Potassium cation, magnesium cation, and hydrogen phosphate anion are the major electrolytes inside cells. Sodium cation and chloride anion are the major electrolytes outside of cells.

29.30 Antihistamines block attachment of the neurotransmitter histamine to its receptors.

29.32 Immunoglobulins are the plasma proteins involved in the antibody-mediated immune response.

29.34 When a T cell recognizes an antigen on the surface of an invader, three kinds of T cells are produced. *Killer* T cells destroy the invader, *helper* T cells enhance defenses against the invader, and *memory* T cells can produce new killer T cells if the invader reappears.

29.36 Memory cells, which are produced from B cells, can quickly produce more plasma cells if the same antigen appears in the future. Memory cells "remember" the antigen and are capable of producing antibodies to it for a long time.

29.38 Vitamin K and calcium ion are needed for blood clotting.

29.40 Blood-clotting enzymes are released as zymogens in order to avoid undesirable clotting in noninjured tissues.

29.42 Hemoglobin iron must be in the +2 oxidation state in order to bind with oxygen.

29.44 When the partial pressure of oxygen drops below 10 mmHg, hemoglobin is unsaturated. When the partial pressure of oxygen is greater than 100 mmHg, hemoglobin is completely saturated. Between these pressures, hemoglobin is partially saturated.

29.46 CO_2 can be transported as a dissolved gas, as bicarbonate ion, or as bonded to hemoglobin.

29.48 CO_2 in the blood raises $[H^+]$ in two types of reactions:

(1) Reaction of CO_2 with nonionized $-NH_2$ groups of hemoglobin amino acids produces H^+.

$$Hb-NH_2 + CO_2 \longrightarrow Hb-NHCOO^- + H^+$$

(2) Carbonic anhydrase catalyzes the reaction of CO_2 with H_2O, producing bicarbonate and H^+.

$$CO_2 + H_2O \underset{}{\overset{\text{Carbonic anhydrase}}{\rightleftharpoons}} HCO_3^- + H^+$$

29.50 Respiratory acidosis occurs when CO_2 generation and CO_2 removal by the lungs are out of balance. Metabolic acidosis results from abnormally high acid generation or from the inability of the body's buffering system to regulate bicarbonate concentration.

29.52 Respiratory alkalosis is due to excessive loss of CO_2 due to hyperventilation. Metabolic alkalosis is due to elevated plasma bicarbonate concentration.

29.54

$$H^+ + HPO_4{}^{2-} \rightleftarrows H_2PO_4{}^-$$

$$H^+ + HCO_3{}^- \rightleftarrows CO_2 + H_2O$$

General Questions and Problems

29.56 A nursing mother's antibodies can be passed to her baby in breast milk.

29.58 Active transport is the movement of solutes from regions of low concentration to regions of high concentration, a process that requires energy. Osmosis is the movement of water through a semipermeable membrane from a dilute solution to a more concentrated solution, a process that requires no energy.

29.60 In the blood, CO_2 from metabolism reacts to form $HCO_3{}^- + H^+$. The H^+ is bound to hemoglobin, which releases O_2, and is carried to the lungs. There, the H^+ is released and O_2 is bound to hemoglobin.

  In the urine, CO_2 reacts to form $HCO_3{}^-$ and H^+. The $HCO_3{}^-$ returns to the bloodstream, and the H^+ is neutralized by reaction with $HPO_4{}^{2-}$ or NH_3.

  Whenever excess $HCO_3{}^-$ accumulates in blood or urine, it can react with H^+ to form $H_2O + CO_2$.

29.62 When blood CO_2 levels drop, the following reaction occurs to restore CO_2 supply:

$$H^+ + HCO_3{}^- \longrightarrow H_2CO_3 \longrightarrow CO_2 + H_2O$$

This reaction uses up H^+ ions and leads to alkalosis. Breathing into a paper bag recaptures the expired CO_2 and restores the blood CO_2 level.

Chemistry in Action

29.64 In an asymmetric transport system, substances can either be transported into a cell or be transported out of a cell, but not both. For example, there exists a system for transport of glycine out of brain cells, but no system exists for transport of glycine into brain cells.

29.66 The metabolic blood–brain barrier is a pathway in which a substance is converted in an epithelial cell to a metabolite that can't enter the brain

29.68 A change in enzyme level in body fluids may indicate organ damage. An automatic analyzer can reproducibly measure the rate of an enzyme-catalyzed reaction to detect the presence of elevated or reduced levels of enzymes.

Self-Test for Chapter 29

Multiple Choice

1. Which oxygen is taken up by heme with the most difficulty?
   (a) the first oxygen   (b) the second oxygen   (c) the last oxygen   (d) All bind with equal ease.

2. Cardiac arrest may result in:
   (a) metabolic alkalosis   (b) metabolic acidosis   (c) respiratory alkalosis   (d) respiratory acidosis

3. Cell-mediated immune response guards against all of the following except:
   (a) cancer cells   (b) transplanted organs   (c) allergens   (d) bacteria

4. Potassium ion is most abundant in:
   (a) interstitial fluid   (b) intracellular fluid   (c) plasma   (d) extracellular fluid

5. All of the following are involved in blood clotting except:
   (a) tissue factor   (b) zymogens   (c) thrombin   (d) memory cells

6. Which of the following disorders is not an autoimmune disease?
   (a) hemophilia   (b) arthritis   (c) lupus erythematosus   (d) diabetes mellitus

7. The amount of water reabsorbed in kidney tubules depends on:
   (a) the amount of sodium reabsorbed   (b) control of membrane permeability by antidiuretic hormone   (c) aldosterone   (d) all three

8. Blood is at its lowest percent saturation with oxygen in:
   (a) peripheral tissue   (b) muscles   (c) veins   (d) arteries

9. All of the following decrease the oxygen affinity of hemoglobin except
   (a) increased $[H^+]$ (b) increased $[O_2]$ (c) increased $[CO_2]$ (d) increased temperature

10. B cells divide to produce all of the following except:
    (a) memory cells   (b) antibodies   (c) phagocytes   (d) plasma cells

Sentence Completion

1. The percentage of heme molecules that carry oxygen is dependent on the _____ _____ of O_2.

2. Antigens can be small molecules known as _____.

3. In the process of blood clotting, _____ are activated to give active clotting factors.

4. Inorganic ions are the major contributors to the _____ of body fluids.

5. Histamine is synthesized from _____.

6. _____ ion and vitamin _____ assist in blood clotting.

7. In _____ _____, substances move from regions of low concentration to regions of high concentration.

8. The three functions of blood are _____, _____, and _____.

9. Bacteria at the site of inflammation are attacked by _____.

10. Arthritis and allergies are known as _____ diseases.

11. _____ is caused by the absence of one or more clotting factors.

12. Fibrin molecules are bound into fibers by crosslinks between the side chains of the amino acids _____ and _____.

True or False

1. The walls of lymph capillaries are constricted so that lymph can't return to surrounding tissues.

2. Homeostasis is the body's mechanism for halting blood loss.

3. O_2, H^+, and CO_2 all bond to heme.

4. Secreted H^+ is eliminated in the urine as NH_4^+ or $H_2PO_4^-$.

5. When the partial pressure of CO_2 increases, the percent saturation of hemoglobin decreases.

6. Allergies and asthma are caused by an underproduction of immunoglobulin E.

7. Blood plasma is the fluid remaining after blood has completely clotted.

8. Blood clotting begins with the release of tissue factor from injured tissue.

9. Reabsorption is the movement of solutes and water out of the kidney.

10. The metabolism of food contributes to one's water intake.

11. Lymphocytes surround and destroy bacteria.

12. Caffeine causes increased output of urine.

Match each entry on the left with its partner on the right.

1. B cells

(a) Foreign substance

2. Active transport

(b) Enzyme that catalyzes the formation of histamine

3. Fibrin

(c) Movement of solute against a concentration gradient

4. Carbonic anhydrase

(d) White blood cells involved in antibody-directed immune response

5. Erythrocytes

(e) Controls reabsorption of Na^+

6. T cells

(f) Blood protein responsible for clotting

7. Antigen

(g) Enzyme that catalyzes reaction between H_2O and CO_2

8. Histidine decarboxylase

(h) Movement of water in response to a concentration difference

9. Osmosis

(i) White blood cells involved in cell-directed immune response

10. Antidiuretic hormone

(j) Red blood cells

11. Antibody

(k) Protein molecule that identifies a foreign substance

12. Aldosterone

(l) Causes a decrease in the water content of urine

Answers to Self Tests

Chapter One

Number questions: 1. (a) micrometer (b) deciliter (c) megagram (d) liter (e) nanogram
2. (a) kL (b) pg (c) cm (d) hL 3. (a) 5 (b) 2 (c) 1 (d) exact (e) 3, 4, 5 or 6
4. (a) 7.03×10^{-5} g; 3 sig. fig. (b) $1.371\,00 \times 10^5$ m; 4, 5, or 6 sig. fig. (c) 1.1×10^{-2} L; 2 sig. fig. (d) $1.837\,100\,8 \times 10^7$ mm; 8 sig. fig. 5. (a) 8.07×10^2 L (b) 4.77×10^6 people
(c) 1.27×10^{-3} g (d) 1.04×10^4 μm 6. (a) 0.564 lb (b) 0.417 m (c) 7.6 L (d) 85.4 in.
(e) 95°F (f) 25°C (g) 5.92 fl oz (h) 6.17×10^{-3} oz 7. 31 cal 8. 217 g
Multiple choice: 1. b 2. d 3. b 4. a 5. c 6. d 7. b 8. b 9. c 10. a
Sentence completion : 1. kilogram, meter, cubic meter, Kelvin 2. number, unit 3. specific heat 4. Bi 5. 3 6. 1 lb/454 g 7. malleable 8. factor-label 9. Specific gravity 10. Celsius, Kelvin
True/false: 1. F (specific gravity is unitless) 2. T 3. F (three sig. fig.) 4. F (0.9464 L/1 qt.)
5. T 6. F 7. F 8. T 9. F 10. T
Matching: 1. e 2. j 3. g 4. i 5. h 6. l 7. f 8. k 9. c 10. a 11. d 12. b

Chapter Two

Multiple choice: 1. c 2. b 3. a 4. c 5. d 6. d 7. a 8. b 9. d 10. d 11. a 12. b
Sentence completion: 1. p 2. dalton 3. protons, neutrons 4. atomic number 5. shells
6. group 7. 13 8. subatomic particles 9. isotopes 10. 18 11. quantized
True/false: 1. T 2. F (5.486×10^{-4} amu) 3. F 4. T 5. F (atomic number indicates only protons) 6. F (They're less reactive.) 7. F (in the same group) 8. T 9. T 10. F (Subshells can contain 2,6,10 ·· electrons.) 11. T 12. F
Matching: 1. h 2. e 3. k 4. a 5. j 6. l 7. c 8. b 9. i 10. d 11. g 12. f

Chapter Three

Multiple choice: 1. d 2. a 3. d 4. c 5. a 6. b 7. b 8. d 9. b 10. d
Sentence completion: 1. Ionization energy 2. potassium phosphate 3. 2 4. polyatomic
5. simplest 6. 8 7. base 8. Hydroxyapatite 9. crystalline 10. 4A or 5A
True/false: 1. F (It forms only Zn^{2+}.) 2. T 3. F (energy needed to form an ion) 4. T 5. F (ions formed may be H^+, $H_2PO_4^-$, and HPO_4^{2-}.) 6. F (Solutions of ions conduct electricity.) 7. F 8. T 9. T 10. F (group 8A) 11. T 12. F
Matching: 1. e 2. l 3. k 4. a 5. h 6. j 7. i 8. b 9. f 10 g 11. d 12. c

Chapter Four

Multiple choice: 1. c 2. d 3. b 4. c 5. a 6. a 7. d 8. b 9. d 10. a
Sentence completion: 1. electronegative 2. biomolecule 3. covalent 4. C≡C, C≡N
5. diatomic 6. trigonal planar 7. d 8. triple 9. Binary 10. organic 11. condensed
True/false: 1. T 2. T 3. F 4. F (valence electrons) 5. F (It's planar.) 6. F (covalent compounds) 7. T 8. F 9. F (Some bent molecules have bond angles that are approx. 109.5°.)
10. T 11. T
Matching: 1. h 2. j 3. f 4. a 5. k 6. i 7. e 8. c 9. b 10. g 11. d 12. l

Chapter Five

Multiple choice: 1. a 2. a 3. c 4. b 5. d 6. c 7. c 8. b 9. a 10. d
Sentence completion: 1. coefficients 2. precipitate 3. spectator 4. aqueous 5. carbonate, bicarbonate 6. Metallurgy 7. reactants 8. +3 9. reducing 10. neutralization
True/false: 1. F (a lithium-iodine battery) 2. T 3. T 4. F 5. T 6. F 7. F 8. F (in blood) 9. T 10. T
Matching: 1. h 2. f 3. k 4. a 5. i 6. c 7. j 8. b 9. g 10. l 11. d 12. e

Chapter Six

Multiple choice: 1. c 2. d 3. b 4. b 5. d
True/false: 1. F (same number of atoms) 2. T 3. T 4. F (Molar mass is the conversion Factor.) 5. F (The mole ratio is 1/2.)
Matching: 1. e 2. a 3. b 4. c 5. d

Chapter Seven

Multiple choice: 1. c 2. b 3. d 4. d 5. b 6. a 7. c 8. a 9. d 10. d
Sentence completion: 1. 1 2. conservation of energy 3. catalyst 4. reversible 5. endothermic 6. equilibrium-constant expression 7. temperature, concentration, catalyst 8. metabolism 9. Reaction rate 10. collide
True/false: 1. F (produced) 2. F (At equilibrium, the ratio of concentrations is constant.) 3. T 4. T 5. F (The size of E_{act} and ΔH are unrelated.) 6. F (not always true for biochemical reactions) 7. T 8. F (Catalysts lower the height of the energy barrier.) 9. F (At equilibrium, the rate of the forward reaction equals the rate of the reverse reaction.) 10. T
Matching: 1. c 2. j 3. l 4. i 5. a 6. k 7. b 8. f 9. d 10. e 11. g 12. h

Chapter Eight

Multiple choice: 1. b 2. c 3. d 4. a 5. d 6. c 7. a 8. b 9. c 10. d
Sentence completion: 1. pressure, volume 2. definite, indefinite 3. Dalton's 4. standard temperature and pressure 5. Avogadro's 6. equilibrium 7. atmosphere, Pascal, mm Hg, pounds per square inch, torr 8. heat of fusion 9. number of atoms, pressure 10. temperature 11. change of state 12. volatile
True/false: 1. T 2. F (Only ideal gases have similar physical behavior.) 3. T 4. F (Doubling pressure halves the volume.) 5. T 6. F (only true in crystals) 7. F (273 K) 8. T 9. F (higher) 10. F (Vapor pressure doesn't depend on quantity of liquid.) 11. F (viscosity)
Matching: 1. g 2. e 3. k 4. f 5. h 6. a 7. j 8. l 9. b 10. d 11. c 12. i

Chapter Nine

Multiple choice: 1. b 2. d 3. a 4. b 5. c 6. d 7. c 8. c 9. a 10. b
Sentence completion: 1. miscible 2. gram equivalent 3. volumetric flask 4. solubility, partial pressure 5. isotonic 6. hygroscopic 7. $M_1 \times V_1 = M_2 \times V_2$ 8. colloid 9. solvent, small solute molecules 10. saturated 11. glucose 12. lower
True/false: 1. F (solvent) 2. T 3. F (A quantity of the second liquid is added to make 100 mL of solution.) 4. F 5. T 6. F (Weight/weight percent is rarely used.) 7. T 8. F (Effect of temperature is unpredictable.) 9. T (It also differs with respect to particle size.) 10. F (hemolysis) 11. F (raise) 12. T
Matching: 1. h 2. f 3. d 4. j 5. a 6. k 7. b 8. i 9. g 10. l 11. e 12. c

Chapter Ten

Multiple choice: 1. b   2. a   3. c   4. d   5. c   6. a   7. b   8. a   9. b   10. d
Sentence completion: 1. equivalent   2. red   3. diprotic   4. strong   5. Dissociation   6. OH^- ions   7. Neutralization   8. pH   9. 30.0 mL   10. conjugate   11. carbonate/bicarbonate   12. amphoteric
True/false: 1. F (60 mL of 0.1 M NaOH)   2. T   3. F (H_2SO_4 is a strong acid.) 4. F   5. F   6. T   7. T   8. F (According to this definition, an acid donates H^+.)   9. F (Ammonia yields ammonium ion, plus the anion of the acid.)   10. T   11. F   12. T
Matching: 1. d   2. e   3. g   4. l   5. a   6. b   7. i   8. j   9. c   10. f   11. k   12. h

Chapter Eleven

Multiple choice: 1. c   2. d   3. c   4. a   5. c   6. d   7. a   8. d   9. b   10. c
Sentence completion: 1. transmutation   2. Gamma radiation   3. tracer   4. background   5. nucleons   6. ^{14}C 7. curie   8. nuclear fission   9. film badges   10. body imaging   11. nuclear fusion   12. critical mass
True/false: 1. F (3/4 will have decayed after 24 days.)   2. T   3. T   4. F (Becquerel)   5. T   6. F   7. F (Atomic number increases by 1.)   8. F (Hazards are due to emissions of radiation.)   9. F (The rem is more common.)   10. T   11. F (Most are synthetic.)   12. F
Matching: 1. f   2. i   3. l   4. k   5. c   6. j   7. d   8. h   9. b   10. a   11. e   12. g

Chapter Twelve

Multiple choice: 1. a   2. c   3. d   4. c   5. b   6. d   7. c   8. a   9. c   10. a
Sentence completion: 1. paraffins   2. triple   3. oxygen   4. distillation   5. condensed structure   6. quaternary   7. lower   8. ring   9. IUPAC   10. isomers   11. Combustion   12. higher
True/false: 1. F (They have different molecular formulas.)   2. T   3. F (It's puckered.)   4. F (3-Methylhexane)   5. T   6. T   7. F (It's polar covalent.)   8. T   9. T   10. F (Reactivity depends on the nature of the functional groups.)   11. T   12. F
Matching: 1. i   2. j   3. f   4. l   5. h   6. c   7. a   8. k   9. e   10. b   11. g   12. d

Chapter Thirteen

Multiple choice: 1. d   2. b   3. a   4. c   5. a   6. c   7. c   8. c   9. d   10. d
Sentence completion: 1. 2-heptyne   2. hydrogenation   3. *para*   4. more, fewer   5. hydration   6. catalyst   7. carbocation   8. unsaturated   9. Toluene   10. substitution   11. Polycyclic aromatic compounds   12. thermal cracking
True/false: 1. F   2. T   3. T   4. F (2-bromobutane)   5. F (Halogenation is the reaction of X_2 with an alkene, where X is a halogen.)   6. T   7. F   8. F (Hydration requires a strong acid as a catalyst.)   9. T   10. F   11. F   12. T
Matching: 1. e   2. k   3. i   4. j   5. b   6. l   7. d   8. c   9. a   10. f   11. g   12. h

Chapter Fourteen

Multiple choice: 1. c   2. b   3. b   4. a   5. d   6. d   7. a   8. b   9. c   10. d
Sentence completion: 1. wood alcohol   2. glycols   3. phenols   4. alkene   5. thiols
6. $KMnO_4$ or $K_2Cr_2O_7$ 7. lower   8. BHT   9. greater   10. free radical   11. peroxide   12. CFC
True/false: 1. T   2. F (A ketone is formed from the oxidation of a secondary alcohol.) 3. T
4. F (carbolic acid) 5. T   6. T   7. F (Ethyl chloride is an anesthetic.) 8. F (two hydrogen atoms)
9. T   10. T   11. F   12. T
Matching: 1. j   2. g   3. f   4. h   5. l   6. b   7. e   8. a   9. k   10. d   11. i   12. c

Chapter Fifteen

Multiple choice: 1. c   2. a   3. d   4. c   5. c   6. a   7. b   8. d   9. a   10. b
Sentence completion: 1. *amino-*   2. quaternary   3. DNA   4. Toxicology   5. heterocycle   6.
Alkaloids   7. hydrogen bonding   8. ammonium   9. free radical   10. nonaromatic amines
True/false: 1. T   2. T   3. F (They're lower boiling.) 4. T   5. F   6. T   7. F (It's synthetic.) 8.
T   9. F (NO lowers blood pressure.) 10. F (*N*-Methylbutylamine)
Matching: 1. d   2. l   3. h   4. i   5. a   6. j   7. b   8. k   9. f   10. g   11. e   12. c

Chapter Sixteen

Multiple choice: 1. c   2. b   3. a   4. d   5. c   6. b   7. b   8. a   9. d   10. b
Sentence completion: 1. carbonyl   2. silver   3. Hydrolysis   4. positive, negative   5. Acetone
6. acetaldehyde   7. more   8. reduction   9. disinfectant or preservative   10. hemiacetal
11. Benedict's   12. Acetone
True/False: 1. F (a hemiacetal link) 2. T   3. F (Ketones don't undergo Tollens' reaction.) 4. F
($NaBH_4$ is used for reduction.) 5. F   6. F (Both aldehydes and ketones form acetals.) 7. T   8. T
9. F (NADH) 10. T   11. T   12. T
Matching: 1. e   2. i   3. d (or l)   4. a   5. h   6. j   7. k   8. b   9. l   10. f   11. g   12. c

Chapter Seventeen

Multiple choice: 1. d   2. c   3. a   4. d   5. b   6. d   7. b   8. a   9. d   10. b
Sentence completion: 1. carbonyl group substitution   2. polyamide   3. carboxylate salt
4. esterification   5. attracts   6. -oic acid   7. propyl propanoate   8. esters   9. Phosphorylation
10. fats   11. hydrolysis or saponification   12. propanedioic acid
True/false: 1. T   2. F (basic hydrolysis) 3. F (Amides are nonbasic.) 4. T   5. F (The products
are acetate ion and ethanol.) 6. F (*N*,*N*-dimethylformamide) 7. F   8. T   9. T   10. F
(Esterification is acid-catalyzed.) 11. F (It's an acid anhydride.) 12. T
Matching: 1. j   2. f   3. k   4. b   5. i   6. d   7. a   8. e   9. l   10. h   11. c   12. g

Chapter Eighteen

Multiple choice: 1. a   2. d   3. c   4. b   5. b   6. a   7. d   8. b   9. c   10. d
Sentence completion : 1. 5.0-6.3   2. enantiomers   3. zwitterions   4. backbone   5. loop
6. glycoprotein   7. Tertiary   8. β-sheet   9. polar   10. sulfur   11. polypeptide   12. Hydrophobic
True/false: 1. F (Glycine is achiral.) 2. T   3. F (Denaturation disrupts all structural elements
except primary structure.) 4. F (They're different.) 5. T   6. F   7. T   8. T   9. T   10. F (Fibrous
proteins are insoluble.) 11. T   12. T
Matching: 1. e   2. g   3. j   4. a   5. b   6. k   7. c   8. l   9. f   10. h   11. d   12. i

Chapter Nineteen

Multiple choice: 1. c 2. a 3. c 4. d 5. b 6. b 7. d 8. c 9. b 10. d
Sentence completion: 1. isomerase 2. Isoenzymes 3. K 4. induced-fit 5. uncompetitive
6. denature 7. turnover number 8. phosphoryl 9. proximity 10. 10^7 11. allosteric 12.
zymogen
True/false: 1. T 2. F 3. F 4. F (a dehydrase) 5. F (Enzyme-substrate interactions are
noncovalent.) 6. F (Minerals, not vitamins, are inorganic ions.) 7. T 8. F (Retinol, retinal,
retinoic acid are all active forms of vitamin A.) 9. T 10. T 11. F (Reaction rate increases.) 12. T
Matching: 1. c 2. h 3. i 4. g 5. k 6. j 7. b 8. a 9. d 10. f 11. e 12. l

Chapter Twenty

Multiple choice: 1. b 2. c 3. a 4. c 5. a 6. d 7. b 8. c 9. b 10. d
Sentence completion: 1. Eukaryotic 2. metabolic pathway or linear sequence 3. ADP and
phosphate 4. unfavorable 5. Krebs cycle, tricarboxylic acid cycle 6. succinyl-CoA, CO_2 7.
NAD^+ 8. one GDP (plus 4 reduced coenzymes) 9. Cytoplasm 10. Catalase 11. succinate
dehydrogenase 12. Basal metabolism
True/false: 1. T 2. F (Only eukaryotic cells are found in higher organisms.) 3. F (Anabolism
is the synthesis of complicated molecules from simpler molecules.) 4. F 5. T 6. T 7. F
($FADH_2$ donates electrons to coenzyme Q.) 8. T 9. F (decrease in order) 10. F (ATP can be
formed in the citric acid cycle) 11. F (a phosphate anhydride) 12. T
Matching: 1. d 2. j 3. f 4. a 5. l 6. k 7. e 8. c 9. b 10. g 11. i 12. h

Chapter Twenty-one

Multiple choice: 1. a 2. d 3. c 4. c 5. d 6. d 7. d 8. c 9. b 10. b
Sentence completion: 1. chiral 2. amylases 3. enantiomers 4. cyclic hemiacetal
5. fructose 6. amylose, amylopectin 7. glycoside 8. Glycogen 9. aldohexose 10. achiral
11. diastereomer 12. Glycoproteins
True/false: 1. T 2. T 3. F (The hydroxyl group on the chiral carbon farthest from the carbonyl
group is on the left.) 4. F (α, not β) 5. T 6. F (Crystalline glucose is the α-anomer.) 7. F
(Sucrose contains only an acetal bond.) 8. T 9. F (An acetal resembles an ether.) 10. F (Maltose
is composed of two glucose molecules.) 11. F (The relationship between the rotations of
diastereomers is not predictable.) 12. T
Matching: 1. e 2. l 3. j 4. h 5. i 6. k 7. b 8. a 9. d 10. g 11. c 12. f

Chapter Twenty-two

Multiple choice: 1. c 2. c 3. b 4. d 5. a 6. b 7. d 8. c 9. d 10. a
Sentence completion: 1. Embden-Meyerhof 2. 6 3. Pyruvate dehydrogenase complex 4.
Insulin 5. glucose 1-phosphate 6. 1 and 3 7. diabetes mellitus 8. GTP, ATP 9. CO_2
10. glucose 6-phosphate isomerase 11. glucagon 12. Hypoglycemia
True/false: 1. F (It produces NADPH.) 2. T 3. F 4. F 5. T 6. F (Glycolysis occurs in the
cytosol.) 7. F (The yield of ATP was formerly considered to be 38 ATP/ 1 mol glucose. The new
estimate is 30-32 ATP/1 mol glucose.) 8. F (glycogen) 9. F (Fermentation occurs only in yeasts.)
10. T (but one results from isomerization of dihydroxyacetone phosphate) 11. T 12. F (It
produces two ATPs.)
Matching: 1. l 2. k 3. i 4. j 5. c 6. h 7. d 8. a 9. f 10. g 11. b 12. e

Chapter Twenty-three

Multiple choice: 1. d 2. c 3. a 4. a 5. d 6. d 7. c 8. b 9. a 10. b
Sentence completion: 1. glycoside 2. Soap 3. hydrophilic, hydrophobic 4. Glycolipids, cholesterol, glycoproteins 5. fluid-mosaic 6. tetracyclic 7. arachidonic 8. micelles 9. Sphingomyelins 10. lipid bilayer 11. Eicosanoids 12. Integral
True/false: 1. T 2. F 3. F (They contain an amide group.) 4. T 5. T 6. F (They form a micelle.) 7. F (Cholesterol is a steroid component of cell membranes.) 8. F (The major difference is in the quantity of unsaturated fatty acids they contain.) 9. F (Cerebrosides are components of nerve cell membranes in the brain.) 10. T 11. T 12. F (In facilitated diffusion, solutes are transported across cell membranes by proteins, but no energy investment is required.)
Matching: 1. l 2. h 3. e 4. f 5. a 6. j 7. k 8. b 9. d 10. g 11. i 12. c

Chapter Twenty-four

Multiple choice: 1. a 2. d 3. c 4. a 5. b 6. b 7. c 8. d 9. a 10. d
Sentence completion: 1. NAD^+, FAD 2. micelles 3. adipocytes 4. dihydroxyacetone phosphate 5. fatty-acid spiral 6. double bond 7. Ketonuria 8. NADPH 9. 3–Hydroxybutyrate 10. lymphatic system 11. mobilized 12. acetyl-CoA
True/false: 1. T 2. F (The products are mainly mono- and diacylglycerols.) 3. T 4. T 5. F 6. T 7. F (Dihydroxyacetone phosphate, not glycerol) 8. F (LDL transports cholesterol.) 9. T 10. F (It occurs in the cytosol.) 11. F (It comes from acetyl-CoA.) 12. T.
Matching: 1. e 2. i 3. a 4. l 5. g 6. j 7. k 8. d 9. f 10. b 11. c 12. h

Chapter Twenty-five

Multiple choice: 1. c 2. d 3. b 4. a 5. b 6. b 7. c 8. d 9. c 10. a
Sentence completion: 1. Replication 2. complementary 3. chromatin 4. retrovirus 5. intron 6. ester 7. nucleoside 8. releasing factor 9. replication fork 10. 2'-deoxyribose 11. Watson-Crick 12. DNA polymerase
True/false: 1. F (61 codons code for the 20 amino acids; the other three are "stop" codons.) 2. F (The amount of adenine equals the amount of thymine.) 3. T 4. F (An anticodon occurs on tRNA.) 5. T 6. T 7. T 8. F (They run in opposite directions.) 9. F (translation) 10. F (Most DNA consists of introns.) 11. F (Two have only one codon.) 12. F (guanosine 5'-monophosphate)
Matching; 1. l 2. j 3. b 4. g 5. a 6. i 7. d 8. c 9. e 10. k 11. f 12. h

Chapter Twenty-six

Multiple choice: 1. c 2. d 3. b 4. a 5. d 6. d 7. d 8. b 9. c 10. c
Sentence completion: 1. "sticky" ends 2. 'junk" 3. restriction endonuclease 4. Taq polymerase 5. bioethics 6. ionizing radiation, mutagens 7. intron 8. single-nucleotide polymorphism 9. proteomics 10. centromere 11. silent 12. autoradiogram
True/false: 1. T 2. F (nucleotide) 3. F (from several people) 4. T 5. T 6. F (starts from base-base sequences at known locations) 7. T 8. F 9. F (missense) 10. T 11. F (adding) 12. T
Matching: 1. b 2. i 3. g 4. c 5. j 6. l 7. e 8. a 9. k 10. h 11. f 12. d

Chapter Twenty-seven

Multiple choice: 1. c 2. a 3. b 4. d 5. a 6. c 7. d 8. c 9. a 10. b
Sentence completion: 1. pyruvate, glutamate 2. Methionine 3. acetyl-CoA, acetoacetyl-CoA
4. carbamoyl phosphate 5. protease 6. pyruvate 7. Transamination 8. arginine
9. phenylalanine, tyrosine 10. urate crystals 11. ALT 12. bicarbonate
True/false: 1. T 2. F (It starts in the stomach.) 3. F (lysine and leucine) 4. F (The human
body can catabolize essential amino acids.) 5. T 6. F (Catabolism occurs in the liver and in the
cytosol.) 7. T 8. T 9. F (One is from aspartate; the other is from ammonium ion.) 10. T 11. F
(Some transaminases have several amino acid donors.) 12. T
Matching: 1. h 2. g 3. j 4. f 5. a 6. b 7. c 8. l 9. k 10. d 11. e 12. i

Chapter Twenty-eight

Multiple choice: 1. a 2. c 3. b 4. c 5. d 6. a 7. d 8. a 9. d 10. d
Sentence Completion: 1. Anaphylaxis 2. adrenal 3. vesicles 4. Histamine 5. cholinergic
6. progesterone 7. enkephalin 8. ethnobotanist 9. synaptic cleft 10. dopamine 11. thyroxine
12. phosphodiesterase
True/false: 1. F (Thyroxine can cross the cell membrane.) 2. F (It blocks reuptake.) 3. T 4.
T 5. F (presynaptic neurons) 6. T 7. F (It increases blood pressure and heart rate.) 8. F (It's a
symptom of iodine deficiency.) 9. T 10. T
Matching: 1. e 2. h 3. k 4. b 5. g 6. a 7. d 8. j 9. f 10. l 11. c 12. i

Chapter Twenty-nine

Multiple choice: 1. a 2. d 3. c 4. b 5. d 6. a 7. d 8. b 9. b 10. c
Sentence completion: 1. partial pressure 2. haptens 3. zymogens 4. osmolarity
5. histidine 6. calcium, K 7. active transport 8. transport, regulation, defense 9. phagocytes
10. autoimmune 11. Hemophilia 12. lysine, glutamine
True/false: 1. F (constructed) 2. F (hemostasis) 3. F (CO_2 bonds to hemoglobin) 4. T 5. T
6. F (overproduction) 7. F (blood serum) 8. T 9. F (tubule) 10. T 11. F (phagocytes) 12. T
Matching: 1. d 2. c 3. f 4. g 5. j 6. i 7. a 8. b 9. h 10. l 11. k 12. e